# Exile in Great Britain

*Refugees from Hitler's Germany*

# Exile in Great Britain

## Refugees from Hitler's Germany

EDITED BY

*Gerhard Hirschfeld*

**Berg Publishers : England**

**Humanities Press : New Jersey USA**

FOR THE GERMAN HISTORICAL INSTITUTE, LONDON

Berg Publishers Ltd,
24 Binswood Avenue, Leamington Spa,
Warwickshire


First published 1984
© The German Historical Institute 1984

Published 1984 in the United States of America by Humanities Press Inc.,
Atlantic Highlands, NJ 07716

**British Library Cataloguing in Publication Data**
Exile in Great Britain
    1. Refugees—Germany   2. Germans—Great
Britain—Social conditions   3. Great
Britain—Social conditions—20th century
I. Hirschfeld, Gerhard  II. Exil in
Grossbritannien. *English*
305.8′31′041    DD256.5
ISBN 0 907582 21 4

**Library of Congress Cataloguing in Publication Data**
Main entry under title:
Exile In Great Britain
   Bibliography: pp. 320
   Includes index.
    1. Germans—Great Britain—History—20th century—
Addresses, essays, lectures.  2. Refugees, Political—
Great Britain—History—20th century—Addresses, essays,
lectures.  3. Refugees, Political—Germany—History—
20th century—Addresses, essays, lectures.  4. Germany—
Politics and government—1933-1945—Addresses, essays,
lectures.  I. Hirschfeld, Gerhard, 1946-
DA125.G4E95  1984    941′.00431    84-10919
ISBN 0-391-03121-X

Printed in Great Britain by Billings & Sons Ltd, Worcester

# Contents

*Gerhard Hirschfeld*

# Introduction

The exodus of hundreds of thousands of men, women and children during the period of Nazi rule has no precedent in German history. The full extent of the human loss cannot be assessed even today – more than fifty years later. This enforced migration also meant a great cultural, academic and economic sacrifice for German society, which has not yet been fully documented. However, basic research has been done in certain areas (including politics, literature and academic life), providing some idea of this human and intellectual blood-letting. The most extensive of these research projects on emigration from German-speaking countries after 1933 is the *International Biographical Dictionary of Central European Émigrés 1933-1945*, published jointly by the Research Foundation for Jewish Immigration in New York, and the Institut für Zeitgeschichte in Munich. These volumes contain short biographies of almost 9,000 individuals active in public life, business and selected professions, as well as in the fields of art, science and literature, and the lives of many more are now well-documented in the archives of both institutions. Several important books have also appeared recently, dealing with the political reaction of governments and public opinion in various countries which accepted refugees. What is still needed are interdisciplinary studies providing an overview of the migration to particular countries and regions. Thus the emigration from Nazi Germany has to be confronted with political, social, economic and cultural conditions in the countries of refuge, and its impact on these described. The collection of essays presented here aims to do precisely this. It is intended both to take stock of present research and to stimulate further work on particular subjects. The volume contains survey articles and

1

pilot studies which, in most cases, are the result of extensive research projects.

During the last months before the outbreak of the Second World War Great Britain became the main country of refuge for German-speaking emigrants, besides the USA. Initially the situation had been different. During the early years of the emigration from Germany, Great Britain was by no means the most favoured country of refuge: France, Poland, Czechoslovakia and even the Netherlands admitted many more refugees. By the end of 1937, Great Britain harboured only about 5,500 of a total of 154,000 refugees who had left Nazi Germany. The British authorities' refusal to admit a more considerable number of refugees from political and 'racial' persecution in Germany was the result of restrictive policies relating to immigration and to aliens, combined with the fear that an influx of refugees would inevitably lead to an increase in existing unemployment. The numbers seeking asylum increased dramatically in the aftermath of Hitler's annexationist policies towards Austria and Czechoslovakia and after the anti-Jewish pogroms of the 'Reichskristallnacht', when restrictions on entry into Britain were considerably eased. At the beginning of the war, there was a total of 74,000 Germans and Austrians in Great Britain, but some of these had received only a provisional residence permit and had to undertake to leave Great Britain immediately after they received permission to migrate to another country. One year later, 55,000 were granted official refugee status. The number of refugees in Great Britain was reduced again by voluntary emigration during the first years of the war and by deportations which took place within the context of provisions for internment. These were, in part, extremely strict. According to British estimates, about 35,000 Germans and Austrians were living in Great Britain in the summer of 1943; more than half of them were either children or too old to work.

It is generally accepted that just under 300,000 people escaped from Germany (excluding Austria and the Sudetenland) between January 1933 and October 1941, before an official ban on emigration was declared. Thus approximately 10 to 15 per cent of them found refuge in Great Britain. The majority of these refugees (about 90 per cent) were of German-Jewish origin. They had left Germany because of the antisemitic coercive measures which had been introduced there and now intended to settle permanently in Great Britain or elsewhere. Apart from the large number of predominantly non-political Jewish emigrants, there was also a small minority of genuine political refugees. For them, Great Britain was only a temporary stop, a 'waiting-room', as it were, in which they planned to establish themselves provisionally until they could return to a democratic Germany after it had been liberated by the Allies. In spite of this difference, the term 'exile' is used for both groups, the passive as well as the actively political refugees, because there was one circumstance which applied equally to all emigrants. Irrespective of the degree to which they were prepared to assimilate or integrate they all, at first, found themselves in a state of insecurity, of uncertainty, of being 'unaccommodated'. In addition, the variations in social consciousness as well as the large number of individual motives do not allow a *universal categorisation valid for the whole period*, of emigrants or exiles according to political convictions or activity (W. Röder). Numerous refugees who fled from political persecution as active opponents of National Socialism, sooner or later felt themselves to be immigrants and wanted to be fully integrated into the society of their country of refuge. On the other hand, many supposedly non-political Jewish emigrants refused to settle down permanently, favouring the idea of returning to their country of origin after it had been liberated from the Nazi menace. Therefore, in these essays, the terms 'émigré', 'emigrant', 'exile' and 'refugee' are used more in a pragmatic and general sense than as strictly-defined concepts.

The demand for an inter-disciplinary approach to this subject, frequently voiced by leading scholars of exile studies, was one of the guide-lines in the choice of these essays on German emigration to Great Britain. There are, however, several fundamental studies concerning the political aspect. These include A.J. Sherman's book on British government policy towards the German and Austrian refugees before the war,[1] Bernhard Wasserstein's fascinating study on Britain and the European Jews, which in a way complements Sherman's book,[2] and Werner Röder's fundamental analysis of Social Democratic exile politics during the war.[3] The emigration of Austrians to Great Britain for political reasons is comprehensively and critically assessed in Helene Maimann's book.[4] Political exile thus appears to be a well-researched and documented field. Nonetheless, many essential aspects have been neglected and important questions still remain unanswered. There is, for example, the relationship between the German Social Democratic Party in London and the British Labour Party, a relationship characterised in general by suspicion and misunderstandings. Its negative implications were probably not without consequences for British policy towards Germany after 1945. The lack of cooperation between the German politicians in exile, who were working for the removal of the National Socialist government, and the Foreign Office in London also requires closer analysis. Representatives of the politically-motivated exiles, primarily German Social Democrats, hoped to be able to influence British deliberations and planning, above all in the question of the long term organisation of post-war Germany. But the German politicians in exile were not granted any influence whatsoever. This applied equally to the matter of the division of Germany into occupation zones, which eventually led to the actual division of the country, and to the cession of the eastern territories, a process involving the expulsion of millions and accepted early by the British. The following contributions offer some new and unexpected insights into this subject. As *Lothar Kettenacker* shows in his essay on the influence of German refugees on British war aims policy, the German politicians in exile were generally regarded by the British Foreign Office as representatives of an exhausted political system that, in the end, had failed miserably. Depriving Germany of all power as permanently as possible, militarily and economically, politically and psychologically, was definitely given precedence over the establishment of a particular political and social order such as many emigrants had hoped for. The emigrants did not share the prejudices held by most civil servants and politicians in the Foreign Office about the militaristic mentality of the Germans. The predominantly negative attitude of the Labour Party towards the German Social Democratic Party (SPD) in exile was also a result of the prevailing Vansittartism (so called after Sir Robert Vansittart, Permanent Under-Secretary at the Foreign Office) much in evidence even among some of Labour's leading representatives. In spite of pressure from the Labour Party, the German Social Democrats refused to make any political concessions that would have meant abandoning their goal of a unified and democratic Germany, let alone to join the popular front advocated by the Communists. As in his recent book,[5] *Anthony Glees* comes to the conclusion that the results of Social Democratic exile in London were, on the whole, positive. The SPD preserved its specific identity during these years, and its firm resistance to the dismemberment of Germany provided it with a good basis from which to operate successfully in German post-war politics.

The political emigrants succeeded in opening up for themselves only a few areas of activity within the framework of the Allied war effort – all of them could be described as more or less non-political contributions to the British war effort. They included intelligence (gathering information by the interrogation of prisoners, press analyses, and the like), psychological warfare, and propaganda. The use of propaganda against Nazi Germany is also the subject of *Conrad Pütter*'s essay. The author shows that, in spite of British control and supervision, it was the political emigrants who largely took responsibility for the clandestine radio stations run by various ministries until the summer of 1941 ('Hier spricht Deutschland' and 'Sender der europäischen Revolution'). Thus political emigrants were given access to a means of disseminating their political ideas, in the hope of encouraging German resistance. The political scope given to the emigrants was narrowed only with the establishment of the central Political Warfare Executive (PWE) in the summer of 1941, and the replacement of information and persuasion by straight propaganda and subversion ('Gustav Siegfried Eins'). The setting up of a Catholic radio station ('Christus König') which was intended to demoralise the Catholic population of South Germany and Austria, revealed again the political exiles' lack of influence in this area.

As *Bernard Wasserstein* points out in his synthesis, by contemporary international standards Britain's record as far as the admission of German refugees is concerned (particularly in the critical years 1938/39) must be regarded as a generous one. British immigration policy on the whole must be seen as an alloy of xenophobic restrictionism and the liberal hospitality traditional (at different periods) in British politics.

While political emigration to Great Britain has been relatively fully researched, there is a lack of basic studies dealing with individual social groups and professions, the development of the arts and literature, and the economic and cultural contribution made by the refugees to their host country which, for many, eventually became a new homeland. In this field, too, the essays in this volume open new perspectives. *John Willett*'s essay on the arts and the emigration combines the writer's objective recording perspective with the committed involvement of a contemporary's personal experience. He suggests, in conclusion, that the multi-racial society of present-day Britain should learn from the experience of the 1930s when facing its own social problems. This suggestion can be seen as a valid contribution towards making good the mistakes of the past and improving social relations in this country.

The flight of scholars and professional people is one of the most fascinating aspects of the exodus from Nazi Germany. On the whole, academics found it easier to fit into their new environment, professionally as well as socially. But the shortage of vacant positions at a time of high unemployment, particularly in these areas, and the lack of prospects for promotion make it obvious why many preferred to leave Britain for the United States and elsewhere, or had to be satisfied with positions which were not necessarily commensurate with their previous experience and training. Naturally this did not apply equally to all professions, and *Francis Carsten* rightly points out in his introductory essay that members of the younger generation who came to Great Britain as schoolchildren or students and were able to finish their education here had an incomparably easier time. As far as the prospects for scholarly and university careers were concerned, Carsten again emphasises the significance of the Academic Assistance Council, founded by the British as early as 1933 and later re-named the Society for the Protection of Science and Learning. That the sciences in Great Britain, particularly the natural sciences and medicine, derived a great deal of profit from the emigrants was largely due to this academics' self-help organisation.

The outbreak of war in September 1939 led to an onerous and often painful experience for the German and Austrian refugees. From one day to the next, the British authorities declared them all without exception to be 'enemy aliens' and imposed certain conditions and considerable restrictions upon those who were not British citizens. The internments and deportations overseas which took place after May 1940 were among the most depressing and shameful events in the relationship between Britain as a host country and the emigrants. *Michael Seyfert*'s essay is a vivid portrayal of internment and of life in the camps, which were often badly, even primitively equipped. Seyfert describes how in spite of these difficulties, an extremely lively artistic, literary and educational milieu developed in the camps. The fact that so many intellectuals were gathered behind barbed wire made this one of the most fascinating episodes in the history of German-speaking exile in Great Britain, and one which had many long-term repercussions. The British authorities changed their restrictive policy after a few weeks, largely because of numerous protests and a change in public opinion. They allowed a number of internees to return – in particular those who were of use for the British war effort – but it was more than a year before the majority of the refugees was granted a limited, but guaranteed freedom.

The emigrants brought their host countries not only great cultural and scientific benefits: their achievements in starting economic and commercial enterprises were also impressive. The Home Office, which was responsible for the settlement of migrants, tended in the years before the War to direct the industrialists among the refugees to the designated Special Areas of the north and north-west, where unemployment was high and industries frequently outdated. The industrialists, welcome in the Special Areas because of the capital they brought with them, established mainly light industries, among them electro-chemical, engineering, chemicals and plastics. The process of establishing these enterprises, and the difficulties as well as the successes which accompanied their development, are described in detail in *Herbert Loebl's* essay. His research, which also includes the period 'after the Second World War, shows that, in 1974, fifty-four firms founded by emigrants in the north-east employed 17,000 workers: a significant contribution towards overcoming the chronic unemployment in this region.

London and England were not the only destinations of German refugees between 1933 and 1945. Thousands of emigrants, predominantly Jews, settled in Scotland, mainly in Glasgow. *Rainer Kölmel* describes how the refugees gradually became integrated into Scottish society, a process which he regards as, on the whole, successfully accomplished. Using the examples of the extensive relief work and the activities of Jewish relief organisations, he points to a fundamental aspect of the refugees' social integration: the initiatives developed, to a large extent, by the refugees themselves and the emergence of a new community feeling on the basis of common experiences.

The long-term consequences of the emigration and the closely related question of the assimilation and integration of the refugees into a culture initially strange to them are the subject of the concluding essay by *Marion Berghahn*, 'German Jews in England: Some Aspects of the Assimilation and Integration Process'. Basing her essay on a social-anthropological study of German-Jewish refugees in London,[6] she attempts to demonstrate that in spite of a high level of integration, both professionally and socially, a specifically German-Jewish ethnicity continues to exist even in the third generation. Undoubtedly, the numerous religious, social and cultural institutions which were established during the period of emigration, and which continue to flourish today, played an important role in this. According to Marion Berghahn, the survival of a specifically German-Jewish way of life has been the decisive factor in the continued existence of cultural and intellectual traditions. These have prevented a complete assimilation of the former emigrants into English society. However, the unique German-Jewish way of life has – paradoxically in an English environment – made it possible for most of them to be what they could not be in another society – German Jews.

An investigation encompassing the political, cultural, economic and social conditions surrounding the emigration to Great Britain would be incomplete without a portrayal of the circumstances which gave rise to the flight of so many German citizens to other countries. In his essay, *John Fox* provides an analysis of National Socialist politics at the time of the seizure of power, and of the action taken against all those groups of which the regime wanted to rid the country, using the means of alignment ('Gleichschaltung'), elimination ('Ausschaltung'), and terror. But the Nazis' destruction of the democratic order and the fight against the 'illegal' opposition did not stop at the borders of Germany. The struggle against refugees, in particular against all political organisations which were established outside Germany, was closely linked with the smashing of the various resistance groups inside the Reich. Fox also deals with the ways and means used by the Gestapo and a number of political institutions (including the German Foreign Office) against emigrants who settled in Great Britain.

The diverse approaches represented in this volume, to a subject as complex as the emigration to Great Britain, make a certain unevenness and occasional overlapping inevitable. Nevertheless, our aim was to retain as far as possible both the originality and distinctive features of the contributions and the interdisciplinary character of the volume. I should like to express my thanks to the contributors for their patience during all phases of the production of this volume. I should like to take this opportunity to express my gratitude for all the helpful advice received while I was looking for suitable contributions. Especial thanks are due to Professor Francis Carsten, both for his advice and for his friendly support of the project. Of course responsibility for the final form of the volume (including all shortcomings) lies with the editor alone.

My thanks are also due to my colleagues at the German Historical Institute in London and particularly to its Director, Professor Wolfgang J. Mommsen, who not only provided initial encouragement for the project, but also followed its progress with helpful criticism and interest. Finally I should like to thank Angela Davies who translated the majority of the German texts.

## Notes

1. A. J. Sherman, *Island Refuge: Britain and Refugees from the Third Reich 1933-1939*, London, 1973.
2. Bernard Wasserstein, *Britain and the Jews of Europe, 1939-45*, Oxford, 1979.
3. Werner Röder, *Die deutschen sozialistischen Exilgruppen in Großbritannien, 1940-1945*, 2nd ed., Bonn/Bad Godesberg, 1973.
4. Helene Maimann, *Politik im Wartesaal. Österreichische Exilpolitik in Großbritannien 1938-1945*, Vienna, 1978.
5. Anthony Glees, *Exile Politics during the Second World War. The German Social Democrats in Britain*, Oxford, 1982.
6. Marion Berghahn, *German-Jewish Refugees in England. The Ambiguities of Assimilation*, London, 1984.

*Francis L. Carsten*

# German Refugees in Great Britain 1933-1945

*A Survey*

During the first years of National Socialist rule in Germany the number of Jewish and other refugees admitted to the United Kingdom was not very large, and the countries bordering on Germany – above all France, the Low Countries and Czechoslovakia – took a proportionately much larger share of refugees from Germany. While in 1933 300–400 a month arrived in Britain, in 1934 the number fell to about 100 per month and even in 1935 it did not increase very markedly.[1] Those who came to Britain often had relatives or friends there who would guarantee their maintenance; others were academics who had contacts with British universities, or independent business people, often with British connections, who could transfer their enterprise or skills and thus could establish themselves without creating any grave problems. The British authorities were willing to admit well-known academics or people who had private means and connections, especially people who were not likely to add to the economic problems of the country, but who might help to alleviate the severe unemployment by establishing new enterprises and factories. They were equally willing to admit on a temporary basis people who intended to migrate overseas. The voluntary organisations established by the Jewish community undertook to support any refugees who might need their help and guaranteed that the refugees would not become a burden on public funds. As late as November 1938 – when the passing of the Nuremberg Laws in 1935 and the occupation of Austria in 1938 had vastly increased the flood of refugees from Central

Europe – the British Prime Minister Neville Chamberlain revealed in the House of Commons that, apart from some 5,000 who had meanwhile left for other countries, only 11,000 refugees had been allowed to enter the United Kingdom since 1933.[2] This meant an average influx of about 2,000 per year, many of whom were able to bring part of their property with them; their absorption was not likely to create any great difficulties, although as early as March 1933 a Conservative MP had claimed in the House that 'hundreds of thousands of Jews are now leaving Germany and scurrying from there to this country.... Are we prepared in this country to allow aliens to come in here from every country while we have 3,000,000 unemployed?'[3] This was, of course, a viewpoint which was always prominent in the debates on the refugee issue in Parliament, in the press and among the public in general.

As far as the British authorities were concerned, considerations such as these remained decisive. In the summer of 1933 an internal memorandum of the Foreign Office stated: 'The number of such refugees is still comparatively small ... but the competent authorities have no desire to see it increased ...'. The 'paramount consideration', wrote the Foreign Secretary, Sir John Simon, in October 1933, was unemployment and the condition of the labour market. In December the British delegate to the High Commission for Refugees set up by the League of Nations was instructed that 'there are no prospects for Germans seeking employment in commerce or industry', that no more students or research workers could be absorbed in the United Kingdom, and that there was 'little or no possibility of finding useful openings in this country for more refugees of the professional classes'.[4] In November the President of the Royal College of Physicians, Lord Dawson of Penn, informed the Home Secretary that a few refugee doctors of special distinction might perhaps be admitted, but added that 'the number that could usefully be absorbed or teach us anything could be counted on the fingers of one hand'. At that time the number of aliens studying at British medical schools was 160, and not all these were refugees.[5] Even one of the most prominent members of the Jewish community, the Marquis of Reading, a former Viceroy of India, declared at a public meeting in London in June 1933: 'We must take care that we do not add to the great unemployment existing in this country'. Apart from the fear of unemployment, there was another fear: that large numbers of Jewish refugees would cause a growth of antisemitism in Britain – at a time when Sir Oswald Mosley was organising the British Union of Fascists and carrying antisemitic propaganda into the East End of London and other districts with a large Jewish population, when antisemitism was virulent all over Europe. Its spread was, of course, fostered by assiduous National Socialist propaganda and British Intelligence believed that a German plot was afoot to export antisemitism by way of the growing number of refugees. As the Home Secretary, Sir Samuel Hoare, told his Cabinet colleagues in March 1938, 'a curious story had reached him (from MI5) suggesting that the Germans were anxious to inundate this country with Jews, with a view to creating a Jewish problem in the United Kingdom'.[6]

Yet the events of 1938, the German invasion of Austria and the atrocities committed there, the occupation of the Sudetenland a few months later and the mass flight of Jews and Socialists from both countries, the German pogroms of November when the synagogues were burnt down, Jewish property was systematically looted and many thousands were thrown into concentration camps, led to a revision of British immigration policy and to the reception of many thousands of the victims. By April 1939 20,300 adult refugees (German, Austrian and Czech) and more than 4,800 children were admitted. By the time the war broke out a few months later, their number had once more doubled, reaching a figure of about 55,000. After the end of the war, about 7,000 or 8,000 orphans from the concentration camps were admitted. Of those who came before the war, the second largest group – about 9,000 – were children under 18 years of age, most of them without their parents whom they had had to leave behind. By far the largest group was formed by women (and men) who were given permits to work as domestic servants – a field where an acute labour shortage existed; there were about 21,000 of them, and they were accompanied by almost 1,000 children.[7] As many of them were not accustomed to this role (and no doubt in many cases had themselves employed domestic servants in Germany), they often felt exploited and humiliated in their new surroundings. Many spoke very little or no English and found it extremely difficult to adjust to such strange surroundings. Many others had stamped in their Aliens Certificates that they were not permitted to accept any work, 'whether paid or unpaid': restrictions from which they were only released after the outbreak of the war, when an increasingly acute labour shortage permitted the economic absorption of the refugees. Although no statistics are available on the social backgrounds of the refugees, there can be little doubt that the majority – the large majority – were of middle- or lower-middle-class origin and that this created problems of integration. The number of Jewish refugees of working-class origin seems to have been very small; only the Communists and, to a lesser degree, the Social Democrats had a number of working-class members in their refugee organisations. The number of political refugees in Britain was not large, although among the Austrian refugees there were a comparatively large number of Socialists and after Munich several hundred Sudeten German Social Democrats were admitted. The vast majority of refugees were Jewish by religion or were so-called 'non-Aryans', who were partly of Jewish origin, or married to Jews.

The admittance of large numbers of refugees, especially during the critical months before the outbreak of the war, was due in no small measure to the incessant lobbying of pro-refugee groups and individuals. These included several Labour MPs, such as Josiah Wedgwood and Philip Noel-Baker, but pride of place went to Eleanor Rathbone, independent member for the Combined English Universities, who earned herself the honorary title of 'Member for Refugees'. Time and again they asked questions in the House, urged the government to take more energetic measures and to grant more visas, and demanded that the conditions of immigration be made less stringent. They soon intervened on behalf of Austrians, Czechs and Spaniards, as well as on behalf of the German refugees. It was due to their efforts that, for example, the Jewish children and the Sudeten German Social Democrats were admitted *en bloc*, just as their efforts later led to the rescision of the policy of general internment of 'enemy aliens'. In November 1938 Noel-Baker opened a debate on the refugee problem in the House of Commons and called for 'an immediate concerted effort amongst the nations' to cope with it, for a statement on government policy and for representations in Berlin to end the persecution. Sir Samuel Hoare replied for the government that any refugees who could maintain themselves or who were guaranteed by friends would 'almost invariably' be given a visa and be admitted. Others could be admitted temporarily pending their migration overseas. But he also mentioned 'an underlying current of suspicion and anxiety' about mass immigration and 'the making of a definite anti-Jewish movement'. As to the number of immigrants, he declined to be tied to any figure or quota system (as the United States were by legislation). In April 1939 Eleanor Rathbone demanded in the *Manchester Guardian* that the government give up its 'selfish isolationism towards the refugees, simplify the conditions of admission and establish temporary reception camps for large numbers'. During the war she continued to attack the passivity of the government in view of the horrors perpetrated in German-occupied

Europe and repeatedly asked what steps were being taken to assist the escape of Jews from there. The then Home Secretary, Herbert Morrison, had to listen to her quoting extracts from his earlier enthusiastic pleas for more Jewish immigration into Palestine.[8] In the House of Lords it was above all George Bell, then Bishop of Chichester, who persistently fought for the same humanitarian ideals.

A number of voluntary organisations looked after the refugees, trying to place them with families and supporting those in need. The most important were the Jewish organisations, such as the Jewish Aid Committee and the Council for German Jewry, which carried the main burden. In addition, there were the Christian Council for Refugees and the Religious Society of Friends (Quakers), as well as the Society for the Protection of Science and Learning (academics), the International Student Service and the Labour Party (responsible for Socialist refugees), while the Communists looked after their own comrades. Between 1933 and 1939 British Jews collected about £3,000,000 for their co-religionists. In 1938 the former Prime Minister, Earl Baldwin, together with *The Times*, launched a public appeal, which within a few months raised over £500,000, most of which was donated to a children's fund. Before the outbreak of the war the British government had refused to contribute to the maintenance of the refugees, but by 1939 the voluntary organisations had reached the end of their funds and there would have been chaos had the government not intervened. Thus in 1940 it contributed £533,000 to the funds of the Central Council for Jewish Refugees and in the following year £264,000. By the end of the war the government bore the entire cost of the refugees' maintenance, a cost that decreased as more and more of them found jobs or continued their migration to America.[9]

Of special importance among the voluntary organisations – for the refugee academics as well as for the British universities – was the Academic Assistance Council, later called the Society for the Protection of Science and Learning. It was founded as early as April 1933 on the initiative of Sir William Beveridge, then Director of the London School of Economics and Political Science, and with the world-famous physicist Lord Rutherford as its president; the vice-presidents were another famous scientist, Professor A.V. Hill, and the Director of the British Museum. Among the members of its council were several vice-chancellors of British universities. Its funds came from 2,000 subscribers, many of them academics who contributed part of their salaries. During the first three years of its existence the Society succeeded in placing fifty-seven refugee scholars in permanent posts and another 155 in temporary positions. Professor Lindemann brought to the Clarendon Laboratory in Oxford a number of well-known German scientists, who rapidly won for the Oxford Laboratory a world reputation in low temperature research. They also worked on other problems, such as the liquefying of helium and the mobility of electrons. At Cambridge, Sir Lawrence Bragg helped numerous refugee scientists. Later the British war effort was to benefit greatly from the activities of so many eminent and less eminent refugees.[10]

The famous Warburg Library, specialising in classical and art history, was transferred from Hamburg to London, where it eventually became a permanent university institute. Perhaps it was easier for well-known academics to find posts in Britain than it was for many others, but there were many less-well-known academics, as well as men with a reputation, who were unable to do so and who had to continue their migration to the United States. Among historians and political scientists the names of Franz Neumann, Arthur Rosenberg, Hans Rothfels and Veit Valentin come to mind; and there were also members of the famous Bauhaus and many others.

If it was difficult for the historians and Germanists to find posts in their own field, it was even more so for the large numbers of lawyers among the refugees. Many of them had to accept minor clerical jobs or almost any sort of work, because their legal knowledge was entirely different from that of a British barrister or solicitor, and very few could afford a lengthy and costly period of new legal training. The position of the doctors was not much better. They were required to study for several years at a British university and even after qualification were admitted only on a temporary basis – until the war made it essential to admit refugee doctors without a British qualification, first on a temporary basis, in hospitals and as assistants to British doctors, and later without any such restrictions. Dentists, however, were admitted without renewed study.[11] Thus there were marked differences between the various professions and the conditions under which the refugees were admitted. Their absorption into British professional life took many years, but it was on the whole successfully accomplished. It was easier, of course, for the younger generation, those who came to Britain while still at school or university and who could finish their education in a British environment. In general, the number of academics and professional people who returned to Germany or Austria after the war was very small, which seems to indicate that the majority became integrated in their adopted country.

In general, academics found it easier to integrate than businessmen – after all, the universities had for a long time integrated very diverse elements and academics were used to co-operating with foreign colleagues. Many businessmen, however, successfully transferred their skills and connections to Britain, as the Huguenots had done on an earlier occasion. As early as 1936 the Home Office stated in an internal memorandum 'that several thousand desirable, industrious, intelligent and acceptable persons have been added to the population. They have brought with them considerable capital, and established industries which have already given employment to more British subjects than the total number of refugees from Germany who are now living in the United Kingdom'.[12] This, of course, was before the mass immigration of 1938 and reflected the British policy of granting admission to certain 'desirable' categories of immigrants and excluding those without private means or special skills. In the early years of National Socialist rule emigrants were able to transfer part of their property abroad, after paying a special tax of 25 per cent before leaving and transferring the rest of their fortunes to a 'blocked' account. They were able to sell these 'blocked marks' in their new country of residence, but at a steadily diminishing rate. Those who left Germany in the early 1930s received a comparatively good price, but by 1938 the value of the 'blocked mark' had shrunk to a small fraction of the original, so that Jews leaving Germany were virtually dispossessed (the export of valuables was also prohibited). The High Commissioner appointed by the League of Nations and Western governments pressed the German government in vain to permit the transfer of at least some of the refugees' property to facilitate their settlement abroad: according to the British government, this was 'the crux of the whole question'. But in July 1938 Foreign Minister von Ribbentrop declined to cooperate with other governments when he was approached by the British ambassador on the refugee issue. When the ambassador asked Ribbentrop whether the transfer of Jewish capital could not be made easier, he refused 'because it would be an imposition for Germany to permit the transfer of the capital amassed by Jews, especially after the war'.[13]

In spite of these difficulties and the strange environment, a considerable number of factories were established by refugees from Germany; according to a statement by the Home Office in February 1939, there were about 300 at that time and many more were established later. In the later 1930s the Home Office tended to direct refugee industrialists to the Special Areas of the north and north-west with their severe unemployment and ageing, run-down industries – to the north Midlands, Wales, parts of Yorkshire, Northumberland, Cumberland, Scotland and Northern Ireland. There they established light industries producing clothing, leather goods, toys and chemical and pharmaceutical products. Most of these firms were small or very small, but some reached a respectable size. According to an evaluation made by the Board of Trade in 1950–1, a total of 163 firms were established in the Special Areas by refugees.[14] To these must be added firms founded in London and the south where the majority of refugees had settled, at least in the early 1930s. Many others established themselves in partnership with British industrialists, or expanded existing firms. It is virtually impossible to assess the total contribution made by the refugees to British industrial life, but there can be no doubt that it was very considerable. The same is true of trade and commercial life, where refugees were able to use and extend their old connections and links with firms in other continents.

Many refugees who came to Britain were only accepted for training in an agricultural or technical occupation pending their migration overseas. As the United States took only a fixed quota of German immigrants and immigration into Palestine was severely limited by the British authorities, they naturally thought of the vast British Empire as offering possibilities for refugee settlement. But all hopes that large, half-empty colonies would offer unlimited possibilities to young, energetic settlers were frustrated. The Colonial Office for some time thought of Northern Rhodesia, which was undeveloped and under-populated, and where the Crown owned vast tracts of land. But the white settlers were opposed to any large influx and no government finance was made available for the purpose; in the end the colony accepted only about 100 refugees. About 500 settled in Kenya as agricultural workers. There were plans to bring several thousands to British Guiana where they were to be settled in the interior. But the government was unwilling to bear even the initial costs of road making and land acquisition and, in the end, the difficulties resulting from the extreme climate and non-existent communications proved so great that nothing came of the whole scheme. At the end of 1939 the Colonial Office had to admit that the total number of refugees who had settled in the British colonies (excluding Palestine) was only about 3,000. Early in 1941 an official of the Colonial Office informed the Foreign Office that 'the hard fact remains that they are not wanted by any Colonial Government, for a number of very good reasons, the most important of which perhaps are [*sic*] that they are certain sooner or later to become a charge on public funds . . . The introduction of a body of people, however small, which is entirely alien in every sense of the word, would be greatly resented by the working classes in the Colony and might well lead to serious trouble . . .'.[15] In general, it was the Colonial Office which often proved the most difficult with regard to the refugee problem; its passive resistance made any progress, urged for example by the Foreign Office, impossible. In default of any other argument it could always be claimed that large-scale immigration presented 'security risks', for the Germans would try to smuggle in 'Nazi agents under the cloak of refugees'.[16] Naturally, it was impossible to prove the contrary, although such agents were apparently never discovered.

Quite distinct from the vast majority of the often quite non-political Jewish refugees was the small minority of political refugees who came to Britain. They were divided according to the parties to which they had belonged in Germany or Austria. There were a few non-Jewish Conservative or Liberal politicians, and there were Social Democrats and Communists, with the latter forming the largest group. The Communists initiated cultural activities on a fairly large scale, with a *Freier Deutscher Kulturbund* (Free German Cultural League) and a *Freie Deutsche Jugend* (Free German Youth) movement which attracted many non-Communists. Before the war a group of the SPD existed in London with Franz Neumann as its chairman, but it remained rather small; and the groups of the *Internationaler Sozialistischer Kampfbund* or the *Sozialistische Arbeiterpartei* were even smaller. Only when these different Socialist groups united in the later years of the war did a large local branch of the SPD come into being. There were considerbaly more Austrian Socialists but they kept their separate entity, as did the Sudeten German Social Democrats.

Immediately after the outbreak of the war the leaders of the SPD were invited by the Labour Party to come to Britain. They did so with the approval of the British government after the fall of France. But, although leading members of the Labour Party consulted the leaders of the SPD and maintained them financially, it cannot be said that they had any influence upon the policies of the Labour Party, not to speak of the British government. This was due to the fact that the International Secretary of the Labour Party, William Gillies, and other Labour leaders were increasingly influenced by the Vansittartites (so-called after Sir Robert Vansittart, the Permanent Under-Secretary at the Foreign Office), a strongly anti-German group which traced Germany's 'black record' back into her Germanic and medieval past.

Exile in Great Britain

This corresponded with a general trend in British public opinion. The longer the war continued and the more the atrocities committed in eastern Europe became public knowledge, the more anti-German British public opinion became.

In spite of the eventual withdrawal of all support by the Labour Party, the leaders of the German Social Democrats refused to make any political concessions, to participate in a 'popular front', or to renounce the idea of a united and democratic Germany. But their influence remained minimal as long as the war lasted. And the same can be said of all other political refugees from Germany, from Conservative to Communist. In the early stages of the war, the Foreign Office on occasion consulted exiled Conservative politicians, such as Hermann Rauschning. Later on, the Russian alliance and the policy of 'unconditional surrender' prevented even such informal contact. British policy rejected the ideas of a German government in exile or a compromise peace. It had to take into account the views of its allies – the exiled governments of the Netherlands, Czechoslovakia and Poland, all established in London – and it dared not risk alienating the Soviet Union. But the government also distrusted all émigrés (whose influence in Germany was questionable) and, above all, it distrusted their alleged nationalism. It was aware that no unity existed among the exiled politicians, that they were divided by many quarrels and splits, that they would be opposed to a partition of Germany and to any large territorial concessions, for example to Poland in the east. It was thus not only opportune, but seemed advisable not to allow the émigrés any political influence. This did not preclude the employment of individual refugees in propaganda or intelligence work without, however, allowing them any say in political matters.

At the outbreak of war, all refugees from Germany and Austria, with the exception of those already naturalised, were classified as 'enemy aliens' and subjected to certain restrictions; for example, they were not allowed to possess any maps, and even those in old guide books had to be handed in. All 'enemy aliens' had to appear before tribunals whose task it was to decide whether or not they were genuine 'refugees from Nazi oppression'. If not, they were to be interned. About 120 of these tribunals, consisting of a judge or retired judge attended by a police secretary, were established. The tribunals were empowered to order the internment of any alien who appeared before them and about 600 were put into category A and interned forthwith. The vast majority (more than 64,000 out of a total of 71,600) were put into category C, classified as 'genuine' refugees and exempted from

20

most restrictions, but they still needed police permits to travel, change their residence or to own a bicycle etc. There was an intermediate category B, comprising nearly 7,000 people who were considered doubtful cases and subject to more severe restrictions. Naturally, the standards applied by the tribunals varied, especially with regard to category B, which undoubtedly included many genuine refugees. In numerous other cases, refugees were classified C without the slightest difficulty and some of the judges even complimented certain refugees on their known anti-Nazi records.[17] This was the period of the 'phoney war' when life in Britain still continued much as it had in peace time.

With the German invasion of the Low Countries and France in the spring of 1940 the general mood changed quickly and became strongly anti-German. Above all, the sudden collapse of Britain's allies was widely attributed to the mysterious working of a Fifth Column which had helped the invader and these rumours were given credence by a memorandum written by the British Minister in The Hague, listing cases of Fifth Column activity in Holland and urging the internment of all Germans and Austrians. Anti-alien sentiment swept the country and was assiduously fanned by the press. Even papers which hitherto had stood up for the refugees, such as the *Manchester Guardian*, began to demand mass internment. In an editorial of 17 May 1940 even the *Jewish Chronicle* advocated internment; it was not possible to argue against it, 'least of all at this juncture when the very life of the nation is at issue'.[18] There was no dissent. The government responded by declaring a belt of country along the eastern and southern coasts 'protected areas' where all male Germans and Austrians between the ages of 16 and 60, irrespective of the category to which they had been allocated, were to be interned. A few days later all male Germans and Austrians who had been put into category B were also interned, followed by all women of the same category. After the defeat of France, at the end of June 1940, the government decided to intern *all* male Germans and Austrians between the ages of 16 and 60, with the exception only of invalids; the women of category C were spared, for reasons unknown. Altogether something like 30,000 people were interned, most of them in makeshift camps, as the preparations for this mass internment at a time of national emergency were extremely scanty and all facilities had to be improvised. About 4,200 refugees were shipped to Canada or Australia, some of them in the most terrible conditions and one of the boats carrying them was torpedoed by a German submarine with heavy loss of life.[19] It was a panic measure decided upon by a government security committee, at a time when a

German landing in Britain was expected daily; it was not a rational move, for the many officers and soldiers used in the operation might have been more usefully employed elsewhere.

In Britain, the majority of the internees was sent to the Isle of Man where they were housed in empty boarding houses and hotels and where their lives soon settled into a routine. At the beginning, however, there was considerable disorder and sometimes worse, because accommodation for so many thousands simply did not exist. At Warth Mill in Lancashire thousands were accommodated in a long-disused derelict cotton mill where the floor boards were rotting and pieces of machinery threatened to tumble down and where the water supply and toilets were of the most primitive kind. What hurt even more was that *all* books and other reading material were confiscated – after all, they might contain a code. Pocket knives, forks, spoons and razor blades suffered the same fate – might they not be used for a treacherous attack on the guards? To compensate the internees for the loss the commandant addressed them on the virtues and merits of the British Empire; among his audience were many eminent and elderly German professors from Oxford.

It was weeks before the internees could communicate with their families and even longer before any books arrived from outside, because all correspondence had to pass through an overworked censorship. At Huyton, hundreds of internees were put into tents and there too the conditions were extremely primitive. The indefatigable Eleanor Rathbone visited Huyton in July 1940 in the company of another MP. According to his report, 'she spoke to them with moving sympathy of our concern for the state in which they were living and our anxiety to do everything that we could to improve conditions in every way possible'.[20]

After a few months, however, the whole cumbersome machinery went into reverse, as public opinion moved strongly in favour of the refugees. The internees were screened again and gradually certain categories of refugees who were useful for the war effort were released. Even those who had been shipped to Canada or Australia were eventually brought back to England. One of those who returned from the Australian Odyssey was the eminent anti-Nazi publicist and writer Franz Borkenau. He and many other refugee intellectuals spent the remaining years of the war in the monitoring service of the BBC. The BBC also employed refugees, including, for example, some leading members of the SPD, as announcers for its German programmes. Political refugees also worked in the various 'secret' broadcasting stations which were domiciled in the villages around Woburn and Woburn Abbey near Bletchley. The journalists Frederick Voigt and Sefton Delmer were responsible for this form of propaganda. Both knew Germany intimately and relied heavily on refugees whom they knew personally. For some time, a group of left-wing Socialists from Germany and Austria was given a free hand to run the 'Station of the European Revolution', which had a strong left-wing bias. Later Sefton Delmer, who preferred to use 'filth and dirt' to destabilise the Hitler regime, ran a station called 'Gustav Siegfried Eins' in which he figured as the 'Chief'. Its broadcasts which dwelt on Nazi corruption and good living were widely heard in Germany and apparently very popular there. Towards the end of the war, there was the 'Soldiers' Station Calais' which to a large extent relied on the services of suitable German prisoners of war, who were also used for broadcasting by the BBC.[21]

Delmer's whole outfit was part of a large government department concerned with propaganda to enemy and enemy-occupied countries on the continent, the Political Warfare Executive (PWE) which had its base at Woburn Abbey from which the owner, the Duke of Bedford, had been removed. The heads of its German section were British, but the lower ranks were occupied almost entirely by refugees. Many of these were German or Austrian Socialists, because Richard Crossman, one of the high-ranking PWE officials, preferred to employ political refugees who had a certain amount of know-how. There were prominent ex-Communists and leading members of the SPD, as well as many others of the Left, all of whom had been specially vetted by MI5. PWE was not only a propaganda department, but in the later years of the war became responsible for other tasks in which the services of refugees were required, as, for example, in preparations for the occupation of Germany. The people working there, however, were not permitted to give any political advice (this function was reserved for the Foreign Office and its Research Department); the refugees' role was limited to the technical and information side.

When increasing numbers of German prisoners of war arrived from North Africa and France, PWE also became responsible for their 're-education'. They were divided into several categories according to their political sympathies. Dozens of lecturers – mainly refugees – were sent to the prisoner-of-war camps to lecture on a wide range of topics. Except perhaps in some of the 'black' camps which were dominated by unrepentant National Socialists, they received, on the whole, a friendly welcome, because they could converse in fluent German. After the German collapse the prisoners were naturally eager to receive information about events at home and the longer their imprisonment lasted, the more they were concerned to know when they would be sent home, a point on which the lecturers could not give them any information. Two refugees, Dr Heinz Koeppler and Waldemar von Knoeringen, were responsible for the establishment of a very special prisoner-of-war camp at Wilton Park near Beaconsfield, where prisoners with a strong anti-Nazi background were brought together and taught in special programmes, and where endless political discussions took place every day. In other camps, too, active groups of anti-Nazis came into being and at Kempton Park a group of young refugees specialised in converting ardent young National Socialists. Refugee lecturers were thus able to establish close contacts with prisoners of war, contacts which in many cases continued over the years, after the prisoners' return to Germany. This was fraternisation of a rather special kind and many refugees found that they could at last do some really useful work.[22]

There was another form of refugee war service of a very different kind. Soon after the outbreak of war, the Auxiliary Military Pioneer Corps was formed as a non-combatant unit and able-bodied younger refugees were asked to join up. At Kitchener Camp in Kent, which housed several thousand young refugees, 'alien companies' of the Pioneer Corps were formed, and early in 1940 five of them were sent to France to work on the British Expeditionary Force's lines of communication. In May, at the time of the French collapse, when the Allied front was retreating before the advance of the German army, these 'alien companies' were issued with arms, without any previous training, and all succeeded in reaching the coast. In the House of Commons, Colonel Arthur Evans, MP, who had commanded them, spoke of their part in the defence of Le Havre and declared, 'they conducted themselves in the best traditions of the British Army ... They were manning machine-guns and anti-tank rifles at the side of the road and at points ...'. In 1940 the headquarters of the 'alien companies' were situated at Ilfracombe in Devon, under the command of the Marquis of Reading and with officers who were mostly re-commissioned from the First World War. At that time refugees could not be given a commission, but could only be promoted to the rank of sergeant. Yet seasoned officers themselves were soon forced to admire the enthusiasm of the new NCOs, whose words of command rang out in true Prussian fashion across the parade ground. It is estimated that a total of more than 9,000 young men and women volunteered for the Forces during the war and that 145 of them died on active service or from wounds (they suffered heavy casualties during the London Blitz). Later it became possible for refugee soldiers to obtain commissions and to be transferred to other units. About 800 of them served in technical units, 650 in combatant units, 450 in the Intelligence Corps and similar units, 300 in the Commandos and Airborne forces, over 100 in the Navy and the RAF. Thus they took part fully in the military effort of the United Kingdom and the risk they ran if taken prisoner by the Germans was certainly much greater, although they were allowed to assume British names if serving in combatant units.[23] After the end of the war a large number of the refugees emigrated to America and other continents, but many others remained in Britain and became British citizens.

Some of the well-known scientists who came to Britain before the war participated in the British scientific war effort, as C.P. Snow and R.V. Jones have described. Some went to the United States to take part in the production of the first atomic bomb and one of them, Klaus Fuchs, a convinced German Communist, communicated his knowledge to the Russians; in 1946, when he was working in Great Britain again (at the Government Establishment for Research on Atomic Energy at Harwell) he was exposed as a Soviet agent. After his release from prison he was sent to the GDR at his own request and he became a leading scientist there at the Central Institute for Nuclear Physics. Of those who remained in Britain, twenty-five were awarded Fellowships of the Royal Society by 1955 and three, Born, Chain and Krebs, won Nobel Prizes. Dr Ernst B. Chain was awarded the Nobel Prize for medicine, together with two British scientists, for the discovery of penicillin. Dr Max Born became Professor of Theoretical and Mathematical Physics at Edinburgh, Dr Otto Frisch the head of the Nuclear Physics Division of the Government Establishment for Research on Atomic Energy at Harwell, Dr Hans Krebs the Director of the Medical Research Council and Dr Rudolf Peierls Professor of Mathematical Physics at Birmingham. Sir Frank Simon was for many years Professor of Thermodynamics at Oxford, Dr Herbert Fröhlich Professor of Theoretical Physics at Liverpool and Dr Erwin Schrödinger – who had won the Nobel Prize for physics in 1933 – Professor at the Institute for Advanced Studies in Dublin. More names could easily be added to this distinguished list and there can be no doubt that British science and medicine profited enormously from the influx.[24]

The same is true of many other fields. It is difficult to think of sociology in Britain without the enormous influence of Karl

Mannheim who was born in Hungary and had taught at Heidelberg and Frankfurt. The Warburg Institute has vastly enriched the life and reputation of London University. Under Professors Fritz Saxl and Ernst Gombrich it became an institute of world renown and trained many dozens of art historians. Gombrich's own books, such as *The Story of Art* (1950) and *Art and Illusion* (1960), became best sellers which allowed many thousands of people to appreciate art and art history. The arts in Britain were stimulated by and benefited greatly from the newcomers and their ideas. Here I need only mention the name of Oscar Kokoschka or that of Kurt Schwitters. In a very different field, the Wiener Library, a large collection of books and pamphlets on German and Jewish affairs, was brought to London in 1939 by Dr Alfred Wiener, after a six-year stay in the Netherlands. Unfortunately, only a remnant of the collection now remains in London. The Wiener Library provided efficient help and valuable information for the British government during the war and later for countless students and researchers in Jewish and German history and politics. After the war, the British universities absorbed many of the younger refugees as teachers and researchers; they were integrated without difficulty into the informal atmosphere of British academic life and contributed their share to the education of the younger generation. If the refugees have retained some of the characteristics of their continental homelands and are integrated only partially into the British environment, this amalgam of different backgrounds and cultures is perhaps not too bad a mixture and has, like the many and very different influxes of more recent years, contributed to the enrichment of the country. After all, in the course of history Britain has benefited from many waves of immigrants, Roman, Anglo-Saxon, Danish, Norman, Dutch and Huguenot, and it seems very unlikely that the twentieth century will prove an exception.

## Notes

1. Figures from A.J. Sherman, *Island Refuge: Britain and Refugees from the Third Reich 1933-1939*, London, 1973, pp. 47-8.
2. Chamberlain on 21 November 1938: *ibid.*, p. 179.

3. E. Doran on 9 March 1933, quoted *ibid.*, p. 28.

4. *Ibid.*, pp. 37, 40, 43, quoting Foreign Office documents of August, October and December 1933.

5. Home Office Minute of 23 November 1933, quoted *ibid.*, p. 48.

6. Cabinet conclusions of 16 March 1938, quoted *ibid.*, p. 88.

7. The figures given in the literature vary greatly: for the children between 9,000 and 10,000; for domestic servants between 4,461 (according to the Home Office in October 1939) and 21,000; for the refugees in general between 49,500 and 60,000. The differences are partly due to the inclusion or exclusion of Czech refugees. See Sherman, pp. 255-6 and n. 104; A. Stevens, *The Dispossessed: German Refugees in Britain*, London, 1975, pp. 141, 150, 158; N. Bentwich, *They Found Refuge*, London, 1956, pp. 38, 45, 80.

8. For Miss Rathbone, see in particular M.D. Stocks, *Eleanor Rathbone: Biography*, London, 1949, especially pp. 257-8, 300, and Sherman, pp. 225-6; for Noel-Baker and the debate in the House on 21 November 1938, *ibid.*, pp. 179-81.

9. Figures according to Bentwich, pp. 32-3, 38, 41, 120, 206; B. Wasserstein, *Britain and the Jews of Europe 1939-1945*, Oxford, 1979, p. 83. In general, see Sherman, pp. 26-7, 226.

10. Bentwich, pp. 17, 34-5; Stevens, pp. 125-6; R.V. Jones, *Most Secret War*, London, 1979, p. 49.

11. Bentwich, pp. 53, 117-18.

12. Home Office memorandum of 8 September 1936, quoted by Sherman, p. 73.

13. Foreign Office document of 8 July 1938, quoted by H.E. Tutas, *Nationalsozialismus und Exil. Die Politik des Dritten Reiches gegenüber der deutschen politischen Emigration*, Munich/Vienna, 1975, p. 236. Earl Winterton in the Cabinet on 'the crux of the whole question', 16 November 1938, quoted by Sherman, p. 175.

14. L. Zeitlin, 'They came to England: the Newcomers in Trade and Industry', in Association of Jewish Refugees in Great Britain (ed.), *Britain's New Citizens: the Story of the Refugees from Germany and Austria*, London, 1951, pp. 25, 31-3.

15. K.E. Robinson, Colonial Office to Foreign Office, 13 January 1941, quoted by Wasserstein, p. 47. In general, see Bentwich, p. 43, and Sherman, pp. 188-92, 234-5, 254-5.

16. The Colonial Secretary, Lord Moyne, to the Foreign Office, 24 December 1941, quoted by Wasserstein, p. 145. Similarly Eden, the Foreign Secretary, in a conversation with Harry Hopkins on 27 March 1943; *ibid.*, p. 188.

17. Stevens, pp. 157-8; Wasserstein, pp. 84-5; personal recollections.

18. Wasserstein, pp. 87-8, 92, with quotations from Sir Neville Bland's memorandum of 14 May and the *Jewish Chronicle* of 17 May 1940; Stevens, pp. 174-6.

19. Wasserstein, pp. 87, 89, 90-1, 96; Stevens, p. 180. The following paragraph is based on personal recollections.

20. Stocks, p. 285.

21. See, for example, G.W. Winkel, *Kriegsgefangene rufen die Heimat. Deutsche Soldaten im Londoner Rundfunk*, Berlin, 1948.

22. These paragraphs are based on personal recollections of the author, who worked in the PWE during the war.

23. Bentwich, pp. 109–12; Stevens, pp. 221–5; personal recollections. According to Bentwich, pp. 110–11, over 10,000 men and 2,000 young women enlisted. But W. Rosenstock, 'The Jewish Refugees', in *Britain's New Citizens*, London, 1951, p. 17, gives a figure of 9,230 for both sexes, excluding Czechs and Spaniards.

24. For details see Z.M. Reid, 'Contributions to Science and Art', in *Britain's New Citizens*, pp. 36–41; W. Rosenstock, *Dispersion and Resettlement – The Story of the Jews from Central Europe*, London, 1955, p. 57.

*John P. Fox*

# Nazi Germany and German Emigration to Great Britain

Emigration from one political society to another has hardly ever been an entirely voluntary process in the true sense of the word. Every instance of emigration in history has resulted from the interaction of the individual with conditions in his society, so that social, economic, religious, or political factors have always made emigration a form of 'involuntary' action. This is true whether the final decision to move is taken by the individual himself because he considers that conditions in society are such that he could hardly survive, economically or even physically, if he remained; or whether his decision to leave comes in the form of a direct order from government or police authorities to him or to the group to which he belongs because that society no longer wants him in its midst. When any society is universally recognised to be in a chronic or even perpetual state of political or economic crisis, it is generally the second of these considerations that comes to the fore.

From 30 January 1933 Germany was such a society in which these factors, among others, directly affected the lives of hundreds of thousands of German citizens who eventually left Germany, and indirectly affected those millions who remained behind to live under one of the worst tyrannies known in the twentieth century. Why was this? What was it about the new situation in Germany after Adolf Hitler became Reich Chancellor which led to nearly 400,000 Germans leaving their own country in the period 1933 to 1939/41? Although figures for emigration from Germany after January 1933 are not totally accurate,[1] nevertheless those available reflect the underlying

29

tendencies and malaise of that society in which the *Totalitätsanspruch des Nationalsozialismus*[2] was the intention and obsession, if hardly and finally a total reality, of Hitler and the NSDAP. The majority of those who left were, of course, Jews but other categories included Social Democrats, Communists, members of other political groups and organisations, Catholics, Protestants, intellectuals and pacifists. As to these people, it is important to bear in mind a significant point of definition[3] which is, in turn, directly linked to the original motivation – whether personal (internalised) or State-influenced (externalised) pressure – for their departure from Germany. Most could be classified as 'refugees', i.e. those fleeing from a situation where economic and even personal security was increasingly placed in jeopardy and who intended to establish a permanent home elsewhere, if and wherever that became possible. Others may be described as 'political exiles', since they considered themselves part of the anti-Nazi movement or resistance and who fled in order to survive, to campaign against the Nazi regime and system and to plan for the day when they could return to a non-Nazi Germany (*das andere Deutschland*).

Fundamental to any discussion, both of the motivations and the fate of those who left Germany, is the question of conditions in that country after 30 January 1933. What was it about the Nazi regime and system of government which led to emigration on this scale? The complexity of the question may be gauged by the fact that initially at least seven questions must be raised. Firstly, what were the initial powers of Hitler's government and how did it set about extending them? Secondly, what was the relationship between the Hitler government, the Nazi movement as a whole, German society and the centres of political, military, bureaucratic, and economic power, and the process of *Gleichschaltung*? Thirdly, what were the domestic policies of the government, especially with regard to those whom it considered opposed Nazism? Fourthly, why did so many Germans feel they had no other choice but to leave Germany altogether? Fifth, how many emigrated in order to work positively for a *neues und anderes Deutschland*, and how many left Germany to start a new and non-political life in other countries? Sixth, what was the effect of Nazi Germany's domestic policies and the waves of emigration on Germany's foreign relations, particularly with those countries who were the initial host societies for German émigrés, for example, Czechoslovakia, France, Belgium, Great Britain, Holland, Switzerland? Finally, how were relations with those countries (for example, Great Britain) affected additionally by Nazi Germany's attempts to stifle the anti-Nazi expressions of politically-active émigré opponents of the regime, by the nefarious practice of continual surveillance of them, as well as the attempt to propagate Nazi propaganda abroad, in order to discredit the anti-Nazi efforts of these émigrés?

From the Nazi point of view such emigration – whatever its character or motivation – was only to be welcomed, on the grounds that this process furthered the 'house cleaning' of German society which the Nazis instituted immediately after the *Machtergreifung*. Yet to appreciate the real nature of the *Machtergreifung* and its consequences, especially in view of the historical controversies surrounding the question of Hitler's role in Nazi Germany,[4] it is as well to bear in mind some of the principles which Hitler and other leading Nazis brought with them when supreme political power in Germany finally became theirs in January 1933. Hitler's fundamental political standpoint, from which everything else flowed and to which it returned, has been described as his 'vulgar Darwinisim'.[5] Hitler's interpretation of the theories of Social Darwinism was reduced essentially to two aphorisms: 'the struggle for existence' and 'the survival of the fittest', both of which were predicated upon the inner value of the race or *Volk*. The question was, since the *Volk* had, perforce, to survive in the real national and political world of the twentieth century, how was one to view the nation or the State *vis-à-vis* the desired functions and purposes of the *Volk*? For Hitler the answer was relatively simple, 'the indispensable prerequisite for the existence of a superior quality of human beings is not the State but the race, which is alone capable of producing that higher human quality . . . the State is only a means to an end'.[6]

Yet Hitler's view of the intended National Socialist State went beyond any of the ideological principles it supposedly embodied. National Socialist principles were to be applied in a State based on the twofold notion of anti-Parliamentarism (with all its concomitants) and the *Führerprinzip*: 'the nature and internal organisation of the new movement make it anti-Parliamentarian . . . it rejects in general and in its own structure all those principles according to which decisions are to be taken on the vote of the majority and according to which the leader is only the executor of the will and opinion of others. The movement lays down the principle that in the smallest as well as in the greatest problems, one person must have absolute authority and bear all responsibility. . . . One of the highest duties of the movement is to make this principle imperative not only within its own ranks but also for the whole State.... Because of this principle, our movement must necessarily be anti-Parliamentarian, and if it takes part in the Parliamentary institution it is only for the purpose of destroying this institution from within.... Hence the People's State must mercilessly expurgate from all the leading circles in the government of the country the Parliamentarian principle, according to which decisive power through the majority vote is invested in the multitude.... In its organisation the State must be established on the principle of personality, starting from the smallest cell and ascending up to the supreme government of the country'.[7]

There is a two-fold significance in these passages, both for the history of the NSDAP and for the German Constitution of the Weimar and Nazi eras. The first is that they are a reflection of Hitler's conviction, after the abortive *Putsch* of November 1923, that the only way to power in Germany was through legal and constitutional means, even if the ultimate intention was to use those same means to destroy the Parliamentary system and thereby all the civil liberties and freedoms usually associated with such a system of government. In his legality oath at the Leipzig Reichswehr trial on 25 September 1930 Hitler spoke clearly about the future legal dismemberment of the Constitution: 'The Constitution only maps out the arena of battle, not the goal. We enter the legal agencies and in that way will make our Party the determining factor. However, once we possess the constitutional power, we will mould the State into the shape we hold to be suitable'.[8] Suitable for Hitler, that is, in terms of the conditions to be established which would enable National Socialist principles and policies to be fully applied and executed.

This path to political power in Germany became known as the 'legal revolution' and it has been said that the concept 'offers the key to the character and development of the National Socialist power seizure'. Although the concept of 'legal revolution' artificially linked two contradictory axioms of political action and behaviour, the fact is that 'this tactic played a decisive role in surrounding this new type of totalitarian power seizure with its seductive aura of effectiveness and made all legal, political, or even intellectual resistance so difficult and, in the opinion of many, well-nigh impossible'.[9] Moreover, according to the *Führerprinzip*, Party and State were to be nothing but instruments in the hands of the Führer for the purpose of achieving his goals: 'This leads to a total inversion of the traditional concept of State, since the ruler is now no longer the servant of the State but, on the contrary, the State is an instrument of the ruler'.[10]

The fact that after 30 January 1933 the 'State' became the 'instrument of the ruler' emphasises the second significant but constitutional point about the passages quoted from Hitler's *Mein Kampf*. The Weimar Constitution was so formulated as to provide for 'the erosion and abrogation of its substance by constitutional means'.[11] The possibility of non- or even anti-democratic rule in Germany was encapsulated in Article 48 of the Constitution which provided for the exercise of Presidential dictatorial powers, and for the setting aside of fundamental rights established in Articles 114, 115, 117, 123, 124 and 163.[12]

As Chancellors Brüning, von Papen, and Schleicher were able to rule in an extra- or anti-Parliamentary manner by invoking emergency powers under Article 48, so Hitler likewise demanded and obtained similar powers for himself in the final negotiations leading to his appointment as Chancellor. On 30 January 1933, therefore, Hitler not only stood on the threshold of power but had equipped himself with the minimum legal and constitutional powers which he needed in order to implement his oft-repeated intention of establishing an authoritarian, anti-democratic and anti-Parliamentary system of government in Germany: 'with that, the real seizure of power got under way; now it was demonstrated how the tactic of gaining power by legal means could be brought into line with the strategy of revolution and blended with the technique of seizing power by over-taking, eliminating, and levelling all political, social, and intellectual safeguards and counterforces'.[13] Within twenty months Hitler felt sufficient confidence to be able to declare, on 20 August 1934, 'beginning with the highest office of the Reich, through the entire administration down to the leadership of the smallest village, the German Reich today is in the hands of the National Socialist Party'.[14] Hitler's claims were, however, exaggerated since the Nazi process of *Gleichschaltung* still took time to be achieved in every facet of German life. Nevertheless, nobody could really deny the overriding 'control and manipulation' of the German State and society exercised by the NSDAP in order to serve 'a regime focused entirely on the one Leader; for the rest, it brought anything but order and security, but rather arbitrariness and frequently internal chaos'.[15]

Whatever the true nature of the Nazi 'revolution', by August 1934 it had been achieved (and continued to be so) essentially in two ways; by the destruction of what had remained of Germany's democratic institutions as of 30 January 1933, 'insofar as their functions could not be accommodated in the new power structure'; secondly, by the creation 'of a total leader State, in which economy, society, and culture through coordination and supervision were to be transformed from free, pluralistic entities into pillars of the untrammelled rule of one Party and a governmental apparatus subordinate to it'.[16]

The execution of these two broad intentions led, *pari passu*, both to Nazi Germany being condemned by most other nations and also to waves of migration on a scale unprecedented in twentieth-century Europe. The three stages of their implementation drastically changed the fundamental bases of German society, making it impossible for hundreds of thousands of her citizens to remain in their homeland. These three stages of the Nazi 'legal revolution' were as follows. Firstly, the massive intensification of executive power by means of Presidential rule, the 'terrorist, profoundly unconstitutional intensification of a power thrust' which reached its apogee in the Enabling Act of 23 March 1933 which abolished the power of the Reichstag and firmly established the dictatorship of the 'national' government. Secondly, through the liquidation of the constitutional pluralistic State by the one-Party regime through the purging of the civil service and judiciary, together with the smashing of the trade unions, democratic professional organisations (April/May 1933) and dissolution of all other political parties, resulting in the legal establishment of the one-Party State on 14 July 1933. In this way, then, fundamental civil rights, guaranteed in the Weimar Constitution, were first suspended and then abolished. Thirdly, the institutionalisation of the Führer dictatorship formed through the alliance with the expanding army (particularly after the destruction of the SA leadership in June 1934), the taking over of the police and its incorporation into the SS, the infiltration and 'alignment' of organisations, and the creation of all-inclusive monopoly organisations in the economic and cultural sectors of society.[17]

'The Enabling Act concluded the first phase of the seizure of power. It made Hitler independent of the alliance with his conservative partners. That in itself thwarted any chance for an organised power struggle against the new regime'.[18] Hitler now possessed all the power he needed to employ against both the Left (however that might be defined) and the Right, in the form of his Nationalist partners. In addition, the Enabling Act placed the entire apparatus of the government bureaucracy at Hitler's disposal (as witness the passing of the Civil Service Law of 7 April); this included the judiciary, control of which was indispensable to his long-term plans. Thereafter, until 14 July 1933 (that other 'black day' when the Nazi Party was declared the sole legal political party and rights of German citizenship were withdrawn from all 'undesirables' and those opponents of Nazism who had fled abroad) the 'rounding-off of power positions already achieved' continued apace. While Communist opposition crumbled 'in an atmosphere of muffled terrorism',[19] the Nazis turned their attention to the trade unions, to other political parties (especially the Socialists) and to the Jews and the Churches. On 1 April 1933 the boycott of Jewish shops and businesses took place, while on 4 April a law was decreed regulating worker representation in trade and industries and authorising employers to dismiss, without right of appeal, employees suspected of 'activity inimical to the State'. Pressure on the trade unions was kept up until on 2 May, without warning, the Free Trade Unions, under Socialist management and boasting some 4,500,000 members were dissolved. SA and SS men, aided by the police, occupied offices, buildings, and banks throughout the country while leaders were summarily arrested and incarcerated in prison or concentration camps.[20]

On 7 April the campaign against 'deviance' in the civil service began with the opening legal salvoes directed against Jewish members of the bureaucracy (still until 1935 referred to under the euphemism, 'non-Aryan'); in reality the first legal step to exclude Jews from all official positions in the country. The 'Law for the Restitution of the Professional Civil Service' authorised the dismissal of any civil servant appointed after November 1918 and adjudged lacking in the proper qualifications for their posts. All civil servants 'not of Aryan descent' were to be retired at once, while those civil servants whose political record failed to give assurances that they would 'always support the National State without reservation' were also to be immediately dismissed. Similar provisions were applied in another law of the same day entitled 'Law on Admission to the Bar', while subsequent decrees expanded and elaborated these basic provisions with which the regime began its ruthless 'house cleaning'.[21]

In other areas as well the political 'house cleaning' continued. On 10 May, throughout Germany, the party headquarters, the newspapers and all other property of the Social Democratic Party and the *Reichsbanner* were confiscated on orders from Göring. At one stroke the SPD was completely crippled, with its leaders imprisoned or forced to emigrate, although it was not until 22 June that it was outlawed as a political organisation 'hostile to the State' and its seats in the Reichstag invalidated. All other political groupings were likewise 'coordinated' and 'sucked into the whirlpool of *Gleichschaltung*'.[22] On

21 June the *Stahlhelm* and the German Nationalist militias led the procession of those announcing their dissolution; the following day it was the turn of all remaining employee and employer organisations. Then came the German National People's Party, the State Party and the German National Front on 28 June, the Centre Association on 1 July, the Young German Order on 3 July, the Bavarian People's Party and the German People's Party on 4 July and, finally, the disappearance of the Centre Party on 5 July. In addition, 'coordination of the various industrial, commercial, artisan, and agricultural associations ran parallel to the break up of the political and para-military groups. But in no case was there any act of resistance'.[23]

The final seal on the National Socialist seizure of power came on 14 July 1933 with the formal establishment of the one-Party State and Nazi dictatorship. Beginning at 11 a.m. and finishing near midnight, the Cabinet approved more than two dozen laws. The most important declared that only a single political party, the NSDAP, now existed in Germany and that anyone attempting to prolong the life of another party or establish a new one would be imprisoned for six months to three years. This law in fact contravened Article 2 of the Enabling Act, which stipulated that no impairment of the Reichstag as an institution was permissible. Another law authorised confiscation of the property of any organisation deemed inimical to the State, that is, Socialist as well as Communist property. Yet another law permitted revocation of the citizenship of anyone who had acquired it under the Weimar Republic and whose citizenship 'is not considered desirable', or of anyone who had emigrated and whose behaviour did not accord with his 'duty to be loyal to the Reich'.[24]

*Pari passu* with the destruction of democratic principles in Germany after 30 January 1933, together with the consequent abrogation of civil liberties, there was instituted the reign of terror which used *Terror als Disziplinierungsmittel*[25] to both intimidate and make powerless all political opponents and to neutralise potential opposition to the Nazi regime. The reign of terror was implemented through such extra-State means as the SA and SS, together with such innovations as Göring's brainchild, the Gestapo, created in April 1933. By 1936 Heinrich Himmler had achieved the position of *Reichsführer-SS und Chef der Deutschen Polizei* which enabled him, through the SS, to exercise almost total control in the area of 'law and order' in pursuit of government policies. Within seven months of Hitler's assumption of power, Nazi terror-tactics had resulted in at least 50,000 people – Communists, Social Democrats, left-wing intellectuals and pacifists among them – being arrested and thrown into prison or the first concentration camps. By July 1933 the SA terror had resulted in, at the minimum, between 500 and 600 deaths.[26]

These developments were bound to affect the lives of all German citizens, whatever their social status and political sympathies, and it would have been truly remarkable had there not been dissatisfaction, at the least, at the new conditions being created in Germany, resulting in many cases in forced or voluntary exile. Those who left Germany, for whatever reasons, were certainly anti-Nazi and anti-Hitler, although this may have been the only thing which many of them had in common. As with the resistance that gradually developed within Germany itself (however active or passive that might have been), one cannot describe as homogeneous the political and other refugees who fled Germany: 'generally speaking, therefore, the dissidence of the German anti-Fascists was greater than their consensus'.[27] The reasons for this become obvious when one categorises the main groups of the émigrés as well as their numbers. According to the League of Nations' figures, around 65,000 people fled from Germany in the period 1933 to the end of 1935. This figure included some 40–45,000 Jews, 5–6,000 Social Democrats, 6–8,000 Communists, 2,000 Pacifists, 1,000 Catholics and some 2,000 individuals who did not belong to any particular category. Up to 1935 more emigrants left Germany for political than for 'racial' reasons. However, the Nuremberg Laws of 1935 imposed almost unbearable legal and economic pressures on Jews and the numbers of Jewish emigrants rose substantially; the widespread pogroms of *Kristallnacht*, in November 1938, resulted in a further dramatic increase in those seeking refuge outside Germany.[28]

Even though the Nazi regime regarded all refugees as being powerless to change anything in Germany once they had left Germany's borders, the Nazi authorities still saw these people as a two-fold menace. Firstly, it was realised that politically active anti-Nazi émigrés, continuing their work from abroad (through various forms of counter-propaganda or contact with like-minded groups remaining in Germany) would work against Nazi efforts to forge a spurious unity between regime and *Volk*. Secondly, by emphasising their own forms of dissent from the Nazi regime, even by the simple fact of leaving Germany without further overt or active opposition when abroad the émigrés refuted Nazi claims of a unified German nation behind Hitler and the Nazi regime. But there was more to this second aspect of the question. Such public forms of dissent with the regime were bound to affect Nazi Germany's relations with other countries, especially those claiming to be democracies. This was particularly so where the refugees were accepted and where support was forthcoming for them from other quarters hostile to Nazi Germany and all that it stood for. This, in turn, was likely to lead to demands to foreign governments that they exert pressure on Nazi Germany to modify its internal policies or to accept that their continuation would adversely affect Germany's foreign relations.

There can be no doubt that the Nazi regime was extremely sensitive to foreign criticisms of events inside Germany; on several occasions considerations of foreign policy or foreign opinion had a direct effect on developments inside Germany. Nonetheless, determined to silence criticism at home which it felt was being encouraged by the more politically active émigrés who were condemning the 'new' Germany from apparently safe havens abroad, the regime decided to mount a direct attack on these exiles. The internal fight against dissidence was pursued externally in several ways: the systematic registration and discrediting of the émigrés; withdrawal of German citizenship; observation and persecution of them through Gestapo agents abroad, with even the German Foreign Office (*Auswärtiges Amt*) and the diplomatic service becoming involved in this nefarious process; political 're-education' (including incarceration in the new concentration camps) of those émigrés who returned to Nazi Germany; as well as more extreme policies such as the taking of hostages, kidnapping and political murder abroad.

The seriousness with which the Nazi regime pursued its fight against anti-Nazi émigrés is revealed by the fact that as early as 4 May 1933 the Gestapo ordered all German State police authorities to maintain detailed lists of émigrés which were to be used as the basis of a central register in Berlin. These orders were supplemented in February and November 1934; the information to be collected included the usual personal details, the last place of residence in Germany and, more sinisterly, an attempt was to be made to establish the new location of the émigrés.[29] These measures naturally remained secret. However, the process of discrediting those who had left Germany was to be as public as possible. This propaganda campaign took several forms – the press and public denunciation among others – and was directed at those émigrés known to be politically active. Nazi propagandists placed the motivation of these people into one or more of at least four categories – cowardice, disloyalty, active enmity towards Germany (high treason) and criminal activities.[30] Since one of the chief Nazi aims was to convince the German people as well as the world at large of the unity of regime and *Volk*, the overall purpose of the Nazi campaign against the émigrés was to discredit (and therefore neutralise) the counter-propaganda they directed both at Germany and at other nations.[31] By describing everything the émigrés said about Nazi Germany as 'lies', the regime used the psychologically effective ploy of attempting to create an identity between the émigrés and all other 'lies' being spread about Nazi Germany.[32]

Even Hitler, Goebbels, and Göring joined in the campaign of vilification of the émigrés. Speaking in his own inimitable style at Hamburg on 16 June 1933, Joseph Goebbels struck the right note for his audience between a defence of the new situation in Germany and sarcastic comments about the émigrés:

> They want to liberate the German people from terror. They want Marxism to rule once more so that it can achieve what it has failed to do in the past fourteen years. But these people fool themselves. These gentlemen are behind the times. They have not understood the signs of the times. Their time has run out. It is only a pity that they are beyond our reach. It is only a pity that now they are able to cause the German people and the German nation so much trouble from abroad. It is thanks to us National Socialists that they lost [political] power. *We* have closed in on them.

Four months later, on 14 October 1933, Hitler himself spoke on the radio about the 'unscrupulous agitators' who had spread about 'a torrent of atrocity stories'. 'Criminal elements' and 'their communist accomplices' were those

> ... who, as émigrés, today tried to set decent and respectable people against each other. The German people have no reason to envy the rest of the world their acquisition. We are convinced that a few years will be enough for the eyes of decent people elsewhere to be opened to the questionable value of such unworthy elements who, under the impressive cover of political refugees, have left the area in which they acted with more or less great economic unscrupulousness.

In a publication widely circulated in 1933 and 1934 Göring spoke about the

> ... flood of vulgar and disgusting slander and atrocity stories which the despicable and unpatriotic creatures who have fled abroad have perpetrated there. . . . The wild incitement to hatred of the émigrés has done its part. Former leaders of the Social Democrats such as

Breitscheid, Wels, and Höltermann call for foreign armed intervention against Germany. They had finally allowed the mask to slip and the German worker can now recognise what scum, and that word is far too generous, has determined their fate in the past decade. These émigrés have so forgotten the Fatherland that they have shamefully revealed themselves as preferring that Germany should be put to flame and fire under a French and Polish invasion rather than being deprived of their sinecure.[33]

Yet another public demonstration of the Nazi regime's determination to discredit the émigrés (and which was, additionally, to prove to the nation how serious a matter was the 'defence' of the Nazi 'revolution') involved *Ausbürgerungspolitik*, expressed in the legal measures passed on the fateful day of 14 July 1933, withdrawing German citizenship from both 'undesirables' and émigrés. This was also to be seen as an additional warning to potential opponents of the regime *within* Germany itself. The Law for the Revocation of Naturalisation and the Annulment of Citizenship of 14 July was directly related to long-term Nazi plans to establish new definitions of German citizenship on purely 'racial' grounds. Shortly after the *Machtergreifung* the Reich Ministry of the Interior began work on measures to define who was German, with the immediate intention of withdrawing citizenship from those who had been granted it between 1919 and 1933, that is, all 'undesirables' but particularly the Jews from eastern Europe, the so-called and hated *Ostjuden*. However, in the preliminary discussions it soon became clear that the regime also intended to use this legislation against the émigrés. In a letter dated 12 May 1933, Reich Minister of the Interior Frick emphasised that the new law under discussion should apply also to those who, 'through their attitude, have proved themselves unworthy of belonging to the German people'. By 10 July the final draft was ready and Frick pressed for its immediate approval by the Reich Cabinet so that the State could immediately act against 'the traitors residing abroad'.[34]

The two main clauses of the law revoking citizenship also showed that arbitrary administrative law had become the rule in Nazi Germany. The revocation of citizenship in Article 1 belonged to the constitutional category of 'banishment on security grounds', by means of which the State sought to protect itself against specific groups considered politically undesirable; in this case 'inferior people', the *Ostjuden*. On the other hand, there can be no doubt that the full weight of Article 2 was to be applied to the émigrés, whom Frick had already described as traitors to the Reich. The revocation of citizenship referred to in

Article 2, therefore, belonged to the constitutional category of banishment of those whom the State wished to punish because their attitudes had offended the authorities.[35] These points are clearly laid out in the pertinent passages of the two articles. Article 1 reads in part that 'citizenship which had been granted in the period between 9 November 1918 and 30 January 1933 may be withdrawn should such citizenship be regarded as undesirable'. Likewise the pertinent parts of Article 2: 'Members of the Reich who are resident abroad may have their German citizenship declared null and void if it is considered that they have harmed German interests by offending against their duty to remain loyal to Reich and *Volk*. The same applies to citizens of the Reich who have failed to comply with an order to return issued by the Reich Minister of the Interior under this provision. With the introduction of revocation proceedings or the issuing of orders to return, their property may be confiscated and, upon revocation of citizenship, will become the property of the State'.[36]

On 26 July 1933 the Reich Ministry of the Interior issued a special decree supplementing the law revoking citizenship. Referring to Article 1 of the original law, paragraph 1 of the new ordinance applied specifically to the *Ostjuden* but granted exemption to front-line soldiers of World War I and those who had rendered particular service to Germany. It thus became clear that Nazi Germany's citizenship laws were to be based on purely *Völkisch*-racial lines: 'whether a denaturalisation is to be seen as undesirable will be dependent upon *Völkisch*-national principles. Above all, racial, citizenship, and cultural factors will determine whether the interests of the Reich and *Volk* can benefit from an increase in the German population through naturalisation'. Likewise, the provisions of the original Article 2 defining loyalty to the new Nazi Reich were expanded and clarified in the new measure: 'it is considered that an attitude of disloyalty towards the Reich and *Volk* is signified when a German renders assistance to hostile propaganda against Germany or has attempted to denigrate Germany's reputation abroad or the measures of the national government'.[37] Together the two measures meant that 'the revocation of citizenship was thought of as a weapon against critics of the regime... suspension of the basic rights of free speech was thus followed by the prohibition of any kind of criticism abroad';[38] while with reference to paragraph 1, sentence 2, of the original Law, 'this blanket authority subjected all German citizens abroad to a slavish obligation; for by Frick's order they had to return to Germany immediately if they did not wish to risk becoming stateless'.[39]

It was also intended that these measures should be applied as quickly as possible. On 22 July 1933 the Reich Ministry of the Interior circulated a letter to the *Auswärtiges Amt* and other authorities requesting submission of proposals for the de-naturalisation of the émigrés. On 16 August an inter-Ministerial discussion took place in the Reich Ministry of the Interior under the chairmanship of *Ministerialrat* Hering. The *Auswärtiges Amt* was represented by Friedrich Gaus, leader of the Legal Department, Senior Counsellor von Bülow-Schwante, head of the newly-constituted *Referat Deutschland*, and *Legationsrat* Kotze. Other participants came from the Political Department of the Ministry of the Interior, the Prussian Ministry of the Interior and the Gestapo. The meeting agreed that by publishing a first de-naturalisation list as soon as possible containing the names of well-known SPD and Communist Party members, Jews and other 'undesirables', an example would be made which could be expected to act as a deterrent against the subversion directed from abroad against 'national Germany'.[40]

The decisive factor, therefore, was to be the attitude adopted by individual émigrés towards the 'national government' in the 'new' Germany. It has been remarked that this definition is of special significance, since thereby 'the usual basis for de-naturalisation proposals, i.e. membership of an outlawed party or organisation, was deemed insufficient and that proof of anti-Nazi activity abroad was required; that meant at the same time a limitation of the basis on which a person could be charged, which had been deliberately omitted from the text of the law as well as the supplementary provisions'.[41] On 23 August State Secretary Pfundtner, as the representative of Reich Minister Frick, signed the de-naturalisation decree which was then published in the *Deutscher Reichs- und Preussicher Staatsanzeiger* of 25 August 1933.

The first *Ausbürgerungsliste* contained thirty-three names and included left-wing writers, publishers, and intellectuals such as Georg Bernhard, Lion Feuchtwanger, Hellmut von Gerlach, Kurt R. Grossman, Alfred Kerr, Otto Lehmann-Russbüldt, Heinrich Mann, Berthold Salomon (B. Jacob), Leopold Schwarzschild, Max Sievers, Ernst Toller and Kurt Tucholsky. University lecturers such as Friedrich Wilhelm Foerster and Emil J. Gumbel were included because of their opposition during the Weimar period to a nationalist and militarist Germany. Social Democrats on this first list included Rudolf Breitscheid, Albert Grzesinski, Philipp Scheidemann, Friedrich Stampfer, Bernhard Weiss and Otto Wels. Communist names included Eugen Eppstein, Ruth Fischer, Friedrich Heckert, Peter Maslowski, Max Hölz, Willi Münzenberg, Heinz Neumann and Wilhelm Pieck. The names on the list represented the 'alternative Germany' and were there because by their denial of Hitler and their fight against him and all that he stood for they were supposed to have harmed and defamed Nazi Germany. Goebbels himself branded these people as 'criminals' and 'outlaws' in the press. On 26 August 1933, for example, the *Völkischer Beobachter* declared that such expulsions would be regarded by the German people 'not only as a benefit and a cleansing [of German society] but also as just deserts for those concerned'.[42]

Interestingly enough, the *Auswärtiges Amt* and the Reich Ministry of the Interior recognised the fact that the policy of de-naturalisation was one which, initially at least, had to be used carefully. They agreed, therefore, that only those political émigrés should be de-naturalised who 'had especially and greatly harmed the people's community [of Nazi Germany]. Further, because of the effect that revocation of citizenship was intended to have on public opinion, it was also considered necessary that the severity of this weapon should not be diminished by too-frequent use. Mass de-naturalisation would only result in an impairment of the whole point of the exercise'.[43] Until the end of 1935, then, only seven such lists were issued, but from December of that year things changed dramatically. In his widely-publicised letter of resignation dated 27 December 1935, James G. McDonald, League of Nations' High Commissioner for Refugees from Germany, described in detail German legislation and its obvious consequences, and called for 'friendly and firm intervention with the German Government' on the part of members of the League and all other members of 'the community of nations' to 'remove or mitigate the causes which create German refugees'. While the letter was at first studiously ignored and then violently attacked in Germany,[44] Hitler's reaction was one of immediate anger. On the morning of 28 December 1935 instructions were issued by telephone from Berchtesgaden to the Reich Ministry of the Interior to prepare, by 30 December, the draft of a law immediately de-naturalising all émigrés.[45]

It has been suggested that Hitler had already been considering such a move *before* the McDonald letter, prompted as ever by his obsession with the *Ostjuden*.[46] The fact is that foreign policy considerations and arguments from the *Auswärtiges Amt* (1936 was the year of the Berlin Olympiade) enabled Frick to dissuade Hitler from the de-naturalisation of *all* émigrés, which at this period would have involved some 80,000 to 100,000 individuals.[47] Nevertheless, Hitler's furious reaction to the McDonald letter and the increasing influence of Heydrich and the Gestapo, and Himmler and the SS were sufficient to counter the attitudes of the *Auswärtiges Amt* and the Reich Ministry of the Interior. From 1936 the way was clear for the mass de-naturalisation of German émigrés, further guide-lines constantly being issued reinterpreting and expanding the original law of 14 July 1933. Furthermore, and given all other developments within Germany, de-naturalisation quickly came to be used as a recognisably anti-Jewish measure.[48] At first on political, but increasingly also on racial grounds, the basic criteria for the inclusion of any name on such a list was that the individual was prejudged to have been 'guilty' of a basic animosity towards Germany and against National Socialism. Following the seven lists issued up to 1936, therefore, a further nineteen were issued in 1937 and fifty-seven during 1938. By February 1939 6,095 German citizens had been de-naturalised, this figure rising to 10,882 by 31 July.[49]

The consequences of Nazi Germany's de-naturalisation policies for the émigrés were, of course, tremendous. Not only were they 'outlawed' from German society but immediately became that horror of horrors in the twentieth-century world, stateless. This unenviable status placed them at the mercy of whichever state they happened to be living in at the time of their loss of German citizenship. Many German émigrés, and especially the Jews, then immediately discovered the brutal truth of the maxim that without citizenship there were no rights of protection. The real tragedy of their new situation first became clear to the émigrés when their passports expired and they found themselves without any kind of official documents. This problem defeated, indeed devastated many émigrés, driving some in desperation to commit suicide.[50] The League of Nations did what it could to help, but such assistance was limited both in extent and effectiveness, while nothing could compensate for the loss of the passport of one's homeland with all the protection this gave the bearer. But there were a number of other consequences for the émigrés attendant on their loss of German citizenship: the confiscation of their property; the extension of de-naturalisation to other members of their families; the cancellation of Doctorates and other academic awards; limitations on rights of inheritance; the withdrawal of all forms of public and private financial assistance and, finally, the categorisation of émigrés as criminals.[51]

The *Auswärtiges Amt* and the German diplomatic service became closely involved, both directly and indirectly, in one of the most nefarious aspects of Nazi policies towards the émigrés – their surveillance and persecution in the countries in which they had found some sort of a haven in their struggle to establish new lives.[52] The surveillance of the émigrés was carried out by both State and Party organisations; the Gestapo, the *Auswärtiges Amt*, the army, the SA, the *Auslandsorganisation* of the NSDAP and so on. Its purpose was to collate systematic information on the organisation, aims, and methods of those political émigrés whose activity was seen as being inimical to the State; the individuals were seen as 'enemies of the State'. As before, the external fight against the émigrés was seen by the Nazi authorities as a necessary means of defence of the Nazi 'revolution' at home: 'one must hunt out the ways and means by which the previously destroyed opposition movements could have re-established themselves, the ways in which information on internal developments in the Third Reich was transmitted abroad and how illegal literature found its way into the Reich. For the Gestapo, therefore, there could be no doubt that the émigrés were an essential part of illegal activity in Germany. The observation of, and systematic information on the émigrés, as a preventive police measure, was seen as a necessary condition for effective counteraction'.[53] Within Germany the émigrés were registered, but abroad they were spied upon and persecuted. This persecution itself took different forms, the most effective being the psychological pressure of being under constant surveillance, of being photographed and, indeed, not knowing who to trust in the émigré community for fear of Gestapo agents, who infiltrated émigré organisations. It has also been suggested that for a variety of reasons some of the 'honest' émigrés even betrayed their compatriots.[54]

Since the 'internal' fight against the émigrés was also to be pursued 'externally' it was inevitable, given the political and constitutional situation within Germany that, increasingly, the *Auswärtiges Amt* and the German diplomatic service as a whole should find themselves acting as the official external arm of the Gestapo in the collection of information on the activities of émigrés. The *AA* department chiefly responsible for this task was the newly (20 March 1933) reconstituted *Referat Deutschland* under the leadership of Vico von Bülow-Schwante, cousin of Bernhard von Bülow, the State Secretary of the *Auswärtiges Amt*. The department's chief function was the surveillance of German internal affairs in so far as these had a relevance for foreign policy. Regarding the émigrés, it acted as the liaison between the diplomatic service and other official Party and security agencies within Germany itself.[55]

However, with State Secretary von Bülow's circular decree of 19 September 1933 there began what has been called 'a shameful chapter in the history of the *Auswärtiges Amt*: the observation of and supply of information about the anti-Fascist émigrés by the German diplomatic service'.[56] Included as enclosures to von Bülow's *Runderlass* to diplomatic missions abroad were the de-naturalisation Law, its subsequent amendments and the first de-naturalisation list. Missions were therefore instructed, at the first opportunity, to deprive émigrés of their passports and thereafter to deny them all forms of protection. The missions were also given standing orders to find out whether there were any resident Germans against whom paragraphs 1 or 2 of the de-naturalisation Law would apply. The instructions emphasised that 'for this purpose it will be especially necessary to follow the activities of the so-called German émigrés with vigilance but in so doing naturally to avoid anything which would harm the [official] representation and its relations of confidence with the German community or which could promote acts of denunciation'. The political activities of the émigrés were to be established by the existence of books, newspaper articles and pamphlets. It was also made clear that in the case of certain individuals Berlin would require an opinion from missions as to whether the appropriate action would be to extend de-naturalisation to other members of the subject's family or to link it with appropriation of his property.[57]

Eight days later, on 27 September, a comprehensive survey of the existing situation and the problems consonant with German emigration to other European countries was drawn up in the *Auswärtiges Amt*. According to this survey, the émigrés had met very often with a positive reception which, as an expression of wider anti-Nazi feelings in such countries, was considered to be significant.

Further, it was noteworthy that when the governments of the countries concerned adopted a neutral attitude towards the political activity of the émigrés, this was the equivalent of practical support. That same day the memorandum containing this survey was forwarded to missions as an enclosure to other instructions requesting further detailed information on the anti-German activity of the émigrés, their connections, leadership, means of support and individual enterprises.[58]

Despite the misgivings of a few missions about this new and, to some, wholly obnoxious role they were being called upon to fulfil and their fears that if news of it became public knowledge it could complicate foreign policy (especially with the countries where the émigrés had settled), neither Foreign Minister von Neurath nor State Secretary von Bülow saw any necessity to cancel or even amend the original instructions. While the *Auswärtiges Amt* was naturally concerned that nothing should be done to compromise the diplomatic service, the fact that Nazi interests were paramount was emphasised in an instruction to the Paris Embassy on 30 November 1933, when it was made clear that its report on the émigrés 'was of particular importance to the appropriate authorities in Germany'.[59] Thereafter, and despite constant expressions of doubt, the *Auswärtiges Amt* passed on to diplomatic missions all requests for information received from the Gestapo.[60]

The expressions of doubt which the *Auswärtiges Amt* in Berlin constantly received from embassies and consulates concerning the role of the diplomatic service in the surveillance of émigrés also reflected their general unease about that other unenviable task imposed upon them as an inevitable consequence of the Nazi *Machtergreifung* in Germany: constant 'defence' of the new situation in Germany, as a means of avoiding undue disruption of the whole range of Germany's diplomatic relations. Inevitably, however, both the diplomatic *and* émigré aspects of foreign policy merged wherever German émigrés were to be found. One of the most important diplomatic relationships for Nazi Germany and one where the émigré question caused complications over and above other questions of European diplomacy and military policy, was that with Great Britain. It would not be going too far, in some respects, to describe the whole history of Anglo-German relations from 30 January 1933 to 3 September 1939 in terms of a 'love-hate' relationship, the vagaries of that relationship being summed up for Hitler at least by his use of the word 'love' when referring to England's rejection of his offers of friendship in his speech of 1 September 1939. From the beginning of the Nazi regime in 1933, therefore, German diplomats in London had the unenviable twofold task of attempting to develop good Anglo-German relations, while at the same time acting as long-distance taskmasters to the German émigrés in Great Britain, on behalf of the Gestapo and the Reich Ministry of the Interior. And this in a country notoriously sensitive to any hint of foreign interference in its domestic affairs and where public opinion was increasingly and vociferously anti-Nazi because of the anti-democratic, indeed inhuman, domestic policies of the Nazi regime.

Without question one of the greatest burdens on Anglo-German relations from January 1933 was Nazi Germany's anti-Jewish policies. There is no doubt that Nazi treatment of the German Jews ensured that English opinion quickly became anti-Nazi if not anti-German. Further complications arose with the efforts of many German Jews to seek refuge in Great Britain. Since this subject and its ramifications for Anglo-German relations has been covered in great detail elsewhere,[61] only certain other aspects of the German emigration and its effect on Anglo-German relations will be referred to here. Nazi attempts to influence British opinion on these issues in a manner favourable towards Nazi Germany will also be examined.

A report, dated 6 June 1933, from Count Albert Bernstorff, Counsellor at the German Embassy in London, emphasised the fact that until that date most of the difficulties in Anglo-German relations had been caused by English protests[62] over Nazi Germany's policies towards the Jews, Communists, and Social Democrats and not, as had been happening elsewhere (Czechoslovakia, Switzerland, France), by the activities of the 'political' German émigrés. As Bernstorff wrote, 'until now it has not been possible to establish that German émigrés in England have engaged in anti-German activity; the numerous Germans here, whether they are simply *en route* or remaining permanently, have often acted with restraint with regard to the English press and to public opinion. Also, in the course of conversations, anti-German activity by the German émigrés has not been brought to the Embassy's notice'.[63] A further report, dated 15 August 1933, from Ambassador Leopold von Hoesch in London confirmed that, for the time being at least, Great Britain's position with regard to the numbers of German émigrés making for her shores was different from other European countries: 'German emigration to England has so far been relatively inconspicuous. Some emigration obviously exists, nevertheless it is numerically somewhat small and in any case is hardly comparable to the great flood of emigrants to other countries, in particular France'. Although Hoesch confirmed Bernstorff's point about the relative lack of 'political agitation' on the part of those German émigrés already in England, he did point out that 'despite the disregard of the émigré problem by British officialdom, various private organisations are involved in supporting the German refugees'.[64]

Nevertheless, the question still remained of how best to deal with the disturbed state of English public opinion *vis-à-vis* developments inside Germany, a matter that Alfred Rosenberg's disastrous visit to London in May 1933 had only exacerbated.[65] While the embassy in London constantly addressed itself to this problem with the long-term objective of achieving a positive and permanent improvement in Anglo-German relations,[66] Ambassador Hoesch's personal advice to the Wilhelmstrasse in Berlin was that in some cases the desired result might best be achieved if a policy of apparent honesty was followed. In a letter of 13 November 1933 addressed to State Secretary von Bülow he had this to say: 'as you are aware, a large number of prominent Englishmen are interested in the fate of some German citizens presently imprisoned in Germany with whom perhaps they had formerly been in contact. Most of the English people thus interested are liberals and socialists who are concerned for imprisoned pacifists and socialists. I have found that in most cases it has a calming effect if one can give the questioner information about the well-being of those in custody since in this way one prevents any public and distorted discussion of alleged atrocities'.[67] However, as Hoesch was at pains to point out in a further letter to von Bülow on 2 December, it was not really a question of satisfying 'inadmissible foreign inquisitiveness and arrogance, but on the contrary is about the problem of countering anti-German propaganda which is of great importance for German interests'.[68]

Nevertheless, for most of the 1930s and apart from the Jewish question, Great Britain's position *vis-à-vis* the question of émigrés from Nazi Germany remained somewhat of an exception, for two reasons. Bernstorff's assessment of 6 June 1933, that German émigrés in Britain were relatively inactive politically, did not change much in subsequent years; in this respect Great Britain differed sharply from France, Czechoslovakia and Switzerland, where most of the trouble for Nazi Germany from 'political agitators' originated. When, however, the Berlin authorities felt particular concern about émigré activity elsewhere – as they did over a conference of the First International held in Paris in August 1933 – the Embassy in London was also instructed to present a *démarche* to the Foreign Office: 'I request you, on the basis of the contents of the enclosed memorandum, which is to be treated confidentially, to draw the attention of the British Government to the seriousness of such proceedings and, with reference to the peace and understanding of the European States which could thereby be endangered, request that they turn their attention to these matters and, should the occasion arise, take steps accordingly'. In reporting the execution of this instruction on 8 December 1933, Prince Otto von Bismarck, Counsellor of the Embassy, added that 'in this instance there was an opportunity to draw attention to propaganda against Germany which had manifested itself on several recent occasions and to an ever-increasing extent'.[69]

Nevertheless, as an incident early in 1934 illustrated, the London Embassy and the authorities in Berlin were obviously interested in whatever level of anti-German activity was pursued by the German émigrés in England. On 3 May 1934 Bismarck reported, for example, that 'in the past week one of the personalities belonging to the émigré circles appeared here and handed over complete and detailed information about the disruptive work of such groups against Germany, as well as names of the principal activists (Lehmann- Russbüldt, Seger, Dr Neumann, Gross and Yaskiel).[70] The name and address of the informant is known – he is a former editor of *Vorwärts*'. Bismarck recommended that the information thus received from the informant be passed to the 'appropriate authorities since it contains in actual fact, and certainly to an extent not previously known to the Embassy, a quantity of important details about the personalities and plans of the pacifists who are part of the London group'. While Bismarck was rather unhappy about the Embassy becoming involved in such 'spying' activities, nevertheless he emphasised that 'on the other hand, the appropriate authorities [in Berlin] will probably want contact with the [informant] maintained, especially since it is certain that the disruptive activities of this group will not decline but will, on the contrary, become more intensive'. As to further contact with this particular informant, Bismarck suggested that if those in Berlin wanted this, 'they themselves should make relevant proposals. Personally, I would not consider it expedient to despatch a German official here but instead recommend that either the informant travels to somewhere neutral or to Germany. If the appropriate authorities should have a confidant in London, something which is not known here, then the informant could go to him'. Apart from this report with its enclosed memorandum on the information received from the London informant, Bismarck despatched further reports and enclosures on 10 and 17 May, and 10 and 18 September 1934. In Berlin the *Auswärtiges Amt* duly passed this material to the 'appropriate authorities' – the Reich Ministry of the Interior and the Gestapo.[71]

The second reason for Great Britain's different position on the German émigré question, as compared with France and Switzerland, was that nearly all of the constant stream of protests about conditions in Nazi Germany with which the London Embassy had to deal were from British and not German sources. These points were neatly illustrated in 1935 and again in 1936. On 10 January 1935 Herr zu Putlitz of the German Embassy was received by C.W. Baxter of the

Foreign Office and, under instructions from the German Ambassador, addressed 'what he described as a purely unofficial enquiry to us about German refugees in this country. Certain of these refugees – he had in mind particularly [the playwright] Herr Ernst Toller – went round the country making speeches against the German Government. *He admitted my comment that very little, if anything, had appeared in the press about Herr Toller's alleged speeches* [author's italics] but explained that other Germans had heard them and were sending furious letters of protest to the German Government and these letters were passed on to Herr von Hoesch with an enquiry as to what action he was taking in the matter. These speeches, Herr zu Putlitz maintained, were having a bad effect on Anglo-German relations, in that they were much resented in Germany. The German Ambassador would be grateful if we could give him any advice'. While Baxter explained the situation with regard to English law and that there was a 'long-standing tradition of freedom of speech in this country and of hospitality to political refugees, and that it was permissible to go very far in criticising the acts of a foreign government', Herr zu Putlitz finally got around to what was obviously the main point of his visit. He mentioned '*inter alia* the possibility of requiring refugees to give an assurance that they would not engage in anti-German activities while in this country; he suggested moreover that they might be expelled, or threatened with expulsion, if they did engage in such undesirable activities'. He was, however, given no reason by Baxter to suppose that any such action could or indeed would be taken by the British authorities.[72]

Some four weeks later, on 12 February 1935, the Embassy in London reported with a degree of satisfaction about 'a significant weakening of interest in refugees from Germany', as well as a definite reduction in the number of books issued by émigrés, resulting in a loss of interest in such publications. Nevertheless, as the penultimate sentence of the report warned, 'this should not be taken to mean that the impetus of the anti-German movement in its uncompromising form has faded'.[73]

In fact, the London Embassy's constant efforts to influence English opinion favourably towards Nazi Germany seemed to result in some degree of success. At the end of May 1936 a group of MPs and other members of the Labour Party, the party which had been in the vanguard of British opposition to developments inside Hitler's Germany, visited Germany after a great deal of preparatory work on the part of the German Embassy in London and after suggestions from the by-then-deceased Ambassador Hoesch. As Cecil von Renthe-Fink of the *Auswärtiges Amt* wrote (27 May 1936), when informing other Ministries of the impending visit, 'the journey is to some degree of special political significance since it is the first occasion on which English politicians and Members of Parliament from the Labour Party have expressed the desire to become personally acquainted with social questions in Germany. The impression they gain can be of decisive importance for the future attitude of other left-wing circles in England towards Germany'.[74]

Although the presence of German émigrés in England caused fewer problems in Anglo-German relations than, for example, in Franco-German or German-Swiss relations (always excluding the Jewish question), there were other areas in which the matter caused difficulties and even embarrassment between London and Berlin. This concerned British reactions to Nazi efforts to establish politically and socially active branches of the NSDAP in Great Britain, together with (from 1933) a fairly intensive campaign of pro-Nazi propaganda. According to reports from the Special Branch and other sources, it was clear that this work was intended not only to win over British public opinion but also to indoctrinate non-émigré German residents in Britain with Nazi ideas. Additionally, and apart from visiting propagandists, it was observed that the task of the resident propagandists was to make 'enquiries into organisations such as the Friends of Europe who are putting out anti-Hitler propaganda'. Yet, as the *Daily Herald* of 6 December 1933 revealed in more detail in an article headed 'Nazi Spy Ring', members of Nazi organisations in the United Kingdom were organised into an espionage service working in direct touch with the Gestapo. Their chief function was 'spying on Jewish and other German refugees in London. Ports and boat trains are watched for persons whose photographs and descriptions have been supplied from Berlin. The work of the relief organisations is kept under surveillance, and boastfully indiscreet members of the service claim that they have their men "on the inside" of all the organisations. In all these ways lists have been compiled of the names, addresses, and occupations of the majority of the London refugees', details of which were forwarded to Berlin. 'But the worst feature of all is that this Nazi spy service does not content itself with getting information. Its real job, the real object of all this seeking of information about refugees, is the harrying of the refugees themselves. Every method, according to the orders from Berlin, is to be used to make the refugees' position untenable and to get them if possible, driven out of the country.

Reputable refugees are being denounced to the Home Office as undesirables, even as criminals . . .'.[75]

Significantly, a Scotland Yard report of 25 April 1934 on the proposed establishment of Nazi headquarters in London pointed out that the motive for acquiring a building large enough to function as a social centre for the German colony and for Germans visiting London, instead of merely serving as Party headquarters, 'is the necessity, from a Party point of view, to get hold of German visitors here and look after them socially in order to keep them as far as possible from contamination by anti-Nazi propaganda whilst in London'.[76]

The position of the British authorities *vis-à-vis* Nazi activity in Great Britain was a difficult one, especially if the activists were careful enough to keep on just the right side of the law. As a Foreign Office memorandum of 20 May 1935 pointed out, 'provided this activity is confined to German nationals and preaching to the converted, and that there is no sign of their becoming militant, we can presumably have no objection, unless they develop the complementary activity of taking action of an illegal nature against émigré German nationals not of the Nazi Party who happen to be in the United Kingdom. (This activity more properly belongs to the Secret Police agents in England, agents provocateurs, such as Herr Wesemann and his ilk.) The Nazi Party in London are particularly careful not to give ground for offence in their normal activities among German nationals and they have been at pains to dissociate themselves from the activities of the Gestapo [ . . . . ] The Nazi Party has hitherto been extraordinarily careful to keep on the right side of the law in its activities, and to render them harmless in appearance. So far as the Secret Police and espionage activities are concerned, those engaged in them probably expose themselves to penalties under English law when caught, by the very nature of their activities. The problem here resolves itself into a question of detection and investigation'.[77]

By the end of the year, however, the patience of the British authorities with one of the chief Nazi propagandists, Dr Thost, London correspondent of the Nazi newspapers, *Angriff* and *Völkischer Beobachter*, came to an end and he was informed that his permit to stay in England would not be renewed. Questions from the German Embassy about the reasons for this decision met with sealed lips at the Foreign Office, although on 1 November 1935 Mr Sargent admitted to Ambassador Hoesch that the real reason was 'on account of other activities which had nothing to do with *bona fide* journalism'. Hoesch himself probably supplied the right answer when he suggested that

53

possibly Thost had been suspected of spying activities.[78]

Whether or not as a result of the successful action finally taken against Dr Thost, it is certain that from early in 1936 constant and serious consideration was given in the Foreign and Home Offices to the possibility of taking action to suppress Nazi and Fascist organisations in the United Kingdom and, thereby, their undesirable activities. The matter was not an easy one to resolve since it involved both questions of English law and political relations with Nazi Germany. One eventual proposal, 'that informal and friendly suggestions should be made to the German and Italian Governments, through their Embassies in London, that they should take steps to secure the closing down of branches of the National Socialist and Fascist Party organisations established in the United Kingdom, the presence of which was considered unusual and undesirable here', was even laid before the British Cabinet on 29 July 1936. The Cabinet concluded, however, 'that the present moment, when His Majesty's Government was trying to promote contacts between the British, Belgian, French, German and Italian Governments, was inopportune for taking the action proposed'. Nevertheless, it was also agreed 'to bring the question up on some later occasion when the moment was more opportune for taking action'.[79]

By October 1936 the general feeling in the Foreign Office was that the moment had become 'opportune' for pressing the matter, particularly with the imminent arrival of von Ribbentrop as Ambassador who, in turn, was expected to press for the decidedly objectionable appointment of Otto Bene, head of the Nazi organisation in Great Britain, as German Consul-General in London. A further reason for considering the moment ripe for moving against such organisations was that while it was expected that the German Government would attempt to link this issue to the negotiations for a Western Treaty, the Foreign Office felt that 'there are less real prospects of any valid or substantial pact'. It was also the opinion of MI5 that the Nazi organisation in London was 'a grave potential danger to this country and that the longer it is left to develop here without interference, the graver will be the potential danger which it constitutes'. Nevertheless on 21 October the Cabinet once more postponed making a definite and final decision on the matter.[80]

The comments by MI5 showed that, for the British Government, questions of national security had begun to loom larger than concern for other aspects of Nazi activities in the United Kingdom – for example the observation and harassment of German émigrés. By 1937, following a new law passed in Germany in January 1937 (it required officials of all kinds to swear an oath of allegiance to Hitler, to recognise the unity of Party and State, and to perform their duties in accordance with the principles of the NSDAP) it was felt in London that 'one effect of these changes is to give a new character to German Embassies and Consulates abroad and to make their members instruments of the Party as well as diplomatic or consular representatives'. The Foreign Office further commented that 'it is undeniable that both the Nazi and the Fascist Party organisations in this country are becoming increasingly active. If they are allowed to continue, their influence over Germans and Italians in this country, and over British subjects of German and Italian extraction, already freely exercised for purposes of propaganda, will inevitably become more powerful, and the greater will be their potential danger as ready-made instruments of intelligence and espionage and – in the event of war – of sabotage'. In March 1937, therefore, the Foreign and Home Office again pressed for permission to make approaches to the German and Italian regimes about the matter of Party organisations in the United Kingdom.[81] Although a meeting of the Cabinet on 14 July 1937 agreed that 'the question could not be allowed to drift indefinitely and must be kept under continuous observation', it was decided that 'in view of the existing difficulties in securing agreement over questions relating to Spain, no drastic action should be taken at the moment'.[82]

A movement in the right direction seemed, however, to be signalled by the non-renewal of the permits of three German journalists in August 1937. This action coincided with numerous press articles about Nazi activities in Britain, epitomised by the *Daily Herald* headlines on 11 August, 'More Nazis May Soon Be Deported. Special Branch Tracks Down Terror System. 500 Agents Busy', and led, not surprisingly, to official German protests at the Foreign Office.[83] International as well as internal developments soon, however, began to play a far more important role, as the conclusion of a memorandum by Frank Roberts of the Foreign Office on 19 January 1939 shows:

... the question has now to be considered in the light of the international crisis of September 1938, leading up to the Munich Agreement and the deterioration in Anglo-German relations since that Agreement. This deterioration and the general international situation suggest the desirability of an even closer watch being kept at all events on Nazi organisations in this country and there would no longer appear to be the same reason to consider the effect of action against such organisations upon Anglo-German relations as in July of last year, when H.M. Government hoped to bring influence to bear in Berlin generally in the direction of European appeasement. On the other hand, any far-reaching action on our part would no doubt be regarded by the German Government as extremely provocative and, as a definite decision has now been deferred for some three years, it is not clear that there would be any definite advantage in now dealing with this question in isolation provided, of course, a very careful watch is being kept upon Nazi activities. In present circumstances the balance of advantage would therefore appear to lie in continuing to follow the course suggested as a *pis aller* by Sir R. Vansittart in September 1937, viz., to watch Nazi activities as carefully as we can and to expel individual delinquents on good causes shown.[84]

The whole question was again brought before the Cabinet on 22 March 1939, when Sir Samuel Hoare, the Home Secretary, strongly recommended that action be taken against three or four known leaders of the Nazi organisations in Britain and that they be deported. In this he was supported by Lord Halifax, the Foreign Secretary, who explained that there were some sixty-one officials of Nazi organisations in the United Kingdom. He was in favour of action on the lines proposed in regard to persons who were found to be engaged in undesirable activities, while he also thought that 'on the whole this was a good time to take this step, since our relations with Germany could hardly be worse than they were at present. It would be a pity to postpone action till a later date when our relations might be improving'. The Cabinet concluded by empowering the Foreign and Home Offices 'to authorise action with a view to the deportation of a limited number of officials of Nazi organisations in this country who were engaged in undesirable activities'.[85] While the Foreign and Home Offices discussed the issue of the sixty Germans whom it was said 'play the lead in organising, i.e. intimidating Germans resident in this country', it was agreed that 'the ideal would be to get rid of them all, and any such drastic action would certainly have a disorganising effect on undesirable German activities in this country'. However, it was also agreed that such a sweeping operation was not possible at the time, but instead a list of 'the six most objectionable Germans in this country' would be drawn up, 'from whom the first batch of three would be selected for expulsion'. On 3 April 1939, therefore, Dr Theodor Kordt, German Chargé d'Affaires, was informed of the names of the three people it was desired should leave the United Kingdom forthwith: Otto Korlowa, *Landesgruppenleiter* of the NSDAP in the United Kingdom; Edmund Himmelmann, formerly Adjutant to the *Landesgruppenleiter* and then organisation leader of the United Kingdom branch of the NSDAP; finally, Johanna Wolf, leader of the Women's Section of the German Labour Front in the United Kingdom.[86]

Other forms of Nazi pressure against émigrés, however, were even more sinister than those already described. The full weight of Nazi oppression was brought to bear against those numerous émigrés who, either because they were disillusioned about life in other countries or because after a time they felt that the worst of the 'revolutionary' excesses of Nazism had burnt themselves out, actually returned to Germany. But the Nazi regime made it clear that the return of émigrés to Germany was not only unwelcome, that attempts would be made to prevent them from entering the country and that if they succeeded in doing so they would be arrested and interned in concentration or 'training' camps. Those émigrés foolish or brave enought to try to return to Germany were classified either as 'political opponents' or as Jews, but as time went on the regulations applicable to returning émigrés became an increasingly important part of Nazi Germany's anti-Jewish policies which, during the 1930s at least, were intended to 'encourage' the exodus of Jews from Germany. In this way, then, Nazi Germany's anti-émigré and anti-Jewish policies ran parallel.[87]

This was demonstrated by the new wave of terror unleashed against the Jews who were returning to Germany in increasing numbers during 1934, as well as by the decree issued by the Gestapo on 28 January 1935. Going further than a previous instruction issued by Göring on 15 January 1934, this new *Runderlass* ordered that *all* returning émigrés were to be placed in concentration camps. Further, during the period of imprisonment there was to be 'a thorough police inquiry into the activity and political attitude' of the émigré whilst abroad. The results of such investigation and a 'guarantee' that the internee would, without difficulty, be integrated into the National Socialist State, were to be the deciding factors leading to release from the concentration camp. While these orders were concerned more with questions of internal security rather than with 'anti-State activity abroad' – the authorities particularly feared contact being made by the returning émigrés with opposition circles in Germany – one thing in particular was clear: the proposals made in the *Runderlass* for the reintegration of returning émigrés into the new Nazi State were not to apply in any way to *Jewish* émigrés who had returned to Germany.

Everything possible was to be done to make their return to the Reich an unpleasant one.[88]

The destruction of all civil and political liberties and the fight against the 'illegal opposition' within Germany by the Nazi regime did not, therefore, cease at Germany's borders. The fight against German émigrés wherever they might be and whatever their activity, but more particularly if it was classified by the Nazi authorities as 'anti-State', was directly related to the prevailing situation and conditions within Germany itself. All measures directed against the émigrés abroad, then, were seen by the regime as necessary *Abwehrmaßnahmen*, as one means of defending, protecting and indeed pursuing that golden dream of the *Totalitätsanspruch des Nationalsozialismus*. Opposition and dissidence, whether at home or abroad, had to be stamped out, irrespective of the methods employed or the repercussions on Nazi Germany's foreign relations. Yet the matter went far beyond internal considerations of politics and security. Unless Nazi Germany was properly disciplined internally, Hitler's foreign policy aims would be more difficult to achieve. This required, therefore, the elimination of Germany's 'opposition' abroad, both because of its contacts and its encouragement of latent opposition within the Reich which, by its very nature, negated the whole *Totalitätsanspruch* of the regime. The means used in pursuit of this aim included blackmail, the taking of hostages, even murder – as shown by the assassination of Theodor Lessing, the philosopher, on 30 August 1933 in Marienbad, Czechoslovakia, where he had lived in exile since February of that year. In general, then, one can say that the 'defensive [political and police] measures of the regime were an indirect element of National Socialist policies of conquest'.[89]

## Notes

1. For the difficulties in attempting to arrive at a precise figure for all those who left Germany from 1933 for a variety of racial, political, or religious reasons, see W. Röder, *Die deutschen sozialistischen Exilgruppen in Großbritannien 1940–1945. Ein Beitrag zur Geschichte des Widerstandes gegen den Nationalsozialismus*, Bonn/Bad Godesberg, 1973, pp. 15–19.
2. H.E. Tutas, *Nationalsozialismus und Exil. Die Politik des Dritten Reiches*

*gegenüber der deutschen politischen Emigration 1933–1939*, Munich, 1975, p. 60.

3. See Röder, pp. 13–14.

4. See G. Hirschfeld, L. Kettenacker (eds.), *The 'Führer State': Myth and Reality. Studies on the Structure and Politics of the Third Reich*, Stuttgart, 1981.

5. See H.W. Koch, *Der Sozialdarwinismus. Seine Genese und sein Einfluß auf das imperialistische Denken*, Munich, 1973, pp. 154–8.

6. A. Hitler, *Mein Kampf*, London 1939, pp. 329–31. .

7. *Ibid.* pp. 288–9, 374–5.

8. K.D. Bracher, *The German Dictatorship. The Origins, Structure, and Effects of National Socialism*, London, 1971, p. 193.

9. *Ibid.*, p. 192.

10. E. Jäckel, *Hitler's Weltanschauung. Entwurf einer Herrschaft*, Tübingen, 1969, p. 107.

11. Bracher, p. 193.

12. L.W. Holborn, G.M. Carter, J.H. Herz (eds.), *German Constitutional Documents Since 1871. Selected Texts and Commentary*, New York, 1970, pp. 28–9.

13. Bracher, p. 194.

14. *Ibid.*, p. 246.

15. *Ibid.*, p. 246.

16. *Ibid.*, p. 210.

17. *Ibid.*, pp. 202, 210. A useful chronicle of important developments in the first stages of the Nazi *Machtergreifung* is to be found in E.B. Wheaton, *Prelude to Calamity: The Nazi Revolution 1933–35*, London 1969. See also M. Broszat, *The Hitler State. The Foundation and Development of the Internal Structure of the Third Reich*, London, 1981.

18. J.C. Fest, *Hitler*, London, 1974, p. 410.

19. *Ibid.*, p. 412.

20. Wheaton, pp. 285, 303.

21. *Ibid.*, pp. 288–90.

22. *Ibid.*, pp. 307, 322; Fest, pp. 413–14.

23. Fest, p. 414.

24. Wheaton, p. 334.

25. W. Wette, 'Ideologien, Propaganda und Innenpolitik als Voraussetzungen der Kriegspolitik des Dritten Reiches', in W. Deist, M. Messerschmidt, H.E. Volkmann, W. Wette, *Das Deutsche Reich und der Zweite Weltkrieg, Bd. 1. Ursachen und Voraussetzungen der Deutschen Kriegspolitik*, Stuttgart, 1979, p. 160.

26. *Ibid.*, pp. 161–2.

27. H.G. Lehmann, *In Acht und Bann. Politische Emigration, NS–Ausbürgerung und Wiedergutmachung am Beispiel Willy Brandts*, Munich, 1976, p. 33.

28. Wette, p. 155.

29. Lehmann, pp. 40–1.

30. *Ibid.*, p. 46.

31. Tutas, p. 18.

32. *Ibid.*, pp. 20–1.

33. Lehmann, pp. 44–6.

34. *Ibid.*, pp. 49–50; Tutas, p. 138.

35. Lehmann, p. 50.

36. *Ibid.*, pp. 275–6.

37. *Ibid.*, pp. 277–8.

38. Tutas, p. 140.

39. Lehmann, p. 51.

40. *Ibid.*, p. 51; Tutas, pp. 140–1.

41. Tutas, p. 141.

42. Lehmann, pp. 54–5; Tutas, pp. 141–2.

43. Lehmann, p. 55; Tutas, pp. 146–7.

44. A.J. Sherman, *Island Refuge. Britain and Refugees from the Third Reich 1933–1939*, London, 1973, pp. 64–5.

45. Tutas, p. 152.

46. *Ibid.*, p. 154.

47. *Ibid.*, p. 153.

48. *Ibid.*, pp. 157–9.

49. *Ibid.*, pp. 157–9. See also Lehmann, pp. 55–8.

50. Lehmann, p. 62.

51. *Ibid.*, pp. 62–5.

52. Tutas, pp. 144–5.

53. *Ibid.*, pp. 68–70.

54. Lehmann, p. 44. See also Tutas, pp. 87–98.

55. Lehmann, p. 60; Tutas, p. 73.

56. Lehmann, p. 61.

57. *Ibid.*, pp. 59, 61.

58. Tutas, pp. 67, 74.

59. *Ibid.*, 74–5.

60. *Ibid.*, pp. 78–9; Lehmann, p. 59.

61. See Sherman, *passim*; J.P. Fox, 'Great Britain and the German Jews 1933', *Wiener Library Bulletin*, 1972, Vol. XXVI, Nos. 1 & 2 New Series, Nos. 26 & 27, October 1972, pp. 40–6.

62. See *Politisches Archiv des Auswärtigen Amtes*, Bonn: Referat Deutschland, Po.5, N.E. adh.I, Lügenpropaganda, Boykottbewegung, 1933, Bericht A.764 mit Anlagen vom 22.3.1933, Hoesch/AA. (Hereafter cited as PA). Also filmed as L1668/L495232–239 (copies at Library and Records Department, Foreign and Commonwealth Office, London. Hereafter cited as AA).

63. PA: Referat Deutschland, Po.5, N.E. adh.4, Nr.1, Bd.1. Deutsche Emigranten im Ausland 1933.

64. AA.5740/HO30985–990. (Abt.Pol.III: Po.2. England: Politische Beziehungen Englands zu Deutschland, Jan. 1932–Jan. 1936.)

65. See *Documents on German Foreign Policy 1918–1945*, Series C, Vol.I, pp. 432–4, Hoesch/AA., London 15 May 1933 (DGFP). See also J.P. Fox, 'Alfred Rosenberg in London'. *The Contemporary Review*, Vol.213, July 1968, pp. 6–11.

66. DGFP, C, I, 751–763, Hoesch/AA., London 16 August 1933; AA.8677/E607163–173, Bismarck/AA., London 19 September 1933 (Presse. Propaganda gegen Deutschland und Gegenpropaganda); AA.5740/HO31673–695, Bismarck/AA., London 12 September 1934.

67. AA.L1808/L522015–018 (Referat Deutschland. Po.5. N.E. adh. 1, Nr.2: Lügenmeldungen über Misshandlungen, Inhaftierungen und Protesteingaben politischer Gesinnungsgenossen 1933–1934).

68. AA.L1808/L522022., L522031–035.

69. AA.8480/E596703–709, Runderlass Bülow mit Anlage/Missionen (Referat Deutschland, 13/5: Po.5. Sozialdemokrat. Partei, 3/1933–1/1934); Bismarck/AA., London, 8 December 1933 (Referat Deutschland. Po.5. N.E. adhr. 4, Nr.1., Bd.4, Deutsche Emigranten im Ausland, 1933).

70. Otto Lehmann-Russbüldt, the writer and pacifist, was until 1926 General Secretary of the German League for Civil Rights and together with R. Olden and Ernst Toller represented the League in Great Britain; Gerhart Seger, a journalist, was until 1928 Secretary of the German Peace Movement, and on behalf of *Sopade* undertook journeys to Czechoslovakia, Sweden, Norway, and Great Britain. Franz L. Neumann, a sociologist, was the author of a penetrating sociological study of National Socialism first published in 1942, *Behemoth. The Structure and Practice of National Socialism 1933–1944* (rev. ed. 1944). Babette Gross, companion and collaborator of W. Münzenberg, was until 1936 proprietor of Editions du Carrefour, founded by Münzenberg in Paris. David Yaskiel, a businessman, established the British International News Agency in London in 1933 as a distribution centre for exile literature; he was also involved in publishing the second 'Brown Book', *The Reichstag Fire Trial* (1934).

71. See AA.K1523 *passim*. (Referat Deutschland, Inland 11.A/B. Deutsche Emigrantentätigkeit im Ausland).

72. Foreign Office Correspondence 371, C671/671/18, Vol. 18874, Minute by Mr Baxter, 11 January 1935 (Public Record Office, London: hereafter cited as PRO FO).

73. PA. Referat Deutschland, Inland II.

74. AA.5764/E420372–375 (Neue Reichskanzlei, England: 1936–1937). See also AA.5730 *passim* (Abteilung Pol. 111. Po.2: Politische Beziehungen zwischen England und Deutschland, 2/1936 – 5/1936).

75. PRO FO C10679/4412/18, Vol. 16751, Colonel Kell/Sir R. Vansittart, 4 December 1933; *ibid.*, C10775/4412/18, unsigned Memorandum, 6 December 1933, with enclosure from *Daily Herald*.

76. PRO FO C2943/75/18, Vol. 17730, Mr Newsam, Home Office/A.R. Dew, 5 May 1934.

77. PRO FO C4321/487/18, Vol. 18868, Memorandum by Mr Creswell, 20 May 1935.

78. PRO FO C7431/487/18, Vol. 18869, Memorandum by Mr Sargent, 1 November 1935.

79. PRO FO C111/3143/4013/4162/5519/6013/576/18, Vol. 19942, Feb.–July 1936; C6014/576/18, Vol. 19942, Cabinet Conclusions, extract, 29 July 1936.

80. PRO FO C7296/576/18, Vol. 19942, Memorandum by Mr Wigram, 8 October 1936, and attached papers.

81. PRO FO C2089/305/18, Vol. 20739, Memorandum by Sir R. Vansittart, Sir Russell Scott, Sir V. Kell, 15 March 1937.

82. PRO FO C5161/305/18, Vol. 20739, Cabinet Conclusions, extract, 14 July 1937.

83. PRO FO C5906/305/18, Vol. 20740, Memorandum by Mr Strang, 11 August 1937; *ibid.*, C5907, Memorandum by Mr Strang, 13 August 1937.

84. PRO FO C4278/94/18, Vol. 23035, Memorandum by Mr Roberts, 19 January 1939.

85. PRO FO C3890/94/18, Vol. 23035, Cabinet Conclusions, extract, 22 March 1939.

86. PRO FO C4820/94/18, Vol. 23035, 3 April 1939.

87. Tutas, p. 111.

88. *Ibid.*, pp. 111–13, 119–27.

89. *Ibid.*, p. 203.

*Bernard Wasserstein*

# The British Government and the German Immigration 1933–1945

The roots of British policy towards the German immigration in the Nazi period can be traced back to the firmly established Victorian tradition of free immigration and political asylum and to the political struggles and legislative action which eventually limited that tradition between 1905 and 1919.

Between 1826 and 1905 there was, in effect, total freedom of immigration to Britain. Although an Aliens Act limiting that freedom was passed by Parliament in 1848 it never took effect and in 1850 the Act expired without any alien having been denied entry or expelled under its provisions. Although the presence in Britain of many radical political refugees occasionally led to diplomatic complications with European powers, these never led the British Government to limit immigration during the Victorian period. Nor was there any significant public hostility to European refugees, such native xenophobia as existed being directed rather at the illiberal European regimes from which the refugees had fled. The prevalent attitude was expressed by the Conservative Lord Malmesbury in 1852 when he declared in Parliament: 'I can well conceive the pleasure and happiness of a refugee, hunted from his native land, on approaching the shores of England, and the joy with which he first catches sight of them; but they are not greater than the pleasure and happiness every Englishman feels in knowing that his country affords the refugees a home and safety'.[1] Against this friendly background the number of foreigners registered in census returns in England and Wales rose from 50,289 in 1851 to 118,031 in 1881.

In 1881, however, a new type of immigration began which was to lead by 1905 to the end of the Victorian liberal tradition of free entry. This was the immigration of Russian Jews. By 1901 the number of aliens counted in the census was 247,758, and it has been estimated that of these about 100,000 were Jews who had entered Britain in the two previous decades.[2] This influx, so much larger in volume than the immigration of the mid-Victorian period and very different from it in social character, helped give birth to what has been described as 'a tradition of antisemitism in Britain' between 1876 and 1939.[3] For much of the period this was confined, particularly in its more virulent forms, to the political fringe. But by the turn of the century there was considerable public opposition to east-European Jewish immigrants, particularly in areas of highly concentrated settlement such as the East End of London. Antisemitism coalesced with a general xenophobia during the Boer War (1899–1902) to produce demands for restriction of immigration. The Aliens Act of 1905 empowered immigration officers to refuse to admit undesirables – the diseased, the insane, the criminal, and the putative public charge. Although passed by Balfour's Conservative Government against Liberal opposition, the Liberal Government administered the Act after 1906. The passage of the Act appears to have had a psychological effect on the volume of immigration which shrank considerably between 1906 and 1914.[4]

The outbreak of the First World War and the bitter anti-German feeling of the war years led to further legislation which greatly limited rights of entry and which, in addition, imposed restrictions upon aliens resident in Britain. Immediately upon the outbreak of the war the Government introduced an Aliens Restriction Bill which passed through all its stages in Parliament in one day, 5 August 1914. The Act, designed 'in time of war or imminent national danger or great emergency to impose restrictions on aliens', required all aliens to register with the police and gave the Home Secretary the power to exclude or deport without appeal.[5] Of an estimated total of 50,000 Germans resident in Britain in 1914 about 40,000 were interned.[6] War hysteria, which compelled the resignation of the allegedly Germanophile Lord Chancellor, Lord Haldane, and led to bans on performances of the music of Beethoven, rendered difficult the position even of long-established and naturalised Germans in England. At the instance of a Scottish baronet, the Crown was induced to bring an action calling upon Sir Ernest Cassell and Sir Edgar Speyer 'to show by what authority they claimed to be Privy Councillors' since they were not natural-born British subjects.[7] German- and Austrian-born British citizens felt obliged to write a series of 'loyalty letters' to *The Times*, asserting their loyalty to their adopted land. There were attacks on shops owned by Germans or by persons with German-sounding names – often Jews.

The restrictive legislation introduced during the war survived its end and was extended by Lloyd George's coalition Government in the Aliens Restriction Act of 1919 and the ensuing Aliens Order of 1920. These provided that, in addition to the restrictions enacted in 1914, no alien might enter the country other than temporaily unless he had a Ministry of Labour permit or had visible means of support; moreover, any alien might be refused admission by an immigration officer; there was no appeal from the Home Secretary's decision. The legislation enacted between 1905 and 1919 remained in effect until after the Second World War: indeed, in its application to immigration from much of continental Europe, it was overriden only upon British accession to the Treaty of Rome, with its provision for free movement of labour within the European Economic Community, in 1972.

The legislative basis for British policy towards the German emigration to Britain between 1933 and 1945 therefore originated in hostility to the immigration and settlement of Jews and of Germans. Of the 49,500 Germans and Austrians (not including trans-migrants passing through the country) admitted to Britain between 1933 and 1939 perhaps 90 per cent were Jews. That such a large number of German Jews were admitted in spite of the anti-Jewish and anti-German roots of the immigration laws in force at the time was remarkable. It is thus hardly surprising that some public opposition to the influx, often couched in the traditional terms of the anti-immigration movements of the early part of the century, surfaced almost immediately. On 9 March 1933, Mr E. Doran, Unionist MP for Tottenham North, asked the Home Secretary in the House of Commons whether he would 'take steps to prevent any alien Jews entering this country from Germany'. The Home Secretary replied that it was

> not within the contemplation of the law that there should be discrimination against aliens on grounds of religious belief or racial origin, but there are adequate powers under the Aliens Order to protect this country from any undesirable influx of aliens.[8]

Although correct as a description of the legal provisions of the Act, the response was, as we have seen, hardly accurate as an explanation of the political origins and purpose of the legislation. Whatever might be 'within the contemplation of the law' the Government, as will be seen, did not don social, political, or religious blinkers in its consideration of the issue between 1933 and 1945.

The initial wave of emigration from Germany of political opponents of Hitler and of Jews (some 37,000 of whom are estimated to have fled the country in 1933)[9] compelled the British Government soon after the Nazi accession to power to review its policy regarding the admission of German refugees. At a Cabinet meeting on 5 April 1933 the question 'of the admission of Jews entering this country from Germany' was considered 'as a matter of urgency', and it was decided to form a Cabinet Committee on Aliens Restrictions under the chairmanship of the Home Secretary.[10]

In a report to the committee on 6 April the Home Secretary noted that over the previous few days there had been a 'marked increase' in the number of aliens arriving in Britain and he added that 'analysis of the records shows that the bulk of this increase is due to an influx of Germans, mainly of the professional classes and probably Jews'. The Home Secretary continued that 'in theory, the Home Office will have power to regulate the stay of such people by refusing to grant further extensions, but in practice it may prove very difficult to insist on their return to Germany while present conditions continue in that country'. Under the current administration of the Aliens Order, 'Jewish refugees from Germany who are unable to satisfy the Immigration Officer as to their means of maintenance would be refused leave to land'.[11]

Appended to the Home Secretary's report was a document signed by four representatives of the Anglo-Jewish community: Neville Laski and Lionel L. Cohen of the Board of Deputies of British Jews, L.G. Montefiore of the Anglo-Jewish Association and Otto M. Schiff of the Jews' Temporary Shelter. This outlined arrangements put in hand by the community to look after immigrants on arrival. The document contained a pledge which was to provide an essential foundation for the Government's willingness to permit substantial immigration from Germany until the outbreak of the war. On behalf of the Anglo-Jewish community the representatives declared: 'All expense, whether in respect of temporary or permanent accommodation or maintenance, will be borne by the Jewish community without ultimate charge to the State'.[12] Indigents would thus not fall on the public purse.

The Home Secretary's memorandum invited the Cabinet Committee to consider 'whether there is any ground for a relaxation of the provisions of the Aliens Order so as to allow of the admission of persons of this class on the basis of the guarantee given by the Jewish community'. The memorandum stated (as it turned out over-optimistically) that 'it may be taken that the Jewish community is willing and has ample means to implement its guarantee of temporary maintenance for the refugees'. The Home Secretary continued that, were Jewish refugees to be admitted on the basis of the guarantee, 'Immigration Officers will continue to exercise their powers to refuse leave to land to any individual alien on medical grounds or on grounds personal to him such as known criminal activities or known association with subversive movements'. This hint of political concern was made explicit in the final paragraph of the memorandum:

> There is, of course, a risk that the influx of refugees from Germany may include a certain number of Communists, but any who are prominent in the Communist Movement are known, and would be excluded by the Immigration Officers. As regards other persons who are suspected on arrival of Communist activities, steps can be taken to see that they are refused leave to land or that the question of giving them leave is referred to the Secretary of State for decision.

The Cabinet Committee considered the issue with particular attention to the number of refugees who might be expected to arrive. The Anglo-Jewish representatives were said to have estimated that the total number expected 'should not exceed three to four thousand, the bulk being members of the professional classes'. However, the committee doubted whether 'it is possible to form any correct estimate at the present time', noting that if anti-Jewish trends in Germany persisted, 'the pressure to migrate will be greatly increased'. 'Grave objections' were expressed to the proposal to relax immigration restrictions on the basis of the Jewish community's guarantee, and the committee's report to the Cabinet stated:

> While it is true that the Jewish Community are prepared to guarantee accommodation and maintenance for the refugees, it is inevitable that sooner or later the Government will be pressed to waive the condition that the refugees must not enter into employment.... It is not possible to forecast the actual effect on unemployment of a waiver of the condition, or the extent to which the refugees might displace British labour, but we agree with the Ministry of Labour that public opinion would be extremely sensitive on the subject, and that if it could be demonstrated in a few

individual cases that British workmen had lost their jobs to Jewish refugees, the demand for a reimposition of the restrictions and their rigid enforcement would be irresistible.

The committee therefore recommended that the existing immigration arrangements should be maintained, that certain further restrictions should be added in order to strengthen controls and that the Anglo-Jewish representatives should be informed that while there could be no question of relaxing entry restrictions, the Government would be prepared to consider extending permission to stay for refugees whose maintenance was guaranteed by the Jewish community.[13]

The Cabinet approved the committee's recommendations in a meeting on 8 April 1933 but its discussion of the issue, as recorded in the minutes, was less negative in tone than that of the committee. It was argued in the Cabinet that it would be in the public interest to

try and secure for this country prominent Jews who were being expelled from Germany and who had achieved distinction whether in pure science, applied science, such as medicine or technical industry, music or art. This would not only obtain for this country the advantage of their knowledge and experience, but would also create a very favourable impression in the world, particularly if our hospitality were offered with some warmth.

As to the dangers anticipated by the Minister of Labour concerning possible displacement of British workmen in competition for jobs, the Cabinet 'were anxious' (so the minutes anonymously proceeded) to avoid 'the other danger of creating an atmosphere in Europe critical to this country'.[14]

Although no formal change in the law issued from these deliberations, the cautiously welcoming attitude of the Cabinet set the keynote for government policy until the outbreak of the war. The emphasis was to be on attracting persons of independent means or those who would not compete in the labour market. The Jewish community's guarantee, initially accepted only in relation to those refugees already in the country, soon broadened to include subsequent arrivals. The numbers of these far exceeded initial expectations and the Jewish community together with the churches and other bodies found it necessary to form special institutions to cope with the flood. Foremost among these were the Council for German Jewry, the Jewish Refugees Committee, the Central British Fund for German

Jewry, and the Academic Assistance Council. Substantial sums were raised by these bodies to finance the integration of refugees; by 1939 the Jewish community alone had raised £3,000,000 (exclusive of contributions by individuals for the maintenance of refugees whom they had brought into the country and guaranteed personally). Large sums were also raised by appeals to the general public. The community's guarantee was maintained until after the outbreak of the war in spite of the fact that the numbers arriving were more than ten times the original estimate. The role of the voluntary organisations in facilitating the influx was thus of critical importance. Moreover, the records of government discussions of the refugee issue between 1933 and 1939 demonstrate that the financial and administrative contribution of the voluntary bodies was the indispensable condition of official readiness to permit the entry of further large numbers of refugees.[15]

In the first phase of the German emigration the countries absorbing the largest numbers of refugees were France (an estimated 21,000 by April 1934), Palestine (10,000), Poland (8,000), Czechoslovakia (3,500), and Holland (2,500). England was estimated in April 1934 to have absorbed 2,000 (although this may have been rather lower than the actual figure).[16] After the initial wave of emigration in 1933 when 300 to 400 German Jews were stated to be entering Britain each month, the volume declined to about 100 per month in 1934.[17] However, after the promulgation of the Nuremberg Laws in September 1935 there was a slight increase in the level of Jewish emigration (which rose from an estimated 21,000 in 1935 to 25,000 in 1936).[18] Meanwhile destinations other than Britain were beginning to close their doors. Out of the total of 106,000 German Jews who emigrated between 1933 and 1936, Palestine was able to absorb 23,963;[19] the outbreak in 1936 of a serious Arab rebellion against the British mandatory government in Palestine led to restrictions by the government on Jewish immigration. In the years 1937 to 1939 the number of German Jews entering Palestine declined to 11,864, out of a total Jewish emigration from Germany of 141,000.[20] As Palestine and other countries raised barriers to entry the pressure on Britain increased.

A memorandum prepared in the Home Office in 1934 reveals some of the preoccupations of offical thinking on the refugee issue. Of particular interest is the definition given to the 'right of asylum':

An individual foreigner has no claim as of right to be admitted to

69

this country on the ground that he is a political or religious refugee. The so-called right of asylum, as defined both in the dictionaries and the legal text-books, is nothing but the competence of every State, inferred from its territorial supremacy, to allow a political or religious refugee to enter.... The right is not the right of a foreigner to admission, but the right of the State if it thinks fit, to receive a foreigner fleeing from persecution.

Foreigners resident in Britain might after a while acquire the right to engage in propaganda against foreign governments. Terrorist activities, however, were a different matter, although the memorandum noted that 'different degrees of public sympathy would be extended to a person implicated in a plot (accompanied by violence) against the present regimes in Germany or Russia, and a person who had made an attack on the President of France'. In general, the document concluded, policy towards political refugees must be decided 'with due regard to two divergent principles – on the one hand the established tradition of hospitality to political and religious refugees, which has been exercised with a good deal of liberality in the past... and on the other the necessity, which is recognised by the powers given under the Aliens Order, of preventing the admission and securing the removal of aliens whose presence in this country is for any reason undesirable'.[21]

The increased pressure on Britain did not, however, lead to the exclusion of significantly larger numbers of 'undesirable' aliens. The number of Germans and Austrians refused permission to land under the Aliens Order of 1920 was 484 in 1933; in 1935 it was 365; and in 1937 it was 438.[22] In the years 1935–7 the efforts of the voluntary organisations, the British Government and the League of Nations were concentrated on seeking to secure an 'orderly' exodus of refugees from Germany. Little progress was made, however, as was evident in the report submitted to the League by the High Commissioner for Refugees coming from Germany, Sir Neill Malcolm, on 1 September 1937:

While there have been no wholesale expatriations from Germany, the placing and final settlement of refugees having already left their country of origin has not made great progress. On the one hand, measures taken by Governments in regard to immigration have brought the numbers of departures from Europe for overseas countries down to a very low level. On the other hand, the lack of the funds required to finance refugee emigration – particularly that of non-Jews – has been one of the chief determining factors in that situation. In consequence, and despite the hopes which had been entertained, steps taken during the year with a view to a solution of the problem of refugees coming from Germany have not been numerous.[23]

Any lingering hopes that an 'orderly' solution might be achieved by international cooperation were to be dashed by the convulsive effects on the international system of German expansion from March 1938 onwards. Following the *Anschluss* on 12 March the numbers of refugees seeking to enter Britain increased sharply. A Home Office memorandum on 14 March considered the new situation arising from the *Anschluss*. It pointed out that it seemed 'certain that economic and political pressure in Austria will lead to a large increase in the number of refugees of Jewish race or ancestry who will seek admission to this country'. There appeared to be a particular 'danger that the small Jewish trader and businessman of limited means will be forced out of business and out of his country, and may be driven by economic and political pressure to seek asylum here'. The question therefore arose:

> . . . as a matter of policy, whether we are to acquiesce in the influx of an uncertain number of refugees, who may not be individually undesirable but may create social and labour problems, or whether a more rigid control is to be set up against new entrants of this type.

A new complicating factor, the memorandum continued, was the news that the Jewish community was now having difficulty meeting the guarantee given to the Government in 1933 and they had 'intimated that they cannot extend this undertaking to new arrivals, though they would still be prepared to make an exception for refugees whom the Home Office or the Ministry of Labour decide to admit to this country after consultation with the [German-Jewish Aid] Committee'. Against this background the Home Office therefore suggested that 'immediate steps should be taken to require that all persons holding Austrian or German passports who seek to enter this country should be in possession of a British visa'.[24]

After inter-departmental discussions and Anglo-German negotiations on the issue, new instructions were issued by the Passport Control Department of the Foreign Office on 27 April 1938. These explained that 'the main purpose of the visa will be to regulate the flow into the United Kingdom of persons who, for political, racial or religious reasons, may wish to take refuge there in considerable numbers'. Particular care was to be exercised in the case of 'persons who describe themselves as visitors':

> Such persons, especially those who appear to be of Jewish or partly Jewish origin, or have non-Aryan affiliations, should be discreetly questioned as to their family circumstances, and how their business or employment has been affected by recent events; and if it is suspected that emigration is intended, the applicant should be invited to say so frankly.

Under the heading 'Potential refugees or emigrants (declared or suspected). Cases in which visas should be refused', the circular stated that 'the test should be whether or not an applicant is likely to be an asset to the United Kingdom':

> Among those who must be regarded as *prima facie* unsuitable will be:
>
> (a) Small shop-keepers, retail traders, artisans, and persons likely to seek employment.
> (b) Agents and middlemen, whose livelihood depends on commission and, therefore, on trade activity.
> (c) Minor musicians and commercial artists of all kinds....
> (d) The rank and file of professional men – lawyers, doctors, dentists.

On the other hand passport control officers might grant visas, without reference to London, to 'Distinguished persons, i.e. those of *international* repute in the field of science, medicine, research or art' as well as certain 'industrialists with a well-established business'. Visas were not to be refused to persons in these categories without reference to London.[25]

The massive new pressure for emigration from the Reich led the United States Government to propose in March 1938 the establishment of an international committee 'for the purpose of facilitating the emigration from Austria, and presumably from Germany, of political refugees'.[26] The British Government agreed to the proposal and, after lengthy diplomatic consultations, it was decided to inaugurate the committee with an international conference which opened at Evian on 6 July 1938. In the weeks leading up to the conference Whitehall officials deliberated at length inter- and intradepartmentally as to the attitude to be adopted at Evian by the British delegation.

The instructions issued to the British delegation reminded them that while the meeting at Evian was to be limited to the problem of refugees from Germany, other 'interested governments' would be watching the proceedings; it was therefore 'important to avoid giving the impression that the meeting was going to create such facilities for emigrants that other countries would with impunity force sections of their population to leave'. On immigration prospects in the United Kingdom the instructions stated:

> It has been the traditional policy of successive British Governments to give shelter to persons who are compelled to leave their own countries by reason of persecution for their political and religious belief or of their racial origin, but His Majesty's Government are bound to have regard to their domestic situation and to the fact that the United Kingdom is not a country of immigration and to recognise that for demographic and economic reasons this policy can only be applied within narrow limits.

Nevertheless, the memorandum continued, within those limits, Britain was prepared 'on the grounds of humanity to adopt an even more liberal policy'. Only a limited number of persons without resources could be admitted, that number depending to a large extent on the help given by the voluntary organisations. A more liberal policy could, however, be adopted towards refugees with capital, students, academics, professional persons and refugees who, with the help of the voluntary bodies, could be trained with a view to emigration overseas.

The memorandum made it clear that neither Palestine nor the colonial empire offered much prospect of space for refugees. The delegation was warned that 'reference to the possibilities of immigration into Palestine should be avoided if possible'. There then followed a discouraging country-by-country survey of the empire. Northern Rhodesia might accommodate at most 500 families, to be settled as farmers 'on a subsistence basis' provided Jewish or other organisations found necessary finance. There were some encouraging reports from Kenya but no final policy had yet been adopted. Barbados offered 'no possibility of refugees in these categories being able to make a living'. In British Guiana there were 'no possibilities'. In British Honduras 'there might be an opening for one veterinary surgeon'. In Ceylon there were 'no possibilities'. In Cyprus there were 'no prospects' save perhaps for 'a few butchers with a capital of £500–£600'. Fiji had openings only for photographers, opticians and oculists with more substantial capital. Hong Kong reported 'no possible openings' and Jamaica 'no possibilities'. Malaya and Mauritius were similarly negative. Nyasaland indicated 'few, if any, possibilities'. Trinidad reported possible openings for two refugees, but added that the Chamber of Commerce was 'strongly opposed to the encouragement of Jewish refugees for work in the Colony'. Finally, Zanzibar conformed to the general pattern with the notation that 'there might be an opening for a German-Jewish dentist later, but at the present time for political reasons the atmosphere is not favourable'.[27]

The generally unpromising tone of the survey of the colonial empire was reflected in the similar attitudes of Dominions' governments and indeed of nearly all governments attending the Evian conference. Save for the establishment of the Inter-Governmental Committee on Refugees, the conference achieved nothing beyond providing an agreeable setting for a lamentable succession of speeches in which delegate after delegate expressed sympathy for the plight of the refugees from the Reich and then proceeded to explain why it was impossible for his government to offer anything other than a token contribution to a solution of the problem. Lord Winterton, who headed the British delegation (the largest at the conference), adhered closely to his instructions, although he put a rather more optimistic interpretation on the possibilities for refugee settlement in Kenya than his instructions (or the future course of events) perhaps warranted. The Evian conference made it clear to the British Government that, in the event of any further surge of German emigration, neither foreign nor colonial governments were likely to offer any succour. The potential pressure on Britain would as a result be all the greater.[28]

The test of the 'even more liberal policy' on immigration into Britain came almost immediately as a result of the incorporation of the Sudetenland into Germany following the Munich conference. On 21 September 1938 Wenzel Jaksch, leader of the Social Democratic Party in the Sudetenland, appealed to the British and French governments to help his followers whose lives were threatened by the German occupation. Herr Jaksch asked whether room might not be found in the British Dominions.[29] However, after consultations with the Dominions' High Commissioners in London, the conclusion was reached that the Dominions were unlikely to take more than a small proportion of the refugees. The suggestion was made that they might be settled in Mexico or the USSR but a Foreign Office official commented that this hardly seemed 'worth serious consideration since Herr Jaksch's people are mostly anti-Communist and we are scarcely in a position to approach either Mexico or the Soviet Union'.[30] The problem was exacerbated by the reported reluctance of the Czech Government to accept German refugees in Czechoslovakia; the Czechs were even threatening to comply with German demands that anti-Nazi Sudeten Germans be sent to Germany. A note prepared by a Foreign Office official, R.M. Makins, on 18 October, pointed out that some temporary visas had already been made available to Jaksch for individuals in imminent peril; these, Makins opined, were 'probably mostly well-known political agitators'. Makins urged that in general mass emigration of anti-Nazis from the Sudetenland 'must be excluded' and that British influence should be used 'to secure that as many refugees are either sent home, if they are willing to go, or else settled in Czechoslovakia'.[31] Under public pressure from the Labour and Liberal parties (plus some Conservatives), the churches, the press, and voluntary organisations, the Government eventually adopted a rather more welcoming attitude towards Sudeten and other ex-Czechoslovak refugees. By the outbreak of the war about 6,000 former inhabitants of Czechoslovakia had been admitted to Britain.[32]

But even while the Sudeten refugee problem was being debated a further massive wave of emigration from the Reich was generated by the Nazis with the forcible expulsion in October 1938 of thousands of Polish Jews and the panic flight which followed the *Kristallnacht* in November. The final year of the peace saw the German emigration reach its numerical peak (40,000 Jews alone emigrated in 1938, and 78,000 in 1939),[33] and there was correspondingly heavy pressure for entry into Great Britain. The discussion of possible outlets for refugee settlement in the colonial empire continued until after the outbreak of the war, and there were occasional bubbles of optimism as to the prospects in Kenya, Northern Rhodesia and British Guiana. A pioneer party of fifty refugee settlers for British Guiana was ready to depart from Britain in August 1939 but they were prevented from sailing by the outbreak of the war.[34] Although this and other such exotic schemes covered reams of official paper no significant scheme of imperial refugee settlement was ever implemented. An offer by the Palestine Jewish community to absorb 10,000 Jewish children from Germany in November 1938 was shelved by the British Government on the ground that it conflicted with its immigration policy in Palestine, which was now moving swiftly towards the strict exclusionism enshrined in the Palestine White Paper of May 1939. In these circumstances the Government felt obliged to make some compensating gesture and it was therefore decided to admit the 10,000 children to Britain.

The Movement for the Care of Children from Germany, the voluntary organisation chiefly responsible for the admission of the children, represented the British liberal spirit at its most effective. The first parties of children began to arrive in Britain in December 1938 and they continued until a few days after the British declaration of war in September 1939. About 90 per cent of the children were Jewish. An appeal for funds by the former Prime Minister, Lord Baldwin, met with donations of over £500,000. Children were, in general, lodged with British foster-parents. The Government, without making any formal change in immigration laws or regulations, did, in fact, in these months modify the application of its policy so as to move closer to the 'even more liberal' position promised at Evian. In a statement to the Inter-Governmental Committee on Refugees on 1 November 1938 the British delegate, Lord Winterton, announced that 'the only limit in fact to the number of refugees who can be admitted is constituted by the ability of the voluntary organisations to provide means for their maintenance and opportunities for their employment'.[35] Although the voluntary bodies reached virtual saturation-point by the summer of 1939, they managed to cope with the flood, and the Jewish community's guarantee was maintained until after the outbreak of the war.

The declaration of war marked a turning-point both as regards the government's policy on immigration from Germany and in official and public attitudes towards refugees already in Britain. If the months between Munich and the outbreak of war can be said to mark a peak of government and public sympathy for the German emigration, the graph of generosity declined to reach a nadir by the summer of 1940. In part this was because of public xenophobia and hysteria not dissimilar to the anti-German outbreaks of the First World War. But it was also the result of sudden changes in government policy upon the outbreak of the war.

At 11.00 a.m. on 3 September 1939, when Britain found herself formally at war with Germany, all visas granted to enemy nationals were automatically invalidated. The Home Office noted that 'apart from the practical difficulties of making contact between the refugee in enemy territory and the refugee organisations in the United Kingdom, which are likely to be almost insuperable, it would be necessary for us to proceed with the utmost caution having regard to the possibility that enemy agents might by this means be introduced into this country'.[36] With few exceptions this remained government policy throughout the war. No refugees emanating from enemy-occupied territory were to be admitted to Britain; although large numbers of citizens of allied countries occupied by Germany were admitted in the course of the war, the policy of exclusion tended to be applied particularly to Germans (and to Jews), with the exception of persons regarded as of value to the British war effort. Nevertheless, no German refugees who actually reached Britain were turned back to Europe. The difficulties of emigration, particularly after the fall of France, and official discouragement of enemy alien immigration combined to reduce the flow of German refugees to Britain to a trickle during the war.

As in the First World War, suspicion of German attempts to infiltrate spies and agents led to restrictive moves against Germans in Britain. In April 1939 the Committee of Imperial Defence approved 'the action taken by the War Office in earmarking accommodation for 18,000 civilian internees'.[37] Secret 'Administrative Instructions for Internment Camps', issued on 25 August 1939, designated a number of sites for proposed camps, among them Northolt Park Racecourse, Butlin's holiday camps at Clacton and Dovercourt, and the Kitchener Camp at Richborough, Kent, which was already occupied by refugees.[38] On 4 September 1939 the Home Secretary, Sir John Anderson, announced in the House of Commons that tribunals were to be established to review all Germans, Austrians and Czecho-Slovaks in the country in order to determine whether they should be interned. The operation was virtually completed by January 1940; by then a total of 528 aliens had been interned and 8,356 subjected to lesser restrictions, while the overwhelming majority (some 60,000, including pre-1933 immigrants and non-refugees) were left at liberty.[39]

The end of the 'phoney war' period in the spring of 1940, however, brought a change in public attitudes, and the rapid collapse of Dutch, Belgian and French resistance to the German invasion heightened the 'fifth-column' panic in Britain. Responding to the public mood, and to a reported order by the newly-appointed Prime Minister, Winston Churchill, to 'collar the lot!', the Government embarked in May 1940 on a policy of general internment of adult 'enemy aliens'.[40] A total of 27,200 were arrested, the majority being refugees from Germany and Austria – 'friendly enemy aliens' as they were dubbed in the jargon of the time. The arrests had their tragi-comic aspects – as when at 1.30 p.m. on 13 July 1940 a group of CID men walked into the Hampstead

Public Library and ordered all Germans and Austrians to leave, quietly. They were presumably acting on the 'known haunts' theory of criminal behaviour. The Isle of Man, which had housed civilian internees during the First World War, was once again turned into a vast metropolis of aliens. About 8,000 Germans and Italians were deported from Britain to Canada and Australia, sometimes suffering robbery and physical ill-treatment en route.

However, the public mood, which initially favoured these measures, soon switched back to a more lenient attitude. The change resulted from scandals in the administration of some internment camps, from complaints that pro- and anti-Nazi Germans were being interned together (fights sometimes following), from a dawning recognition that the internment of refugees served no rational purpose and from such events as the sinking by a German torpedo of the liner, *Arandora Star*, with the drowning of 600 German and Italian deportees, many of whom, it was subsequently shown, were refugees.

Once again the Government responded to the mercurial change in public mood; hardly a month after issuing the order for wholesale internments the Home Secretary announced that he was considering the release of certain classes of internees. By August 1941 as many as 17,745 internees had been released, and some of the deportees were permitted to return to Britain; by April 1944 only twenty-five refugees were still reported interned.[41] Although subject to continuing restrictions the lot of German exiles in Britain improved steadily in the later part of the war, many being permitted to join the British armed forces or to make contributions in other ways (as by broadcasting) to the British war effort.

Towards the end of the war, however, as British troops moved into western Germany, the question of the future disposition of German exiles in Britain once again became a live issue in Whitehall. There was a strong tendency in official quarters to regard the German emigration in Britain as a temporary rather than a permanent addition to the population. With the collapse of Nazism and the British occupation of part of Germany, this view was expressed by the Home Secretary, Herbert Morrison, who told the Cabinet Committee on Refugees, on 16 May 1945:

We ought to act on the assumption that those who had come here had done so temporarily, and ... they should eventually go back whence they came. It was often said that the Jewish refugees in this country were terrified of returning to Germany. We should not be influenced by this attitude. It was possible that post-war Germany would abandon antisemitism altogether. If the Jews were allowed to remain here they might be an explosive element in the country, especially if the economic situation deteriorated.[42]

This view was not, however, translated into an official policy of encouraging the repatriation of German refugees, the majority of whom (particularly the Jews among them) were to remain permanently settled in Britain.

British policy towards the German emigration may therefore be seen as an alloy of the elements of xenophobic restrictionism and liberal hospitality traditional (at different periods) in British politics. There were very few formal changes in policy, the shifts occurring rather by administrative fiat, often in response to public pressure. The British record as regards admission of German emigrants between 1933 and 1939 was (particularly in the critical years, 1938-9) a generous one by contemporary international standards. With the outbreak of the war what had become a 'half-open-door' policy was abruptly reversed. The internments of mid-1940 marked the low point of British policy towards emigrants in Britain. Thereafter the treatment of refugees improved, although they remained subject to the provisions of the 1920 Aliens Order as well as other restrictions. The tremendous contribution to British public, economic, academic and cultural life by the German immigrants during and after the war demonstrated the wisdom of the British Government's cautiously compassionate policy towards the German immigration between 1933 and 1945.

## Notes

1. Quoted in B. Porter, *The Refugee Question in Mid-Victorian Politics*, Cambridge, 1979, pp. 1-2.

2. V.D. Lipman, *Social History of the Jews in England 1850-1950*, London, 1954, pp. 87-90; the difficulties in making such an estimate are discussed *ibid.* and in L.P. Gartner, 'Notes on the Statistics of Jewish Immigration to England 1870-1914', *Jewish Social Studies*, XXII, 2, April 1960, pp. 97-102.

3. C. Holmes, *Anti-Semitism in British Society 1876-1939*, London, 1979, p. 233.

4. Bernard Gainer, *The Alien Invasion: The Origins of the Aliens Act of 1905*, London, 1972, pp. 199–202.

5. *Ibid.*, p. 207.

6. H. Kellenbenz, 'German Immigrants in England' in C. Holmes (ed.), *Immigrants and Minorities in British Society*, London, 1978, pp. 63–80.

7. C.C. Aronsfeld, 'Enemy Aliens, 1914–1918: German-born Jews in England During the First World War', *Jewish Social Studies*, XVIII, 1956, pp. 275–83.

8. Quoted in A.J. Sherman, *Island Refuge: Britain and Refugees from the Third Reich 1933–1939*, London, 1973, p. 28. This monograph is the best analysis of British policy on the German immigration up to the outbreak of the Second World War.

9. H.A. Strauss, 'Jewish Emigration from Germany – Nazi Policies and Jewish Responses (I)', *Leo Baeck Institute Year Book*, XXV, London, 1980, p. 326.

10. Report of Cabinet Committee on Aliens Restrictions, 7 April 1933, Public Record Office (PRO), Kew, CAB 24/239.

11. Home Secretary's Memorandum to Cabinet Committee on Aliens Restrictions, 6 April 1933, *ibid.*

12. 'Proposals of the Jewish Community as Regards Jewish Refugees from Germany', *ibid.*

13. Report of Committee on Aliens Restrictions, 7 April 1933, *ibid.*

14. Quoted in Sherman, p. 32.

15. For a general discussion of the role of the voluntary organisations see N. Bentwich, *They Found Refuge*, London, 1956.

16. 'Comparative Table of Distribution of Refugees' (based on information collected by the League of Nations High Commission for Refugees), PRO FO 371/17700/178.

17. Strauss, p. 354.

18. *Ibid.*, p. 326.

19. *Ibid.*; D. Gurevich (ed.), *Statistical Handbook of Jewish Palestine 1947*, Jerusalem, 1947, p. 104. This figure refers to German citizens (or former citizens) and does not include Jewish refugees from Germany holding Polish or other foreign citizenship.

20. *Ibid.*

21. 'Memorandum respecting Foreign Political Refugees in the United Kingdom', 30 November 1934, PRO FO 371/18553/196.

22. Sherman, p. 270.

23. Report submitted to the Eighteenth Ordinary Session of the Assembly of the League of Nations by the High Commissioner, Sir Neill Malcolm, League of Nations Document No. A.17. 1937. XII.

24. Home Office Memorandum, 14 March 1938, PRO FO 372/3282/22.

25. Foreign Office Circular, 27 April 1938, PRO FO 372/3284/9.

26. Memorandum communicated by the United States Embassy in London to the Foreign Office, 24 March 1938, PRO FO 371/21747/109.

27. Memorandum of instructions for the United Kingdom Delegation to the Evian Conference, July 1938, PRO FO 371/22529/66.

28. For a fuller account of the Evian conference, see Sherman, Chaps. 4, 5.

29. Foreign Office memorandum, 13 October 1938, PRO FO

371/21583/231-6.

30. *Ibid.*

31. Note by R.M. Makins, 18 October 1938, PRO FO 371/21584/407-11.

32. Sherman, p. 255.

33. Strauss, p. 326.

34. Bentwich, p. 42.

35. Statement by Lord Winterton, 1 November 1938, PRO FO 371/22536/237.

36. E.N. Cooper (Home Office) to A.W.G. Randall (Foreign Office), 18 September 1939, PRO FO 371/24100/120 ff.

37. Extracts from minutes of CID meeting, 6 April 1939, Home Office papers, 144/1262 (700470/2).

38. Home Office papers, 144/21258 (700463/39).

39. For a fuller account see B. Wasserstein, *Britain and the Jews of Europe 1939-45*, London, 1979, Chap. 3.

40. See P. and L. Gillman, *'Collar the Lot!': How Britain Interned and Deported its Wartime Refugees*, London, 1980.

41. See Wasserstein, pp. 107-8.

42. Minutes of Cabinet Committee on Refugees, 16 May 1945, PRO CAB 95/15.

*Anthony Glees*

# The German Political Exile in London 1939–1945

*The SPD and the British Labour Party*

Wartime London was the centre of a shadow world whose name was exile. It was inhabited by the representatives of some of the great democratic movements of Europe which Hitler and the Nazis had tried to destroy. These political exiles had one central purpose common to them all: to maintain a political existence. Many of them showed great courage and high idealism in pursuit of this and nowhere, perhaps, was this more apparent than in the case of the exiles from Germany. They were the people who had not capitulated to the Nazis and had chosen exile rather than risk torture, imprisonment or death. Even though they were now in relative safety, they were regarded by many as enemy aliens, secret representatives of an odious regime, whilst their erstwhile supporters at home could too easily see them as cowards or traitors.

Yet despite all of this, despite the great difficulties inherent in exile life – the isolation, the feuding, the strangeness – exile could be a worthwhile activity. It did not necessarily mean political extinction, as many have supposed; for every Napoleon III there is a Lenin. The Second World War was no exception. The way in which General de Gaulle was being built up in exile and was himself using it in order to become a major wartime figure, served as an example to many.

There were exiled members of most of the German parties of the Weimar era in London, old Liberals like Fritz Demuth or August Weber and even former Nazis like Hermann Rauschning; the most important were those who represented the political Left. They were important for a number of reasons. Firstly, both the Social Democratic Party and the Communist Party had amassed a large membership before 1933. Secondly, these were the only parties that had officially refused to accept Hitler's dictatorial constitutional arrangement. Thirdly, even though the supporters of these parties would be unable to offer their leaders any allegiance for the duration of the Third Reich, if Hitler were overthrown and a freely democratic situation established, a sizeable number of them would be able to return to the party fold. Although many Britons were of the opinion that, if and when Hitler was defeated, German politics would require a fresh start with new political movements, it was unthinkable that in free conditions an organised labour movement would not reappear.

It must, however, be noted that the political significance of the Left exiles was not always accepted by those British authorities with the most serious interest in the matter, that is by the British Foreign Office and the British Labour Party. The explanation for this fluctuating attention is a major part of the history of exile; as a specific form of political activity, exile consists not only in the preservation of a party identity but also in the gaining of official recognition of the party's legitimacy by the authorities of the host nation. It was not enough for the leadership to marshal all available exiled supporters, it had also to gain acceptance as the spokesman on policies which affected the home country.

The role of the Social Democrats in exile in London is especially interesting. They had possessed a vested interest in the Weimar Republic and we should not forget that much of what Hitler did, was directed against the SPD. The Nazi regime presented itself as the alternative to Social Democracy and its concept of politics, to Marxism and class conflict, to parliamentary democracy and liberty. Thus, even in exile, the SPD had political meaning as the *opposite* of Nazism. But there is another reason for regarding the SPD as more important than the Communists. From 1941 until the end of 1945 London was the official headquarters of the SPD in exile, where policies were made and ideas formulated. The KPD, on the other hand, was officially based in Moscow and although German Communists in London were certainly not inactive, they were always only the mouthpiece of Moscow and wholly subservient to the Soviet Union. The SPD was able to act autonomously and its status was accepted by all other Social Democratic communities (of whom the most significant were those in the USA and Sweden).

For the SPD to make a success out of its exile, it had to ensure that the party's identity remained intact and it had to gain some measure of recognition from the British Government via the Foreign Office and the British Labour Party. It managed to do all these things for some, but never for all, of the time and this is why the SPD's London years were only a partial success. The Party had possessed the sympathy of the Labour Party before 1941, but then proceeded to lose it; it managed to win the attention of the Foreign Office after 1940 but it lost that too. Yet despite this, it was able to preserve its distinctive identity during almost the entire period in exile, although it did face a major internal crisis in its dealings with the Communists from 1943 until 1944.

To have succeeded even in part was a remarkable achievement. It should not be forgotten that the SPD survived the war and was able to return to Germany. It had managed to fight off the Communists despite the fact that their exile membership was almost double the 100 or so Social Democrats in London and despite their financial support from Moscow; this feat certainly helped the SPD to fight the KPD after 1945. It overcame the isolation from its loyal followers inside the Reich, which was after 1939 almost hermetically sealed off from the outside world. It had not capitulated to the ever-increasing British desire to put an end to independent German political activity even though, as the terrible crimes of the Nazis became public knowledge, the claim by Social Democrats and others that 'another' (better) Germany existed, one which deserved fair treatment, became very, very difficult to uphold.

There can be no doubt that the years in London were very different from those the Social Democratic leadership had spent in Prague (1933–8) and Paris (1938–40). In neither city did exile generate any positive results with the sole exception of the production of the *Deutschland-Berichte*, which were widely read. Much of the time in Prague was spent arguing rather fruitlessly about the ideological causes for the success of fascism. Hitler was seen as little more than the lackey of capitalism whose mismanagement of the German economy was bound to lead to his overthrow.[1] Although SPD leaders exhorted their membership inside the Reich to carry out 'a revolutionary policy', they did not draw up any blueprints for revolution and they remained basically uncertain as to whether a revolutionary stance was the best means of defeating Hitler. It was of course important to fit the phenomenon of Hitlerism into some kind of conceptual framework but it was not always easy to see what practical steps the SPD could take, first to gain and then to keep power. After all it had, during the Weimar period, gained considerable experience of the exercise of political power on both a *Land* and a Reich level and a number of SPD leaders realised that ideas were no substitute for action.

The time spent in Paris (1938–40) was no happier. The SPD leadership had been asked to leave Prague by Eduard Beneš. One of the reasons Hitler gave for threatening his state was that Czechoslovakia harboured the 'enemies' of Germany.[2] The Socialist Prime Minister of France, Léon Blum, had offered the SPD asylum and it seemed wise to move to Paris. But by the time the Social Democrats arrived, Blum had fallen and his replacement (E. Daladier) was on the political right and not over-anxious to help the SPD. The fall of France altered the party's position immediately. By virtue of the armistice signed at Compiègne in June 1940, the French authorities were obliged to hand over German political exiles to the Gestapo. The SPD executive (which since Otto Wels's death in September 1939 had been led by Hans Vogel) decided to flee the country and they set off for the south. *En route* Rudolf Breitscheid and Rudolf Hilferding were arrested by the French police and handed over to the Gestapo. They were both deported to their deaths, a grizzly reminder to their fellow SPD leaders of the fate that awaited them in Nazi Europe.[3]

The SPD was forced to choose between fleeing to Britain or America. They chose Britain. It was the obvious choice; there had been links between individual SPD members and the British Labour Party for a number of years. Figures like Viktor Schiff, Otto Kahn-Freund, ex-*Reichsbanner* leader Karl Höltermann and Wilhelm Sander, prominent Social Democrats, had built lives for themselves in London. On a more official level, there existed close and cordial relations between the International Secretary of the Labour Party, William Gillies, who was also the Chairman of the National Executive's International Sub-committee, and the SPD leadership in Paris. Gillies had proved a most generous friend of the party: in July 1939 for example he donated £150 to the party to finance the printing of 20,000 leaflets and he also gave the SPD 15,000 *Reichsmark* towards the cost of having them distributed.[4] At this time, German Social Democrats were always treated as full and trusted comrades by the British Labour Party (and, incidentally, by their fellow Socialist parties in the Socialist Workers' International). The enemy was fascism, and it was an enemy common to all nations. The SPD was simply one of its victims.

As early as September 1939 secret invitations had been issued to the SPD leaders to come to London and set up their official headquarters there. Later, in the winter of 1939, Hans Vogel and Erich Ollenhauer were invited to England to have talks with some of the most important leaders of British Labour, namely Clement Attlee, Hugh Dalton, William Gillies, Philip Noel-Baker, Ernest Bevin and Arthur Greenwood. Financial aid was offered to the SPD in return for which German Social Democrats promised to supply information about Germany to the Labour Party.[5]

During this visit, William Gillies arranged a highly important and 'most secret' meeting between Hans Vogel, Erich Ollenhauer and Gladwyn Jebb of the Foreign Office, Private Secretary to the Permanent Under-Secretary, Sir Alec Cadogan.[6] The Labour Party was concerned because it believed that the Foreign Office was badly informed about the status of the political Left in German political life, both before and during the Third Reich, since it had no contact with exiled Social Democrats, dealing only with representatives of the Right and Centre. It was true that men like the ex-Nazi Rauschning were carefully listened to by the Foreign Office; Gillies was understandably concerned about this and feared that the Foreign Office might be persuaded to make a compromise peace with reactionary forces in Germany in order to forestall the 'Bolshevisation' of Germany. Like the SPD, the Labour Party argued that radical social changes were necessary in order to destroy the basis of Hitler's position. Both Labour and SPD wanted Social Democrats to be Germany's new leaders.

There was no doubt that the Foreign Office was very badly informed about the SPD. It was, for example, thought by them that Otto Strasser, the renegade Nazi, was the editor of the SPD's *Deutschland-Berichte*. But the Foreign Office was willing to learn and, after a full discussion, Gladwyn Jebb was able to arrange for Vogel and Ollenhauer to meet a very influential figure, Sir Campbell Stuart, at that time the virtual overlord of British propaganda to Germany. The meeting took place on 15 January 1940 and they discussed a number of ways in which the SPD might both influence and help with the British propaganda campaign against Hitler.

The Foreign Office did not want simply to increase its knowledge of the enemy; it wished also to maintain some authority over the groups which might take power should Hitler be overthrown. Some historians have seen this motive as suspect, implying a reluctance actually to fight the Nazis and a readiness to construct a patched-up peace with them. None of the evidence, however, supports this view. Even Sir Robert Vansittart, the Government's Chief Diplomatic Adviser, on whose orders a number of contacts with Germans were made, remained convinced that the war could only be won by fighting and not by dealing with 'a fat Field Marshal or phantom generals'.[7] Vansittart, of course, was no friend of the German people in any case. As he wrote to his colleagues in the Foreign Office in March 1940: 'Eighty per cent of the German race are the moral and political scum of the earth. You cannot reform them by signatures and concessions. They have got to be hamstrung and broken . . . they are a race of bone-headed aggressors and we should certainly aim at splitting Germany up if we possibly can'. It should, however, be pointed out that Vansittart's views were not widely shared at this time and they did not have the results they had three years later. Wherever German exiles could play any useful role in British policy-making, they were encouraged to do so, even at the expense of more celebrated allies of longer standing. An example of this is the considerate treatment accorded to Wenzel Jaksch, the Sudeten German Social Democratic leader, *vis-à-vis* Eduard Beneš. Despite the fact that Beneš (by now himself in London) did not wish to negotiate with Sudeten Germans, the Foreign Office insisted that he do so if he wished to maintain influence in Britain.

Other exiled Germans the Foreign Office liked to consult included Rauschning, who appears to have had personal access to Lord Halifax the Foreign Secretary and was consulted by William Strang; ex-Reich Chancellors Joseph Wirth (in Switzerland) and Heinrich Brüning (in the USA) were also listened to. The latter was regularly interviewed by the personal assistant to HM Ambassador in Washington, John Wheeler-Bennett, who also maintained contacts with SPD exiles in North America. Other links between German exiles and influential British circles were forged by Patrick Gordon-Walker, a lecturer at Oxford University, and Richard Crossman, who worked for the BBC.[8] They, like Campbell Stuart, were anxious to use exiles, especially Social Democratic ones, to assist in the propaganda war. One reason they often gave for seeking this assistance, apart from the political ones, was that the British believed the non-political exiles who were Jewish spoke German with 'Jewish accents' and could thus not be used to give radio talks on the BBC.

Out of all this emerged two important British ideas. The first was that an émigré 'clearing-house' should be set up as a semi-official committee consisting of the English contacts of various exile groups who would then relay their views to the authorities. The second was that a 'government in exile' be created in London, a proposal very strongly supported by no less a figure than the Liberal Leader in the

Lords, Lord Clement Davies, who had been PPS to Lloyd-George. Underlying these two immediate plans was the view that the war was primarily a war against an aggressive and dangerous political doctrine (rather than against Germans or Germany). Implicit in this view was the existence of 'two Germanies', one 'good' and one 'bad', a Nazi Germany and 'another' one. A number of Britain's allies disliked this view intensely, notably the French who totally opposed the creation of a German government in exile.[9]

There thus seemed every indication that if the SPD leadership were to come to London, real and exciting possibilities for political work would exist there. It would be a chance for them to help fight against Hitler and it would enable them to forget sterile and introspective ideological discussion. As the situation in occupied Europe deteriorated the SPD leaders made their way to neutral territory in Lisbon, in order to attempt a passage to England.[10] As early as 10 July 1940 Gillies had cabled to the SPD leaders that they should come to England 'by any means possible, visas unnecessary'. This had proved too difficult and so, on 17 December 1940, at the express wish of the Minister for Economic Warfare, Hugh Dalton, visas were telegraphed to Lisbon; at the end of that month Hans Vogel and his wife were flown to Bristol in an RAF Liberator, to be followed a few days later by Erich Ollenhauer and his family and by Curt Geyer and Fritz Heine in June 1941. They had been rescued on the highest authority and for a very high purpose – to assist in the British war effort. From what had gone before, the exiles had every reason to expect that such assistance would be worthwhile. It would permit the SPD to stay alive and politically active and place it in a good position to play a vital role in German affairs once Hitler had been defeated.

There was, however, an important internal obstacle to meaningful political work and that was the factional splitting that had occurred within the SPD's ranks during its exile. Apart from the SPD proper, there also existed the ISK (*Internationaler Sozialistischer Kampf-Bund*) and the *Neu Beginnen*, (the New Beginning Group). The first task for the SPD leadership in London, then, was to re-unite these factions. Talks to this end were initiated in the Labour Party headquarters, Transport House, on 25 February 1941. Vogel and Ollenhauer made it plain to their fellow Social Democrats that the British Labour Party was very anxious to see the emergence of a unified front and despite some serious disagreements, voiced in particular by Willi Eichler of the ISK, full agreement was reached on 6 March 1941.[11] This brought together under one roof all the 160 or so

SPD members in London. They included not only personalities who had been important in the past but also those like Eichler himself who were to be important in the future – Erwin Schoettle, Richard Löwenthal, Dr Susanne Miller, Erich Brost, E.F. Schumacher, Heinrich Fraenkel and many others. This important feat of unification had barely been achieved when the first difficulty presented itself. Having agreed on a common organisational base, the exiled German Social Democrats immediately began to plan for the future. As Hans Vogel phrased it, 'it is not possible for Social Democrats inside Germany to discuss the problems of post-war Germany so we must do it for them'. SPD members knew, however, that one central problem was likely to prove more tricky than any other; their relationship with the exiled German Communists.

There were a number of people, both British and German, who believed that Hitler's success had been in large part due to the divisions within the organised German Labour movement, the split between Communists and Social Democrats. Most SPD leaders, it should be noted, did not take this view, stating that no common front with Communists was possible because during the Weimar years and then again after August 1939 Communists and Nazis had been acting in concert. However, with the USSR's entry into the war in June 1941, the matter was again thrown wide open.[12] With 300 members the German Communists were numerically the largest group in exile and they had two important sources of support. The first came directly from Moscow, the second from those in Britain who were either openly or covertly Communist supporters. Officially, of course, the USSR was part of the Grand Alliance and an ally of the Western democracies (even if this fact is sometimes ignored today).

Since 1935 German Communists had tried to come to an arrangement with the SPD to produce a Popular Front, but such proposals had always been turned down by the SPD. Now, however, their overtures were more weighty. Even the BBC asked Vogel to make some positive mention of the USSR in his broadcasts to Germany. In August 1941 Vogel reported to his colleagues that a KPD leader, Heinz Schmidt, had 'offered the SPD a great deal in return for very little'. This offer was, however, not pursued.

The theme was taken up again in 1943 when Stalin decided to disband the Comintern (the overt way in which Moscow controlled the various Communist parties of the world) and to recognise a German exile movement. On 12 and 13 July a National Committee for Free Germany (*Nationalkomitee Freies Deutschland*) was formed in

Moscow. Its president was Erich Weinert, a Communist and a poet and its members included Walter Ulbricht, Wilhelm Pieck and Colonel von Einsiedel, who was said to be a nephew of Otto von Bismarck. The Soviet intention was to create a Communist-led umbrella organisation to encompass the entire anti-Nazi spectrum. This was not simply a re-run of the Popular Front idea but something more robust – a coalition government in exile for post-war Germany and one which was Communist-dominated.

One of the first people to realise the significance of this move was, surprisingly, George Bell, Bishop of Chichester, who argued that if this notion were allowed to thrive, the KPD would succeed in uniting all anti-Nazi Germans in Britain as well. His plea was ignored, although Eden did order the British secret service to carry out a check of the various exile movements in London in order to see whether they were likely to succumb. Bell appeared to believe that groups like the SPD might well fall for Communist flattery since the treatment they were receiving from the British authorities was so appalling. The US State Department took a similar view, noting that 'the best way to fight Bolshevism (in post-war Germany) is to deal with those who are as anti-Russian as they are anti-Nazi' – which meant first and foremost dealing with the SPD. Yet the Foreign Office took no steps to encourage Social Democrats in London. They certainly could not know that the SPD would not, in the end, go along with the KPD, since the SPD did not know this itself; indeed, a number of leading SPD members did join with the KPD.

It is possible that the attitude taken by the British authorities (which did, as Bell predicted, at least initially, drive a number of Social Democrats and others into the arms of the KPD) was simply the result of overwork or of ignorance. But it is also possible that it was the result of Communist influence on British policy making and that Soviet agents within the British Foreign Office and within the British secret services may have manipulated events. In his memoirs, Kim Philby points out that British policy on these matters was non-existent.[13] Not only was he in a position to know, however, he was also in a position to ensure that any policy which did not serve the interests of his true masters, the Soviet Government, would never see the light of day. Thus, whether intentionally or by accident, there can be little doubt that, unlike the SPD in exile, German Communists were able to count on a helping hand from the British authorities as well as the Soviet ones. Indeed, in June 1943, Vogel had been approached by Professor Robert Kuczynski on behalf of the Communists in order to gain the

SPD's entry into a so-called Free German Movement. Another leading Communist, Siegbert Kahn, had also approached a number of other prominent Social Democrats so that by the summer of 1943 Viktor Schiff, Heinrich Fraenkel, Adele Schreiber-Krieger, Otto Lehmann-Russbüldt, Leopold Ullstein and Irmgard Litten were ready to help the KPD set up a Free German Movement. The SPD leadership was thereby put in a most awkward position. It appeared to be losing the initiative in exile politics yet, at the same time, it believed that any joint action with the KPD would have a disastrous result on democratic socialism in post-war Germany.[14]

On 25 September 1943 at the Trinity Church Hall in London the Free German Movement was brought officially into existence at a meeting attended by over 400 people. The SPD was pushed into the shade and it appeared that the Free Germans would prove the most important group to emerge from exile, with their place in post-Nazi German politics assured. KPD leaders such as Hans Fladung, Hugo Graef, Wilhelm Koenen and Karl Becker gained in stature and were able to discover support for their venture in wider British circles. A branch of the Amalgamated Union of Engineering Workers (AUEW), for example, went so far as to ask the Foreign Office to give the Free Germans official recognition. Yet the wisdom of the SPD's refusal to have any dealings with the Communists was not slow to show itself. For as the USSR's territorial ambitions in Central Europe became increasingly plain, the Free Germans began to disagree seriously on whether or not they should be supported. KPD supporters believed that whatever policy the USSR wished to pursue regarding German national sovereignty should receive their full approval but an increasing number of Social Democrats disagreed. Vogel, Ollenhauer and the rest of the official party leadership had always opposed the dismemberment of Germany, so their refusal to work with Communists combined with their stout defence of self-determination for Germans enabled them to speak for all those who were opposed to a second Versailles. By May 1944, however, the Free German front had collapsed. The SPD was able to establish itself as an effective (but not aggressive) supporter of German nationalism and the KPD demonstrated that it had remained Moscow's puppet. Indeed, it could be argued that the SPD gained a number of important tactical advantages from the incident. At the same time, however, the close surveillance of both SPD and KPD by MI5 and MI6 was less than helpful to the SPD in its other dealings: a number of MI5 reports noted the SPD's opposition to German dismemberment and the fact that this was increasingly bringing them into serious conflict with Churchill's post-war plans.[15]

Despite the hopeful start, the SPD's dealing with the Labour Party did not thrive. After the autumn of 1941 relations between German Social Democrats and their British colleagues had begun to deteriorate. The ostensible reason for this was the difficulty created by Walter Loeb,[16] an influential rank and file SPD member. Loeb, who had many friends in high places, was once described by Lord Vansittart as the 'most intelligent and courageous of all the SPD members in London'. This was, however, only because Loeb was determined to prevent the SPD from adopting any policies other than those supported by the British Labour Party. And that was the source of the difficulty, for it would be no exaggeration to say that Loeb wanted the SPD to become the German-speaking mouthpiece for British Labour.

It was not without irony that the more Loeb pressed his case, and the more Vogel and Ollenhauer rejected it, the more suspicious Labour leaders (including Gillies himself) became of the SPD's motives. What the SPD in exile considered to be a degree of independence necessary for it to remain politically credible, the Labour Party took as chauvinism inappropriate to the actions of fellow-countrymen of Hitler and the Nazis. The fact that the SPD had in some sense been fighting the Nazis for even longer than Britain did not mitigate this.

Loeb gained the support of one of the most important Social Democratic leaders, Curt Geyer, who like Vogel, Ollenhauer and Heine received a modest salary from the Labour Party. Loeb and Geyer argued that the history of the SPD after 1914 and during the Weimar era proved that Social Democrats were inherently nationalistic and aggressive and one of the causes of National Socialism. This simplistic assessment of complex matters accorded with the prejudices of a number of Labour Party members and so petty disagreements among the exiles were elevated into a battle for the survival of German Social Democracy.

There was, in addition, an increasing acceptance of a Vansittartite view of Germany and the Germans. This was, perhaps, understandable.[17] Britain was, after all, fighting Germany for the second time in a generation; the war of extermination that the Nazis were waging was bound to cause hatred and disgust. Yet the spread of Vansittartism amongst the Labour Party leaders should not have affected their political judgement of the SPD, if only because they themselves had initially accepted the complexity of the issues involved and shown sympathy with the situation the SPD had been faced with since 1914.

Gillies's personal position was that at best the SPD might hope to be the agent of British Labour policy in Germany; the crimes of the Nazis made any free political behaviour inappropriate. As the arguments about this developed during 1942, he and the Labour Party in general adopted an increasingly hostile stance towards the SPD. The chairman of the 1941 Labour Party conference, James Walker MP, who went on to found the Fight for Freedom Association, had declared bluntly that 'the German people are just as responsible for the acts of their government as the government itself'. His attitude was opposed by a minority of men such as Harold Laski and Philip Noel-Baker but they were not able to prevent Vansittartite notions gradually becoming official party policy.

It must also be accepted that the cause of the exiled SPD had not been helped by the visit to Britain, in the autumn of 1941, of one of its most controversial figures, Friedrich Stampfer,[18] who had fled to New York. Stampfer was a good propagandist but he lacked political tact. He believed the SPD had a duty to oppose openly any Allied policy which might interfere with German territorial sovereignty. This was a not unreasonable position; unfortunately Stampfer's truculent manner was considered quite inappropriate to the SPD's position.

Stampfer was given two major interviews in London. One was with Gillies and the other with Hugh Dalton, the Minister for Economic Warfare. Stampfer wished to gain Dalton's support for greater SPD participation in propaganda. Dalton had been instrumental in getting the exiled leadership to London and was also the man who had argued that it had been 'to the discredit of Britain and France that they'did not openly go out of their way to make friends with the democratic leaders of Weimar Germany' and that after the present war Germany should not be made an outcast. 'The most far-sighted . . . policy is to seek to win the co-operation as an equal partner of a Germany governed by a political system whose aims and needs run parallel to ours'.[19] But the interview with Stampfer shows how much Dalton had changed his stance since those words had been written. He refused either to assist the SPD or to accept that the SPD could help the war effort in any way.

Stampfer's visit was also subject to a fierce attack in the British press. On 23 November 1941 an editorial in the *Sunday Times* attempted to accuse him of subverting the war effort. Curt Geyer even went so far as to suggest that Stampfer had really come to London to have secret talks with certain German generals, although there is no evidence of this whatsoever. At his meeting with Gillies, Stampfer received no greater satisfaction than he had received from Dalton. His attempt to get the SPD taken more seriously as an ally against Hitler was now treated with grave suspicion.

Gillies now believed that the time had come to attempt to force the SPD to concur with the Labour Party's wishes. If he could prove that the SPD was not worthy of exercising political independence on account of the historical errors it had committed, then the Party would admit its guilt and, possibly, fall in with his plans. To this end, Gillies prepared a document on the SPD's post-1914 history which he submitted to the National Executive Committee International sub-committee for ratification. The SPD's case was put by Philip Noel-Baker and the NEC sub-committee considered it on 25 November 1941.[20] Noel-Baker argued that the Labour Party should hope '... for the revival of German Social Democracy and ought to encourage now all German Social Democrats and to prepare to give every assistance to a Social Democratic Government in Germany after the War'. On 26 March 1942, the sub-committee met again to come to some decision. A motion stating that Gillies's interpretation of the history of the SPD – that it was nationalistic and para-fascist – 'was true in all essentials' was carried with only Laski and Noel-Baker dissenting.

Yet this stricture did not make the SPD leadership more amenable and so Gillies tried a rather tougher tactic. On 2 October 1942 he sent for Ollenhauer, Geyer and Heine and told them the Labour Party would no longer support them. Vogel and his wife, on account of their age, would for the time being receive financial aid but the rest should give up their political work for the SPD and find a job. The hardest hit by this was Ollenhauer, for Geyer had his journalistic work and Heine was by now working for Richard Crossman. Since Ollenhauer was the real driving force behind the SPD in exile, Gillies's decision augured political death for him and for the SPD as a whole. Ollenhauer was only saved by donations from Swedish Social Democrats (who recognised the value of his work) and a part-time post for a secret American agency.

Although not every British Labour leader agreed with Gillies's views, they were implemented until 1946 (when he was succeeded by Denis Healey). Individuals such as Patrick Gordon-Walker and Austin Albu (who founded the pro-SPD Socialist Clarity Group) as well as the Fabians continued to sympathise with the SPD but it remained the concern of a small and powerless fringe. A comment made by Ivone Kirkpatrick about Ernest Bevin in this connection should not be forgotten, that 'one thing which left its mark upon him was the bellicose attitude of the German Social Democrats in 1914 for which he never forgave them. He felt betrayed and it made him more anti-German than anything else the Germans ever did'.[21] In exile, the SPD had gained some formidable opponents.

Despite the great bitterness that was thereby engendered and the serious rift between English and German Social Democracy that it caused, it should not be forgotten that the practical differences between the two parties were not very great. The SPD accepted that it had made mistakes in 1918/19 and it knew that many Germans, including many from the working-class, were prepared to offer Hitler support, either through conviction or because they were afraid to do otherwise. The SPD also accepted that the whole German people would require an extensive education in liberal democratic values after Hitler's defeat; but it could not support the view that fascism was a peculiarly German phenomenon or that the correct punishment for Nazi crimes was the dismemberment of Germany. The SPD knew there would be a working-class movement after the war; the only doubt was who was to lead it and it was better that it be led by the SPD than by any other political grouping.

The British Labour Party, however, was ready to follow the mainstream of British public opinion, of which an ever-increasing percentage was, possibly understandably, not able to dissociate the terrible crimes of the Nazis from the ordinary Germans who seemed ready to tolerate them. In addition, the impact that Churchill had made on the British public was important. They could readily understand the Churchillian formulation that Britain was fighting a war of national survival against a series of hostile nations of whom the most odious was Germany. This became an important factor in the making of British policy towards Germany.

It therefore comes as no surprise to note that the chances of the SPD achieving fruitful co-operation with the British Foreign Office diminished rapidly. The Coalition Foreign Secretary, Anthony Eden, mirrored completely the 'hard' line on Germany. As early as July 1941 he wrote: 'I have no confidence in our ability to make decent Europeans of the Germans and I believe that the Nazi system represents the mentality of the great majority of German people'.[22] He refused to allow the BBC to distinguish between 'good' and 'bad' Germans. It was plain, therefore, that during the early war years much had changed in the Foreign Office's attitude towards exiled politicians from Germany. The chances for SPD influence on British policy-making towards Germany were becoming increasingly dim.

Crude Vansittartism was by no means the only explanation for this. It should also be remembered that there were in London the 'governments in exile' of a number of the countries which had been invaded by Germany and subjected to terrible treatment. The Foreign Office was bound to be extremely cautious in any dealings with German exiles which could have caused insult to such governments or which might have implied bilateral commitments to Germany. Most importantly, the USSR was now a member of the Grand Alliance; this meant that neither the British nor the Americans could afford to add to Soviet suspicions about the true motives of Allied war policy. It would have been very easy to see serious dealings with German exiles as the first stage of a secret peace offensive.

Churchill's directive that 'nothing should be decided about Germany' until Hitler was defeated had simplicity to commend it even if it made relations with German exiles awkward. At the same time, however, it is necessary to be sceptical about this policy and about its consequences. The division of post-war Europe into two rival blocs has been hardly satisfactory from the Anglo-American point of view, and the official Foreign Office attitude that 'the Germans would be likely to regard the leaders of German exile movements as traitors in enemy pay',[23] who would command no following in post-war Germany was quite wrong as far as men like Ollenhauer, Eichler and Heine were concerned. Even Willy Brandt, though vilified by Konrad Adenauer for his active resistance to Nazism, did not appear to have suffered from this taunt in any political sense. Strategic considerations, too, made encouragement of anti-Hitler Germans a sensible move; twice in 1944, for example, General Eisenhower asked President Roosevelt to state that their enemy was Nazism and not the German people. Roosevelt refused.

Above all, the Soviet Union itself was actively pursuing a quite different policy. Stalin had always gone out of his way to stress the distinction between Nazis and Germans and in the summer of 1943 Moscow Radio announced the formation of a National Committee for Free Germany, a pro-Soviet German government in exile. Although the USSR subsequently tried to assuage Western fears by saying this was simply a propaganda move, there can be no doubt that this Committee *was* designed to be the nucleus of a future German government and that Soviet foresight in this area is one reason why their political control of their own sector of post-war Germany was so complete. In other words, British failures in the sphere of the politics of exile allowed the USSR to score a number of tactical advantages. Whilst it is quite true to say that the USSR policy-makers did not have to take Russian public opinion into account in the same way as the Foreign Office, the criticism of the Foreign Office must nevertheless stand.

By 1945 Foreign Office knowledge about German political exiles in general and the SPD in particular was so sparse that its attitude towards post-war Germany may be described as one of ignorance. British interests were bound to suffer. It must remain a matter of speculation to what extent this ignorance stemmed from more sinister causes. Subsequent discoveries of Communist agents in the Foreign Office highlight the fact that such ignorance proved most useful to the Russians. What might have been achieved through sensible co-operation between the SPD on one hand and the Foreign Office and the Labour Party on the other was not simply help in the war against Hitler; it would have extended British influence over post-war German political development and it might have helped to create a Social Democratic order throughout Europe. If necessary such co-operation could have been conducted in great secrecy.

As it was, the reality produced a depressing chronicle of events. The SPD was nevertheless able to weather both the disciplinary actions of the Labour Party and Foreign Office disinterest; it also managed to avoid the suffocating embrace of the German Communists and did so on a basis (namely the refusal to accept the dismemberment of Germany) which gave it a useful platform in post-war German politics. SPD leaders in London demonstrated considerable personal courage in a very difficult situation. Their past was scrutinised and their future denied, while their political statements were regarded with suspicion and subject to the monitoring of the British secret services. Yet the SPD survived exile even through the final, bitter irony that Hans Vogel lay dying at the very moment when Ollenhauer and Heine were meeting with Kurt Schumacher at Kloster Wennigsen.

The balance sheet of exile in London was not one of failure. The party retained a distinctive Social Democratic identity. Its leadership was accepted back home in Germany and a number of the ideas it brought with it from England became party policy. It is true that it failed with the British Labour Party and with the Foreign Office; but success would have been an impossible achievement under the existing circumstances. Above all, the confidence gained during the years of exile enabled the party to face up to the difficulties of postwar German politics and subsequently to play a central role in the overcoming of an appalling past.

## Notes

1. See L. Edinger, *German Exile Politics*, Berkeley, 1956.
2. *Ibid.*, p. 203.
3. SPD archives (Friedrich Ebert Foundation), File 18.
4. SPD archives, File 11.
5. Labour Party archives, Middleton Papers, Box 8.
6. Public Record Office (PRO) Foreign Office (FO) 371.2442c897.
7. PRO FO 371 24389c34389.
8. PRO FO 371.23105c16461/24387c1424.
9. PRO FO 371.23058c171104.
10. PRO FO 371.24419c13495.
11. SPD archives, File 4.
12. SPD archives, File 12.
13. See Kim Philby, *My Silent War*, London, 1968.
14. SPD archives, File 62/13; PRO FO 371.34416c1160.
15. PRO FO 371.34414c10609.
16. SPD archives, File 42.
17. See T.D. Burridge, *British Labour and Hitler's War*, London, 1976.
18. See F. Stampfer, *Erfahrungen und Erkenntnisse*, Cologne, 1957; SPD archives, File 44; Labour Party archives, Middleton Papers, Box 8.
19. See Hugh Dalton, *Hitler's War*, London, 1940.
20. Labour Party archives, Int. Sub-committee 1941.
21. I. Kirkpatrick, *Inner Circle*, London, 1959, p. 205.
22. L. Woodward, *British Foreign Policy*, London, 1976, pp. 22, 31, 76, 209, 222.
23. PRO FO 371.26559c2951.

*Lothar Kettenacker*

# The Influence of German Refugees on British War Aims

It has always surprised Continental Europeans that one of the most famous and influential German emigrants in England, Karl Marx, changed the world with his revolutionary ideas, but not the socio-economic conditions of the country on which his analysis was largely based. Even a cursory survey of the history of German minorities in Great Britain[1] shows that this is not a unique phenomenon. The decision of German emigrants to settle in Britain in the 1840s was determined predominantly by economic interests, while in the following period their social impact was also largely restricted to economic or scientific activities. Germans might establish commercial firms and some, such as Hanseatic merchants or the Hanoverian purveyors to the British Court, even enjoyed certain privileges. They might found branches of banks and hold professorships, but parliamentary seats and official government positions generally remained beyond their reach. Nevertheless, any charge of deliberate discrimination cannot be upheld. German emigration to Great Britain as a result of Hitler's seizure of power has no parallel in history, but it confirms historical experience that in this country of unlimited contradictions, a liberal and humanitarian immigration policy could easily coexist with political exclusiveness.

The great majority of Germans who fled to Britain before the outbreak of the Second World War suffered persecution on racial grounds;[2] they were not political refugees, although the two groups cannot always clearly be separated. It is certainly more appropriate to speak of 'exile' than of 'emigration' for the nucleus of the political group, because there was no question of their leaving voluntarily, or being willing to integrate permanently. Never before had there been so many German politicians in exile in Britain, attempting to influence the course of German politics with the help of their host country. The truth was, however, that they lacked legitimacy and were politically powerless. In short, the experience of the political exiles in Great Britain was one of frustration. The processes of political decision-making within the framework of a democratic constitution seemed to have been reversed. Whoever claimed some sort of representative status, rightly or wrongly, whoever claimed to speak for Germany, for Bavaria, or for a particular party or pressure group, was considered in Whitehall to be a thoroughly suspect individual, and was seen as someone who, while not necessarily intending to compromise the government, certainly ran the risk of doing so. However, more use was made of German experts in various fields, as individuals who could put their specialist knowledge at the disposal of the government without political considerations playing a part. The following essay sets forth the factors which influenced the British Government in their decision to keep the German politicians in exile at bay. At the same time it anticipates, albeit in a somewhat simplified form, an answer to the question of what part German emigrants played in British plans for Germany after the war.

When Britain responded to Hitler's attack on Poland with the declaration of war on 3 September 1939, it had already admitted approximately 50,000 refugees from Germany and Austria.[3] There were few prominent politicians from the Weimar Republic among them; the former Chancellor of the Reich, Heinrich Brüning, had emigrated to the USA,[4] Joseph Wirth to Switzerland, and the executive committee of the Social Democratic Party had moved its headquarters from Prague to Paris. External conditions did not favour the formation of a German émigré government in London. But there were much more important reasons why London, which offered a refuge to so many European governments in the course of the war, was not to become the seat of a German alternative government. Unlike the governments of the countries occupied by Hitler's armies, a government consisting of German politicians in exile would have had no legitimacy to which it could have appealed. It would have owed its existence to toleration and recognition by one of the two enemy states, not to a political act of the German electorate. De Gaulle's long struggle to achieve political recognition in London[5] shows that the question of political legitimacy was taken seriously by the British government. It was not only a matter of international law; public opinion also had to be taken into consideration.

The hope that it would come to a revolt of the old élites against Hitler, who had recklessly plunged the Reich into war, was still widely-held in Great Britain, not least by the Prime Minister.[6] A petition to Lord Halifax, in which a Member of Parliament declared himself in favour of the formation of a German émigré government, evoked the following terse comment from the Foreign Office: 'An émigré German Government under allied auspices would cut little or no ice in Germany in present circumstances and would weaken our own position *vis-à-vis* the German people.'[7] Any group of men from the Weimar 'system' discredited by National Socialist propaganda would have been exposed to ridicule by Hitler. Apart from this, the reaction of the only group which could still pose a threat to Hitler had to be considered. The conservative élites who, together with the old Reichswehr generals, had helped Hitler into a position of power, might now wish to put an end to the nightmare; it was assumed that they would favour something akin to military dictatorship rather than face a repetition of the Weimar débâcle. A German émigré government, on the other hand, would have to consist predominantly of leftist anti-fascists, if it was to be at all representative of the political exiles.[8] The numerous secret feelers for peace which were put out in the first months of the war frequently mentioned highly-placed Wehrmacht generals who were ostensibly awaiting their hour. 'These gentlemen', reports a Foreign Office review, 'were said to fear the outcome of the pact with the Soviet Union and to favour a peace of compromise, accompanied by the removal of Hitler and his replacement by a more moderate government.'[9]

Of the efforts made by Germans to establish contact, the mediation attempts made by Pius XII in the winter of 1939/40,[10] through the agency of the former leader of the Centre Party Monsignor Kaas, appeared to be somewhat more credible than others. According to this plan, the National Socialist regime was at first to be replaced by a military dictatorship, which would later give way to a conservative democratic government. The Foreign Office regarded both the likelihood of a coup d'état taking place, and the question of whether such a development would serve British interests in the long run, with the greatest scepticism. Nevertheless, during the 'phoney war', which was being waged primarily against Hitler and not against the German people, the immediate objective of British policy remained the removal of the dictator. Whether a successor government, perhaps under Göring,[11] would inspire enough confidence for the British government to enter on peace negotiations, remained an open question.

It is not surprising, therefore, that government circles showed more interest in conservative emigrants who were closer to the centre of power in Germany than in leftist exiles who, it was believed, would not be able to stage a successful comeback without foreign help. This preference is explained by the government's assessment of the situation in Germany, and it also reflects the attitude of a Cabinet which did not yet have to show consideration for the ideological sensitivities of the Labour Party. The attention received by Hermann Rauschning in London during the first few months of the war, even from certain circles within the Labour Party,[12] is illustrative of this state of affairs. Rauschning was a bourgeois landowner and a former President of the Senate of Danzig, who had dissociated himself from the National Socialists and exposed the emptiness of their pretensions. He could claim both a thorough knowledge of Hitler's 'court' and, at the same time, to be in close touch with the old ruling classes of Prussia. Rauschning warned of the dangers posed by the proletarian-isation of the middle classes and by the bolshevisation of Germany as a result of the pact with the Soviet Union. The Prussian Junkers, by now discredited in Britain, were presented as gentlemen with a Christian conscience. He also advocated, as an interim solution, a military dictatorship supported by the bourgeoisie and including right-wing Social Democrats. The Foreign Office was most ambivalent about his advice to aim for the removal of Hitler. Military reversal should induce the General Staff to stage a coup d'état, but without weakening the army to such an extent that it lost domestic control. 'This advice is clearly difficult to carry out', was Sir Alexander Cadogan's comment.[13] Nevertheless, Rauschning's thoughts were taken seriously enough for his views to be summarised by the historian E.L. Woodward and subsequently printed by the Foreign Office, a treatment reserved for particularly important documents only.

In the period which followed, it was Robert Vansittart who argued strongly against the idea of ending the war without completely discrediting Prussian militarism, to which no fewer than five wars in the last hundred years were attributed.[14] The opinions of his Chief Diplomatic Advisor did not, however, prevent Lord Halifax from giving Rauschning a private audience on 15 December 1939, on the advice of the Labour politician Hugh Dalton. The Foreign Secretary was immediately charmed by the personality of Rauschning who was, by now, a well-known author; he found Rauschning 'an agreeable and interesting person'.[15] While Halifax remained non-committal and only repeated the Government's general statements on the question of exiles, Rauschning made no secret of his strongly-held opinions. The German people should be administered a policy of alternate hope and fear. Only if peace was made in time could they count on generous conditions. The threat of a hard peace if the Germans did not soon come to their senses did in fact become a constant theme of British propaganda. Rauschning appeared to confirm that the old ruling class was disillusioned with Hitler and his regime, but did not quite know how to get rid of them. 'There was a general desire', the transcription of their meeting reads, 'among the highest ranks of the army, big business, landowners, and others who represented the old order, to see the end of the Nazi regime, but the army could not move unless and until there was such popular discontent in Germany as to be producing something like civil war, in which case the army could come down and, under the guise of restoring order, take over the government.' It helped Rauschning's credibility that he did not attempt to create any illusions by prophesying an imminent collapse, because a memorandum of the Political Intelligence Department of the Foreign Office about the situation in Germany after the first two months of war warned the government not to expect an imminent revolt in Germany. 'There is no reasonable prospect of a revolt in Germany, nor are there any important signs that the Germans as a whole have lost faith in Hitler's lucky star.'[16] The Foreign Office was particularly interested in destroying any illusions the Germans might hold that their policies would be successful. The completely disrupted balance of power could not be restored without a decisive weakening of Germany.

After the outbreak of war, this traditional aim of British politics again took precedence, at least in the Foreign Office, in a deliberate departure from the prevailing policy of appeasement. On the one hand, the government did not want to undertake anything which was likely to prevent a possible revolt in Germany, such as the recognition of an émigré government on English soil; such an action could only lead to further solidarity with Hitler. On the other hand, it was just as unwilling to stipulate minimum conditions and thereby facilitate a compromise peace which would leave Germany intact and capable of again challenging the status quo in Europe. For these reasons, the government deliberately took care not to define its war aims very precisely. This resolution had already been passed by the Cabinet on

9 October and, although it was frequently challenged, it was not revised in principle for the duration of the war.[17] This course also seemed advisable when France's position was taken into consideration. France's importance among the Allies increased with the certainty that all hopes of Hitler being overthrown were idle, and that the 'phoney war' would be followed by a bloody one. By October 1939 France was even less willing than the Foreign Office to re-establish peace after a mere change of government in Berlin, without 'garanties materielles efficaces, destinées à prévenir tout retour offensif de l'impérialisme allemand'.[18] This point of view had largely been adopted in the Foreign Office, although the more extreme war aims aired in the French press, such as the dismemberment of the Reich and the cession of the Rhineland, met with little approval in London.[19]

It was only the question of the long-term shaping of Germany which offered German emigrants some opportunities of exerting influence via public opinion in Great Britain. At no time did the exiled politicians exert any appreciable influence on the immediate conditions of the armistice, although it was precisely in this area that decisions of the greatest importance for the future were made – as the results of the zoning of Germany testify. However, they were free to consider the constitutional future of Germany. A certain consensus emerged in this area among those conservative and liberal emigrants (at least those who were not tied to any party political organisation) who were best able to get a hearing at the beginning. They were convinced that Germany's recovery was possible only on the basis of a federal, if not confederal, reconstruction. Rauschning too tried to convince Lord Halifax 'that the future constitutional position of Germany should be based upon a return to the federal principle, in which the Reich would be composed of the old German states in federation'.[20] After the fiasco of the Empire and the failure of the Weimar Republic, democracy was to develop from below, perhaps within the framework of a Rhineland Republic, or the Kingdom of Bavaria.

Sebastian Haffner advocated similar constitutional ideas in his book *Germany: Jekyll and Hyde*, which was published in 1940. It found a certain echo in British public opinion.[21] However, it was precisely his reservations about a compromise peace with the old ruling classes which distinguished his position from that of Rauschning and gave his liberal views weight in official circles. Moreover he did not, like many emigrants and emmissaries of the Resistance,[22] repeat the arguments for a powerful Reich controlled by the Wehrmacht as a bulwark against Bolshevism. The British knew full well who had helped the Bolsheviks to power in Moscow. Haffner's challenge was directed at Bismarck's Reich, which was sacrosanct even for many patriotic Social Democrats.[23] 'What distinguishes the Third Reich from the German Reich are nuances', he wrote, 'for the world at large they are identical, the spirit of aggression, aggrandisement, and world domination, which constitute the means, soul, and demon of this state.'[24] The generals who embodied the Prussian-German tradition of power politics might be more likeable, cultured and intelligent than the National Socialists, but both served the principle, 'Deutschland über Alles', which had resulted in ever more crises and wars. German history had come out of joint in 1866. Peace could only be secured in Europe if Germany returned to a federal constitution. Germany had been the Hellas of Europe before Prussia, the new Macedonia, had destroyed its vital nerve centre. Prussia had to be lopped back to its extent at the time of Frederick II for the sake of a sound development of the reconstituted German territorial states. Haffner rejected the charge that he favoured the dismemberment of Germany because, firstly, he argued for economic unity and, secondly, he opposed any form of punishment in order not to make life difficult for the new confederation by burdening it unjustly. One may object that in the end this solution amounted to a dismemberment of the German Reich. However, Haffner's proposals contained positive initiatives for the reorganisation of Europe on a federal basis, an idea which was to play a crucial role in all British plans for Germany and for Europe as a whole. Basically, Haffner's recommendation was to dissolve the Prussian Reich into its historical constituent parts, instead of dividing Germany by force according to foreign agreements and interests. The federal ideas of southern German resistance circles followed similar lines. Robert Vansittart, who was impressed by them, advised: 'Don't break up Germany; break up Prussia, and do it good and proper'.[25] Another emigrant of conservative leanings, Edgar Stern-Rubarth, even advocated the exclusion of Prussia from the German confederation.[26] The idea of a peaceful pre-Bismarckian Germany was a *fata morgana* – 'all this lay very much in the future', as Lord Halifax indicated to Rauschning.[27] British public opinion did not need the writings of German émigré historians[28] to be convinced that Prussia's history was indeed a macabre story.

If Haffner strongly advocated that the emigrants should have the right to a say in the re-structuring of Germany – he had in mind working committees for the re-establishment of the individual

German states[29] – there was a rude awakening in store for him and other German emigrants. The internment of all 'enemy aliens' after the German attack on France was the expression of a war psychosis which did not last long, but was felt to be deeply humiliating, especially by the political refugees. Before this 'general round-up', only about 300 people who were suspected of pro-Nazi activities had been taken into custody.[30] Even though almost all the political refugees were soon released, the shock of internment was so enduring that all dreams inspired by the idea of joint responsibility for the future of Germany came to an abrupt end.

The change of government in May 1940 proved to be even more decisive for the refugees. Churchill's purely military conception of the war, and his determination to pursue it to a victorious conclusion, left the emigrants with only two alternatives: either to withdraw totally from politics, or to contribute to the 'war effort' in the hope, but without any certainty, that by doing so they would also be able to influence post-war conditions. With Churchill's coming to power, the 'balance of power' doctrine, already well established inside the Foreign Office, prevailed in the Cabinet: rejection of a compromise peace not only with Hitler's regime, but also with a military dictatorship led by the old élites, which would not have changed the predominant position of Germany in Europe. From now on, possible political upheavals in the Reich were seen primarily as opportunities for a military weakening of Germany; Churchill's assessment of the events of 20 July 1944 was perhaps the most striking illustration of this attitude.[31] Consequently, the conservative emigrants too lost much of their political influence.

A distancing from this group of emigrants was also in line with the internal political situation, because the Labour Party had accused Chamberlain's government of fawning on the rightist politicians in exile, while ignoring the Social Democrats. Now it was the left liberal and Social Democratic emigrants who were called upon for war service, or, more precisely, for employment in psychological warfare, which was organised in a completely new, much more efficient manner by Churchill.[32] Chamberlain's government had been relatively cautious in this field, not least because it was aware that too vigorous a tone might produce an undesirable solidarity in Germany. In the spring of 1940, Haffner had complained about the coolly temporising attitude of the government *vis-à-vis* the émigrés: 'Why is no use made of them, of their experience of internal German politics, their knowledge of German political psychology, and their still countless underground ties with Germany? Why are they not at least used in the propaganda campaign against Hitler?'[33] Already in November 1939, Vansittart had recommended that German emigrants be employed on matters relating to propaganda. In a note to Lord Halifax he wrote: 'I feel strongly that Herr Rauschning and Herr Höltermann [*Reichsbannerführer*, L.K.] should be consulted on all our broadcasts in German. Rauschning has the confidence of what remains sound in the German bourgeoisie, and Höltermann commands the confidence of the Left. Consultation would involve no obligation on our part'.[34] The last sentence is particularly indicative of the purely marginal nature of any influence which the emigrants were permitted to exert.

This was not, however, to deter the true anti-fascists from their commitment to British propaganda. Moreover, many emigrants (including, for example, Sebastian Haffner) assumed that large-scale involvement in psychological warfare would necessarily result in their participation in the political re-organisation of Germany at the end of the war. This was an essential illusion for every politically active German, considering the precarious wartime situation in which they found themselves. The hope that they would be able to have a say in political matters as soon as the time was ripe may also have motivated the leaders of the SOPADE when they first took up contact with the Foreign Office in December 1939. It was only at the insistence of the International Secretary of the Labour Party that the Foreign Office condescended to instruct a young expert on Germany to listen to the views of the Social Democratic leaders. Ivone Kirkpatrick spoke to Hans Vogel and Erich Ollenhauer, 'a companion whose name I was unfortunately unable to catch'.[35] Contrary to expectation, both seem to have made a sensible impression, but did not have much that was new to report. Apparently they declared themselves satisfied when it was explained to them that they could be employed in propaganda.

Even though Great Britain alone continued to fight against Germany's new continental supremacy, conceptually the struggle had assumed the character of a large-scale coalition war even before the German attack on the Soviet Union and the entry into the war of the USA. The Prime Minister was aware that the war, which could not have been prevented without the 'Grand Alliance' with Moscow he had demanded consistently ever since Munich,[36] could not now be won without the support of the USA. Even if Great Britain were to be among the victors at the end of the war, this would not ensure that the British government would be in a position to implement its own ideas about the political future of Germany. While with every political initiative Churchill considered primarily the reactions of the USA (particularly since the Atlantic Charter, which had been formulated precisely with the American public in mind), since Eden's visit to Stalin in the same year the Foreign Office increasingly gave consideration to the political interests and sensitivities of Moscow. It would be only a slight exaggeration to say that the Foreign Office was as much the agent of its Soviet ally's interests in Whitehall, as the advocate of the British government *vis-à-vis* Moscow.

It was indicative not only of the careful diplomacy of the decision-making élite, taking the interests of the allies fully into account, but also of their uncertain approach to power politics, that they avoided all contact with the 'other Germany' in order not to arouse the suspicion that they were, after all, aiming for a compromise peace. By his explicit opposition to 'the slightest contact' Churchill rejected all the German opposition's overtures for peace, referring expressly to the negative repercussions in Washington and Moscow.[37] As it was never possible to be certain whether the German emigrants were in touch with Resistance circles in Germany or not, this directive applied in principle to all political arrangements with German politicians in exile. The fact that the Peace Treaty of Versailles had been overruled by the United States Congress, because the secret agreements among the European powers during the war violated the right of self-determination, was seen as one of the most important lessons of the past. Assessment of the international isolation of Moscow in the 1930s was a similar case. The ideological antagonism between German Social Democrats and Communists at the end of the Weimar Republic, which was also manifested in the decision to take refuge in the West and East, made it seem inadvisable to associate in any way with the Social Democratic emigrants in London, known to be anti-Communist. Open cooperation with bourgeois politicians in exile was out of the question for reasons both of internal and external politics, since this would lend countenance to the Left's theory of conspiracy based on capitalist class solidarity. Moreover, the fact that the liberal bourgeoisie in Germany could only form a majority government with a partner from the Right or the Left also had to be taken into consideration.

Apart from the major Allies, on whose military efforts a successful continuation of the war depended, it was also necessary to take the security needs of the European allies into account, especially those of France and Poland. Their claims on Germany could never be reconciled with the ideas of the anti-fascist, but nevertheless patriotic

German emigrants. Poland and France not only contributed actively
to the war effort – Polish pilots had proved to be of great value in the
hour of greatest need during the air battle over England in September
1940 – but after the war their diplomatic and military potential was
also an indispensable factor in Britain's long-term planning for the
maintenance of peace and stability. Britain could only hope to be an
equal partner among the new great powers of the future with the
support of her middle-sized and smaller allies, whose governments
had taken refuge in London.

It was, above all, out of consideration for the Reich's neighbours to
the west and to the east that international control of the industrial
centres on the Rhine and the Saar was envisaged at an early stage,[38]
together with a generous rounding-off of Poland's western border, at
Germany's expense, and a large transfer of population to the west.[39]
No German politician in exile could be expected to identify with war
aims which endangered the territorial integrity of the Reich. Seen
from this point of view, it was to the advantage of the German
emigrants to be excluded from post-war planning and thus protected
from the charge of collaboration. This assessment of the post-war
situation was based on the assumption that the majority of the German
population would be as recalcitrantly nationalistic as they had been
after the First World War. It was this pessimistic outlook which
determined the whole of British post-war planning. Consequently,
unconditional surrender and the complete occupation of Germany
were seen as necessary prerequisites for a complete re-orientation of
the German political mentality.[40] The demand for unconditional
surrender, settled at an early stage though only proclaimed publicly at
the Conference of Casablanca,[41] was the final confirmation for the
German emigrants that a negotiated peace with the 'other Germany',
that is, with those Germans inside or outside Germany who opposed
Hitler's regime, was in principle out of the question.

All the serious complications which precluded the German
emigrants from exerting influence were aggravated by their own
political fragmentation. The British propaganda machine made
cautious efforts to co-ordinate the various groups of German
emigrants – a semi-official committee of their British patrons was
considered. Their efforts failed, however, and not least because of the
dissension among the German politicians in exile, who continued in
their differences of opinion while abroad. A Foreign Office note of 16
January 1940 reads: 'The difficulty of getting émigrés together under
one umbrella, however large, is no doubt almost insuperable'.[42] Even

the coalition of all the Socialist groups in Great Britain in a new organisation was not able to convince the government of its political coherence. A note made by Eden in January 1942 refers to a talk with the Soviet ambassador, in which the latter enquired about the attitude of the German emigrants in Great Britain and the USA: 'In general, the position here is that early last year the four main émigré groups joined together to form the Union of German Socialist Organisations in Great Britain. As its decisions have to be unanimous, the Union has not found it possible to publish many declarations of policy. Indeed, the only declaration of importance was issued last December and did little more than express opposition to National Socialism and the general desire to set up a new economic and social order in Germany. And it supported the Atlantic Charter'.[43] One civil servant dealing with Germany felt that it would do no harm to let Maiski know that German emigrant groups were not considered to be of any importance. 'We need not perhaps tell him that they are generally speaking, though left-wing, anti-communist.'[44]

In fact, of course, the predominantly leftist emigrants were divided into numerous groups which ranged through all the intellectual shades of the left-wing spectrum.[45] Many made no secret of their anti-Communist opinions, which were primarily directed against the Soviet Union. From the British point of view this was a reason for caution, because the pact with the Soviet Union,[46] greeted as a triumph of British diplomacy when finally signed in May 1942, could be undermined from this quarter. It did nothing to increase the influence of the political emigrants in Great Britain that, during the period which followed, the Social Democrats and the Communists could not combine to form the sort of 'popular front' in exile which, so it appeared, had been successfully created in Moscow and was known as the National Committee for Free Germany (*Nationalkomitee Freies Deutschland*).[47] When the *Freie Deutsche Bewegung*,[48] which had come about primarily as the result of Communist emigrants' activities, proved to be a failure, Moscow began a systematic campaign aimed at discrediting the Social Democrats.[49] The Soviet government assumed, with some justification, that the political activities of all those groups of exiles in the West which it did not control were aimed at reducing Communist influence in post-war Germany. As long as Soviet imperialism had not revealed its true face in Eastern and Central Europe, the Russians' distrust of the German emigrants seemed perfectly legitimate to the Foreign Office. It could not be ruled out that Moscow might take advantage of the inevitable chaos at the end of the war to achieve a sovietisation of the whole of Germany. The only way to prevent this, it was thought, was not to allow any doubts of British loyalty to arise in Moscow, while at the same time laying down the general conditions of a common Allied occupation policy, even before the war had ended.

The British government saw itself as the political headquarters of an alliance of highly heterogeneous partners. As a result of this perception, British diplomats soon began to encourage a pro-Soviet policy in the USA, warning the Americans against any form of familiarity with exiled German politicians. While it is generally accepted that Roosevelt's attitude to Stalin, and the aims he pursued, were naïvely optimistic, the Foreign Office feared, during the war, that the anti-Communist attitude of the American public could, in the end, endanger the Soviet Union's participation in the arrangements for peace. These were based on the long-term weakening of Germany, for which the Soviet Union's participation was seen as indispensable. Even civil servants, who were normally far from making prognoses along Marxist lines, now began to suspect that a disastrous alliance between American 'Big Business' and the German conservative élites might suddenly emerge. The attempts to bring about peace undertaken by American businessmen after the outbreak of war were a bad omen.[50]

In the same way that France had warned Chamberlain's government of the subversive activities of the nationalist conservative politicians in exile, Strasser and Rauschning, London now took exception to the activities of the same emigrants in the USA. Soon after the USA's entry into the war, London felt bound to warn Washington against the *Frei Deutschland-Bewegung* which had been founded a year before in the Bermudas by Otto Strasser, Rauschning, Treviranus and others. Strasser had telegraphed Hull, the American Secretary of State, to say that his movement endorsed the United Nations' declaration concerning the common struggle against Hitler and his regime. 'The State Department are quite capable of falling for this,' commented the Foreign Office.[51] In London, similar attempts did not have the slightest hope of official recognition. 'We see little prospect of wishing to recognise any foreseeable Free German Movement,' Sir Orme Sargent wrote to Harold Nicolson at about this time. Nicolson showed an interest in the aims of a predominantly Social Democratic Free German Committee.[52] He was informed that the committee did not represent all the German emigrants, let alone those Germans who were still far from giving up their belief in Hitler.

A year later, the dangers posed by the German lobby in the USA were pointed out to the British Embassy in Washington. German-American voters numbered more than 8 million; the widespread fear of a bolshevisation of Europe ostensibly favoured agitation by German emigrants and organisations such as Loyal Americans of German Descent, for a moderate peace, or even a compromise peace with an acceptable successor government. A memorandum of the Political Intelligence Department dated 21 January 1943 states disapprovingly: 'The general feeling in the USA towards the German people is one of pity rather than anger.... There thus exists a very fruitful field for those German-Americans, Americans of German origins and German refugees, who are already working to create a feeling in the United States that will produce American intervention to protect Germany from the consequences of defeat'.[53]

One of the most determined opponents of a compromise peace was the historian John Wheeler-Bennett, who worked in New York for the British government's propaganda service and had the confidence of a great many emigrants who were in favour of just such a compromise peace as an end to the war. Wheeler-Bennett thought that he could discern a new form of appeasement in the United States, since the recognition was not yet as widespread there as it was in Great Britain, that there were no groups within the socio-political spectrum in Germany to which the responsibility of governing could be entrusted *per se*, 'before the process of political and ideological "delousing" of Germany has been completed'.[54] Wheeler-Bennett saw forces at work in the State Department, in certain business circles and in the military establishment, which were driven by a fear of the bolshevisation of Europe and were therefore prepared to negotiate with any reactionary groups in Germany, even the General Staff, provided that the formula of Casablanca was accepted willy-nilly. While power politics were the primary consideration for the Right, the democratic Left, not yet won over by Vansittartism, was moved by a belief in the 'other', that is, the 'better' Germany (in the jargon of the Foreign Office, the 'good German' theory). Dorothy Thompson, the American columnist, was considered to be one of the most dangerous protagonists of this view because she was well-meaning. She advocated negotiating with the German 'patriots',[55] that is, with opponents of the regime both inside and outside Germany, who feared nothing so much as a bolshevisation of their country in the wake of the chaos which would accompany the fall of the Reich. When the Italians were freed of the stigma of being 'enemy aliens' in 1942 and the

US Department of Justice considered similar measures for German nationals, the British government intervened in Washington to check this development. On 30 October Eden wrote to Halifax, the ambassador: 'We are concerned lest any concessions to German émigrés may increase the pressure from the United States government for recognition of a Free German Movement'.[56]

British objections were always the same: they had to take their European allies into account, in view of the patriotic and anti-Communist attitudes of the majority of the German emigrants, and they were convinced that politicians who had been in exile would not be able to achieve much in Germany after the war as they must necessarily appear to be quislings. This policy was based in part on the prognosis that the national recalcitrance of the Germans, observed after the First World War, would not be very different after another catastrophe which they had brought upon themselves. It was also the expression of a liberal understanding of democracy which did not allow the necessary re-education of the 'master race' to begin with the imposition of discredited politicians. For a while the legal status of the German emigrants in the USA remained unchanged, but the establishment of a Council for a Democratic Germany in 1944 gave cause for renewed unease. British diplomats in the Embassy in Washington considered which form of 'anti-soft peace publicity' would most effectively immunise American public opinion against the activities of German emigrants. Their report to the Foreign Office stated that they had all agreed to continue to refrain from using the sort of directly anti-German propaganda which had been issued in the First World War. Instead, they preferred to use methods of indirect influence which would avoid giving the impression that there was an organised campaign behind it.

The European allies too should be encouraged 'to do everything possible to spread the light'.[57] Washington requested help in this matter from London, which provided a list of talking points designed expressly with the American business mentality in mind. The leaders of public opinion, politicians, journalists and scientists on the East Coast were not only to be disabused of their belief in 'good Germans', but also to be warned against the conservative emigrants' defence of the German General Staff. The warning was directed not least against the belief 'that you can do good business with Germany'.[58] Thus it was stated, in line with an argument which is still familiar today and which has always been better known for its propaganda value than for its historical validity:

Germany is and always has been as selfish in trade as in politics. And they are smart too. Last time they paid reparations with money borrowed from England and America and then defaulted from the loans. And it was these same industrialists and financiers who put Hitler into power.

The support given to the Soviet Union, prudently referred to as 'Russia', is particularly revealing, because the activities of German emigrants in arch-capitalist America were seen as posing a threat to the future of the British alliance with Moscow. The naïve idea that after the war the Soviet Union would open its borders to American consumer goods as naturally as it did now to lorries, tanks and military aircraft was deliberately promoted. 'You may have to choose', it was suggested to the Americans, 'between the German market and the Russian market. And the Russian market is going to be bigger.'[59] In any case, it is certain that in 1943 and 1944, when in Central Europe the course was being set for future developments, British diplomats tried everything to diminish American distrust of the Soviet Union. Some of the younger and more idealistic officials, in particular, believed that Britain had an historical role as mediator between the centres of capitalism and socialism since she was already on the road from 'War Socialism' to the 'Welfare State' of the future.[60] From this point of view the German emigrants, whether of conservative or Social Democratic leanings, who constantly conjured up the spectre of a Bolshevist Germany, were the true saboteurs of a new 'Pax Britannica', because their propaganda threatened to destroy the alliance of heterogeneous partners and evoked the danger of renewed confrontation. It seems that this softening-up strategy had the greatest effect at the apex of Washington's political pyramid, on the President and his closest advisers, Sumner Welles and Harry Hopkins.

It is typical of the British government's planning for Germany during the war that priority was given, not to the political and social order itself, but rather to the general conditions under which new structures could emerge. Though the liberal and pragmatic ideals of British parliamentary democracy justified the defeat of an aggressive Germany and thus of Hitler's regime, these were seen to be incompatible with the imposition of a particular social order thereafter. The main principle, however, underlying the government's wartime activities was that any potentially controversial issues which might prejudice the coalition as well as the political understanding between the 'Big Three' had to be deferred until after the war.[61] But what was more controversial than the question of Germany's new social order? Did this issue not also implicate Great Britain's domestic politics? And could it not be assumed that the Americans and the Russians had completely different ideas concerning the future role of German entrepreneurs and union leaders? Concentrating on the general framework or, more precisely, developing mechanisms by which the victorious powers would control Germany after the war was an attempt to evade this dilemma. Occupation policy thus became dependent on the occupying powers reaching a consensus.

Unfortunately, even on this path of least resistance, an insurmountable obstacle was soon encountered when it became evident that Churchill, Roosevelt and Stalin were in favour of dividing Germany into two or more independent states.[62] The Foreign Office and the State Department by contrast had only gone so far as to recommend a decentralised reconstruction of the Reich, shrinking from the more drastic measure of carving up the Reich into separate entities. Indeed, they totally rejected this policy as one which might rekindle German nationalism. The planning committees increasingly turned towards a policy of decentralising power in Germany, especially of dividing Prussia along the lines suggested during the Weimar Republic, as an alternative to the short-sighted policy of radically dividing Germany, advocated by the politicians.[63] There is some evidence that moderate emigrants played a part in this decision-making process, even if the extent of their contribution cannot be established exactly. However different the emigrants' ideas concerning Germany's future social order might be, most of them (with the exception of a few rather eccentric outsiders who hoped for a restoration of the House of Wittelsbach)[64] agreed that Germany's national unity should be preserved. As early as mid-1942, a Foreign Research and Press Service (FRPS) discussion paper for talks with Lord Halifax argued: 'Decentralisation is advocated in various quarters, partly on the grounds that the tradition of local self-government is much stronger in Germany than the tradition of democracy at the centre, and partly because with suitably designed regional units, it would curb the power of Prussia'.[65] A common interest was emerging between the more reasonable politicians in exile, who envisaged a decentralised reconstruction of the Reich, and the British decision-making élites who had been moulded by the First World War and for whom Prussia was synonymous with militarism and the supremacy of the Junkers. There was also agreement between the two coalition partners, and especially between Churchill and Attlee, in diagnosing the Prussian *bacillus* as the cause of the *furor teutonicus*. The concept of decentralisation was defined so loosely, however, that initially all possible solutions were left open, from a confederation to a federation, depending on which pressure group prevailed. Since quite a few politicians supported a dismemberment of Germany, the Foreign Office, as a compromise solution, in the spring of 1943 recommended encouraging separatist tendencies.[66] But all practical measures were subsequently boycotted, largely on the advice of German emigrants.[67]

The question of Germany's constitution was also totally open as far as the British government was concerned. This is illustrated by its changing position on the issue of the retention of a German national government or at least a central administrative machine. Historical analysis gradually evolved into political expediency, and this development also throws light on the significance that indirect control held for the British government. This fundamental principle of imperial domination, perfected by the British, would, as a matter of course, be applied in Germany presupposing a readiness to make use of tractable individuals. It might be thought, therefore, that in this respect the British government would welcome the help of those German politicians in exile who had found both refuge and material support in London. That this was not the case requires explanation, especially as the Soviet government later used this method successfully to achieve its aims.[68]

The problem posed by the continued existence of a German central government seems to have been introduced into the debate for the first time in the summer of 1942. A memorandum by T.H. Marshall, the FRPS's adviser on Germany, launched a debate on the German question within the Foreign Office that went beyond purely technical military considerations. In 'What to do with Germany', Marshall declared categorically that 'I am opposed to the dismemberment of Germany', but at the same time, he suggested that 'during the period of occupation which might last for a period of two years, there would be no central government in Germany'.[69] The failure of the Weimar Republic was attributed primarily to the Berlin government. The lesson to be learnt from this experience was that the rebirth of a democratic Germany would have to take place on a regional basis. A later memorandum by Marshall reads: 'The only way to encourage decentralisation is to build up the powers of the regional authorities before a German central government comes into existence'.[70]

Meanwhile, the Foreign Office had adopted the views of its experts on Germany. In order to facilitate the process of decentralising

Germany, the Allies were to announce immediately after the armistice that 'no recognised central Government existed' and 'that the occupying forces would deal with the regional or provincial authorities'.[71] When in September 1943 Eden explained to the Cabinet the objections to recognising a central government in Germany, he emphasised among other things: 'In the absence of potential democratic leaders after ten years of Nazi repression any such government would probably only be representative of the old Germany and might well ensure the survival of those very elements of militarism which it is our fundamental aim to destroy'.[72] There was no mention of the expelled democratic politicians in exile in London who represented the 'other Germany' and who might, after the fiasco into which Hitler and the generals plunged the Reich, have a better chance to make a fresh start than they had had in 1918.

In view of Great Britain's worldwide responsibilities after the war, the Cabinet was most reluctant to be encumbered with the administration of Germany. The minutes of a Cabinet meeting of 5 October 1948 refer to 'the heavy and invidious tasks involved in assuming responsibility for the administration of Germany after the war'.[73] The well-tried principle of 'indirect rule' had enabled the seemingly insignificant island to control a huge empire.Now it was to be applied to Germany, as the triumphant conclusion of a centuries-old tradition. The British conception of a 'Control Commission' assumed as a minimum requirement the existence of an intact administrative machine in Germany. The British saw that without the support of German officials, they would be facing an impossible task. It seemed uncertain, however, whether a German administration would cooperate with foreign occupation authorities, except through the medium of a German government, because 'collaboration might be a dangerous game. The Germans are old hands at underground murder clubs'.[74] It was to be anticipated that the politicians in exile, who had collaborated with the enemy during the war, would be the first victims of a nationalist vendetta, or even more strongly denounced as *Erfüllungspolitiker* (lackeys of the victorious powers). The best improvisation seemed to be some sort of puppet government of unsullied experts, 'without political colour and without connections abroad through which sympathy could be organised'.[75]

The adoption of these criteria, obviously derived from experiences after the First World War, meant that a government consisting predominantly of exiles must appear as the worst of all possible choices. It would lack any political legitimation; assassination attempts would pose a constant threat; it would represent political parties which had long since disappeared from the German scene. At the same time it would make heavy demands on the occupying powers, either because it was not compromised by association with the previous regime, or because it would seek to demonstrate its political independence. Apart from all this, it would have connections abroad (such as those of the SPD with the Labour Party) which would make it easy to mobilise Allied public opinion in favour of better conditions for Germany. The British view of the German mentality led them to believe that the Germans would have greater respect for any Allied NCO than for any one of their own exiled politicians. When Wirth, former Chancellor of the Reich, expressed interest in taking an active part after the war on condition that adequate food supplies would be guaranteed for the starving population, the Foreign Office backed off: Wirth's name was associated with inflation and with deference to the Allies.[76]

Indeed, this negative description applied to almost all of the prominent politicians in exile: they represented a political system which had lost all support and had failed miserably in the end. The British did not want the re-establishment of democracy in Germany to be associated with the unfortunate past. If the British planners took an interest in the experiment of Weimar, it was only with the aim of avoiding the obvious mistakes and failures of the past. In the final analysis, British policy towards Germany was not shaped by a burning desire to spread democracy; rather, it aimed to preserve the security of a nation which had been forced to make a supreme effort to defend itself against Germany twice in one generation and which now wanted nothing so much as to be left in peace. A permanent destruction of Germany's military, economic and psychological power took definite precedence over the establishment of a particular political or social system as desired by many of the emigrants, who did not share British prejudices about the militaristic spirit of the Germans.

British officials who were concerned with the future of Germany did not take it for granted that a democratic or socialist Reich would necessarily abandon the idea of power politics. A Cabinet paper which speculated about German reactions to defeat stated: 'We must so condition the evolution of Germany that the claws of militarism become rudimentary and finally drop off. We must leave them no alternative to peace. Then, by necessity, they may become as peaceful as the Swiss'.[77] Liberal democracy did not allow any intervention in this process of evolution beyond the establishment of a general framework, denazification and demilitarisation. Any attempt by the occupying powers to direct this development for their own ends by using German agents would lead only to a discrediting of both. In spite of Vansittart's propaganda, which had clearly left its mark, there was still too much respect for the German people, their diligence and their potential for recovery for them to be kept permanently in a state of tutelage. Germany was not a kindergarten which could be kept under control by a carefully selected staff.

In conclusion, there is the question of what function the emigrants would be permitted to exercise if they were not to have an official one. As the files of the Control Commission are not yet available to the public *in toto*, it is not possible to say with any certainty whether, when, and to what extent emigrants were selected for government and administrative positions at municipal and regional level.[78] It is certain, however, that 'enemy aliens' were, in principle, excluded from appointment until at least March 1945, about one year after the first appointments were made by this authority.[79] It has already been suggested that the assistance of German emigrants was particularly welcomed in those areas which were seen as having contributed to the war effort without having had any political consequences. These included both intelligence (that is, the collection of information by the interrogation of prisoners, press analyses, and so forth) and the wider field of psychological warfare and propaganda. Now, however, it was Social Democratic emigrants rather than Conservatives or those associated with the Centre Party who found employment at the BBC or PWE, with the help of Labour Party intellectuals such as Patrick Gordon-Walker[80] or Richard Crossman.[81] The emigrants developed a strong sense of national responsibility which brought them into conflict with official British policy, or what it was imagined to be, both during the war and, more often, after it. They were motivated by the suspicion that a new, harsher version of the Treaty of Versailles was in store for Germany. If this was the case, it would only encourage the re-emergence of untrammelled nationalism. Programmes broadcast to Germany by the BBC had to be agreed with the Foreign Office, and therefore they did not contain any promises for the future which the government could not keep. Nevertheless, some broadcasts were frequently criticised for being 'too soft' or 'too friendly'[82] by Members of Parliament who had been influenced by Vansittart, or by émigré governments such as the Polish, which saw its territorial claims on Germany endangered. It was common knowledge that the propaganda agencies employed a large number of 'enemy aliens', and this repeatedly gave rise to suspicion. On the other hand, it was the only area in which the British felt that they were dependent on the know-how of German emigrants. Bruce-Lockart, the General Director of PWE, reports that almost all parliamentarians thought of themselves as experts on propaganda and, often enough, they were advised by their 'pet German émigré'.[83] More than anything else, the word 'pet' reveals the position of the German emigrants who were striving for influence.

In many respects, efforts in the field of psychological warfare were part of the 're-education' of a nation which had been perverted by the ideology of National Socialism. During the war German emigrants had been called upon to help in the re-education of prisoners of war,[84] and, later, they were used as teachers in Germany. Nevertheless, their attempt to influence the conception of British cultural policy in Germany during the planning phase was, on the whole, unsuccessful. As early as 1941, a group of British teachers under the leadership of a prominent civil servant in the Ministry of Education tried to persuade the government to prepare German teachers in exile for a return to their homeland. The attempt failed and it was decided to continue this work, which later became well-known as GER (German Educational Reconstruction), under the auspices of a private association.[85] Later, one of the leading officials in the education branch of the military government was to sum up the British attitude thus: 'It would be the height of arrogance to assume that victory somehow gave us the moral right to impose our way of life'.[86] Rather, victory served British security interests which included the policy of re-education, that is, the attempt to teach the Germans the lesson that 'war can never pay them'.[87]

Leaving aside the internal discussion about the division of Germany, where the emigrants may well have wielded a certain amount of influence, the Germans living in exile were given no right to a voice in the making of the decisions which were of vital importance for the future of their country. This applies both to the division of Germany into occupation zones, which was to lead to a divided nation, and to the cession of the eastern territories which implied the uprooting of millions of Germans according to decisions taken early in the war. Yet, it must be recognised that it was precisely their lack of influence during the war which enabled many emigrants to make a successful political comeback after 1945, in spite of all the British predictions to the contrary. Since exile had strengthened their national identity many emigrants were led to believe that the same was true for the rest of Germany – which did not, in fact, correspond to the psychological realities of the post-war situation. During the war, the dream of becoming a great power had turned into a nightmare and after the population had woken up, their first concern was simply to survive.

## Notes

1. Cf. H. Kellenbenz, 'German Immigrants in England', in C. Holmes (ed.), *Immigrants and Minorities in British Society*, London, 1978, pp. 63–80.

2. See A.J. Sherman, *Island Refuge. Britain and Refugees from the Third Reich 1933–1939*, London, 1973.

3. Cf. Migration Statistics, *ibid.*, p. 271.

4. On the influence of Brüning and other German emigrants in the United States see J. Radkau, *Die deutsche Emigration in den USA. Ihr Einfluß auf die amerikanische Europapolitik 1933–1945*, Düsseldorf, 1971.

5. C. de Gaulle, *Memoirs de Guerre*, Vol. 1, *L'Appel (1940–1942)*, Paris, 1954, esp. the chapter 'Londres'.

6. M. Cowling, *The Impact of Hitler. British Politics and British Policy 1933–1945*, Cambridge, 1975, pp. 355–65.

7. Robert's comment on V. Adams's and Lord Halifax's question in Parliament, 27 October 1939, Public Record Office (this applies also to following references in similar form), FO 371/22985/C17562.

8. See W. Röder, *Die deutschen sozialistischen Exilgruppen in Groß-britannien 1940–1945*, 2nd ed., Bonn/Bad Godesberg, 1973.

9. 'Summary of Principal Peace Feelers, September 1939 – March 1941', FO 371/26542/C4216. Printed in L. Kettenacker (ed.), *Das 'Andere Deutschland' im Zweiten Weltkrieg*, Stuttgart, 1977, p. 164.

10. Documented by P.W. Ludlow, 'Papst Pius XII, die britische Regierung und die deutsche Opposition im Winter 1939/40', *VfZG*, 1974, pp. 299–341. See also the memoirs of J. Müller, *Bis zur letzten Konsequenz*, Munich, 1975.

11. For Göring's role, and assessments of him abroad, see the Ph.D. dissertation by S. Martens, Münster, 1983.

12. Röder, p. 79.

13. Comment on Woodward's note to Kirkpatrick, 9 October 1939, FO 371/22986/C18421.

14. See esp. Vansittart's memorandum, 'The Origins of Germany's Fifth War', 28 November 1939, *ibid.*, C 19495.

15. FO 371/22947/C20493.

16. 'PID Memorandum on the First Two Months of the War', 27 October 1939, FO 371/22986/C18065.

17. Cf. L. Kettenacker, 'Die britische Haltung zum deutschen Widerstand während des Zweiten Weltkriegs', in Kettenacker (ed.), p. 52.

18. See the French government's *aide-mémoire* of 23 October 1939, FO 371/22946/C17105. Also printed in Kettenacker (ed.), pp. 157–8.

19. British government's reply of 20 December 1939, WP (G) (39) 150, CAB 67/3. Also *ibid.*, pp. 159–61.

20. See n. 15.

21. S. Haffner, *Jekyll and Hyde*, London, 1940. The manuscript was completed in April 1940 and printed immediately, thus Haffner was not able to comment on the internment which began a short time later. The publishers (Secker and Warburg) described the author as follows: 'The author is an "Aryan" German under forty years of age' – both important for the book's success – 'who has lived all his life in Germany. He was trained as a lawyer and worked for six years under the Nazi regime. Having been brought up in the liberal tradition he determined to leave the land of his birth'.

22. For the critical assessment of the military opposition see K.-J. Müller, 'The German Military Opposition before the Second World War', in W.J. Mommsen and L. Kettenacker (eds.), *The Fascist Challenge and the Policy of Appeasement*, London, 1983, pp. 61–75.

23. Otto Braun, Minister President of Prussia, is representative of many Social Democrats of the Weimar period. H. Schulze, *Otto Braun oder Preußens demokratische Sendung*, Frankfurt, 1977.

24. Haffner, p. 289.

25. Vansittart's note of 20 January 1940, referring to a memorandum by the southern German resistance movement, passed on to him by Colonel Christie, an intelligence agent living in Switzerland (FO 371/22986/C19495).

26. E. Stern-Rubarth, *Exit Prussia*, London, 1940.

27. See n. 15.

28. Special mention should be made of Erich Eyck and Veit Valentin among liberal committed historians. See H.-U. Wehler (ed.), *Deutsche Historiker*, Göttingen, 1973.

29. Haffner, p. 326.

30. 'Control of Enemy Aliens', WP (G) (40) 115, 29 April 1940, FO 371/244420/C6845. See also, Peter and Leni Gillman, *'Collar the Lot!' How Britain interned and expelled its Wartime Refugees*, London, 1980; and the essay by Michael Seyfert in this volume.

31. Kettenacker, p. 69.

32. Cf. M. Balfour, *Propaganda in War 1939–1945. Organisations, Policies and Publics in Britain and Germany*, London, 1979, pp. 80–7.

33. Haffner, p. 248.

34. FO 371/22986/C18287.

35. Kirkpatrick's note of 19 December 1939, FO 371/24420/C897.

36. Cf. M.A. Gilbert, *Winston S. Churchill*, Vol.V (1922–1939), London, 1976, p. 1073. Also Cowling, pp. 223–53.

37. FO 372/26543/C10855.

38. 'Direct Means of Preventing German Rearmament', 9 April 1942, FO 371/30931/C6599. See also the Archbishop of Canterbury's article 'Ending the Prussian Tradition', *Manchester Guardian*, 8 July 1942.

39. 'Memoranda on Frontiers of European Confederations and the

Transfer of German Populations', 20 February 1942, FO 371/30930/C2167. Summary: 'The Eastern Frontier of Germany', 29 June 1942, FO 371/31500/U276. At first, only the separation of East Prussia, Danzig and Upper Silesia was considered.

40. See E.H. Carr, *Conditions of Peace*, London, 1942, pp. 210–36.

41. J. Wheeler-Bennett and A. Nicholls, *The Semblance of Peace. The Political Settlement after the Second World War*, London, 1974, pp. 51–64. In addition, Michael Balfour, 'Another Look at "Unconditional Surrender"', *International Affairs* 46, 1970/4, pp. 719–36.

42. Makin's note of 16 January 1940, reference as for n. 35.

43. Communication to Sir Stafford Cripps, 16 February 1942, FO 371/30929/C405.

44. *Ibid.*

45. See Röder, pp. 20–89, and the memorandum 'Main groups and some personalities among refugees from Germany and Austria', 15 December 1941, FO 372/30929/C2098.

46. Cf. L. Woodward, *British Foreign Policy in the Second World War*, Vol. II, London, 1971, pp. 244–54. The text is on pp. 663–5.

47. See A. Fischer, *Sowjetische Deutschlandpolitik im Zweiten Weltkrieg 1941–1945*, Stuttgart, 1975, pp. 53–9. For an interpretation of this step, see V. Mastny, *Russia's Road to the Cold War*, New York, 1979, pp. 80–5.

48. Röder, pp. 198–215. Eden replied to a question in Parliament on 7 June 1944 that the government was not considering recognising this movement, either at present or in the near future (Hansard, House of Commons, 400, 1331).

49. Article in *Pravda*, 16 July 1944 (Report from the embassy in Moscow), FO 371/29119/C9324.

50. See the information in 'British and United States Oil and Other Business Men', in 'Summary of Principal Peace Feelers' (n. 9). In addition, B. Martin, *Friedensinitiativen und Machtpolitik im Zweiten Weltkrieg 1939–1942*, Düsseldorf, 1974, pp. 132–53. Also, by the same author, 'Friedensplanungen der multi-nationalen Großindustrie (1932–1940) als politische Krisen-strategie', *Geschichte und Gesellschaft* 2, 1976, pp. 66–88.

51. Makin's comment on the *Daily Telegraph*'s report of 6 January 1942, FO 371/30929/C239.

52. Sargent to Nicholson, 12 January 1942, *ibid.*, C1173.

53. J.A. Hawgood, 'The German Lobby in the United States', in Kettenacker (ed.), pp. 218–21.

54. J. Wheeler-Bennett, 'The New American Appeasement', February 1943, FO 372/34451/C4055.

55. R.I. Miall/PWE, 'Dorothy Thompson and the "Patriots"', 18 January 1943. G.W. Harrison of the Central Department held the following opinion of this: 'Miss Thompson believes the "opposition" will be able to oust the Nazi Regime. We don't. Miss Thompson would like a compromise peace (a) in order to save bloodshed and (b) more particularly because she is afraid of Bolshevism in Europe (Dr Goebbels' line). We are all out for complete victory'. Roberts too was anxious (21 January): 'There are many signs that the German Junker class are looking more and more to fooling the Americans with a compromise peace and I think we have good cause to be anxious' (FO

371/34456/C770). They therefore resolved to point out to the Americans the 'good German danger', appealing to high places and proceeding 'with a light hand'. A selection of Dorothy Thompson's radio broadcasts was published as a book: *Listen Hans*, Boston, 1942.

56. FO 371/30929/C10442.

57. Campbell to Harvey, 26 June 1944, FO 371/39119/C8883.

58. 'Talking Points', *ibid.*, also ff.

59. *Ibid.* These ideas were also disseminated by Harry Hopkins. Besides Sumner Welles, he was one of Roosevelt's chief advisers. See R.E. Sherwood, *The White House Papers of Harry L. Hopkins*, Vol. II, London, 1949, pp. 639–42.

60. The diary entry made by Eden's private secretary on 7 January 1942 exemplifies this attitude: 'America far more old-fashioned and anti-Russian than Great Britain – a hundred years behind in social revolution'. J. Harvey (ed.), *The War Diaries of Oliver Harvey 1941–1945*, London, 1948, p. 85.

61. The decision not to define war aims precisely for the present had already been taken by the War Cabinet on 9 October 1939 (WM 42(39) 8, CAB 65/1), see above, pp. 105–6 and n. 17.

62. On this question, see especially R.G. Webb, *Britain and the Future of Germany: British Planning for German Dismemberment and Reparations 1942–1945*, Ann Arbour, London, 1981; also K. Sainsbury, 'British policy and German unity at the end of the Second World War', *English Historical Review* 94, 1979, pp. 786–804. See also L. Kettenacker, 'Preußen in der alliierten Kriegszielplanung 1939–1947' in L. Kettenacker, M. Schlenke and H. Seier (eds.), *Studien zur Geschichte Englands und der deutsch-britischen Beziehungen, Festschrift für Paul Kluke*, Munich, 1981, pp. 312–40.

63. See esp. Kettenacker, 'Preußen in der alliierten Kriegszielplanung'.

64. There was a 'Bavarian Council' in the USA. Sir John Wheeler-Bennett reported regularly on its activities. See the memorandum 'Plan to Prevent a Prussian Dominated State' by Dr F.W. Proewig, who was particularly active in these circles. The FO did not think much of him: 'a doctrinaire with an anti-Prussian complex', 'a slippery customer', 'his economic arguments (i.e. penchant for Adam Smith liberalism) very childish' (FO 371/34460/C10018).

65. 'What is the future of Germany', 29 June 1942, FO 371/31500/U276.

66. WP (43) 421, 27 September 1943, FO 371/34460/C11296.

67. Thus the FO opposed a directive by Churchill to the Special Operations Executive (SOE) concerning encouragement of separatist tendencies in Germany. See Harrison's note of 22 November 1943, FO 371/39079/C178.

68. See Fischer, *Sowjetische Deutschlandpolitik im Zweiten Weltkrieg*; Mastny, *Russia's Road to the Cold War*, pp. 233–9.

69. FO 371/31500/U360, 9 July 1942.

70. 'Confederal or Federal Germany', 1 October 1943, FO 371/34460/C11429. See also 'Federalism in Germany', FRPS/Oxford, 16 February 1943, *ibid.*, Vol. 34456/C2233.

71. 'The Future of Germany', WP (43) 96, 8 March 1943, FO 371/34457/C2864.

72. See n. 66.

73. WM 135(43), 5 October 1943, Confidential Annex CAB: 65/40.

74. 'Recognition of a German Government', 15 July 1944, FO 371/399116/C9330.

75. *Ibid.*

76. Butler's comment, 30 October 1944, FO 371/39080/C14671.

77. The next sentence reads: 'And let us remember that if there were 70,000,000 Swiss they might not be so peaceful after all' (WP(45)18, 10 January 1945, FO 371/46791/C150). This sentence reveals how widespread Vansittart's notions of a specific German national character, with roots reaching far back into history, were among the British governing élites.

78. U. Schneider's dissertation ('Britische Besatzungspolitik 1945. Besatzungsmacht, deutsche Exekutive und die Probleme der unmittelbaren Nachkriegszeit, dargestellt am Beispiel des späteren Landes Niedersachsen, April bis Oktober 1945', Hanover, 1980) shows that at least emigrants referred the occupying officers to politically reliable people who could be entrusted with public office.

79. Troutbeck to the British Council, 29 March 1945, FO 371/46865/C861.

80. See Lord Gordon-Walker's Foreword in Kettenacker (ed.), p. vi and pp. 108–9.

81. On Richard Crossman, 'Director German Region/PWE', see Balfour, pp. 88–102 and Röder, p. 35. Crossman, who later transferred to the Political Warfare Department at SHAEF, was considered to be pro-German. On 25 February 1945 Murphy wrote to Matthew (State Department), 'Crossman wanted and wants a tender treatment of Germany so that the Reich can be won over to a Western Bloc which Britain can use to counter-balance Soviet power' (National Archives/Washington: RG 59/C118).

82. For example, the Polish ambassador complained on 22 February 1943 that in their propaganda, the BBC differentiated between the National Socialists and the German people. Count Raczynski pointed to Soviet propaganda as a model to be emulated. There were clear differences between broadcasts in German and in Russian. 'In their internal propaganda the Russians describe matters more realistically and they speak of German and not only Nazi imperialism; especially emphasising that the present war is but a continuation of the war of 1914–1918 and represents the same phenomenon of German aggressiveness.' The Foreign Office pointed out that the BBC's propaganda operated within a democratically constituted society, and therefore had to be 'consistent'. A BBC 'Output Report' of January 1943 reads: 'We have made it clear then that the main purpose of the United Nations is the destruction of the German war machine rather than the German people, and though this distinction has been qualified, it has always been maintained' (FO 371/34444/C2385).

83. R.H. Bruce Lockart, *Comes the Reckoning*, London, 1947, p. 159.

84. See H. Faulk, *Die deutschen Kriegsgefangenen in Großbritannien. Re-education, Geschichte der deutschen Kriegsgefangenen des Zweiten Weltkriegs*, Vol. XI/2, Munich, 1970. See also M.B. Sullivan's popular account, *Thresholds of Peace. German Prisoners and the People of Britain 1944–1948*, London, 1979. Leading German figures were the late Sir Heinz Koeppler, Herbert Sulzbach and Waldemar von Knoeringen.

85. See G. Pakschies, *Umerziehung in der Britischen Zone 1945–1949*,

Weinheim and Basel, 1979, pp. 80–5, and J. Anderson, '"GER". A Voluntary Anglo-German Contribution', in A. Hearnden (ed.), *The British in Germany. Educational Reconstruction after 1945*, London, 1978, pp. 253–67.

    86. G. Murray, 'The British Contribution', in Hearnden (ed.), p. 66.

    87. 'German Reactions to Defeat', see n. 77.

# Conrad Pütter

# German Refugees and British Propaganda*

*The Activities of German Refugees in Secret British Broadcasting Stations*

## I

On the evening of 1 June 1940, the radio monitoring station of the Supreme Command of the German Armed Forces intercepted for the first time the programme of a German-speaking broadcasting station transmitting on 30 metres short-wave. It announced itself with the words, 'Hier spricht Deutschland auf der Welle 30.2'[1] ('This is Germany on 30.2 metres'). Four months later another short-wave transmitter could be heard in the Reich on 31 metres, using the words 'Hier ist der Sender der Europäischen Revolution!...' ('This is the broadcasting station of the European Revolution! We speak for all those damned to silence. We are calling the masses to a political and social revolution. We are fighting for a peaceful Europe.')[2] Although both broadcasting stations tried to create the impression that they were located within the Reich itself, the German monitoring services, with the help of radio bearings, could quickly make out their position as being somewhere in the south-east of England.[3]

Great Britain joined the broadcasting war against Germany for the first time in 1940, using the so-called 'grey' or 'black' broadcasting stations, that is, stations which concealed their actual geographical location. More than half a dozen additional broadcasting stations of

---

* Translated by Meinir Wynne Davies

this kind were to follow in the course of the War, joining in the battle for influence on public opinion in the German Reich.

Daniel Lerner, a former member of staff of the Western Allies propaganda institution, Psychological Warfare Division, has put forward the thesis that psychological warfare can only be successful if it runs parallel to successful military action.[4] If this is accepted, then it is clear that the first two British underground broadcasting stations were established at a most unfavourable time.

The period between September 1939 and June 1941 was a time of great military success for the Reich and its leadership. Belgium, Holland, France, Denmark and Norway, as well as parts of the Balkans had had to capitulate in the face of German troops and were under military occupation. Great Britain was fighting for sheer survival with its back to the wall in the Battle of Britain. The German Reich, or at least the vast majority of the German population, was flushed with victory. In the summer of 1940 scepticism and pessimism predominated among the British population as they contemplated their situation. Even the transport home of British troops from Dunkirk did not in any way inspire confidence in their own victory; on the contrary, they were preparing themselves for a long and bloody war.[5]

However, the British felt that they could detect signs of scepticism on the German side too. A survey carried out by the Ministry of Information (MOI) in February 1940 among the few German prisoners of war then held in Britain, showed that the mood among the German population seemed to be shifting from 'We shall be victorious' to 'We shall never capitulate', but that they nevertheless felt strongly enough to last out a war successfully to the end.[6] The British also thought that they could discern a growing discontent in the Reich among industrial workers, owing to the growing pressure of work. However, the National Socialist system and, above all, the person of Adolf Hitler still seemed to be accepted by the large majority of the population.

What should or could a black broadcasting station hope to achieve in such a situation? Why set up an underground broadcasting station at all, when the BBC had already installed a German service that openly broadcast propaganda and to which, it seemed, many Germans listened regularly?

The reason was that Goebbels' Ministry of Propaganda had already adopted the business of war on the air on a grand scale. In February 1940 it had begun to broadcast to England with a powerful transmitter, the New British Broadcasting Station (NBBS). Its announcer, known as Lord Haw-Haw, quickly achieved a somewhat macabre celebrity. He succeeded in amusing many of his listeners, while at the same time spreading uneasiness among the British population because part of his information was evidently based on a sound knowledge of the situation in the country.[7] Three additional black broadcasting stations were set up at short intervals during the summer of the same year, aimed at a variety of social and national groups in Great Britain. Many black transmitters were known to be functioning in France until the capitulation. Thus Great Britain also took up the weapon of psychological warfare; perhaps for no other reason than for political prestige. During the battle for France, indeed, such political considerations coincided with the aspirations of many German, or German-speaking refugees (Austrians and Czechs). After their flight from Germany or from German troops, they had found temporary refuge in England and were seeking a new platform for their battle against German fascism.

Unlike the production of pamphlets and magazines, for which the refugees required only a typewriter, paper, envelopes and stamps in order to spread their information, the production and transmission of radio broadcasts presented extreme difficulties, both technical (tape recorders did not yet exist) and legal. For example, it has never been possible to set up and use a transmitter in any European country without official permission and supervision. No state allowed foreigners to broadcast propaganda to their population without exercising some form of control and, of course, the unsupervised use of 'enemy aliens' in programmes aimed against that enemy was out of the question. Broadcasts for foreign countries (and in most cases those for the home population) were, if not produced by the authorities, then at least strictly supervised and censored by them.

# II

Until the second half of 1941 Britain possessed no effective propaganda authority; such organisation as there was, was in a miserable state. Compared with the gigantic and successful propaganda operations that the Third Reich had at its disposal, under the direction of Goebbels' Ministry of Public Enlightenment and Propaganda, the British were lagging hopelessly behind.

Responsibility for foreign propaganda (the initial intention was only to produce leaflets) was given to the Department of Propaganda in Enemy Countries, a secret organisation known as EH after its original quarters in Electra House on the Embankment. At the same time, in February 1939, it was decided that in the event of war with Germany the staff should be evacuated to Woburn Abbey in Bedfordshire, there to continue their 'magic tricks' protected from both bombs and curious glances.[8]

Initially there were frequent quarrels about who should actually be in charge of EH; from the spring of 1939 to the summer of 1940 responsibility for the organisation shifted three times between the Ministry of Information (MOI) and the Foreign Office (FO).[9] On the initiative of the coalition Prime Minister Winston Churchill a new organisation, the Special Operations Executive (SOE), was founded in July 1940. Its function was 'to coordinate all actions by way of subversion and sabotage against the enemy overseas'.[10] However, this organisation came under the control of yet a third minister, the Minister of Economic Warfare, Hugh Dalton. Dalton divided SOE into two departments. The first, SO1, took over from EH the black and white propaganda, a move which EH resisted strongly.

Continual disputes over areas of jurisdiction, personal and political intrigues among the individuals involved and, last but not least, the necessity of centrally co-ordinating and supervising propaganda against the enemy in the face of the escalating violence of the War, led to the setting up of the Political Warfare Executive (PWE) in the summer of 1941. PWE was intended to take over the planning, execution and direction of all forms of psychological warfare against the Axis powers, which until then had been carried out by the Foreign Office, Ministry of Information, Ministry of Economic Warfare and, at least in formal terms independently, by the BBC. Since all four bodies had one representative on the Directing Committee of the PWE, they were forced to work together. It was only with the creation of this secret organisation that British psychological warfare began to function really efficiently against the Third Reich.

## III

The history of the origin and organisation of the broadcasting station 'Hier spricht Deutschland . . .' is largely unknown. Its former German members of staff are dead and there is a paucity of British documents which could give more exact details of its planning and alleged aims. The following account brings together the few facts which can be considered as certain.

In the first months of 1940 several underground transmitters were operating from Paris against the Third Reich, for example 'Freier Deutschlandsender' and a 'Deutscher Freiheitssender', as well as the 'Österreichischer Freiheitssender' from Fécamp in Normandy. Through the possession of shares the British were involved in the private Austrian company which was also broadcasting programmes to the British Expeditionary Force in France.[11]

The fact that the German Radio Counter Intelligence Service was using strong jamming stations against these transmitters made it clear to EH and SOE that the Germans were alarmed by the broadcasts, doing everything in their power to prevent them from reaching German ears. The British therefore considered it worthwhile to start broadcasting from British territory on stations known as German Freedom Stations. They were in possession of a very useful shortwave transmitter near Woburn in Buckinghamshire.

After the German invasion of France the transmitters on French territory were, one after the other, forced to stop broadcasting and those of the staff who could manage it fled from the advancing German troops to England. One of those who escaped was the German Carl Spiecker, a former politician of the Centre Party and press agent of Reichskanzler Marx, as well as *Sonderbeauftragter zur Bekämpfung des Nationalsozialismus* (Special Commissioner for the Combating of National Socialism) under Brüning. Spiecker had been in contact with the British Propaganda and Secret Service Agencies even before his flight to England. Together with the SPD officials Jakob Altmeier and Ernst Langendorf he had installed a 'Sender der Deutschen Freiheitspartei' (Transmitter of the German Freedom Party) on a cutter in the English Channel as early as 1938. British agencies were involved in this venture through the provision of money and information.[12]

When on his arrival Spiecker contacted F.A. Voigt, the British journalist, he was no longer unknown to the British. Voigt, who had been a correspondent for the *Manchester Guardian* in Germany before the war, was no longer working as a journalist, but for EH. Spiecker's

133

wish to carry on his struggle against National Socialism with the help of radio broadcasts from Britain was quickly approved. After the initial difficulties with organisation and spheres of authority, the first German-speaking black broadcasting station was set up on British soil in May 1940. Voigt himself was appointed Head of the Transmitter by EH,[13] and later became the German adviser on British psychological warfare.[14] Hans Albert Kluthe was persuaded to become both producer and announcer.[15] Spiecker and Voigt were able to agree very quickly on the content and orientation of the station's programmes, the political content aimed at being consonant with the convictions of both men.

The broadcasting station Hier spricht Deutschland . . . saw itself as the voice of the true Germany and devoted itself primarily to patriotic themes. Spiecker, Kluthe and Voigt hoped to find their public among the nationalistically- and conservatively-minded bourgeoisie. Their assignment was to make it clear to these circles that one could not be a true German and a Nazi at the same time.[16] However, right from the start, programming was based on a number of incorrect assumptions and Hier spricht Deutschland . . . quickly came to an end.

Firstly, the evening programmes originally lasted for forty-five minutes, far too long to keep the interest of the listeners for the whole time.[17] News items occupied a very small percentage of total broadcasting time, the greater part of which was devoted to commentaries. None of the broadcasting stations which were to follow ever broadcast such long programmes. Moreover, the longer the broadcasting time, the greater the danger for the listeners of being caught committing the punishable crime of listening to foreign transmitting stations. In addition, Spiecker had probably lost the public he was trying to reach – those who had formerly voted for the liberal and regional parties of the Weimar Republic. Again and again he explained to them his nationalist standpoint and his commitment to the national interests of Germany,[18] but it is likely that they had long ago aligned themselves with the extremely successful National Socialist regime. They therefore no longer represented a public for a broadcasting station which was not only secret, but also nationalistically orientated.

Was not also Spiecker's idea of speaking personally as a 'considered and experienced political adviser', and of appealing to the humanitarian conscience, the prudence and the reason of his listeners somewhat misjudged, at a time when Hitler and Goebbels could use their demagogical powers of rhetoric to whip up nationalistic ecstasy in hundreds and thousands of Germans? Could the following plea really hope to succeed in forcing the excited German public to stop and think for a moment: 'The fate of the individual might be difficult, might be terrible and unbearable, but the only thing that counts today is the fate of the German people. It remains questionable whether the bloody sacrifice which Hitler demands from the German people is justifiable and necessary'.[19] Such a statement represents a point of view which was politically obsolete in the summer of 1940; it had lost all reference to reality and, in this form, had absolutely no chance either of supporting or instigating any effective opposition to fascism in Germany. Listening to foreign transmitting stations was in itself a small act of resistance, a form of dissociation from the National Socialist regime. Would listeners, faced with such statements, really turn on the radio to listen to these programmes again? The German Service of the BBC with its solid information, offered a programme much more suited to this purpose.

The fact that Spiecker and Kluthe could make such statements at all, that they could make even more far-reaching demands for a 'strong Germany' and for the 'retention of most of the areas won through military action'[20] (whatever they meant by that), also shows that, at least in the beginning, they had a great deal of journalistic and editorial independence from their British supervisors and censors. It should have been foreseeable that a transmitting station of this political orientation would not survive for very long. Before outside criticism of the statements made in Hier spricht Deutschland . . . could become too strong, the problem solved itself. Spiecker became very ill in the spring of 1941 and was no longer available for editorial work. Either there was no one who could replace him, or SOE, having realised that the work put into the station did not pay off, did not seriously try to find a substitute.[21]

Moreover, new and basically different plans for radio propaganda to Germany were ripening in the corridors of SOE.

## IV

At about the same time as Hier spricht Deutschland . . . began broadcasting, a number of German émigré socialists gathered around Waldemar von Knoeringen and Paul Anderson. They were all members of the *Neu Beginnen* group, or at least sympathised with it,[22] and they also tried to get permission from the British to start their own broadcasting station. Their contact in SO1 was Richard Crossman. During long discussions with him they worked out the ideological basis for a new broadcasting station, which was to address itself mainly to the German working class. Because of his position at SO1 F.A. Voigt also took part in these planning sessions.[23] After the group around von Knoeringen had heard of the existence of Hier spricht Deutschland . . ., their efforts to establish a broadcasting station for German workers became even stronger; in this they were helped by the political orientation and personal ambition of Richard Crossman.

During the summer of 1940 SOE also came to the conclusion that it would be logical to try to reach not only right-wing Germans, but also German workers and to attempt to encourage them to oppose the regime.[24] Technically this would not be a problem, since the existing equipment still had enough free capacity to establish a further short-wave station. After SOE, on the recommendation of Voight and Crossman, had given permission for the operation of the station, the 'Sender der Europäischen Revolution' began transmitting on the evening of 7 October 1940.[25]

From the very beginning it was planned on a larger scale than Hier spricht Deutschland . . . and was allocated more transmitting time (up to nine 20-minute programmes daily).[26] From the beginning, therefore, the regular staff included a great number of German emigrants. During the course of its existence the following belonged to the staff of the transmitting station – Paul and Evelyn Anderson, Karl Anders (alias Kurt Naumann), Fritz Eberhard, Julie and Waldemar von Knoeringen and Richard Löwenthal as well as Kurt Mandelbaum and Werner Klatt, the latter engaged on a freelance basis.[27] Almost all members of the team worked not only as announcers, but also as editors. Crossman, who had become a station head, together with Anderson and von Knoeringen, undertook the selection of suitable staff on an informal basis. Before the venture could really begin all the members of staff had to be vetted by the British Secret Service. Sender der Europäischen Revolution made it quite clear to its potential audience that they were listening to German Socialists. Its main thesis was that the 'problems on the Continent could be solved only by a revolution of the entire European industrial working class'.[28]

Although the station took neither a Communist nor a Social Democratic position, nor was trade union-orientated in the traditional way, its assignment was to appeal to a broad spectrum of the working population. SO1 presumed that many workers had lost all confidence in the traditional parties of the workers' movement as well as being disappointed by National Socialism. The British propaganda machine felt that it might be able to provide a new political direction for these sections of society, and that therefore the station's image should be European rather than internationalist. It was planned that the station should work independently at first, but that it should later work closely with other secret left-wing stations which were transmitting from England, France, Italy, Holland and Belgium.[29]

The setting up of these two stations furthered the main purpose of psychological warfare, that is, to weaken the enemy through the infiltration of material critical of the regime. It also proved to the War Cabinet that great advances were being made in the propaganda war against the Third Reich. (The significance of this proof, which justified its existence, was not underestimated by SOE.) In addition, the existence of these clandestine stations was a vehicle for the political ambitions of the British Labour Party leaders Voigt and Crossman. Voigt, who belonged to the right wing of the Labour Party,[30] carried on a vehement feud with Crossman, without the knowledge of their German staff, at SOE and later at PWE. In internal memoranda they accused each other (naturally without naming any names) of proceeding from false premises concerning the political and social situation in Germany, as well as of being unequal to the task of leading the stations either politically or organisationally.[31] It was a battle which Crossman finally won.[32]

When, on the other hand, one sees with what ambition, enthusiasm and courage both groups set to work, it becomes obvious that both the British and the Germans working in these stations hoped to achieve more than just the placing of a spoke in the wheel of Hitler's war machinery. Their ambitions and their hopes looked beyond the distant day of the War's end, believing that with this work they were making a positive contribution to a democratically-organised rebuilding of Germany.[33] A great number of discussion papers written by the group involved in Sender der Europäischen Revolution have been found. They include suggestions, designs and plans for a Socialist rebuilding of post-war Germany, but the Utopian nature of the majority of these papers is another story.[34]

The composition of the staff and the working conditions at Sender der Europäischen Revolution were ideal. Never again was the staff of a broadcasting station working for the Western Allies chosen according to political alignment and never again was a staff so homogeneous in its ideological composition. In the work of putting together programmes, the staff received a surprising amount of journalistic freedom. This was due, among other things, to the fact that until then the Ministry of Information (MOI) and the Ministry of Economic Warfare (MEW) had issued regulations only for the BBC and only editors working there had to keep to them.[35] For the first two secret radio stations these regulations initially did not exist. There was a certain framework within which the broadcasting station should function, but the German members of staff had been involved to a very great degree in the construction of the framework; this was their broadcasting station, on which they could express their political opinions. The fact that these same stations were also part of the British psychological warfare machine was at first subsidiary. Within this fixed framework, the German staff were subject to very few restrictions.

The two ministers responsible for these secret radio stations were too busy with an abundance of other tasks (which included the strengthening of their own positions) to supervise the two teams closely. SOE was involved in a feud with EH, and was trying to initiate new propaganda projects at the same time; Crossman and Voigt held the same political views as their respective members of staff so that (at the beginning at any rate) they saw no cause to interfere greatly in their work. Also, of course, they both had a great number of other tasks (for example, Crossman was a commentator with the German Service of the BBC). Additionally, both EH and SOE may have felt at the beginning that the opportunities for psychological warfare through the media of these two secret broadcasting stations were not great enough to make any closer involvement necessary.

The teams had no contact with each other. At first, some members of the staffs lived freely in London and later in Aspley Guise. They were, however, bound to secrecy concerning the stations and, in most cases, they honoured this in relation to politically like-minded colleagues and friends.[36] Every morning the members of staff met for editorial meetings in which the themes to be dealt with were discussed in great detail. Voigt or Crossman often took part in these discussions, in order to pass on information, advice and suggestions, sometimes also to make sure that regulations which had originated outside the teams were adhered to. They did not write any contributions themselves. All the texts were written and spoken in front of the microphone by the German members of staff.

According to Fritz Eberhard open censorship of the scripts did not take place. The staff of Sender der Europäischen Revolution often had to submit their reports or commentaries to their chief, Crossman, to be checked for correctness and suitability for propaganda purposes. Reports were never absolutely refused.[37] However, it was a standard rule during the War that broadcasts were never transmitted live, and this also applied to the secret broadcasting stations. They worked on the basis of mutual trust. It went so far that some members of staff were paid in cash by Crossman so that their fellow exiles would not suspect that they were working for the British Secret Service.[38] As far as access to information was concerned, the editors of Sender der Europäischen Revolution enjoyed privileges which no other staff of a secret radio station later enjoyed in this form. (The German members of the BBC staff too, did not have at their disposal such a mass of material at any other time during the War – at least officially.)[39] At this time they regularly received all obtainable German newspapers and magazines and the daily edition of the BBC-monitoring service. In addition – through Richard Crossman – they had access to the reports which were published by the Political Intelligence Department of the Foreign Office (PID). Through their personal contacts with various Labour ministers they were even partially informed about important proceedings in the War Cabinet.[40]

The rich flow of information and the freedom in the planning of the programmes was not to last long. With the tightening up of British propaganda operations and the establishment of both the British propaganda apparatus and the PWE, most of the privileges of the staff of the Sender der Europäischen Revolution came to an end. From the autumn of 1941 PWE published daily instructions, which often dictated in the most detailed terms the subjects and even the expressions which the broadcasting stations should use.[41]

Like Hier spricht Deutschland..., Sender der Europäischen Revolution saw its task as not so much in the transmission of news, which took up about a third of its broadcasting time, but in encouraging its listeners to resist the regime. It attempted to achieve this by analyses of the political situation, comments on current news items and calls to battle. Its most important statements may be summarised as follows:

— German fascism can successfully be fought and defeated by the united resistance of broad sections of the population and sabotage in the factories and in the transport system as well as by disobediences in daily life.
— Even before the German attack on the Soviet Union, the war was a lost cause, because of the military superiority of the West over the Third Reich. The sooner the war is ended the less blood will be on

German hands and the easier it will be to return to peace. Every means is justified to stop the German war machine.

— The absolute elimination of fascism can succeed only if it is desired by the whole of Europe. Lasting peace is thinkable only as the result of a 'European revolution' and not a purely national one. All European countries must eliminate 'capitalism and imperialism, nationalism and militarism', the true enemies of a dignified human existence.[42]

— The champions of the revolution can only be the industrial working class allied with the technical intelligentsia. In the Reich itself the natural allies of the workers are the foreign workers abducted from their countries and taken to Germany. The resistance movements in the German-occupied zones are a glowing example for the battle for freedom from National Socialism.

Furthermore:

— Sender der Europäischen Revolution and Hier spricht Deutschland... were the only broadcasting stations on British territory which offered their listeners a prospect for the future which was more than the punishment of war criminals and the occupation and demilitarisation of Germany. Apart from a number of social changes, a basic democratic model in the form of a soviet [council] system was to take the place of a parliamentary system which had become obsolete.[43]

— While the broadcasting station Hier spricht Deutschland... devoted itself mainly to home affairs, Sender der Europäischen Revolution gave much more time to questions of foreign policy. As a compliment to its host country, it showed great respect for the British democratic process.

— The staff set their hopes on the dissension which they expected between the armed forces (generally felt to have more integrity) and the party and state apparatus. The working class should, wherever possible, ally itself with the armed forces, without, however, letting itself be corrupted by them. The leadership of a possible rebellion against National Socialism should always be in the hands of the working class.[44]

— The station often reported on deeds of cruelty and massacres carried out by the SS and the Gestapo in the Reich or in the occupied zones, always finishing with the warning, 'German workers, always remember – all these crimes take place in your name – they take place in the name of the German people!'[45]

— As the editors saw themselves as 'independent Socialists' they took a critical view of other Socialists, especially of orthodox Marxist groups and parties. A favoured target for their criticism was the Soviet Union and here mainly the person of Stalin. They liked to call him the 'Bolshevist Chief' and said that his dictatorial misuse of power was in no way better than Hitler's.[46]

After the Nazi attack on the Soviet Union in June 1941 the broadcasting station had to change radically its attitude towards the USSR. They did not, however, do this immediately and then only under pressure from the British propaganda offices.[47] From the winter of 1941 all anti-Soviet polemic disappeared almost completely from their programmes. Eberhard reports that the Russian Ambassador had made several representations to the Foreign Office because of the criticism of the Soviet Union broadcast by Sender der Europäischen Revolution and had demanded that the programmes be stopped.

One can say that, in general, the political statements made by the station's journalists became more obviously careful from the winter of 1941/2. The influence of the newly-founded PWE and the resulting tightening-up and centralisation of planning and carrying out of psychological warfare gave the staff of Sender der Europäischen Revolution less and less scope for the production of anti-fascist programmes, which they had felt was their *raison d'être*. Their freedom of expression was subject to more and more restrictions; their access to information noticeably decreased. Increasingly, this station, with its decidedly political commitment, did not fit into the changing British concept of propaganda against the Third Reich. The promises of an independent self-determined future for Germany which the editors had been making up until then were no longer desired to be heard.[48] The German staff, however, did not wish their political and journalistic freedom to be restricted to the extent that PWE was now demanding. To be merely implementing the work of the PWE without the political line in which they believed was absolutely unacceptable to them. They preferred to take the risk of their station being closed down completely rather than produce propaganda in the style of the new black broadcasting station, 'Gustav Siegfried Eins'.[49] This rigid attitude rendered them intolerable to PWE.

The Soviet Ambassador's intervention accomplished one more thing; it speeded the decision to close down the station completely. Even Richard Crossman, who had risen to the position of leader of the German section of PWE, neither could nor would support the editors any longer. At the end of June 1942, after almost two years of activity,

141

Sender der Europäischen Revolution closed down without either comment or advance notice. Its staff was fired. Most of them, Anders, Anderson, von Knoeringen, Löwenthal and Klatt,[50] found other positions, at least on a part-time basis, with the German service of the BBC, where their main responsibility was for the production of programmes aimed at the working class and at prisoners-of-war.

It should be stressed once again that the initiatives for creating these first two British secret broadcasting stations did not come from the British alone. To a large extent, they originated in German émigré circles which were seeking, and finally found, a temporary partner for their ideas in the British. The establishment, laying down of conditions, as well as the choice of German personnel, was carried out by the British in the other German-speaking black and grey broadcasting stations to be discussed below.

# V

At the beginning of 1941 a man who was making regular contributions to the German Service of the BBC came to the notice of SOE. With his gruff diction and rough speech he had very quickly become famous in the Reich too. This author and speaker was Sefton Delmer, a former Beaverbrook journalist. Born in Berlin of British parents he spoke perfect German with a Berlin accent and knew Hitler and most other Nazi leaders personally from his time as a correspondent in Germany. SOE easily succeeded in recruiting this most valuable colleague for their work. The recruitment of Delmer as the future leader of all grey and black stations shows that British psychological warfare against the Axis was entering a new and active phase.

From now on, the broadcast war against the Third Reich was to become more effective since it was to be fought by professionals. Many organisational changes resulted from the tightening-up and centralisation of British propaganda during the winter of 1940/1. All non-British workers involved in black and grey propaganda, including French, Belgians, Dutch, Norwegians, Romanians, Czechs, Yugoslavs, Germans, Austrians and many more were moved out of London and brought to various houses (according to their nationalities) in Woburn Abbey, Aspley Guise, Simpson and other villages in Bedfordshire. They were not allowed to visit their families, who had to stay in London. They were not even allowed to leave the premises; a visit to the local pub was forbidden as was the private use of telephones and cars. Private visits to London were allowed only with the express permission of the respective British authority; permission for the train journey was not given unless the staff member spoke good English and was not conspicuous in any other way. Naturally, they were forbidden to speak to anybody about their work.[51] Obviously not all members of staff followed these orders. Spiecker and Kluthe from *Hier spricht Deutschland...* did not have to comply with these regulations, because by this time their station no longer existed.

SO1 converted a house in Waverdon (cover name Simpson, another village nearby), belonging to the Duke of Bedford, into a sound and recording studio in which, in future, all the programmes of the black broadcasting station were to be recorded so that they could later be brought to the actual transmitter.[52] The studio times were arranged so that members of the different teams, who were brought by car from their accommodation to the recording studios in Simpson by different routes according to exactly contrived plans, could never meet. Not only were the different nationalities kept apart, but teams who worked in the same language but had different political sympathies were not supposed to meet either.[53] (On one occasion when the French Socialist team (F2) met the Gaullist team (F4) in the studio in Simpson a fight broke out between the two groups which ended, however, with both teams accusing the British of deception, and F2 refusing to cooperate any more with 'perfidious Albion'.)[54]

The planning and leadership committees of the propaganda aimed at different countries were divided, according to nations, into sections, whose leadership was always in British hands. These national sections were made up of teams, or Research Units (shortened to RU), which then wrote and read the texts for their respective stations. The station itself was never known by its real name in internal transactions, but received a consecutive code number with a letter designating the language it was broadcasting (e.g. F for France, G for Germany and Austria, Y for Yugoslavia).[55]

There was a general rule in force that the staff of any Research Unit never learned of the existence of another RU unless it was an absolute necessity. Only with special permission from the highest security authorities and then 'only in especially urgent circumstances' was a member of a team permitted to be told the name of a colleague in another RU.[56] It is obvious, therefore, that these changed circumstances led to a severe restriction of the journalistic freedom previously enjoyed by the staff.

Not only was there a reorganisation of the administrative side of radio propaganda against the Third Reich, the content of the programmes also changed. Sender der Europäischen Revolution, which at this time was still active, had originally aimed its programmes at a left-wing public, at listeners who, because of their social status and tradition, sympathised with the SPD and KPD. It was felt by the British authorities that this was a public which would have been totally out of sympathy with Hitler and the NSDAP. Towards the end of 1940 this group still rejected, or at least was sceptical of, the Nazi system and the Party despite, or perhaps because of, its military success. The 'conservative' element in the German population, who would have had as much reason to distance themselves from Hitler and his clique, were served, at least until the spring of 1941, by the 'conservative' station Hier spricht Deutschland.... The large majority of the German people who applauded Hitler were not addressed at all. This enormous potential audience was now to become more important to British black propaganda.

The first two British secret broadcasting stations worked on the principle of honest propaganda, that is, the staff tried to convince the listeners of the justness of their convictions through the superiority of their arguments; they wanted to enlighten their public on the dangers of National Socialism, they encouraged them to criticise, both openly and secretly, and sometimes even to resist the regime itself. If the listeners were not opponents of the regime already the broadcasting station wanted to make them so. At the request of SOE this approach was soon to come to an end.

# VI

When Hier spricht Deutschland ... ceased broadcasting in March 1941 it became necessary to create a new station, again aimed at conservative and petty bourgeois circles in Germany. For reasons of internal politics, and so that there would be a proper balance, the Minister responsible, Hugh Dalton, ordered the establishment of a right-wing station to go with the left-orientated Sender der Europäischen Revolution.[57]

Sefton Delmer seemed to be the right man for this task. The clear intention right from the start was that Delmer, after the apparent failure of Hier spricht Deutschland ..., would no longer work according to the principle of 'convincing the public'. The first vehicle for this new policy was the black radio station he established, Gustav Siegfried Eins, nicknamed GS1, which listeners could interpret as 'Geheimsender Nummer 1' (secret transmitter number 1). Its internal code number was G3.[58]

With the creation of Gustav Siegfried Eins, German-speaking propaganda using lies and subversion as a means of undermining German morale at the front and at home took the place of 'honest' attempts at convincing the population of the danger of Hitler's plans: 'The Party leaders are corrupt, they live in luxury, they demand everything from ordinary people without making any sacrifices themselves'.[59] It was hoped that by revealing details of real or invented scandals the German 'man in the street' would be persuaded to try to follow the example of the Party chiefs. In this way SOE hoped to put a spoke in the German war machine's ideological wheel. It was no longer the aim of British propaganda to the Reich to encourage resistance among workers but rather to spread discontent. It wanted, in this way, to exert a destructive force on German discipline 'especially on the discipline forced on the ordinary person by the Party'.[60]

In his memoirs, Sefton Delmer describes how this was to be achieved: 'To stimulate the Germans into thoughts and actions hostile to Hitler before this stage had been reached they would have to be tricked'.[61] 'Convincing' propaganda came to an end with the start of transmission by Gustav Siegfried Eins on 23 May 1941.[62] All other British black broadcasting stations which followed used methods of consciously misleading, using half-truths and manipulation. The idea of 'never tell a lie' and 'honest propaganda' was left to the white broadcasting stations, that is, in Britain, to the BBC German Service alone.

A very important role in the deliberations leading to the establishment of Research Unit G3 was played by the fact that the Germans had a station already functioning in the summer of 1940 which was aiming its propaganda at the British working class (Workers' Challenge) and which enjoyed great popularity among the people. Its success must be attributed partly to the plain language it used – including slang expressions and obscenities. It was this language and content level which had proved to be so successful that the new British black broadcasting stations were to take it over.

The right-wing image of Gustav Siegfried Eins was established because Hugh Dalton, the MEW Minister in Charge, felt that this 'dirty work of manipulations and lies', although an effective method of psychological warfare, should not be carried out in the name of the labour movement or Socialism.[63] This style of right-wing gutter-press journalism also suited the personality and political convictions of Sefton Delmer, the head of this station.

Gustav Siegfried Eins worked according to the principle of a one-man personality show. Its hero was the Chief, assisted by an aide, whose task it was to announce and to end the programmes, as well as to read number and letter combinations aimed at confusing the Gestapo and SD. The whole sequence of the broadcast was put together in such a way as to frighten the listener. For its programmes, which were broadcast hourly between 5 o'clock in the afternoon and 4 o'clock in the morning for seven to twelve minutes,[64] Gustav Siegfried Eins used a signature tune (the first broadcasting station to do so) and even this was supposed to send a cold shiver down its listeners' backs. While the official Deutschlandsender used the melody of the first line of the song 'Üb immer Treu und Redlichkeit...' ('always be loyal and sincere'), Gustav Siegfried Eins answered with a second line 'bis an Dein kühles Grab...' ('until your cold grave'). The Chief himself then spoke to 'his people'. Delmer described his invention of the Chief as follows, 'a die-hard of the old Prussian school would use the transmitter to give the members of the organisation his caustic and salaciously outspoken views of what was going on. Views, which while being spiced with plenty of inside information, would show him as loyal and devoted to the Führer, but scathingly contemptuous of the "rabble" that had seized control of the Fatherland in the Führer's name'.[65]

The main target of his attacks was the Party bureaucracy and its clique of functionaries whom he described as 'lecherous, greedy, immoral, lacking in scruples and parasitical'.[66] He accused them of using the power given to them for their own base purposes, getting rid of their enemies by murder and slander. If they ever appeared at the Front they behaved like cowards. They used their connections with the Party to further their own careers. One of these career-minded people was, for example, Field-Marshal Rommel, the stooped, incapable SS protégé. The Chief never grew tired of these descriptions.[67] The Nazi organisation he hated most was the SS, that 'gang of criminals' under the leadership of 'pale Heinrich with the pince-nez', whom he loved to call 'looters, war-profiteers and pompous arseholes'.[68] The Chief left out Hitler and Göring from his attacks at first, presuming correctly that too many Germans still identified themselves with them. From September 1942, however, he began to attack Hitler himself, at first indirectly, by describing him as a sick, badly-advised man who had fallen under the influence of his SS clique. The statements culminated in the demand that 'Germany needs a competent military commander-in-chief'.

The totally destructive line of the Chief's propaganda was also obvious when he devoted a great deal of his time to both praising and defending officers like Rundstedt, Kesselring, Halder and Thomas, defending them from the *Parteikommune*. However, he then gradually began to point out to his listeners that the old Prussian virtues had no chance against the ruthlessness of the NSDAP and the SS. These heroes, formerly so highly praised, suddenly appeared either as losers down on their luck or in the more miserable role of being politically and morally impotent.

In order to attract his public, Gustav Siegfried Eins presented the whole range of 'Great German' and reactionary prejudices: the French were lousy soldiers and seducers, the Italians were the most dreadful and cowardly comrades, he called Jews sub-human and bastards and spoke of the Soviets as a barbaric red gang and man-eating Bolsheviks (which did not stop the Soviets from establishing their own station based on Gustav Siegfried Eins, 'Sender der SA-Fronde' with the SA man Weber as the main figure, in the same year).[69]

The Chief never attacked institutions and values directly; he discredited them by slinging mud at people who represented them, always calling these people by their full names. It was part of his technique to use so many details, dates and names in his reports that it became impossible to assess how much truth there was in one piece of news. His reports were never completely invented and always contained a grain of truth. Every broadcast was devoted to one theme only, which was presented in the most glittering and brightest colours possible. News, in the usual sense of the word, never featured.

Gustav Siegfried Eins did not become so popular solely because of its incredibly detailed knowledge of happenings in the Reich and its inside knowledge of events in the troops. The Chief gained his great reputation through being the 'pornographer of the air'. 'Sex and violence' was the recipe according to which the staff put the programmes together. They enjoyed uncovering and describing in obscene detail scenes from the private lives of Party and SS functionaries; scandals, sexual passions and aberrations, corruption and ruthless battles for personal gain made up more than three-quarters of the whole broadcast. All this was transmitted in crude and rough language, words such as 'pig' and 'shit' being among the milder expressions used. While today's audiences are used to such expressions, to hear such words on the radio in 1941 must have been shocking. Even the British found this 'scandal-sheet of the air' embarrassing sometimes – as, for example, when the Intelligence Department of the Foreign Office described its crude expressions euphemistically with the words 'uses very plain and original language'.[70] The American monitoring service FBIS got round this problem elegantly by having monitors omit all the obscenities, substituting (in the English translation) all four-letter words either with empty brackets or the addition 'follows a very dirty word'. Gustav Siegfried Eins became a 'peep-show of power politics' for the FBIS, who could not believe that the puritanical British were responsible for it, even though soundings proved that it was situated on British terrritory.[71] With a show of moral dismay the American monitoring service analysed the broadcasting station and its possible public as follows: 'For a man speaking, at least by implication, for decency, honour and law, the Chief talks with devastating frankness about sex, crime and repulsive disease. His is a kind of vulgar radio literature which continues a tradition of effective literary trash. His broadcasts resemble the shoddy pamphlets and books in which the depravities of courtiers, monks and secret societies were sensationally "revealed" to a curious and ignorant public. This public was composed of political illiterates rather than of responsible citizens. Similarly, in Germany today where the participation of the masses in politics is confined to passive acceptance of decisions made on high, the Chief's broadcasts offer a vicarious participation in the "real" life of the powerful. For this reason, the Chief is possibly quite successful among listeners of inferior status and power, and he may generate in them a blind hatred for certain sections of the German ruling class. In the long run, his propaganda probably will not build any constructive ideology or organised opposition, but rather nihilism and anarchy'.[72]

At the beginning all the work was done by three people. In the first three weeks of the existence of G3 Sefton Delmer, undeniably the boss of the whole undertaking, wrote most of the texts for the Chief himself. He could not read the texts, however, because he was known by name to German listeners as a regular commentator for the BBC German Service. Had he done so, the myth that the broadcasting station was a purely German undertaking based somewhere in the Reich would have been uncovered. In his broadcasts, the Chief made several statements which were meant to support the story. Especially after the beginning of the Russian campaign he tried to convince the listeners that the station was somewhere on the Eastern Front, complaining bitterly the whole time that his broadcasts were being continually blocked by the Russians and Germans.[73] The German defence system had, of course, quickly discovered the approximate location as being in the Oxford-Cheltenham area.[74] They could not very well publish this piece of information, as it would only have created even more publicity for the Chief.

In his memoirs, Delmer names Paul Sanders as the voice of the Chief and a certain Johannes Reinholz as his aide.[75] Delmer, however, used pseudonyms for both. The real people were Frank Lynder as announcer and Peter Secklemann as the voice of the Chief.[76] Both were involved later in writing the broadcasts after Delmer had carefully briefed them. Secklemann was mainly responsible for the fruity language and Lynder more for the clever combination of truths and half-truths. All the information they needed for this work was passed to them directly by Delmer who, after agreement with his own superiors at SOE and later at PWE, had sifted out what was necessary. He decided what themes were to be dealt with and was given the relevant texts to be checked before Lynder and Secklemann could go to Simpson to record the programmes. If the texts did not seem good, or 'hot' enough, Delmer wrote strong comments on them, improved them or completely rejected them. Delmer himself had all the say in questions of content, editorial work and politics: 'The Germans . . . would say and do what you tell them to say and do. No more nonsense about freedom and independence'.[77]

Lynder and Secklemann had already learned obedience. Both had had to flee from Germany to England before the War, more because of Hitler's obsession with racial problems than for political reasons, and at the beginning of the War they were members of the British Pioneer Corps, as were many other refugees. It was there that SO1 and Delmer came across them and engaged them, after the usual check by the secret service and a test of their suitability for black propaganda purposes. With them a new type of broadcaster entered the scene in the psychological battle against the Third Reich. Neither of them were committed anti-fascists, as von Knoeringen or Eberhard were. For them the work at SOE was a welcome change from the dull service with the Pioneers. They were faced with an exciting task, and that they could also thereby harm Hitler was, of course, 'fantastic'. Neither of them had tried to become involved in, or applied for, this work. They belonged neither to a political party nor to any other organisation and possessed no experience in the field of political warfare.[78] Because of this, they did not demand any journalistic freedom and did not run the risk of being censored because of some political slip of the tongue. Their wish was to fight Hitler; how was initially totally irrelevant, or only a secondary consideration. In a word, they were the ideal members of staff for the purposes of SOE/PWE and Delmer.

Soon Delmer, Lynder and Secklemann could no longer deal with all the work that had to be done. There were personnel and factual archives to be planned, as well as newspaper material to be looked at and catalogued. With the growing confidence that Delmer had in them and their work, they were also allowed to see the regular reports of the British secret service. When the black broadcasting stations G5 ('Wehrmachtssender Nord'), G6 ('Astrologie und Okkultismus'), G7 ('Christus König') and G8 ('Arbeitssender') started to broadcast in 1942, they also had to work there. In return, members of the new teams helped both of them in writing scripts for the Chief.

Important material concerning the response to Gustav Siegfried Eins in the Reich was provided by the British consulates in Lisbon, Berne and Stockholm. Besides newspapers and magazines, secret information (for example, about meetings with business people) as well as reports on agents and defectors came out of these consulates. Sometimes they even made suggestions for scripts, as for example in the case of the British consulate in Stockholm, which employed the German refugee Werner Lansburgh. On the basis of newspaper analyses which he had to make there and of rumours from Germany which were collected in the consulate, he wrote drafts of stories for Gustav Siegfried Eins which were then sent on to Woburn Abbey where they were developed into broadcasts.[79]

Delmer and his staff felt themselves to be especially successful when Hans Fritzsche himself, the German chief commentator, dealt with Gustav Siegfried Eins twice in July 1942 in his regular broadcasts on the Reich radio, pointing out that this was an 'especially perfidious example of an English enemy radio station'.[80] It had very soon earned the name 'mucky station' among the German people and the troops because of its partly obscene content.[81] The listeners seemed to enjoy hearing the Chief, either in spite (or precisely because) of his vulgar way of expressing himself, and many apparently believed that his reports about the conditions behind the scenes in the Party and Reich were true. Through systematic questioning of prisoners-of-war in 1943, the British were sure that Gustav Siegfried Eins was very popular in the Reich and at the Front.[82] Because of this the station was a headache for the German authorities; it headed the list of enemy transmitters to be jammed[83] and they even considered the advisability of answering the Chief's comments directly, as the following document from the High Command of the Baltic Navy proves: 'Since these broadcasts are presumably being listened to by many Germans, despite the fact that this is strictly forbidden, and because the facts at first sound very credible to most of the listeners who are very receptive, accepting this sort of rumour uncritically and being easily impressed by them (thus, unlike most of the other obvious propaganda methods of the enemy, this station is very dangerous) – the High Command recommends countering its actions. This could be done in such a way that immediately after each of these broadcasts a counter-broadcast follows on the same wavelength without a break and ridiculing the preceding comments in a similar tone'.[84] This suggestion was, however, never carried out. It would have been the best of all possible reactions which Delmer and his team could have wished for.

However, by carefully questioning prisoners-of-war, the British soon found out that the majority of the listeners had seen through Gustav Siegfried Eins' cover of being a German transmitter and had recognised it as a British propaganda radio station. Although they did not take its comments very seriously, this did not prevent them from listening to it for their own entertainment. In the spring of 1944 Gustav Siegfried Eins, which until then had been the best-known of all secret stations, was closed down, because, as was noted at the time, 'it has blown its cover by its success'.[85] Apart from that, a number of other black stations had started broadcasting, some of them with a similar degree of success.

## VII

With the foundation of the Political Warfare Executive in the summer of 1941, British radio propaganda for the continent dramatically increased its output. At the height of psychological warfare, from the middle of 1943 until the end of 1944, PWE maintained up to twenty-three Research Units in various languages from Woburn Abbey, with only four short-wave transmitters.[86] Of these twenty-three, only eight were in German. None of these black broadcasting stations enjoyed the freedom which the first two German-speaking stations had had. Their task was only to carry out orders and the staff was subject to a very strict policy which was seldom its own.

The political aims of the British differed considerably from those of the national staff members of the new black station Christus König which started broadcasting religious propaganda to Germany on 19 September 1942 and continued for two and a half years.[87] Its planners and staff were confronted with a number of complicated problems.

151

From the very beginning, the question of whether religious themes should be used at all in propaganda was debated in the relevant British circles. On the one hand, it was believed that religious themes could be used as effective propaganda subjects; on the other hand it went against the grain, from a religious point of view, to use such themes in war, be it only a radio war. In January 1940 the Religious Broadcasting Department of the BBC[88] had already suggested transmitting church broadcasts to Germany, on condition that only religious topics (and under no circumstances political questions) be touched upon. With an eye to the possibility of the War being a long one it was important to begin religious broadcasts immediately, otherwise it could be said that the British were misusing religion for political purposes. Both PWE's predecessor EH and the BBC rejected such broadcasts as being politically unwise, although they tried at the same time to work out possible models and to make suggestions on how to present effective religious propaganda. Hitler, therefore, should not be presented (as was later the case) as the Anti-Christ. Neither should one, under any circumstances, employ such expressions as 'heathen' or 'agnostic', since one could also regard Goethe or Kant, in the broadest sense, as such. In order to show that National Socialism also manifested religious traits – albeit false ones – expressions such as 'substitute religion' should be used.

Propaganda using religious themes could only be imagined, if it should ever be used at all, as propaganda for 'conservative' groups. Precisely this argument was taken up by a number of members of the leading bodies responsible for psychological warfare. They maintained that official British white propaganda, put out by the BBC, as well as the black and grey varieties, were based upon false premises in that they assumed that only the German working class was capable of getting rid of the National Socialist regime. This view of the situation was much too narrow. Wider sections of the German public should be made the target of radio propaganda, which should try to reach the 'mass of loyal, patriotic and moderate Germans', the greater part of which were the thirty to forty million German Catholics. The actual wording on this subject contained in a memorandum dated 1 February 1940, from T.F. Burns, leader of the Catholic Section of the BBC, was as follows: 'One must make particularly sure in these broadcasts that the patriotic feelings of the Germans are dealt with especially accurately'.[89] All these were at the beginning little more than thoughts for memoranda. Only the German Service of the BBC occasionally transmitted broadcasts with a religious content, especially on High Church holidays. It could, therefore, be maintained with a clear conscience that officially there was no propaganda with religious and Christian content. Religion was only mentioned in so far as the programmes rightly claimed that National Socialism was not compatible with true Christianity.[90] The British would have preferred to carry on in this way. Religious propaganda was much too sensitive an issue to be left to those in charge at Electra House or at SOE.

Circumstances began to change in August 1940 when the Germans tried to reach the British public with the black broadcasting station 'Christian Peace Movement'. This station, whose speaker posed as a priest, tried to get through to its listeners using their understandable wish for peace. Peace could begin tomorrow if only the British people would refuse to obey 'Churchill, the incarnation of evil, who began this war in the interests of a godless aristocracy'. Using a number of Biblical quotations, the Christian Peace Movement tried to prove that Germany was waging 'a just war' against the powers of evil, which wanted to destroy it.[91]

With the appearance on the scene of this station, the taboo on the use of religious themes for propaganda was broken. It strengthened the case of those on the British side who thought that it was also necessary to fight with a 'Christian black station'. The fact that such considerations were not acted upon immediately was due not only to the low level of organisation in the British propaganda machine, but also to the fact that too many people who, up to that point, had had nothing to do with psychological warfare felt themselves competent to intervene in the planning of such a radio station. The Catholic Church, for example, not only wanted to be informed in detail of all movements in this direction, but also wanted to be substantially involved in the event of such a station being set up. This was totally unacceptable to those working secretly for psychological warfare.[92]

When Gustav Siegfried Eins began its work in May 1941, aiming its programmes at a more conservative public, SOE felt that it was no longer necessary to establish another broadcasting station aiming at a Catholic audience. Nevertheless, plans to use religious motifs in radio propaganda continued, plans in which various bodies were involved, but at no point were German refugees asked to help. Only one individual suggested that the responsibility for such a station should be put in the hands of a committee made up of Church representatives and German and Austrian refugees, and that was George Bell, the Bishop of Chichester. He suggested Dr Schütz and Dr Müller-Sturmheim, among others, as possible members of this committee.[93] It was probably the fact that the Bishop had omitted to suggest either members of the BBC or leading members of the black propaganda organisations as committee members, that led Richard Crossman, head of the German section at SOE, to recognise that the suggestion was unfeasible, and he indignantly rejected it.

Long before it was at all clear if and when such a station as Christus König would be set up, all the bodies involved were thinking about possible speakers and staff. T.F. Burns, from the Department for Catholic Broadcasts in the BBC, imagined a future member of staff as follows: 'Only those who are filled with a true Christian feeling can become speakers and staff members – those who are Christian and humanist and conservative in the true sense of the word – not extremists or orthodox believers in any party sense – they must also come from spiritual or cultural spheres . . . the choice of staff must lie in pure and healthy hands.'[94] That the choice of staff eventually landed in the hands of Sefton Delmer is a stroke of irony. Indeed, it was pure luck that those finally chosen did fulfil all the requirements. The suggestion list for future members of staff included such illustrious names as Father Friedrich Muckermann, who had been a respected theologian and well-known speaker in church broadcasts during the Weimar Republic in Germany, and Father Leiber, German speaker for Radio Vatican for many years.[95] Both refused the task, partly because they would have been too well-known in the Reich for such an undertaking and partly because they had scruples about working under the direction of Sefton Delmer and in a team using his style of work. It had been clear from the spring of 1941 that a religious RU would be led by Delmer.[96]

The Bishop of Chichester repeatedly argued that not only the reading of religious texts, but also the writing of them, should be done by German and Austrian refugees because they alone knew 'with what spiritual attitude one could deal with Germans, what form of address to choose and how to bring in German tradition and history'. He suggested Sebastian Haffner as someone who possessed the necessary integrity and knowledge.[97] This suggestion, however, like most of the others which had come from the church, found no response in those chiefly responsible for psychological warfare. As far as black propaganda was concerned, Church representatives were gradually excluded from the planning since the leaders of psychological warfare felt it was not their task to carry out revival work in Germany, as the Catholic Church seemed to want, but to spread subversive thinking, for which any means were justified.

By the middle of 1942, four Research Units were broadcasting in

German under the direct leadership of Sefton Delmer (G3, G5, G6 and G8). The idea which Goebbels had also had, for Britain, that there should be a secret station designed for each of the large sections of the population, had become popular at PWE. Preparations for the planning and the technical side of the running of a black radio station posing as a religious one were more or less finished by June 1942. From the fact that the planned station was given the code name G7 – numbers were allocated according to the sequence in which the stations were put into action – it can be seen that the search for suitable staff had been more difficult than previously expected, so that G8 (the workers' station) could begin broadcasting only on 16 June 1942.

PWE and Delmer finally chose as the sole speaker and writer a young Austrian refugee called Elmar Eisenberger. While Delmer writes that Eisenberger had been a real cleric, a father in a holy order,[98] Lynder maintains that he was only a member of a worldly Maltese order.[99] Who had actually suggested Eisenberger for the work, or rather the manner in which he was recruited into Sefton Delmer's team, cannot be ascertained. Once engaged, he seemed to have adjusted to his task extremely quickly, for just one week after his arrival at Woburn Abbey he had already compiled, written and recorded programmes for the radio station Christus König for several days. This fast and apparently smooth acclimatisation to the conceptions of PWE surprised even his superiors.[100] Thus Christus König began broadcasting Christian programmes on 15 September 1942. RU G7 was to become the longest-lasting secret station of British origin; it closed down on 29 April 1945.[101]

In Woburn Abbey Eisenberger had greater journalistic freedom than most of his German-speaking colleagues. Naturally the framework within which he had to function was given from outside through PWE; he had not been able to work on its creation. He wrote most of his scripts himself and the function of censor was carried out by Delmer. Eisenberger, who was treated with great consideration, could take it upon himself, for example, to reject scripts suggested to him by German members of other RUs if he thought that they were not compatible with his Christian tasks, which even in this work he felt to be important.

If the directives came from Delmer himself, however, even Eisenberger could not ignore them. Frank Lynder reports that there were often great battles over certain texts or statements which were meant to demoralise the German population. Eisenberger often suffered under the 'devilish' work required of him by PWE, for example, applying psychological and spiritual pressure to people even in their air-raid shelters, instead of comforting and encouraging them.

It was often the case that he had to read prayers which were not his, and which were anything but hope-giving. As a consequence of this struggle with his conscience he apparently even left his Order after the War.[102]

Contrary to the original plan, non-denominational propaganda stations aimed at both Protestants and Catholics were set up alongside Christus König. It was felt at this point that the Germans, especially the North German Protestants, were no longer suitable partners. They were thought to be incapable of gathering enough strength to develop a strong opposition to Hitler's regime. The original idea to aim above all at German youth was abandoned[103] in view of the massive and obviously successful influence exercised on them by Goebbel's Ministry for Enlightenment and Propaganda. Only the German Catholics remained. It could be assumed that they had resisted the temptation to support Hitler. They were among the few organised sections of the population which still had the chance of creating difficulties for the regime.[104]

The people who were directly addressed by Christus König as 'dear Catholics' were not only from highly-placed or intellectual circles. The planners of the station imagined their ideal listener as the 'simple man or woman' who went to Mass on Sundays, perhaps had relatives at the Front whom they worried about, and who were expecting comfort and consideration from the Church. On both a language and content level, the programmes were tailored to an audience in a small town or village, who had voted for the Centre or a regional party before the seizure of power. They would therefore be likely to have reservations about the Nazi Party, but strong connections to the Church and its institutions. The ideal listener was not an open enemy of the regime, but was someone who perhaps expressed his discontent in the intimate circle of friends and relatives. The broadcasts tried, above all, to reach a South German public, Bavarians and Austrians, who were to be strengthened in their separatist aspirations.[105] With its emphasis on Southern Germany, Christus König moved in the course of 1943 towards becoming a regional station for Bavaria and Austria. Delmer thought this policy was so successful that in December 1943 he suggested turning Christus König into a purely Austrian station. A 'left-wing worker, giving exact instructions for sabotage, and a middle-class civil servant preaching the merits of a constitutional state' should join the existing 'Catholic priest'.[106] This plan of Delmer's was not, however, put into action. Subsequently, the South German image of the station tended to diminish.

In language, style, pathos and composition, broadcasts by Christus

König always constituted a homogeneous whole. All contributions were of a largely religious nature. The language was full of Biblical quotations and kept close to a Biblical style.[107] The texts were in the form of a sermon and tried to link the happenings of the day, the problems and needs of the listeners to the very cleverly chosen Biblical quotation used to introduce the programme. News, even church news, was never a part of the programmes. Eisenberger often reported on the battle between the Church and Christians against the regime, but all this was embedded in the sermon. He hardly ever used the real names of people or places but preferred to present them to the listeners by means of Biblical comparisons, such as 'in this time of temptation', 'in this time of trial', 'our new Herod', 'Moloch', 'Baal', 'the worst of the godless', 'the godless prophet' and so on.[108] The speaker took on the role of the Good Shepherd who was worried about the spiritual well-being of his flock.

Each sermon lasted about six to nine minutes, followed by a prayer which summarised and intensified what had gone before in a brief and meaningful way. From the middle of 1943, the 'priest' gave thanks in his prayers in the morning programmes, that the listeners had survived the night unharmed by bombs. In the evening prayers, he asked for God's help that the listeners might survive the night. The transmissions ended with a hymn and the final saying 'Christ, the King, lives!' ('es lebe Christus der König!').

Christus König had a special position in the extensive British network of, at times, more than twenty black and grey radio stations, inasmuch as it was the only one whose propaganda statements were exclusively based on religious themes. Its assignment, to have a demoralising effect on the German population, was hidden behind an anti-fascist image which was compatible with its Christian convictions. Anti-fascism of this kind was no longer considered to be the most important element of radio propaganda. The Christus König station was the result of a policy whose only concern was how most effectively to disrupt the war machine in the Third Reich. The original mainspring and concern of the Sender der Europäischen Revolution had become a subsidiary matter under the leadership of Delmer at PWE. The question concerning those in charge of black broadcasting stations was not, 'How can Germany free itself from the yoke of fascism?', but rather, 'How can psychological warfare contribute to the Third Reich not winning the War?' If anti-fascist policies or programme content were, by chance, the result of these considerations, all the better. In any case, they motivated the German-speaking staff in their work. From the very beginning, anti-fascist policies were not considered in the planning of these broadcasting stations. They proved to be a hindrance in the political supervision of the staff and, unfortunately, not particularly successful with the German listeners.

When the German 'priest', as Eisenberger referred to himself in his programmes, repeatedly called on his listeners, in no uncertain terms, to resist the Party, State and Army, the appeals did not arise from an honestly-meant attempt to help the Germans free themselves, but were inspired by the British wish to weaken the fighting morale of the enemy on the battlefield, using all means at their disposal.

## Notes

1. 'OKW/WNV-Chi: Rundfunkpropaganda-Lagebericht, für die Zeit vom 28.5 – 4.6.1940', Berlin, 10.6.1940. Bundesarchiv-Militärarchiv Freiburg (BA-MA) RW 4/v.247.

2. 'OKW/WNV: Wehrmacht-Propaganda-Lagerbericht, für die Zeit vom 1 – 15.11.1940', Berlin, 21.11.1940. BA-MA RW 6/v.168.

3. 'OKW/WNV-Chi: Chi-Nachrichten, Rundfunkpropaganda-Lagebericht vom 1.3.1941'. BA-MA RW 4/v.249.

4. D. Lerner, *Psychological Warfare against Nazi Germany. The Sykewar Campaign, D-Day to VE-Day*, Cambridge, Mass./London, 1971, p. 285.

5. C. Cruickshank, *The Fourth Arm. Psychological Warfare 1938–1944*, London, 1977, pp. 62–3.

6. 'Political Warfare Executive, Preliminary Organisation', 10 February 1940, Public Record Office, London (PRO) FO 898/9, p. 203.

7. J.A. Cole, *Hier spricht der Großdeutsche Rundfunk*, Vienna/Hamburg, p. 164.

8. 'Propaganda in Enemy Countries', February 1939, PRO PREM 1/374, pp. 4–6.

9. 'PWE/Preliminary Organisation, 1.6.1940', PRO FO 898/1.

10. 'Ministry of Information, Propaganda relating to enemy and enemy-occupied countries', H. Dalton to Duff Cooper, 15 December 1940, PRO INF 1/893.

11. *Sunday Dispatch*, 26 November 1939; interview with R. Bauer, Washington, 8 December 1979.

12. E. Langendorf to Deutsches Rundfunkarchiv (DRA), 13 April 1976 and 28 March 1978.

13. See B. Bouvier, *Die Deutsche Freiheitspartei*, Frankfurt/M., 1978, p. 117.

14. 'Germany and occupied countries', memorandum, 14 April 1941, PRO FO 898/181.

15. See papers of C. Spiecker, Hauptstaatsarchiv, Düsseldorf, RWN 26.

16. 'PWE/Preliminary Organisation', memorandum, 6 September 1940, PRO FO 898/9, pp. 218–19.

17. See n. 1.

18. 'Hier spricht Deutschland . . .', broadcast of 24 July 1940, Papers of C. Spiecker, Hauptstaatsarchiv, Düsseldorf, RWN 26.

19. See n. 1.

20. *Ibid.*

21. See S. Delmer, *Black Boomerang. An Autobiography*,Vol. 2, London, 1962, pp. 37–8.

22. See W. Röder, *Die deutschen sozialistischen Exilgruppen in Großbritannien*, 2nd ed., Bonn/Bad Godesberg, 1973, pp. 184–5.

23. Letter from R. Löwenthal to DRA, 25 September 1979.

24. Questionnaire, Prof. F. Eberhard, Berlin, 20 December 1975.

25. 'Political Intelligence Department (PID), Research Units, Underground Broadcasting Stations', PRO FO 898/52, pp. 87–8.

26. 'OKW/WNV-Chi: Zusammenstellung ausländischer Rundfunksender, die Nachrichten in deutscher Sprache bringen, Stand 30.9.1941, vom 15.10.1941', BA-MA RW 4/v.305.

27. For the list of members of staff see, among others, Röder, p. 184; questionnaire F. Eberhard; letter, R. Löwenthal.

28. Papers of F. Eberhard, Vol. 1, Institut für Zeitgeschichte (IfZ), Munich, ED 117/1.

29. See n. 16.

30. Interview with F. Eberhard, Berlin, 28 February 1979.

31. See, among others, 'PWE/Germany and occupied countries', 14 April 1941, PRO FO 898/18.

32. *Ibid.*

33. Papers of C. Spiecker and F.Eberhard.

34. Papers of F. Eberhard.

35. 'Plans and Propaganda', PRO FO 898/4.

36. See letter from W. Auerbach in papers of F. Eberhard.

37. Interview with F. Eberhard.

38. *Ibid.*

39. Interview with Patrick Gordon-Walker, London, 28 April 1979.

40. Interview with F. Eberhard.

41. Letter from R. Löwenthal.

42. 'OKW/WNV-Chi: Rundfunkpropaganda-Lagebericht für die Zeit vom 23.2 - 1.3.1941', Berlin, 3 March 1941. BA-MA RW 4/v.249.

43. See Röder, p. 184.

44. 'On the wireless', papers of F. Eberhard, 18 May 1942.

45. 'Sender der Europäischen Revolution', broadcast of 27 February 1941, in *Seehausberichte*, Vol. 1, Part II, 28 February 1941, Sendungen Rundfunksender, Library of Congress, Washington, USA.

46. 'OKW-Chi: Chi-Nachrichten: Rundfunkpropaganda-Lagebericht für die Zeit vom 9 - 17.10.1940', Berlin, 21 October 1940. BA-MA RW 4/v.248.

47. Interview with F. Eberhard.

48. 'EH and SOE, Organisation, Policy and Aims', Memorandum, 25 February 1941, PRO FO 898/4.

49. Interview with F. Eberhard.

50. Information in BBC archives, questionnaire and other sources.

51. 'Special Security Precautions for Research Units', 26 July 1941, PRO FO 898/51, pp. 39–40.

52. 'Proposal for revised arrangements at Simpson', n.d., PRO FO 898/51, pp. 105–6.

53. 'Note on the Operation of PID Research Units', 4 October 1945, p. 1; PRO FO 898/51, p. 41.

54. *Ibid*.

55. 'RU Programme Procedure', 6 October 1943, PRO FO 898/51, pp. 390–1.

56. See n. 51.

57. R. Seth, *The Truth-benders: Psychological Warfare in the Second World War*, London, 1966, p. 55.

58. 'PID Research Units, Underground Broadcasting Stations', PRO FO 898/51, p. 80.

59. See Delmer, pp. 41–2.

60. Federal Communications Commission (FCC)/Foreign Broadcast Monitoring Service, '"Gustav Siegfried 1" (The Chief)', Special Report No. 15b, 28 August 1942, National Archives (NA), Washington, USA, Record Group 262.

61. See Delmer, p. 40.

62. See n. 58.

63. See Delmer, pp. 37–8.

64. 'O.V.: Mitschriften Geheimsender "GS1" vom 25. und 26.7.1941', BA-MA RW 4/v.252.

65. See Delmer, p. 42.

66. See n. 60.

67. FCC/Foreign Broadcasting Intelligence Service (FBIS), 'Clandestine Radio Stations', Special Report No. 58, 22 March 1943, NA, Washington, RG 262.

68. *Ibid*.

69. Fritz Erpenbeck, 'Hier ist der Sender der SA-Fronde . . .', *Beitr. z. Geschichte des Rundfunks*, Issue 8, No. 4, Berlin (East), 1974, p. 7.

70. See n. 58.

71. See n. 60.

72. See n. 67.

73. 'Report on the Operation of RUs', 11 October 1943, pp. 186–7; PRO FO 898/51, p. 7.

74. 'Stab WNV/Fu: Bericht über einen G-Sender', 19 September 1941. BA-MA RW 4/v.304.

75. See Delmer, p. 49.

76. Interview with F. Lynder, Berlin, 2 March 1979.

77. See Delmer, p. 38.

78. Interview with F. Lynder.

79. Letter, W. Lansburgh to DRA, 26 October 1979.

80. See n. 73.

81. American Friends of German Freedom, 'Inside Germany', No. 21, New York, February 1942, pp. 9–10; Eliasberg papers, Archiv für soziale

Demokratie, Bonn.

82. See n. 73.

83. 'Anlage zum Abkommen über die Zusammenarbeit des italienischen und deutschen Funkstördienst gegen die feindliche Propaganda, 30.1. – 4.2.1942.' BA-MA RW 4/v.305.

84. Oberkommando der Marine Ostsee (OKMO): Bericht über feindliche Zersetzungspropaganda, 30 July 1941. BA-MA RW 4/v.252.

85. Draft, 'On the work of Research Units', 15 November 1943, p. 160; PRO FO 898/51, pp. 157–62.

86. See n. 53.

87. See n. 58.

88. Memoranda of 31 January, 12 February and 28 March 1940, PRO FO 898/177.

89. T.F. Burns, 'Broadcasting to German Catholics', 1 February 1940, PRO FO 898/177.

90. Memorandum from R. Crossman, 24 June 1941, PRO FO 898/177.

91. 'Notes on Propaganda to Germany', 31 October 1942, p. 2, PRO FO 898/67.

92. Memorandum from R. Crossman, 5 July 1941, PRO FO 898/177.

93. See n. 90.

94. See n. 89.

95. *Ibid*.

96. Interview with F. Lynder.

97. Memorandum by the Bishop of Chichester for the Conference on Broadcasts to Germany dealing with Religious and Spiritual Issues, 30 July 1941, PRO FO 898/177.

98. See Delmer, pp. 122–3.

99. Interview with F. Lynder.

100. Memorandum from Mr Wilson, 26 September 1942, PRO FO 898/67.

101. See n. 87.

102. Interview with F. Lynder.

103. See n. 97.

104. Memorandum, 26 July 1941, PRO FO 898/177.

105. 'Catholic Broadcasts', memorandum, 8 November 1941, PRO FO 898/177.

106. Minutes of Black Meeting, PWE, 16 December 1943, p. 3, PRO FO 898/61.

107. See n. 67.

108. FCC/FBIS: transcript of shortwave broadcasts: Catholic Clandestine (German Priest), 13 July and 30 July 1943, NA, Washington, RG 262, Box 162.

# Michael Seyfert

# 'His Majesty's Most Loyal Internees'

*The Internment and Deportation of German and Austrian Refugees as 'enemy aliens'.*
*Historical, cultural and literary aspects.*

## I

In his autobiography, *The World of Yesterday*, Stefan Zweig describes the deeply disturbing effect which the news of the outbreak of war early in September 1939 had on him. He writes of his premonition that he and 55,000 other refugees from Germany, Austria and the Sudetenland would now be subjected to 'restrictions': '...it seemed unlikely that I would be allowed to sleep in my own bed that night. Again I had dropped a rung lower, within an hour I was no longer merely a stranger in the land but an "enemy alien", a hostile foreigner; this decree forcibly banned me to a situation to which my throbbing heart had no relation'.[1] Zweig, of course, was to experience neither these restrictions and the internment, nor the feeling of being excluded again, of not being wanted, which was soon to affect those refugees classified as 'enemy aliens'. At the beginning of 1940 he received British citizenship and, shortly afterwards, was able to leave Europe.

The experience of internment, the deportations overseas, the rapid reversal of this aspect of British policy on asylum as well as the cultural, artistic and literary achievements of the refugees from Hitler who were detained in camps have received scant attention so far in the research done on exile. Two contemporary investigations of British internment policy are in fact polemics against it, based on insufficient evidence because the authors lacked access to government papers.[2]

Some surveys[3] and articles on legal aspects[4] have appeared, and there have been marginal treatments of these topics in books which concentrate on other aspects of exile in Great Britain, or British politics during the war.[5] Since 1980, however, two books on this subject have been published: Peter and Leni Gillman's *Collar the Lot!* and Ronald Stent's *A Bespattered Page?*[6]

These books are based primarily on British government documents generally available in the Public Record Office. However, the majority of Home Office documents relating to the internment remain closed for an indefinite period of time and the Gillmans and Stent found – as did the author of this article – that even in response to special application, the Home Office allows only a very limited number of additional documents to be viewed. Thus, it is still not possible to reconstruct completely the decision-making process within the British government. But sufficient source material is available in accessible documents of the Foreign Office and the Dominion Office, in Cabinet minutes and War Office and Colonial Office records to make a reliable account possible.

## II

Contrary to the popular view, the British government was not totally unprepared for the problem of internment. The Committee of Imperial Defence (CID) had discussed it as early as 1923 and decided that, in the event of a future war, enemy aliens would be expelled and not interned in large numbers as they had been during the First World War. Only a limited number of places (about 5,500) for the accommodation of internees were to be made available for those foreigners who did not leave the country before the declaration of war.[7] At that time it was not possible to foresee that fifteen years later more than 50,000 refugees from Germany, Austria and the Sudetenland would be seeking asylum in Great Britain. The CID reacted to the changed situation by establishing a Sub-Committee on the Control of Aliens in War. The minutes of a meeting in February 1939 reveal that there was little doubt about the refugees' loyalty: 'While most of these refugees would be technically alien enemies, most of them can be presumed to be more favourably disposed to this country than to those they have been forced to leave'.[8] Nevertheless, the committee recommended that the War Office should have quarters prepared for

18,000 internees. This indicates the extent of the inconsistency marking internment policy in the next few months. On the one hand, it is stated that 'it is not proposed to undertake an automatic internment . . . immediately on an outbreak of war', but on the other, 'we concur with the Home Office view that some measure of general internment would become inevitable at a very early date'.[9] Only a few days before Britain entered the War, the CID resolved to distinguish clearly between refugees and hostile enemy aliens, to intern both groups separately and to entrust to the Home Office the administration of any camps which might be established for the internment of refugees.[10]

The documents from this planning stage of the internment show clearly that the Home Office was not in favour of a general internment such as had been carried out in France, for example. The Home Secretary, Sir John Anderson, gave explicit reasons for his attitude in a letter to the Foreign Secretary Lord Halifax on 7 November. He emphasised that:

> It was felt that any wholesale measure of internment would be an inappropriate method of dealing with the problem, both because it would be a wasteful method and because it would be wrong to treat as enemies refugees who are hostile to the Nazi regime, unlikely to do anything to assist the enemy and often anxious to assist the country which has given them asylum.[11]

Even before the War broke out, MI5 had been authorised to arrest all suspect enemy aliens as soon as hostilities began. The reliability and loyalty of the others were to be examined by special tribunals and, if suspicions remained, the persons concerned were to be interned. If the verdict was positive they were to remain free.

Even these proceedings, however, were plagued by mistakes and misunderstandings. For example, MI5 included among those classified as 'dangerous' Eugen Spier and Alex Natan, both of Jewish origin and both antifascists who wrote detailed accounts of their experience of internment.[12] Spier reports that after his arrest on 1 September 1939, he was taken to the Olympia exhibition halls in Kensington, which were being used as a collecting point, and designated 'Prisoner of War No. 2'. There he encountered former Nazis like Hitler's friend Ernst (Putzi) Hanfstaengl and Captain Fischer, Himmler's predecessor as Head of the Prussian Secret Police, as well as opponents of National Socialism such as Edgar Stern-

Rubath, who had been Stresemann's secretary, and Bernhard Weiss, former Deputy Commissioner of the Berlin Police who was wanted by the National Socialists. According to Spier, Jews and antifascists were in the minority, and they were insulted and threatened by their fascist antagonists.[13] Natan reports that forty-one prisoners spent the first days of the War at Olympia, joined later by thirty-seven crew members of a captured German merchant vessel.[14] Olympia was only a reception camp, and the internees were transferred to a closed-down British holiday camp at Clacton-on-Sea. Stern-Rubath writes in his memoirs:

> Of course, everything which was not absolutely necessary, including bed linen, had been removed, and it was surrounded by barbed wire and guards. A military commander, stiff as a poker, had had all dangerous instruments, including pocket knives, razors etc., removed from us, so that after a few days, we looked like unshaven tramps.[15]

During the first few months of the War, 112 tribunals, most of them chaired by a member of the legal profession, screened more than 73,000 Germans and Austrians all over the country. The majority were refugees, some were old-established residents, and others owed their presence in Great Britain at the outbreak of war purely to chance. The tribunals had been issued with guide-lines for their operation by the Home Office. They were to classify enemy aliens in three categories. Category A was for those whose loyalty was suspect, which indicated that they represented a potential security risk and resulted in immediate internment. Category C was for those whose reliability was not in doubt. People in category C were subjected only to the same restrictions which applied to aliens in peacetime. Category B was an intermediate one which involved neither internment nor complete freedom from restrictions (such as stricter rules for registration). In addition, the tribunals had to decide who were to be classified as 'refugees from Nazi oppression'. Of the 73,800 aliens screened, less than 1 per cent were interned and 64,200 were put into category C.[16] Not all of the tribunals displayed an understanding of the refugees' position, or were fully aware of the political situation in fascist Germany. Thus some put everyone into category B, which later made renewed screenings necessary. Communists, Socialists and veterans of the Spanish Civil War sometimes suffered discrimination and were interned as a security risk. The case of the economist Jürgen Kuczynski, who was put into a camp in January 1940, is one example.[17]

There were denunciations, too. Kurt Hiller reports that the German Communist Party (KPD) in exile, assisted by a woman staff member of the Czech Refugee Trust Fund, sent denunciations to some of the tribunals' chairmen, accusing no less than seventy refugees (including Hiller) of being Gestapo agents during their exile in Prague.[18]

Many who were interned at this stage were put into a closed-down Warner's holiday camp in Seaton, Devonshire. Contrary to the original intention antifascists had to share this camp with interned National Socialists. Kuczynski reports that the prisoners were able to earn some money by carving shuttles for weaving. According to his description, the Communists dominated the organisation of camp life. 'We set the tone in the camp; we controlled the most important jobs, and we were the ones who represented the interests of all the internees to the English armed forces guarding us.'[19] The inconsistency in the internment of some of the refugees put into category A is illustrated particularly clearly by the case of Sebastian Haffner, who was interned at Seaton in February 1940. During his stay there, his book *Germany: Jekyll and Hyde* was published in London. In it, he sharply criticised the mass internment of German and Austrian refugees in France and advocated emigrants taking an important part beside the Allies in the struggle against National Socialist Germany. Shortly thereafter the House of Commons declared Haffner to be giving important support to the Allied war effort, but he had to remain in the camp until the end of April. He was released with the assistance of his publisher – only to be returned later during the general internment.[20]

## III

With the German occupation of Denmark and Norway in April 1940, Britain's position in the War deteriorated markedly. Within the military leadership, in Parliament, in the Cabinet and in the press unmistakable warnings were heard about a Fifth Column which could come to the assistance of the Germans in the event of an invasion of Britain. On 4 May 1940, the British Chiefs of Staff accepted the views of the Joint Intelligence Committee which coordinated work done by the secret service, and advised the Cabinet and the General Staff. The Chiefs of Staff decided that the British Union of Fascists, Communists, the IRA and, above all, aliens represented a security risk, and recommended that 'adequate steps' be taken.[21] The newspapers owned by Lord Rothermere (*Daily Mail*, *Sunday Despatch*) and the Kemsley group (*Daily Sketch*, *Sunday Chronicle*) had followed the rise of fascism in Germany during the 1930s with undisguised sympathy, thus providing publicity for Mosely's British Union of Fascists. Now they turned their readers against the refugees. An article by Ward Price in the *Daily Mail* on 20 April 1940 is typical of this sort of agitation:

> Act! Act! Act! Do It Now! The rounding up of enemy agents must be taken out of the fumbling hands of local tribunals. All refugees from Austria, Germany and Czechoslovakia, men and women alike, should be drafted without delay to a remote part of the country and kept under strict supervision.[22]

The results of an opinion poll showed that the public mood towards the refugees was already very negative among the middle and upper classes by the end of April 1940. The press campaign was having an effect, and it had become almost socially acceptable to be anti-refugee.[23] The press campaign being waged against the immigrants became so aggressive during the following weeks that the Ministry of Information stated in a confidential memorandum that local governments and refugee committees were disturbed by the increasingly antisemitic attitudes which they could observe among the general public.[24]

The Home Secretary at the time, Sir John Anderson, is usually held responsible for the mass internments which soon followed. Peter and Leni Gillman, and Ronald Stent, however, refute this widely-held assumption. The Gillmans discuss the altercations between the Home Office and the War Office, the Chiefs of Staff and the Joint Intelligence Committee, in which the Home Office eventually had to yield, but not without delaying proceedings and even taking recourse to obstructionism.[25] In the first Cabinet meeting presided over by Churchill as Prime Minister on 11 May 1940, a strip of land along the eastern and southern coasts was declared a Protected Area. Anderson had to concur in the internment of all male enemy aliens between sixteen and sixty years of age in this area, regardless of the category into which they had been put. About 2,000 refugees were taken into custody by the police during this mass round-up, and handed over to the military authorities for internment.

Only a few days later, on 15 May, the Netherlands capitulated. The British Minister to the Dutch government in The Hague, Sir Neville

Bland, was able to escape to England and reported that a Fifth Column which existed in the country had assisted German parachutists in the occupation.[26] Sir Neville Bland's report, in which he warned that no German or Austrian should be trusted, was broadcast by the BBC and provided politicians with solid arguments. Churchill now unequivocally supported internment:

> ...there should be a very large round up of aliens and suspected persons in this country. It was much better that these persons should be behind barbed wire, and internment would be probably much safer for all German speaking persons themselves since, when air attacks developed, public temper in this country would be such that such persons would be in great danger if left at liberty.[27]

On the next day the Home Secretary, Anderson, ordered the arrest of all male enemy aliens in category B. In a meeting on 15 May, however, the Joint Intelligence Committee decided that these measures were insufficient and demanded the internment of *all* enemy aliens between the ages of sixteen and seventy.[28]

Anderson was still against mass internment. His report, 'Invasion of Great Britain: Possible Cooperation of a Fifth Column', underlined the differences in the situations of Great Britain and Holland, and emphasised again that the majority of the 73,000 Germans and Austrians were refugees who were opposed to the fascist regime.[29] The relevant Ministry and Cabinet documents show that there was a faction in the War Office, Cabinet and the Secret Service which aimed to provide the government with an opportunity to assume extraordinary powers.[30]

The Home Office, however, still opposed mass internment. It was supported by MI5, which argued that all suspect aliens had been taken into custody or interned by the tribunals on the outbreak of war. However, an insignificant espionage affair[31] which did not involve any refugees at all weakened the position of MI5 and the Home Office to such an extent that Anderson concurred in the arrest of all British citizens who were in any way prominent within the British Union of Fascists. Whereas enemy aliens could be arrested without a court order under the Royal Prerogative alone, British citizens could only be arrested on the legal basis of the emergency legislation.[32] According to the Gillmans, the War Office exerted so much pressure on the Cabinet through Chamberlain, Lord President of the Council in Churchill's government, that Anderson agreed to the arrest of all women in category B.[33]

Meanwhile, Great Britain's position in the War had become disastrous – Belgium had capitulated on 28 May, large contingents of French troops were surrounded by German units and the evacuation of the British expeditionary forces from Dunkirk was beginning. All this made an invasion of Britain itself seem more and more likely. The Chiefs of Staff again expressed their concern that the refugees were in a position to undertake subversive actions such as sabotage. On the same day, therefore, the Cabinet approved the proposal that Chamberlain should set up a committee for the preservation of domestic security. The result of Chamberlain's efforts was the creation of the Home Defence (Security) Executive under the chairmanship of Lord Swinton. As the Gillmans show, this committee had almost unlimited powers. With only one exception, no documents relating to its operations are yet available to the public. The minutes of one meeting, however, reveal the committee's membership.[34] Decisions about the question of internment no longer rested with the Home Office, but with 'a tiny body of men whose very existence was a secret, whose members were not responsible to Parliament or even to Cabinet, among whom MI5 and the War Office were in clear ascendancy'.[35]

The next step towards mass internment was not dicussed in the Cabinet, which indicates that the Home Defence (Security) Executive was acting entirely on its own responsibility. Thus on 31 May the regional police authorities received instructions to intern all aliens in category C whose reliability was in any way in doubt – thus leaving the police a completely free hand.[36]

The last stage of the mass internment was decided upon in a Cabinet meeting on 11 June 1940. On the previous day, the government had decided to imprison more than 4,000 Italians as enemy aliens after Italy's entry into the War. The military leadership and the secret service exerted such strong pressure that Churchill decided 'that as a general principle, we should endeavour to round up all enemy aliens as quickly as possible, so as to place them out of harm's way, and that we should subsequently examine individual cases and release those who were found to be well disposed to this country'.[37] But Anderson only informed the Cabinet ten days later that they would make as many arrests as could be accommodated. The Home Office's instructions to the police show that the first stage of the general round-up began on 25 June 1940.[38]

## IV

The internment measures now applied to almost all male refugees, 4,000 women in category B and several hundred children whom they had brought with them into the camps. Excluded were those under sixteen and over seventy years of age, as well as the invalid, the infirm, refugees who had an important function in the war economy and a few who were under the special protection of a government ministry.[39] But even here there were inconsistencies and misunderstandings and it soon became apparent that among the approximately 30,000 people interned, there were a certain number who, according to the authorities' declared intentions, should not have been put behind barbed wire at all.

For thousands of refugees, watching friends, acquaintances and relatives being arrested, and constantly expecting to be arrested themselves, these weeks were a difficult psychological test. The fear of uncertainty and the daily threat of separation are repeatedly expressed in the literary documents of those days. But the immediate difficulties of life as an immigrant, a life which was full of problems anyway, were not the only causes of distress. What was at stake was the refugees' whole position, their status and acceptance in their country of refuge which many already regarded as a new home. Max Herrmann-Neisse touched on this problem in his poem 'Wie lange noch?' ('How much longer?'):

> Als hätte ich mich frevelhaft vergangen,
> bin, ohne Schuld, ich peinlich in Verdacht,
> vielleicht im nächsten Augenblick gefangen
> und um den Schein an Freiheit noch gebracht,
> der Freiheit, derentwegen ich entsagte
> und mich der heimatlichen Hut entschlug,
> die Flucht in das mir Unbekannte wagte,
> der Fremde Unzulänglichkeit ertrug,
> um hier nun, in der Freiheit Mutterlande,
> in dem ich mich in Freundesland gemeint,
> zu meiner und der ganzen Menschheit Schande
> mißtrauisch gleichgesetzt zu sein dem Feind![40]

Most of the 'enemy aliens' were arrested at home, some even at work. Some attempted to delay or evade internment by leaving their homes very early in the morning and only returning in the evening. Soon the police made the rounds of the parks and visited the public libraries in which some of the immigrants spent their days.

The internees were first taken to the nearest police station or to a collecting point, and after being handed over to the military authorities, sent to reception camps. One of the internees describes his arrival at Kempton Park race-course which had been adapted for this purpose: 'While we were still detraining, we were roared at by a fierce sergeant.., told to "fall in by fours" and to hurry up about it.... From the railway platform to the race-course, i.e. to the camp, there is a covered walkway about 200 metres long – it seemed to me and all the others that we were running the gauntlet between two rows of weapons; every three steps, on both sides, a heavily-armed soldier...'.[41] After registration and a baggage check, the internees' passports and visas were taken away. This was a severe blow for many because during their years of exile they had come to know the vital importance of these documents and did not want to lose them under any circumstances. Their total isolation from the outside world was equally depressing. Receiving and writing letters was forbidden in the camps. It was often a week before families had any news of the internees and even this was only a signed official form. Because radios were not installed during the first weeks and no newspapers were available in the reception camps, rumours circulated about the war situation and a supposed German invasion, increasing the internees' anxiety.

The refugees spent only a short time in the reception camps before being transferred by rail or coach and under military guard to camps arranged by the War Office. Because all the relevant documents have not yet been released, it is not possible to make a list of all the camps, which ranged from Southampton to Knapdale in Scotland. Conditions in the camps varied enormously, from the tents of Prees Heath Camp in Shropshire to the terraced houses of a newly-built council estate in Huyton near Liverpool. Holiday camps, schools, army barracks, underground car parks, manor houses, shut-down factories and even the winter quarters of the Bertram Mills Circus were used. In addition, several camps were specially set up with wooden barracks and Nissen huts. Without doubt the worst camp was at Warth Mills in Bury, Lancaster, a disused cotton mill which lacked every necessity. Hans Friedmann kept a diary of his internment, and in it he describes his arrival at Warth Mills on 4 July 1940:

The factory buildings... are all at ground level, covered with broken, slanting glass roofs. . . . In front of a pair of barbed wire gates fashioned from beams, we come to a halt. In a dirty courtyard paved with worn-out cobble-stones, single figures move about and observe us through the fence. . . . Behind us lies a gloomy building several storeys high. Dirty, dank passages and slimy, slippery stairs take us to the first floor. What surrounds us is a weirdly dismal side-show set, and only the soldiers with bayonets at the ready provide a link with reality. A huge factory absorbs us. There too, the floor is covered with a slimy mess of oil and dirt. . . . A draught whistles through numerous blind, broken windows. . . . Puddles of water on the floor suggest that the roof leaks.[42]

The living conditions in this camp were certainly an extreme case, but there were also complaints and difficulties at other camps.

The majority of the 'enemy aliens' were accommodated in camps on the semi-autonomous Isle of Man, where civilian internees had been sent during the First World War. (There were several people who, like the journalist Heinrich Fraenkel, had been interned there before.) Camps on the island were in small towns, mostly along the coast, and consisted of terraces and squares, separated off by barbed-wire fences. The internees were housed in hotels and guest-houses which, in peace time, were frequented by holiday-makers. The owners, evacuated by the War Office, had locked their possessions in their attics and had left only the most basic necessities for the use of the internees – beds, sparse furniture and kitchen utensils. Hutchinson, Central Promenade in Douglas, Onchan, Peveril and Peel were male camps; female internees were accommodated at Port Erin and Port St Mary which together made up the women's camp Rushen. Unlike the men, the women received their meals from guest-house proprietors and had more freedom of movement. For many who had had to spend weeks in prison cells because of a lack of adequate accommodation, this was naturally an improvement. The camp almost completely incorporated the two small towns which had been surrounded by barbed-wire fences. The women had close contact with the Manx population (which of course was equipped with passes to allow freedom of movement) and were under the supervision of the matron-in-charge of the Red Cross, Dame Joanna Cruickshank.

The camps on the Isle of Man and those on the mainland were soon administered by the internees themselves, who elected spokesmen, *Reihenväter* (block fathers) and *Lagerväter* (camp fathers). (The use of the title *Führer* was, of course, strictly taboo.) These spokesmen represented the interests of the internees *vis-à-vis* the camp military command responsible for guarding the camps, counting the prisoners every morning and evening and making sure the black-out regulations were adhered to, etc. Prisoners were adequately nourished. In most cases they received the equivalent of army rations, and even Kosher food was provided to orthodox Jews.[43]

On the Isle of Man and in most of the mainland camps the refugees were soon separated from National Socialists and their sympathisers. Newspapers and letters – often held up for weeks by British censorship – now reached the internees, and a lively cultural life began to develop in the camps. Nevertheless, they were increasingly engrossed by two problems: securing their release, and the threat of deportation overseas.

## V

As early as 24 May, Churchill had remarked in the Cabinet that he strongly favoured removing all internees from the United Kingdom.[44] As the Home Defence (Security) Executive also began to press for the deportation of all civilian internees, Chamberlain initiated administrative preparations.[45] There are many Foreign Office and Dominion Office documents which show what efforts the government made to persuade Canada, Australia, New Zealand and Newfoundland (via their respective High Commissions in London) to accept civilian internees and prisoners of war. Canada initially replied in the negative and was won over only by dramatic representations of the dangers ostensibly posed by the prisoners remaining in Great Britain. The Canadian authorities saw admitting prisoners of war, as less of a problem than admitting civilian internees, which suggests that the British government supplied misleading information.[46] On 14 June the British government received confirmation that Canada would admit 2,633 German internees in category A, 1,823 prisoners of war, and 1,500 pro-fascist Italians.[47] Representatives from the War Office, the Foreign Office, the Canadian High Commission and MI5 participated in a Conference on the Move of Prisoners of War and Internees to Canada held on 17 June in the War Office, at which details were discussed. Sailing dates for the transport ships were decided upon, as were security measures and cooperation with the Canadian authorities.[48]

As the camp commanders began to look for volunteers and it became increasingly obvious that deportation was going to be compulsory, uneasiness spread amongst the internees. For some of the younger people without family commitments and ties, deportation seemed to offer some advantages – at least it would take them out of the path of a possible German invasion, which would have had the most dire results for the refugees. However, the majority did not want to leave Europe in this way, especially as it was uncertain whether their wives and children would in fact be able to join them overseas, as the government promised. Thus the possibility of deportation represented another severe psychological burden. It was not only the fear of being attacked by German U-boats during the voyage and the uncertainties posed by a long separation from family and friends which depressed many internees, but also the fact that they were to be forcibly driven out of Europe 'like a consignment of livestock' (A. Natan). When news reached them that the *Arandora Star*, a transport ship, had been sunk by a German U-boat on 2 July 1940 with the loss of more than 700 prisoners including not only Nazi sympathisers, as the government insisted at first, but also antifascists, deportation took on the dimensions of a very real threat to their continued existence. Frederic W. Nielsen heard of the sinking just before his own compulsory embarkation for Canada, and noted in his diary: 'We hear the news with horror, not only because of the danger which faces us . . . I am thinking of our relations, who, after this bad news, will be worried about every one of us . . . and then my thoughts go to the many defenceless and innocent victims who were sent to their deaths by a really criminal policy of internment and deportation'.[49]

The first ship taking internees to Canada was the *Duchess of York*, which put to sea on 21 June with category A civilian detainees and 500 prisoners of war. The *Arandora Star* followed on 30 June, bound for Canada and carrying 1,000 internees for Newfoundland. The sinking of this ship was one of the biggest shipping disasters of the War: of 479 Germans and Austrians, 175 lost their lives, and only 226 of the 712 Italians on board could be saved. On 3 July, the *Ettrick* set out with 1,307 category B Germans and Austrians and 407 Italians. The Polish ship *Sobieski*, which was under the control of the Royal Navy, followed on 7 July and took 983 Germans and Austrians of categories B and C, and 405 Italians to Canada. By this time Australia had also declared its willingness to admit civilian internees. The troop-ship *Dunera* set out on 10 July with 2,288 Germans and Austrians of categories B and C, 244 of category A and 200 Italians on board – including all the survivors from the *Arandora Star*.[50]

During the voyage, friction developed between antifascists on the one side, and National Socialists and prisoners of war on the other. The guards usually expressed undisguised sympathy for the latter. Nielsen reports about his crossing on the *Sobieski*: '...captured German officers converse jovially, almost chummily, with the captain. The enemy, who is shooting at their fishing boats, bombing women and children, murdering their brothers and sons, is treated politely, charmingly...but the rest of us, who neither shoot, rob, nor murder, but are only simple people wanting peace and understanding – we are treated at best impartially'.[51]

The internees on the overcrowded troopship *Dunera* were treated particularly badly during the crossing to Australia. The guards were hostile and threatening to the prisoners, stealing the possessions which they had brought on board with them. These excesses were later strongly condemned by Parliament and punished by military courts, and those who had suffered losses were compensated. Max Zimmering's poem 'Die Luke' ('The Porthole') expresses the desolate mood of the prisoners penned below decks and suffering from lack of fresh air, exercise and food:

> Der Luke Kreis begrenzt die Welt, das Licht;
> Davor ein Menschenknäul mit hohlen Augen,
> In denen sich des Himmels Farbe bricht,
> Die sich verhungert an die Wolken saugen,
> Als ob der letzte Tag gekommen wär –
> Und durch die Luke siehst du nichts als Meer.[52]

In the Australian camps at Hay and Tatura, refugees were immediately separated from prisoners who were Nazi sympathisers, but it was months before the same conditions were provided by the Canadian authorities. The antifascists held in Canada repeatedly had to insist on their status as refugees from Nazi oppression and refuse any contact whatsoever with the representatives of the Swiss Protecting Power, who, on instructions from Berlin, offered the so-called 'German nationals' their support.

By the late summer of 1940, the call for release went up from the Canadian forests, the Australian desert, coastal villages on the Isle of Man and various mainland camps – and could no longer be ignored in London.

## VI

The sinking of the *Arandora Star* provided the critics of internment policy with strong reasons to press for a revision of government measures. Many people in Britain had only just become aware that thousands of refugees from Hitler had been interned and shipped overseas. When the mass internments began, it was mainly the unionised workers and Communists who opposed them, suspecting that this policy posed a threat to the bourgeois liberties of the British people too. François Lafitte is representative of this attitude. In his book *The Internment of Aliens* he writes:

> We cannot blind ourselves to the fact that an authoritarian trend has been developing recently in our home life, a trend which manifests itself not merely in the treatment of 'enemy aliens', but also in the indefinite detention in custody of British citizens without charge or trial, in attempts at widespread censorship of opinion...and in other ways. In this sense the 'enemy aliens' problem cannot be dissociated from the problem of the British community itself, in its struggle for personal liberty, democracy and a new order.[53]

Emigrants' organisations, refugee committees, Jewish and Christian religious communities, politicians of all parties as well as various public figures now demanded an immediate revision of internment policy and, at the same time, supported the interned refugees with relief funds and donations of goods.

Joining the Auxiliary Military Pioneer Corps was one way in which category C internees could secure their release, and more than 4,000 had availed themselves of this opportunity by the end of 1940. Interned women, however, were permitted to join the Auxiliary Territorial Service only from mid-1941 onwards.[54]

In Parliament too, voices were raised against the policy of internment. The government was severely criticised in long debates on 10 and 23 July and on 3 December. On 22 August, the Home Secretary, Sir John Anderson, explained in the House of Commons that mass internments had been carried out at the instigation of the military leadership. Although regrettable mistakes had been made, essentially the measures were necessary and had to be maintained for the present.[55] In view of the harsh criticism, the Cabinet decided that administration of the camps should pass to the Home Office, and that the War Office should only be responsible for their security. The Cabinet ordered that the necessary committees should be formed to advise the government on matters relating to internment, and these were set up by the end of July.

Sir Justice Asquith chaired an Advisory Committee which advised the Home Secretary on the general principles of internment policy. An Advisory Council chaired by Lord Lytton and under the control of the Foreign Office was to devote itself to the welfare of the internees and bind them closely to the cause they had in common with Great Britain. A separate committee chaired by the former British Ambassador to Rome was formed for Italian internees. In addition, the Dummett Committee was created to review the unsatisfactory classifications in category B.[56]

At the end of July 1940, the Home Office produced a White Paper detailing eighteen categories of internees to be released. The immediate reaction was critical, however, because it provided for the release only of internees who could be useful for the British war effort. Gerhard Leibholz's reaction was typical. In a letter to his friend George Bell, Bishop of Chichester, he criticised the new measures and drew a comparison with National Socialist Germany:

> The new regulation is based on the utilitarian principle to release a small number of refugees who might be useful to this country. No scope is left to deal with the case of internees according to their loyalty. In Germany of today the Jews, for instance, who are engaged in war work are being kept separated from other workers and wear an armlet with the inscription 'useful Jew'. Is this not the same principle?[57]

In August, the government's attitude towards the refugees relaxed. On 1 August, Churchill spoke in the Cabinet of Britain's more secure position which made it appropriate 'to take a somewhat less rigid attitude in regard to the internment of aliens'.[58] Because of public criticism levelled at the first White Paper, a second White Paper was produced, on the advice of the Advisory Committee, at the end of August. It contained an additional category under which people who had distinguished themselves by political or journalistic work in the struggle against fascism could also be released.[59] A newly-created body under the chairmanship of the former president of the International Court of Justice in The Hague, Sir Cecil Hurst, reviewed applications for release under this new category and made recommendations to the

Home Office. For the first time, this committee was assigned a commission of advisers, comprising German and Austrian Social Democrats and trade unionists.[60]

A revised and expanded version of the second White Paper was published as a third White Paper in October 1940.[61] Three further categories had been added and more followed which, however, were announced only in Parliament. Now the cases of artists, scientists and writers came up for discussion, as did those of students whose university education had been interrupted by internment. Those internees who had long been resident in Great Britain and others, who could not join the Pioneer Corps for health reasons, were also to be released. Numerous committees reviewed applications and petitions, and revised the original classifications. By mid-January 1941, nearly 500 government employees, semi-official and honorary advisers, had effected the release of 8,700 internees.[62] As early as October 1940, the Home Office had sent a Commissioner, Alexander Paterson, to Canada and in January 1941, Major Julian Layton travelled to Australia. Internees were to be recruited for the Pioneer Corps and applications for release were to be processed on the spot.

Refugee committees, emigrants' organisations, official British agencies such as the British Council, various religious communities and individuals continued to work for the welfare of those refugees who were still in camps awaiting release. Those who had been shipped to Canada and Australia had to stay in camps for many months, some even until the end of 1942, as no space on board ship was available to bring them back. As late as December 1941 the *Frei Deutscher Kultur-bund* (Free German League of Culture) was working actively for the release of interned antifascists, and sent donations of money and goods to the camps. A revue called *Eine Reise nach Castralien (A Journey to Castralia)* was performed shortly before Christmas 1941 in London for the benefit of the internees. It received a mention in *Zeitspiegel*, an Austrian refugee paper: 'The island Castralia is situated partly in the northern and partly in the southern hemisphere. Its most northerly point is in England (around the Isle of Man) and its most southerly in Australia (around Camp A,B,C or D). In the west it reaches as far as Canada. It is inhabited by a tribe, classified in 1940 by scientists as "homo detained", but commonly known as "the internees". The population practises the arts and sciences, especially drawing and poetry'.[63]

## VII

Shortly after his release, one of the exiles defined what was most important to him about the experience of internment: 'The most interesting point in the internment problem is not how much the interned have had to suffer – for suffering is general all over the world at present – but how far they have been able to stand up, spiritually, to their trial, and to transform their adversities into productive experience.'[64] Most of the people who shared this experience are of the same opinion. The cultural achievements in British camps of Germans and Austrians who fled from Hitler deserve particular mention. In almost all camps, artistic, literary and educational activities developed during the very first days of internment – in many cases within a few hours. This made it easier for all concerned, the producers as well as the consumers of cultural activities, to bear their loss of liberty. It was not only well-known and established writers, artists, actors and theatre people, and internationally recognised scientists who participated in these activities. Hitherto unknown and undiscovered talents also contributed greatly to their success and helped the performances, cabarets, concerts, camp schools, lecture series, readings, art exhibitions, camp newspapers and camp universities to attain a high standard.

On the first day of the internment confusion, depression and countless wild rumours were making the situation unbearable for many of those who had just arrived at the reception camp at Kempton Park. It was here that Jack Bilbo (Hugo Baruch), an adventurer, painter, art gallery owner, writer and good-natured braggart (later, in Hutchinson Camp, he claimed to be B. Traven) immediately began to cheer up his fellow prisoners with an impromptu cabaret, which later became a regular and popular event.[65] Max Zimmering reports that soon after the *Dunera* sailed, Siegfried Lohde, an actor from the Austrian émigré theatre *Laterndl*, set up a theatre *Interndl* on board, and the actors Josef Almas and Leo Bieber organised recitations. 'The driving force behind this activity was only to a very small extent a desire for self-importance; it was much more something I should like to call social responsibility.'[66]

Very few written records exist of these performances, which were mostly improvised, the repertoire being recalled from memory. When the internees became accustomed to life in the camps, performances were given which more resembled similar events outside, involving as they did rehearsals, stage sets, musical composition, directors, and even programmes and tickets (which were occasionally exchanged or sold on the camps' internal black markets).

One of the first performances of this sort was the bilingual camp revue *What a Life!*, which was given its première on 26 September 1940 in Central Camp on the Isle of Man. The programme lists ten scenes about aspects of camp life – and comments 'Perhaps less, perhaps more, perhaps nothing'.[67] This revue was directed by the film and theatre producer G.M. Hoellering, who had collaborated with Brecht on the film *Kuhle Wampe* and after the War became the owner of the Academy Cinema in London's Oxford Street. The authors of the revue were Richard Hutter, Norbert Elias and Otto Erich Deutsch, whose 'Ballade vom deutschen Refugee' ('Ballad of the German Refugee') was a hit in other camps too. The music was composed by Hans Gal who, while in Huyton Camp, had written a *Huyton Suite* which was also successfully performed after the War.[68] *What a Life!* stands out among the numerous performances given in the camps because it was produced by Hoellering at the suggestion of the camp commandant.[69] All the other performances which took place in camps on the Isle of Man, on the mainland, in Canada and Australia were the result of the internees' own initiative.

In the camp at Onchan, recitations from *Faust*, *Wallensteins Lager*, and *A Midsummer Night's Dream* were on the programme of an event called *Auf der Festwiese* (In the Carnival Grounds). A Grand Concert soon followed, as did an art exhibition with paintings, drawings and sculptures by interned artists.[70] It was not long before the internees put on complete plays. Hans J. Rehfisch directed Shakespeare's *Julius Caesar*, which had its première in the Gaiety Theatre, Douglas, on 23 November.[71] The acting group in Hutchinson Camp on the Isle of Man was particularly active. Between spring and September of 1941 they performed an adaptation of Chesterton's *The Man who was Thursday*, Steinbeck's *Of Mice and Men*, Lessings' *Nathan der Weise*, Schiller's *Die Räuber*, Galsworthy's *The Silver Box*, Sternheim's *Kassette* and Ardrey's *Thunder Rock*. In the women's camp, Rushen, revues, puppet shows and Christmas plays were performed.[72] Camp Huyton had the opportunity to see *Septembertage*, a play by the young Kuba (Kurt Barthel) who was interned there. Louis Fürnberg's *Böhmische Passion* was also performed there.[73]

In Australia, the revue *Erinnerung an Europa* (*A memory of Europe*), put on by interned artistes from the *Frei Deutscher Kulturbund* at Camp Hay enjoyed great success. It was written by Max Zimmering, Jacques Bachrach and Wilhelm Russo. Zimmering later wrote about this performance: 'The content of this revue attempted to put the fate of the internees, in their own minds at least, back into a European context, to give them hope for a better future, in spite of the less than rosy world situation, and to show them that even here, in the Australian desert, behind barbed wire and far away from Europe, they should not give themselves up for dead'.[74] This revue was performed again in revised form under the title *Hay Days*. A *Schweik* dramatisation by Rolf Stein followed, which was put on again in the camp at Tatura. In December 1940 there was a performance of *Faust* consisting of recitations and acted scenes.[75] There was a performance of R.C. Sheriff's *Journey's End* in the autumn of 1941, and Kurt Sternberg produced his *Snowwhite Revue* for New Year 1942.[76] Apart from these larger productions, there were many readings of literature written in the camps, musical evenings, and a performance of Handel's *Israel in Egypt*, specially arranged by the pianist Peter Stadlen.[77]

The theatre played an important part in the everyday life of the internees in Canada as well. In Camp C (Sherbroke) readings from Shakespeare and a commemoration of Stefan Zweig with readings from his works were held. In Camp A (Farnham) an internee wrote a parody of Hofmannsthal's *Der Tor und der Tod* (*Death and the Fool*), performed under the title *Tropf and Trommler* (*The Drip and the Drummer*). In addition, Chekhov's *The Proposal* and Wilde's *The Importance of Being Ernest* were performed here, as well as Sheriff's *Journey's End*. Finally, the performance of Shaw's *Androcles and the Lion* in Camp B (New Brunswick) should not be forgotten.

Camp 'universities' and schools were important institutions in everyday camp life. Informal individual lectures and discussion circles soon developed into highly-planned programmes. In Camp Onchan, there had been 600 hours of teaching and more than 300 lectures with a total audience of 16,250 people by the beginning of August.[78] Fred Uhlmann remembers how difficult it was, sometimes, to make a choice from the lectures on offer: 'What could one do if Professor William Cohn's talk on the Chinese Theatre coincided with Egon Wellesz' Introduction to Byzantine Music? Or Professor Jacobsthal's talk on Greek Literature with Professor Goldmann's on the Etruscan Language? Perhaps one felt more inclined to hear Zunz on the *Odyssey* or Friedenthal on the Shakespearean stage.'[79] There is only one known case of this work being impeded by a camp administration. In the women's camp, Rushen, where antifascists had long been having altercations with Nazi sympathisers, disputes arose about who was entitled to give lectures. The camp commander finally forbade those without formal academic qualifications to give lectures.[80] In most camps, however, commanders actively supported the cultural activities of the inmates.

It was not only academic knowledge that was passed on in the camps. Technical schools and 'Youth Universities' were also organised for young people. The older people felt a responsibility to compensate the young for the interruption to their education represented by internment. In the women's camp, Rushen, a kindergarten and a school were set up for children who had come into the camp with their mothers. Later, Minna Specht established a second school there, giving the camp the benefit of her experience and ideas in the field of education.[81] The 'enemy aliens' deported overseas soon began holding lectures and training courses. As early as the second day on board the *Dunera*, lectures were being held on topics from the humanities as well as the sciences.[82] Not long after the deportees' arrival in the Australian camp at Hay, a well-organised university was functioning:

> Apart from a huge number of English, six French and four Spanish courses, it was possible to learn Latin, Greek, Russian and Japanese, and there were lectures on the history of art as well as English and German literature.... Apart from numerous beginners' courses in Algebra, Mechanics, etc., there were lectures on Group Theory, Matrices, Tensors, Vector Analysis, Projective Geometry, Differential Equations, Optics, Theoretical Physics, Radio Engineering and Electronic Gauges.[83]

From the end of 1941 onwards, refugees interned in Australia could take examinations at the University of Melbourne, while those who had been deported to Canada could be examined at McGill University.

Camp libraries played an important role and supplemented the activities of camp universities, although the shortage of books in many areas of the humanities was often lamented. The libraries also provided well-used centres for individual study, for entertainment and relaxation in everyday camp life. 'Walking along the shelves', wrote an internee, 'one reads the titles and the name of the authors – and suddenly forgets the barbed wire which cuts through our lives only a few metres away.'[84] He is speaking of the library in Camp Onchan, which was built up on a basic stock of books brought in by the internees themselves, and expanded by donations from emigrants' organisations, British institutions and individuals. This library was created in July 1940 and by the end of April 1941 it already had a stock of 5,000 books. The YMCA, the Jewish Refugee Committee, the German Emergency Committee, the British Council, Rev. John Duffield (an Anglican clergyman on the Isle of Man) and Camp Commander Shaw are all mentioned as donors. In addition, the library received loans from the National Central Library and the Victoria and Albert Museum in London.[85]

A significant function of the daily, weekly, fortnightly or monthly camp newspapers was to create a public forum in the camps. Some of these papers were duplicated from stencils, others were available only in the form of carbon copies, while in some cases there was only one copy which was displayed on a wall or a post. In the first weeks of internment, newspapers from outside were not yet available for camp inmates and the most dreadful rumours were rife. During this period, camp newspapers produced with official permission were a great help to the prisoners in coming to terms with their detention. In Hutchinson on the Isle of Man, a newspaper called *The Camp* appeared, and the *Sefton Review*, the *Mooragh Times*, the *Central Promenade Paper* and the *Onchan Pioneer* were produced in the other camps. The women of Camp Rushen published the *Rushen Outlook* and the *Awful Times*, and (for a time illegally) the *Frauenruf*. Immediately after their arrival in the Australian camp at Hay, a 'Group of Journalists' among the internees put out the *Camp News*, which first appeared as a news-sheet for display only. Soon after, *Lagerspiegel* (*Camp Mirror*) and *Boomerang* also came out. In Canada, there was a newspaper called *Stacheldraht* (*Barbed Wire*) in Camp A, a *Camp L Chronicle* and *Die andere Seite* (*The Other Side*) in Camp B. Although the various teams determined their individual editorial standpoints, it is possible to make certain generalisations. All the camp newspapers saw their main task as reporting topical political questions which directly concerned the internees – for example matters concerning their status, their release, the improvement of conditions in camps and so on. In addition, camp newspapers provided information about military developments and discussions of the political situation. The conditions under which refugees lived in other host countries were of particular interest. Furthermore, camp newspapers were a source of information about various activities in the camps, and provided interned writers with a forum for the work they produced during internment.

## VIII

When considering literary production in the internment camps, it would be wrong to limit the investigation merely to those who had already made a name for themselves as professional authors, and to ignore the works of hitherto unknown writers (some of whom have remained anonymous). The literature of internment, including that produced retrospectively, is as heterogeneous as is the literature of exile in general (in which context it should be seen). This is not surprising since the spectrum of internment literature reaches from young authors whose work was published for the first time in camp newspapers, to professional journalists and writers such as, for example, Richard Friedenthal, and from the Dadaist Kurt Schwitters to orthodox Communists like Kuba (Kurt Barthel) and Max Zimmering. To the latter we owe interesting observations on the cultural life of the camps.[86] According to Zimmering, three clear tendencies emerged: firstly, the expression of a close connection with the German cultural heritage; secondly, the attempt to give artistic form to the expression of internment; finally, the desire to blot out the experience of imprisonment, either by references to events outside the camps or by trying to exclude topical references altogether. These three tendencies can undoubtedly be discerned in the literature of internment, although the artistic shaping of the actual experience of internment is clearly predominant.

As with the collective consumption of literature, so its production had, in many cases, a consolidating effect. Often enough the two activities overlapped, when literature produced in the camps was read there, or published in camp newspapers. It followed that, in speaking about the literature of internment, we are dealing mainly with poetry, songs, sketches, short stories and other modest forms. In many cases these take the form of texts for immediate use and should not therefore be measured only by the standards of aesthetic innovation. On the other hand, some of the works produced in the camps are among the important artistic achievements of exile literature.[87]

Heinrich Fraenkel's book *Help us Germans to Beat the Nazis*,[88] which was published in London a few days before his release, is a rare example of a longer piece of literary work produced in a camp. It served to familiarise the British with the aims of the refugee anti-fascists, and to promote their common struggle against National Socialist Germany. Fraenkel was permitted to rent a typewriter and a

185

study was set up for him in the hospital barracks of Hutchinson Camp. A department within the Foreign Office even provided him with source material from Nazi Germany by supplying him with copies of the *Völkische Beobachter*, *Stürmer*, *Schwarze Korps* and *Militär-wochenblatt*.[89]

Besides giving artistic form to the experiences of everyday camp life and of imprisonment, the themes of establishing an identity and the relationship of the internees to their host country appear frequently in the literature of internment. They are often associated with reflections on the time before internment, on the fate of being a refugee and on the everyday life of an emigrant, as well as on experiences of fascism. 'Wer sind wir?' ('Who are we?') asks the title of a poem written in the Australian camp, Hay.

> Wir sind keine
> Kriegsgefangenen
> aber man bewacht uns
> und obwohl wir keine Nazis
> hat man in Verdacht uns.[90]

The answer to the question is a resigned 'Wir sind die Genarrten' ('We are the ones they have made fools of') in this poem, but in 'Brief aus dem Lager' ('Letter from the camp'), a poem by the young Kuba, individual resentment (Man hat mich angekackt/Ich sitz im Drahtgeflecht – They have shat on me/I am sitting in a tangle of wire) is combined with thorough-going criticism of the internment policy which hampered the fight against fascism:

> Die sollten lieber Stangenbohnen ziehn
> an all dem vielen Draht.
> Das wär für etwas gut
> und hülf dem Staat!
> Gemüse macht doch Blut!
> Baut Bohnen an,
> statt daß ihr Draht vertut![91]

Often the decision to write in English was itself a means of dissociating oneself from fascist Germany, or of demonstrating a commitment to Great Britain. This was so particularly if the text was for camp use only and not, like Fraenkel's book, for example, intended for English readers. One example of this is Oswald Volkmann's poem 'Loyalty', in which he draws the following conclusion:

> We have been Hitler's enemies
> For years before the war
> We knew his plans of bombing and
> Invading Britain's shore,
> We warned you of his treachery
> When you believed in peace,
> And now we are His Majesty's
> Most loyal internees.[92]

Volkmann's ironic poem stands for a large number of similar poems in which the authors reveal 'das Absurde' – 'the absurdity' (Kurt Hiller) and 'das Groteske' – 'the grotesqueness' (Hans Jaeger) in the fact that German and Austrian antifascists, persecuted by the National Socialists, found themselves behind the barbed wire of their British allies. This paradox, it seemed, could only be expressed in irony and satire.

## IX

One year after the beginning of mass internment, Hans Jaeger, who had then already been released, wrote: 'Certainly, in retrospect, the proportions shift. The happy ending casts its conciliatory light on everything which once appeared black. The mists part, and difficulties, which one believed could hardly be overcome, dissolve. One stops debating the question of whether it was all necessary'.[93] The internment was certainly a serious problem for many of the immigrants in Great Britain. It gave rise to depressions and was even – in Camp Huyton – the cause of suicides. Those who died in the *Arandora Star* catastrophe were not the only indirect victims of the internment and deportation policies. Rudolf Olden must also be reckoned among them. He would have liked to remain at Oxford, and would not have left Britain – if he had not been interned. Friends procured a lectureship for him in the USA in order to secure his release from the British camp. During the crossing, his ship was torpedoed and Olden drowned.[94]

In spite of the mental strain, separations and uncertainty caused by the internment, the judgements of those who experienced it are, on the whole, conciliatory. Tristan Busch (Andreas Schütz) called the internment 'a war crime', but he is alone in this judgement.[95] The first book published in Great Britain in which an 'enemy alien' released from a camp put down his experiences in the form of a novel is entitled *Never mind, Mr Lom! or The Uses of Adversity*.[96] This captures the feelings of most of the refugees, who could now continue in their attempts to assimilate. Reports and novels published later and based on the experiences of internment hardly change this picture.[97]

The question of the necessity of, or rather, the reason for the internment has occupied the minds of many of the immigrants. The explanations generally given refer to the panicky reactions of the British government and the Armed Forces and, sometimes, to their decision that it was necessary to demonstrate resolve to the British people. Nevertheless, the suspicion persisted that certain anti-democratic circles inside the government had urged the detention of antifascist refugees in order to divert attention from their own existence and, in the event of a German invasion, to ensure that a large number of determined opponents of the Nazi regime were behind lock and key. So far, research has not been able to uphold this view. In Britain, as in other countries, there was no pro-fascist Fifth Column worth mentioning. Thus it may be assumed that uncertainty, ineffectiveness and a certain amount of xenophobia were responsible for the internments and deportations.

However, the establishment of the Home Defence (Security) Executive and its largely autonomous mode of operation, uncontrolled by Parliament or even Cabinet, show that even democratic governments are prepared, in the case of a national security threat (be it genuine or a fabricated one), to restrict civil liberties, to violate democratic rights and to withdraw the making of important decisions from public and parliamentary scrutiny.

## Notes

1. S. Zweig, *The World of Yesterday*, Cassell: London, 1943, p. 326.

2. See F. Lafitte, *The Internment of Aliens*, Harmondsworth, 1940; 'Judex', *Anderson's Prisoners*, London, 1940.

3. See, for example, H. Jaeger, 'Refugees' Internment 1939–1940. A Survey of Literature', I, *Wiener Library Bulletin (WLB)* 3/4 (May/Aug. 1955), pp. 31, 33; II, *WLB* 5/6 (Sept./Dec. 1955), pp. 49, 51.

4. See E.J. Cohn, 'Legal Aspects of Internment', *The Modern Law Review* 4 (1941), pp. 200–9; H.J. Feist, 'The Status of the Refugees', *The Modern Law Review* 7 (1941), pp. 51–3; R.M.W. Kempner, 'The Enemy Alien Problem in the Present War', *The American Journal of International Law* 43 (1940), pp. 443–58.

5. To mention only a few: W. Röder, *Die deutschen Exilgruppen in Großbritannien 1940–1945. Ein Beitrag zur Geschichte des Widerstandes gegen den Nationalsozialismus*, Hanover, 1968; H. Maimann, *Politik im Wartesaal. Österreichische Exilpolitik in Großbritannien 1938–1945*, Vienna, 1975; B. Wasserstein, *Britain and the Jews of Europe 1939–1945*, London, 1979; A. Clarke, 'Die Rolle des Theaters des Freien Deutschen Kulturbundes in Großbritannien im Kampf gegen den deutschen Faschismus (1938–1947). Ein Beitrag zur Untersuchung des deutschen antifaschistischen Exiltheaters', Ph.D. dissertation, Berlin (East), 1972.

6. P. and L. Gillman, *'Collar the Lot!' How Britain interned and expelled its Wartime Refugees*, London, 1980; R. Stent, *A Bespattered Page? The Internment of His Majesty's 'most loyal aliens'*, London, 1980.

7. See Gillman, p. 23.

8. Public Record Office (PRO) CAB 16/211 Committee of Imperial Defence. Sub-Committee on the Control of Aliens in War. Proceedings, 20 February 1939.

9. PRO CAB 16/211 Committee of Imperial Defence. Sub-Committee on the Control of Aliens in War. First Report (CAW 21) 1 April 1939.

10. See PRO CAB 16/21 Committee of Imperial Defence, Sub-Committee on the Control of Aliens in War, Minute 6, Meeting of 25 August 1939.

11. Letter from Sir J. Anderson to Lord Halifax, 7 November 1939, PRO FO 371/22941.

12. See. E. Spier, *The Protecting Power*, London, 1951; A Natan, 'Barren Interlude. The Story of my Detention' (typescript, with handwritten corrections), in the archives of the Institut für Zeitgeschichte (IfZ) Munich.

13. See Spier, p. 24.

14. See Natan, p. 36.

15. E. Stern-Rubath, *Aus zuverlässiger Quelle verlautet... Ein Leben für Presse und Politik*, Stuttgart, 1964, p. 278.

16. See Gillman, pp. 45–6.

17. See J. Kuczynski, *Memoiren. Die Erziehung des J.K. zum Kommunisten und Wissenschaftler*, 2nd ed., Berlin, 1975, p. 360. Cf. also Lafitte, p. 64: 'Tribunal chairmen put "dangerous bolshevists" into category A'.

18. See K. Hiller, *Rote Ritter. Erlebnisse mit deutschen Kommunisten*, Gelsenkirchen (n.d.), (Schriften zum Zeitgeschehen, Heft 3), p. 100f.

19. Kuczynski, p. 361.

20. See S. Haffner, *Germany: Jekyll & Hyde*, London, 1940. According to a communication from Haffner of 2 August 1978, he was interned from February to April as a member of category A. After his release he was put into category B, which meant that he was interned again from May until August 1940. Mr Parker, MP, asked the Home Secretary a question concerning Haffner in the House of Commons on 23 July 1940. See Hansard, Parliamentary Debates, 363, 623, 23 July 1940.

21. See Gillman, p. 88.

22. *Daily Mail*, 20 April 1940.
23. See 'Judex', p. 109.
24. See Stent, p. 51.
25. See Gillman, chaps. 10–13.
26. *Ibid*., pp. 101–4.
27. PRO War Cabinet 123 (40).
28. See Gillman, p. 108.
29. PRO War Cabinet 128(40); Anderson's Report: (W.P. [G] 40.131).
30. See Gillman, p. 126.
31. The case of Kent/Wolkoff. Cf. *ibid*.
32. For the legal position, see the articles listed in n. 4. The Royal Prerogative of Power over Enemy Aliens which, by British Common Law, was vested in the Crown could only be used as the legal basis for the internment of enemy aliens. Further legal means for the detention of aliens – not only nationals of enemy states, but also of neutral and allied states – were provided for by 'Detention after Refusal of leave to land' and Article 12(5A) of the Aliens Order of 1920. Defence Regulation 18B was based legally on the Emergency Powers (Defence) Act of 1939. Under this, aliens as well as British citizens could be interned if they were considered by the authorities to be a threat to the security of the state.
33. See Gillman, p. 133.
34. *Ibid*., p. 142.
35. *Ibid*., p. 145.
36. *Ibid*.
37. PRO CAB 65/7. Cabinet Minutes W.M. 161/40 of 11 June 1940.
38. See Stent, p. 74.
39. Karl Höltermann, Bernard Menne and Wilhelm Sander, for example, were spared internment through their close contacts with trade unionists and Labour Party politicians.
40. As though I had wantonly committed an offence,/I am, without fault, painfully under suspicion,/perhaps, in the next instant, captured/and deprived of even the appearance of freedom,/the freedom for which I renounced/and did without the protection of home,/dared the flight into what was unknown to me,/bore the inadequacies of a strange place,/in order, now, here in the mother-land of freedom,/where I thought I was in a friendly country,/to the disgrace of myself and the whole of humanity/to be suspiciously equated with the enemy! [ed. transl.] The poem has the subtitle 'Aus der Zeit der Internierungen' ('From the period of internment'), Free German League of Culture/Austrian Centre/Young Czechoslovakia (eds.), *Die Vertriebenen, Dichtung der Emigration*, London, 1941, p. 26. Max Herrmann-Neisse was not interned.
41. Unpublished account by Willy Hess, 23 pages, typescript, dated 20 October 1940. In the possession of the author.
42. H. Friedmann, 'Internierungstagebuch. 25/7 – 21/8/1940' ('diary of the internment'), 48 pages, typescript, deposited in the Dokumentationsarchiv des Österreichischen Widerstandes, Vienna (DÖW), p. 24.
43. See PRO FO 916/36. This contains a 'Dietary' of the camps on the Isle of Man, dated 20 July 1941, signed by B.E. Sergeaunt, Government Secretary. The exact rations of foodstuffs are listed, followed by an appendix: 'In the

event of Kosher meat not being obtainable, to those internees who decline other meat, the following may be issued in lieu ... '.

44. See Gillman, p. 133.

45. *Ibid.*, p. 161.

46. See PRO FO 916/2580. Letter from the Canadian High Commissioner, Vincent Massey, to the Dominion Office, dated 6 June 1940, re 'Transfer to Canada of German Prisoners of War and Internees'. This letter states that 'the Canadian Government assume that civilian internees present a greater military risk in the United Kingdom'.

47. See the letter from the Canadian High Commission, dated 14 June 1950, signed by Ritchie, to the Dominion Office, in PRO FO 916/2581.

48. See PRO FO 916/2581: Minutes of the 'Conference on Move of Prisoners of War and Internees to Canada', 17 June 1940.

49. F.W. Nielsen, *Emigrant für Deutschland*, Darmstadt, 1977, p. 177.

50. See Stent, pp. 96–7.

51. Nielsen, p. 182.

52. The circle of the porthole delimits the world, the light;/In front of it a throng of people with hollow eyes,/In which the colour of the sky is refracted,/Eyes which, starved, suck at the clouds,/As though the last day had arrived – / And through the porthole you see nothing but sea. [ed. transl.] The poem appears in M. Zimmering, *Im Antlitz der Zeit*, Berlin, 1948, p. 61.

53. Lafitte, p. 27.

54. See the letter from A.K.J. Pigott (War Office, Director of Recruiting and Mobilisation) to the Secretary, Council of Aliens, 22 January 1941, PRO FO 371/29173.

55. See Hansard, Parliamentary Debates, 364, 1433–42.

56. The tasks of the various committees are given in detail by Stent, pp. 205–8.

57. Letter from G. Leibholz to George Bell, Bishop of Chichester, Oxford, 20 August 1940. The original is in the Lambeth Palace Library, London: Bell Papers, Vol. 30.

58. Churchill in the War Cabinet, meeting of 1 August 1940. PRO CAB 65/8, 217 (40).

59. The first White Paper issued by the Home Office: 'German and Austrian Civilian Internees. Categories of Persons Eligible for Release from Internment and Procedure to be Followed in Applying for Release'. Cmd. 6217, HMSO, July 1940. This was followed, a month later, by 'Civilian Internees of Enemy Nationality. Categories of Persons Eligible for Release from Internment and Procedure to be Followed in Applying for Release'. Cmd. 6223, HMSO, August 1940.

60. See Röder, p. 120.

61. See 'Civilian Internees of Enemy Nationality. Categories of Persons Eligible for Release from Internment and Procedure to be Followed in Applying for Release', HMSO, October 1940.

62. See Stent, p. 213.

63. *Zeitspiegel* 49, 6 December 1941.

64. W. Zander, *Adventures in Reconciliation. The Power of the Spirit in Internment*, International Fellowship of Reconciliation, leaflet No. 7, n.p., 1941.

65. See *Onchan Pioneer* 1, 27 July 1940. Bilbo himself reports in J. Bilbo, *Rebell aus Leidenschaft*, n.p. (Horst Erdmann Verlag), 1963, p. 287.

66. M.Zimmering, 'Kunst hinter Pfählen', in Kulturbund zur demokratischen Erneuerung Deutschlands (ed.), *Aufbau. Kulturpolitische Monatsschrift* 1, 1948, p. 254.

67. *What a Life!*, programme in the possession of the author.

68. See H. Gal, *Huyton Suite for Flute and two Violins*, Op. 92, Simrock, Hamburg/London.

69. Personal communication by the late G.M. Hoellering, 11 July 1978.

70. *Grand Concert*, programme in the possession of the author.

71. *Julius Caesar*, programme deposited in the DÖW, Vienna.

72. See Clarke, p. 191. Clarke surveys the theatrical and cultural scene in the camps.

73. *Böhmische Passion/Septembertage*, programme deposited in the DÖW, Vienna.

74. Zimmering, *Kunst hinter Pfählen*, p. 254.

75. See W. Russo, 'Faust auf der Camp-Bühne', *Camp News* 50, 11 December 1940.

76. *Snowwhite*, programme in the possession of the author.

77. Personal communication from P. Stadlen, London, 30 June 1978.

78. See 'Der Campreporter meldet' ('The camp reporter announces'), in *Onchan Pioneer* 2, 9 August 1940.

79. F. Uhlman, *The Making of an Englishman*, London, 1960, pp. 232–3.

80. See Clarke, p. 159.

81. See M. Kelber, 'Auch Haus Schwalbach hat zu danken', *Erziehung und Politik*. Minna Specht zum 80. Geburtstag, n.p. (Verlag Öffentliches Leben), 1960, p. 330.

82. See H. Eichner, 'Internierungslager und Lageruniversität', E. Schwarz and M. Wegner (eds.), *Verbannung. Aufzeichnungen deutscher Schriftsteller im Exil*, Hamburg, 1964, p. 117.

83. *Ibid.*, p. 118.

84. 'Allein mit Büchern. Die Library der Popular University', *Onchan Pioneer* 4, 23 August 1940.

85. See 'Die Camp Library', *Onchan Pioneer* 27/28, 9 March 1941.

86. See Zimmering, *Kunst hinter Pfählen*, p. 256.

87. For example, works by Theodor Kramer, Kuba, Max Zimmering, Hans Eichner, Arthur Zanker, Kurt Schwitters, Karl Weisselberger.

88. See H. Fraenkel, *Help us Germans to Beat the Nazis* (Gollancz Victory Book No. 14), London, 1941. Of particular interest in this context is 'Epilogue in Camp', pp. 104–18.

89. See H. Fraenkel, *Lebewohl, Deutschland*, Hanover, 1960, p. 49. (Original edition in English: *Farewell to Germany*, London, 1959.)

90. We are not prisoners of war/ But they watch us/ And although we are not Nazis/ They hold us in suspicion. [ed. transl.] An anonymous poem from Camp Hay. Handwritten copy in the possession of the author.

91. It would be better if they grew climbing beans/ on all that wire./ That would be of some use/ and would help the state!/ Vegetables build up the blood!/ Grow beans,/ instead of wasting wire! [ed. transl.] Kuba (pseud. Kurt Barthel), E. Scherner (ed.), *Brot und Wein. Gedichte – Lieder – Nach-*

*dichtungen*, Leipzig, 1973, p. 54.

92. O. Volkmann, 'Loyalty', in E. Barcs, 'His Majesty's Most Loyal Internees...', *Quadrant* 53, May–June 1968.

93. H. Jaeger, 'Rückblick auf's Internment', unpublished manuscript dated 17 July 1941, in Jaeger, 'Materialien zur deutschen politischen Emigration', deposited in the archives of the IfZ, Munich.

94. See R. Greuner, *Gegenspieler, Profile linksbürgerlicher Publizisten aus Kaiserreich und Weimarer Republik*, Berlin (East), 1969, pp. 276–8.

95. See T. Busch (pseud. Andreas Schütz), *Major Kwaplitschka. Entlarvter Geheimdienst*, Vienna, 1950, p. 256.

96. See A. Lomnitz, *Never mind, Mr. Lom! or The Uses of Adversity*, London, 1941.

97. See, for example, L. Laurent, *A Tale of Internment*, London, 1942; L. Kahn, *Obliging Fellow*, London, 1946; R. Friedenthal, *Die Welt in der Nußschale*, Munich, 1956. Also numerous autobiographies, in which experiences of internment are described, as well as short stories and articles.

# John Willett

# The Emigration and the Arts

A few years ago there was a thoughtful and provocative article in the *New Left Review* in which Perry Anderson, its editor, argued that all the more radical émigré thinkers – particularly the political thinkers – had gone to America, leaving his and my country with the painlessly assimilable residue. The United States got Marcuse, in other words, while we got Popper and Wittgenstein, who, in Anderson's view, were closer to our own intellectual tradition and less immediately subversive. Leaving aside the question of what is or is not likely to be subversive in the long run (and what needs subverting, for that matter), a similar thesis could be put forward with respect to the arts. The leaders of the mid-European avant-garde tended to finish up in America, even if they had spent some years in Austria, France, and/or England on the way.

Of the Bauhaus masters, for instance, Gropius and Moholy-Nagy were in England for a few years during the mid-1930s, then settled in Harvard and Chicago respectively; Mies van der Rohe, Albers and Herbert Bayer never lived here. Nor did Schönberg, Hindemith, George Grosz, Piscator or Brecht. Of the various exiled leaders of the main avant-garde movements of the 1920s – functional architecture, dodecaphonic music, the epic theatre, abstract or socially critical art – very few came to Britain and not one remained there. Why this was is not easy to say. Of course we were in those days a very traditional country, and even if our better traditions included that of accepting political exiles we were less open-minded about the value of modern art movements. Of course too the Americans, once admission was granted, could accept and absorb anything – for, as Brecht had already observed:

> This inexhaustible melting-pot, so it was said
> Received everything that fell into it and converted it
> Within twice two weeks into something identifiable.*

However, it was more complicated than that, since at the same time one could – and still can – live in America in an enclave of one's own kind, to an extent that is hardly possible in Britain. Forty years ago in California the Manns, Feuchtwanger and Alfred Döblin were like a small Olympus of German literature in exile, and were taken by their hosts very largely at their own valuation. There was the film industry, which was already full of central Europeans. And there was the money. America had the resources and the cultural openness needed to set up such new enterprises as the Chicago Bauhaus. Britain had not.

And yet today it is hard to say which country has been more deeply affected by the ideas which the exiles brought with them. Wherever you go today in the English-speaking world, Brecht, Kafka, serialism and the Bauhaus are familiar topics of highbrow chit-chat, much as were Proust, Post-Impressionism and the Russian Ballet in the London of the 1920s. The rise in our esteem of the Weimar and pre-Weimar German cultural heritage over the past two decades has been astounding, particularly for those who recall the primacy formerly given to any movement or artist coming from Paris. In England's case, far more than in America's, it seems even more astounding in view of the neglect suffered by some of those same exiles at the time. I listen today to the recording of Kurt Gerron singing the 'Moritat' from the *Dreigroschenoper*, or admire Meidner's pre-1914 portrait of Max Herrmann-Neisse, and I recall being told (mistakenly, it now turns out) that Gerron was working as a barber in the Strand, and wish bitterly that I had made contact with either Meidner or Herrmann-Neisse in the days when they were living in our city, ignored. I was too unimaginative to realise what such contact might have meant.

No doubt the sheer size of recent West German expenditure on the pre-Nazi arts and their propagation has helped to bring about this change in our critical values. What is surely more fundamental, however, is the parallels that now exist between London (and to a lesser extent other large British cities) and pre-Hitler Berlin. For since about 1960 there have been signs of a growing social similarity, some of them superficial (haircuts, boots, leather, porn- and sex-shops, overt

---

* From *Bertolt Brecht Poems*, transl. John Willett and Ralph Manheim, with the cooperation of Erich Fried, Eyre Methuen, London, 1976, p. 167.

homosexuality, dominance of the colour black), others more profound (satire of a destructive and even sadistic kind, vandalism and violence, the revival of agitprop, graduate unemployment and racial tensions more serious than this country has ever known). Such parallels have made the culture of that period accessible to a much wider swathe of British society than ever used to converse about Proust and Diaghileff. So in the *New Musical Express* of 31 January 1981 – the weekly pop music paper where the all-significant 'charts' of record sales appear – a writer under the name Biba Kopf (shades of *Berlin-Alexanderplatz*) welcomed her(?) readers' shift of interest from Nazi symbolism and war souvenirs to the positive achievements of pre-Nazi days. David Bowie sings the Brecht-Weill 'Alabama Song' and performs *Baal* on BBC television; a group forms under the name Bauhaus (or 'Bauchraus', as the *NME* happily misprints it); another uses the symbol AIZ; yet another puts a picture of an agitprop group of the 1920s on one of its record sleeves.

Somehow the ideas of the anti-Nazi émigrés have taken root here, despite all our conservatism, our insularity, our weather and our more incomprehensible folkways (like rhyming slang or cricket). We may have lost their avant-garde to America; we may have sent others to internment in Canada or Australia; we may have ignored the reputations and achievements of those who stayed. Yet the gist of the message has got through, to an extent that I for one would never have dreamed possible in the dark days between the fall of Red Vienna and the recapture of Stalingrad in 1942. So how did the change come about: how much real continuity was there between the emigration itself and the present rehabilitation of its culture? How much did the émigrés do, either directly or indirectly, to help us to understand the very different, far harsher and more precarious world from which that culture arose? And what do we owe to those who battled it out and settled for good in this country despite all its disadvantages, like that friend of Georg Heym, member of the pre-1914 Expressionist *Neuer Club* and collaborator of Piscator, who still lives by himself high above Oxford Street, a 90-year-old man running a photographic agency on his own? It is time to look back and see.

# I

In England, unlike France or Russia or America, there was never a coherent nucleus of German literature in exile, just individual exiled writers who remained more or less displaced. This was partly because the exiled publishing houses – Querido, Bermann-Fischer, Carrefour and the rest – were all based elsewhere apart from Wieland Herzfelde's Malik-Verlag, which was only technically registered in London, c/o Margaret Mynatt and the foreign book department of Selfridge's store. Nor did we house any of the major anti-Nazi magazines, such as *Mass und Wert*, *Internationale Literatur*, *Das Wort*, *Die Sammlung*, *Die Neue Weltbühne* and other more or less miraculous survivals. After 1933 the *Schutzverband deutscher Schriftsteller* had set itself up in Paris and the library of exiled publications which it gathered there fell, like Paris itself, into the hands of the Nazis in 1940. There was the international PEN whose secretary, Herman Ould, was certainly sympathetic to the German writers (and himself translated Toller's plays); and an anti-Nazi German section of that body was founded by Ernst Toller, Rudolf Olden and Herrmann-Neisse. There were some active and efficient émigré booksellers, such as Hans Preiss, near the British Museum, Joseph Suschitzky, formerly at Swiss Cottage, and Dr Fritz Homeyer and Miss Eva Dworetsky in the foreign department of J. and E. Bumpus (who no longer exist). Martin Schor at the London Library saw to that institution's exceptionally good holding of modern German books. But generally the exiled writers were left without either a local outlet or a spiritual home. There was the *Freier Deutscher Kulturbund*, presided over by, among others, Oskar Kokoschka but largely run by the Communists; there was the rival *Gruppe unabhängiger Autoren* which Kurt Hiller set up, but which remained relatively obscure. Cafés, let alone literary cafés, were virtually unknown – thus Jakob Hegner, writing wistfully to America from London in 1940: 'In der neuen Welt wird es wieder eine alte Mampe-Stube geben. Hier gab es und gibt es nichts dergleichen – wenigstens nicht für unsereinen'.* Only Elias Canetti, bulging briefcase under his arm, could somehow turn the ordinary English teashop into such.

The writers were thrown back on themselves, and not all of them

---

*'...there will be another old *Mampe-Stube* in the New World. There is not and never has been anything of that sort here – at least not for the likes of us'. [Ed. transl.]

were happy there. They were lost among the disorderly subtleties of the language – the 'feuchtklimatische, wolkengefächelte englische Sprache', ('damp-aired, cloud-caressed English language', JW), as the Prague German poet Rudolf Fuchs called it in his late *Gedichte aus London* – they missed what Herrmann-Neisse, in another posthumous volume, termed 'Die Kleinigkeiten, die nicht viel bedeuten', ('The little things that do not count for much', JW), like large porcelain stoves or civilised drinking hours; they were dumbfounded by our political complacency. Once again, from Herrmann-Neisse's unfinished cycle 'Zwischenzeit':

> Da klang, was wir erzählten, übertrieben,
> man lauschte zweifelnd, wenn auch wohlgesinnt:
> man war noch immer Gentleman geblieben,
> als welcher jede letzte Schlacht gewinnt.*

Much the same depression seized even so successful a writer as Stefan Zweig, who had had a second home in London since well before the fall of Austria and whose sales in English translation were comparable with those of Feuchtwanger and Thomas Mann. He too looked backwards to more congenial times and forward to nothing much but his own death. And indeed Fuchs and Herrmann-Neisse died in England in the early 1940s, aged respectively fifty-two and fifty-five, while Zweig killed himself, aged sixty, after moving on to Brazil in mid-1940. 'London ist jetzt für mich furchtbar geworden', he told Hermann Kesten on the eve of the war,

> seit sich die ganze Emigration hierher wendet und zwar ihre letzte und ich darf wohl sagen, schlechteste Welle – alle jene, die nicht von Deutschland fortwollten, alle Schriftsteller, die nie wirklich Schriftsteller waren. Ausser Körmendi [a Hungarian novelist], Fülop-Miller [author of *Geist und Gesicht des Bolschewismus*], Robert Neumann, Zarek und Friedenthal machen fast alle im billigen Radikalismus und agitieren gegeneinander. Wie bei jedem Zersetzungsprozes bilden sich in der Emigration notwendigerweise giftige und stinkige Gase... †

---

* What we told them sounded exaggerated,/ Well-meaning as they were, they listened sceptically:/ They were, after all, still the *gentleman*/ Who always wins the last battle. [Ed. transl.]
† 'London has become unbearable for me... since the whole of the emigration

Of this handful of writers of whom Zweig approved, Robert Neumann was exceptional in that he learnt to write in English – an English of a somewhat idiosyncratic sort, but none the less readable for that – and also became an adviser to a London publishing house: Hutchinson's. Richard Friedenthal too (who was later Zweig's literary executor) had a very perceptive understanding of his insular hosts, about whom he wrote both amusingly and accurately – and without any kind of self-pity – in his postwar novel *Die Welt in der Nusschale*, the nutshell in this case being the internment camp on the Isle of Man to which so many assorted members of the emigration were sent in 1940. Indeed Friedenthal, an upright and apparently non-political Prussian who emigrated of his own free choice, in due course settled in London even though his great post-war successes – the Goethe and Luther biographies – were primarily with German publishers. Finally, unmentioned in Zweig's list and some ten years younger than these two writers, Elias Canetti too was – and still intermittently is – genuinely at home in England, where his massive and complex pre-war Viennese novel *Die Blendung* (*Auto-da-fé*) had a great critical success in 1946 in Dame Veronica Wedgwood's translation. Alone among the writers of the emigration he had a perceptible influence on our own literature, since it was largely he who persuaded Iris Murdoch to publish her first novel *Under the Net*. Its successor *The Flight from the Enchanter* is dedicated to him.

Others came and went without leaving much mark on their surroundings: Kurt Hiller, Karl Otten, Hans Rehfisch, Felix Braun, Jan Petersen from the Communist underground within Germany. Brecht made two brief visits in 1934 and 1936, during the second of which he established some slight contact with our own anti-Nazi writers (inviting Auden, for instance, to come and see him in Denmark). To these trips we owe a handful of poems of which 'Der Kaledonische Markt' with its echoes of Kipling is the most attractive and 'Die Hölle der Enttäuscher' ('The Hell of the Disenchanters') the most intriguing: was it the Londoners or the emigrants themselves

---

descended on it – the last, and I dare say worst wave what's more: all those who did not want to leave Germany, all the writers who were never real writers. Apart from Körmendi [a Hungarian novelist], Fülop-Miller [author of *The Mind and Face of Bolshevism*], Robert Neumann, Zarek and Friedenthal, they are almost all cheap radicals agitating against each other. Poisonous and foul gases are as natural a part of the emigration as of any other process of decay....' [Ed. transl.]

who 'had crumbled under threats'? and could be seen to 'show one another their letters of credit/ And point at the many stamps and signatures/ Using their thumb to cover the places/ Where the year had been scratched out'.* We also have Hanns Eisler's recollection of his visit with Brecht to Stefan Zweig's comfortable apartment, where the two men gave their host a personal rendition of their new song 'Von der belebenden Wirkung des Geldes' ('On the stimulating impact of cash'), ill-manneredly emphasising its relevance to their immediate surroundings in St John's Wood. This not uncharacteristic bit of 'Schärfe' or (by English standards) wanton aggressiveness may help to explain the older writer's growing distaste for 'Radikalismus'.

Radical writers, however, have the enormous advantage in such circumstances – a psychological as well as a literary advantage – of always looking forward. They are too busy with the future, and with the meaning of what is going on around them, to be able to lament a past which their readers may see as hopelessly foreign or remote. And so the outstanding émigré author for us was, until his sad death in 1983, a man who shared much of Brecht's background and political interests, even though he had turned against the Communist Party soon after coming here and was now anathema to the extreme left. This was of course Arthur Koestler, the former Berlin journalist and collaborator of Willi Münzenberg in Paris who, with the publication of *Darkness at Noon* in December 1940, became a major English novelist. Koestler's great strength was that he had not merely been close to, or had himself experienced, the desperately extreme situations of which he wrote, but was able to bring them home to English readers. He wrote without overstatement; he had a nice sense of irony and a good eye for the comic or curious detail; his most minor characters were often vividly and understandingly sketched. Moreover he knew how to construct a story; the different episodes, flashbacks and reflections were well balanced and economically set down. And he thought for himself, not along a party line. All these are qualities which would anyway carry over into a translation, but on top of that he was remarkably lucky in the translator of that first novel, the sculptor Daphne Hardy, for her English had just the right unobtrusive momentum, and from then on his works all appeared as original English books.

Koestler's clarity, like his all-consuming curiosity, sprang from his

---

* From *Bertolt Brecht Poems*, transl. Willett *et al.*, pp. 230–1

journalistic training; the emigration also brought England other central-European journalists of whom the finest was probably Rudolf Olden, who was drowned when the ship carrying him to America went down in 1940. Many of these people worked (as did Friedenthal and Hans Flesch, an eminent radio producer, some of whose novels appeared under the name 'Vincent Brun') for the wartime BBC or for the officially-backed weekly *Die Zeitung*, among them being Peter de Mendelssohn, his wife Hilde Spiel and Sebastian Haffner who was to hold a leading position on *The Observer* for some years after the war. Three had been outstanding theatre critics in glittering, republican Berlin: Alfred Kerr, Lutz Weltmann and Monty Jacobs. Another, Frank Warschauer, had been an early friend of Brecht's. Heinrich Fraenkel ran the chess column in the *New Statesman*. But the only one to make a lasting impression on the face of British journalism was the former editor of the *Münchner Illustrierte*, Stefan Lorant, whose work for the Hulton Press papers *Picture Post* and *Lilliput* set a new standard for photo-journalism and the intelligent juxtaposition of pictures with text. It was these two journals that featured the drawings of Erich Kästner's chief illustrator, Walter Trier, and introduced the British magazine public to the work of John Heartfield who a few years earlier had been laying out the exiled *Arbeiter-Illustrierte-Zeitung* for Willi Münzenberg. As for book production proper, it remained as yet virtually untouched by the German influence. Like the whole business of publishing it would only seriously begin to reflect the impact of the emigration once the emigration itself was at an end.

## II

The visual artists should on the face of it have been in a much less difficult position than the writers, since their work was not constricted by language and had no need of a German publishing or theatre apparatus for its communication. Art, like music, is supposed to speak to everyone. But, of course, it frequently does not, and the fact that the resident art-lovers were not merely ignorant of the development of Central European art since – well, certainly since the mid-nineteenth century and possibly even since Dürer's time – but positively resistant in most cases to its more recent movements, made the life of even the most eminent of its exponents difficult indeed. Only one of the émigré painters was indisputably of the first rank: that was Kokoschka, who had the double advantage of being a Czech subject (hence a wartime ally) and having the loyal and generous support of the family of Brigadier-General Sir Henry Page Croft, Conservative MP for Bournemouth for many years. Yet even Kokoschka – of whom nobody could say, for instance, that he 'couldn't draw' – never penetrated the self-satisfied defences of the British art world. There is a splendid episode in his autobiography where he describes his first visit to Sir John Rothenstein, the director of the Tate Gallery. Rothenstein, he says, offered him a cup of tea and some sandwiches, asked if he would care to donate a picture to the gallery, and that was that. Henceforward he had his private patrons (especially for portraits) and exhibited the occasional landscape of Cornwall, where he went to live like many English painters before him; he was best known to the public, however, for the drawings and statements which he now and then made on behalf of Europe's children or the exiled Czech government. In due course he even became a British subject and in 1959 was made a CBE. (This is the award given to second- or third-grade figures in the arts and to the dimmer brigadiers. In any other country he would have had the equivalent of a knighthood and/or the OM.)

In 1940 Kurt Schwitters arrived from Norway and was promptly interned on the Isle of Man. He figures in Friedenthal's novel under the transparent disguise of 'Baby Bitter', the exponent of the 'Stottergedicht' or 'stutter poem'; and Friedenthal gives a wholly credible picture of the British camp commandant's reactions – amiable, patronising, then appalled – to the art exhibition put on by his charges. Here, in this mid-European nutshell half-way between England and Ireland, Schwitters was happy for more than a year painting mainly portraits; after his release, however, a certain depression seems to have set in. At first he lived in Barnes with his Norwegian son, seeing a few friends like Naum Gabo and the Polish philosopher-publisher Stefan Themerson, who later compiled a book called *Kurt Schwitters in England*. 'In any case', he was to write in 1947, 'nobody in London cares about good art. Only a few friends know what art is, and the only critic who amounts to anything – Herbert Read.' E.L.T. Mesens of the London Gallery that year organised two *Merz* performances to which representatives of the BBC were invited, but they are said to have left early, unimpressed. Nonetheless, and despite ill-health (Schwitters had a stroke in 1944), this unquenchable individualist went on writing stories in English – for instance, 'Maro the old cat of Hjertöya', 'Five girls on the switchboard' (July 1942), 'So shall we always be with the Lord' (about English landladies, as is another story), 'Twopenny novel about an ugly girl' and 'She is singing in the wireless'. And he wrote poems like the 'London Symphony' about the signs around him in Barnes:

> Halt, we are specialists.
> To be let
> To be sold
> High class clothiers
> Apply first floor
> Artistic plumber
> Enough said, we save you money...

and so on. It was only at the end of the war that he moved to the Lake District with Edith Thomas, started his third and last *Merzbau* and died.

Others remained more or less in obscurity until after the war, when they either found some sort of niche in the English art world or returned to pick up the threads of their pre-1933 reputation in the altered (and not always all that welcoming) West Germany of the economic miracle. Meidner, for instance, came to England in 1939 and left in 1953, still totally unknown; it is only in the past ten years that we have begun to appreciate the passion and skill of his work. John Heartfield arrived after the fall of Prague, when he was known at least to British Communists; he was befriended by the Carline family of artists in Hampstead (whose most distinguished member-in-law was Stanley Spencer) and did a certain amount of work for Lindsay Drummond and other book and magazine publishers; it was very noticeably below his best standard. Moholy-Nagy too worked in London for two years before setting up the New Bauhaus in Chicago: he designed posters, including a striking cross-section of a London Underground escalator, arranged displays for Simpson's clothing store in Piccadilly, had a show of his paintings at the London Gallery (as did Herbert Bayer) under Lady Norton's regime, and took photographs for two exceedingly British books – John Betjeman's *An Oxford University Chest* and Bernard Fergusson's account of Eton. His Light Modulator or *Lichtrequisit* can be seen functioning in the special effects for Alexander Korda's film of H.G. Wells's *Things to Come*. On a more conventional level there were Hans Feibusch, a pupil of Carl Hofer's, who came to specialise in murals, and the sculptors Siegfried Charoux, Uli Nimpsch and Georg Ehrlich, while the former Stuttgart lawyer Fred Uhlman developed in exile into a successful, semi-naïve painter on more or less Utrillesque lines. Like Canetti, he stayed on in

England to become a well-known Hampstead figure, incidentally giving the Heartfields house room for five years. His wife Diana Croft was a leading organiser of the Artists' International Association and served as that body's representative on the Artists' Refugee Committee, along with Margaret Gardiner, Roland Penrose and its secretary, Stephen Bone.

The fact was that in the 1930s and 40s scarcely anybody in England was accessible to Expressionism except possibly in its more abstract (or *Blaue Reiter*) forms, while the socially critical wing of *Neue Sachlichkeit* seemed positively detestable. Scotland perhaps was less resistant, since Jankel Adler and a number of Polish near-Expressionists established themselves there, as for a time did Josef Herman. But the angular distortions, the crude colours and harsh contrasts, the strong elements of squalor and hatred in much modern German art were all very remote from English tradition and, indeed, from those trends in continental art which we had been beginning to absorb: the worldly gaiety of Impressionism, the sensual vitality of Picasso and Matisse, the coolness of Mondrian, even the creepy titillations of the Surrealists. It was only in the summer of 1938, under the impact of the Degenerate Art exhibition in Munich the previous year, that a first major showing of the modern Germans was held in London at the New Burlington Galleries. Chaired by Herbert Read, with Edith Hoffmann as his secretary, and organised primarily by Irmgard Burchard and Herbert Einstein, this 269-exhibit show included two paintings by Dix, four Max Ernsts, three Grosz watercolours, four Kirchners, seven Modersohn-Beckers, three Schlemmers and two Schwitters among more extensive selections of Corinth, Kandinsky, Klee, Kokoschka, Lehmbruck, Liebermann, Marc and Rohlfs. Otto Bihalj-Marin wrote the special commentary, which was published by Penguin. Prices were low – I bought a beautiful Klee watercolour on silk for £25 – yet the British public galleries seem to have bought nothing. Their first modern German pictures, in fact, were given to the Leicester Art Gallery (famous for its collection of fox-hunting paintings) during the 1940s by my friend Hans Hess, son of the Erfurt industrialist-cum-collector, who had helped edit the paper *Inside Nazi Germany*, been sent to internment in Canada and returned to a job on that gallery's staff. Nor were many of the lenders to the exhibition English: Sir Michael Sadler with five pictures, the Earl of Sandwich with a Lehmbruck head, and one of the organisers, John Harrison, with two Schlemmers, being the only clearly identifiable names. The rest came from the continent or from the emigration itself.

Yet the nucleus of a better understanding was coming into being. This took three forms. Firstly, there were the embryonic dealers, with their special knowledge of the mid-European collections and the mid-European artists: Lea Bondi-Jaray from the Galerie Würthle in Vienna who took over the St George's Gallery in London early in the war, with Erica Brausen and the bookseller Harry Fischer who joined her there; Heinz Roland and Gustav Delbanco, who were to become pillars of Cork Street; not to mention those who dealt privately or became advisers to the main auctioneers. Secondly, there was the influx of eminent art historians and critics, largely associated with the shift to England of the Warburg Institute: Ettlinger, Antal, Wind, Gombrich, Münz, Hodin and others among whom Nikolaus Pevsner soon stood out with his book *Pioneers of the Modern Movement from Morris to Gropius* (1936) and his ensuing associations with the *Architectural Review* and with Penguin Books. Finally there were the art book publishers who were to introduce us to an entirely new conception of that genre: scholarly, amply illustrated and well-produced volumes at a low price. So Ludwig Goldscheider and Bela Horowitz in 1937 brought us the Phaidon imprint and Bruno Cassirer set up his firm in Oxford, then moved under Faber's wing, while Wolfgang Foges formed the book production firm called Adprint which introduced British publishing to the concept of picture research and the close integration of illustration and text. With Walter Neurath as production director and the poet W.J. Turner as editor, this pioneering outfit designed the wartime 'Britain in Pictures' series for Collins, followed by a series of poetry anthologies for Frederick Müller which had lithographs by such expressive artists as John Piper, William Scott, Michael Ayrton and the Adler-influenced Glaswegian Robert Colquhoun.

All three of these developments were long-term ones, barely perceptible during the emigration years proper. In architecture, by contrast, the modern English movement was open to mid-European influences from the outset. This was due partly to the organisation in 1933 of the British MARS group of architects who owed allegiance to the international CIAM and its outstanding figure Le Corbusier. At the same time there were a number of well-informed individuals like Morton Shand, the architectural historian, Bobby Carter, the RIBA librarian, and J.M. Richards, the outstanding editor of the *Architectural Review*, who were all well aware of the new German architecture; there was also Jack Pritchard, who was ready to give its leading exponents employment in his Isokon furniture firm. Gropius arrived in England in 1934, and was widely welcomed; his book *The New Architecture and the Bauhaus* was published by Faber the following year and, in partnership with Maxwell Fry of MARS, he designed the Impington Village College in Cambridgeshire and the elegant house in Church Street, Chelsea, lived in by the playwright Benn Levy and Constance Cummings. But in 1937 he moved on. Similarly with Erich Mendelsohn, whose temporary partnership with Serge Chermayeff (the Broadcasting House architect) produced the neighbouring Chelsea house for the actress Diana Wynyard and her husband, and the big De La Warr Pavilion at Bexhill-on-Sea; he likewise left and in 1941 settled in the United States. Marcel Breuer too, who had been perhaps Gropius' most brilliant pupil at the Bauhaus, designed an interior in Bristol with the English architect F.R.S. Yorke; also the standard Isokon chair. With Yorke he produced a model of a 'Concrete City' for the MARS exhibition which followed in the same gallery a year after the modern German art show; then he too moved on to the USA. These three, together with Mies van der Rohe, were probably the best-known of all the architects to emigrate from Nazi Germany, though Bruno Taut in Turkey and Ernst May in Russia and East Africa had been almost as famous in their way (the last-named having oddly enough been partly trained in England). It was thus the less prominent who stayed, even though by comparison with the artists they were much more productively absorbed. The Hungarian Ernö Goldfinger for instance was by 1938 an active member of MARS; he designed one of the earliest cooperatively owned blocks of London flats (near Cecil Sharp House in Regents Park Road) and in due course came to rank as a leading member of the modern movement in this country. The Berlin architects Arthur Korn and E. Kaufmann also qualified to practise in Britain, as did the town planner Walter Bor. Of course these and other foreign-born recruits to the profession (like the Russian constructivist Berthold Lubetkin) were grist to the mills of those who wished – and perhaps wish even more vehemently today – to persuade us that CIAM-type modern architecture is un-English. Such xenophobes, however, forgot that the same architects were even then being mocked by the Nazis as un-German. The fact is that the most advanced architecture at that time was international, in a way that other avant-garde art movements were not. As a result the architectural emigration could enter a practical working fraternity such as was virtually unknown in the other arts.

# III

In the theatre the problem was in some ways similar to that of the writers. There was the same language barrier – all the more severe in the actors' case since it involved matters of pronunciation which an author is happily spared – and there was much the same lack of outlets. In the USA, in Palestine, France, Russia and of course in Switzerland a more or less professional German-speaking theatre was at least a possibility; in England there were only amateur groups, operating on an amateurish scale. In effect, therefore, the productions of the German *Kulturbund* and the Austrian *Das Laterndl*, for all the talent of their organisers and collaborators – Albert Fuchs and Martin Miller, Friedrich Richter, Betty Loewen, Hugo (Königs-) Garten and the musician Georg Knepler for instance – were not much more than cabarets; nor did the major exiled dramatists like Brecht and Toller ever let their new works be performed there. Toller was himself often in England in the mid-1930s, and was indeed much better known than Brecht: he spoke at PEN meetings, and had his plays performed in both London and the provinces. The Irish writer Denis Johnstone collaborated with him on a successful adaptation of his *Die blinde Göttin*, while a number of younger English writers liked and respected him; Stephen Spender, for one, translating his last play, *Pastor Hall*, while Auden translated the lyrics for *No more peace* and wrote that moving poem on his suicide which calls him 'egotistical and brave', and apostrophises him affectionately:

> Dear Ernest, lie shadowless at last among
> The other war-horses who existed till they'd done
> Something that was an example to the young.

Walter Hasenclever too, who married an Englishwoman, had two of his later plays performed in the London West End – his *Ehekomödie* in 1937 under the title *What should a Husband do?* and *Konflikt in Assyrien* (*Scandal in Assyria*) for which he disguised himself under the pseudonym Axel Kjellström in 1939. Neither was a success. In fact the only major émigré dramatist to have left much mark on the London theatre at that time was Carl Sternheim with his very conventional play *The Mask of Virtue*. And that was because it happened, through no fault of the writer, to provide our first glimpse of Vivien Leigh.

It cannot be said, then, that the vital theatrical innovations of the Weimar Republic penetrated far enough even for us to reject them as we rejected so much of its visual art. Brecht's *Senora Carrar's Rifles*, widely performed by Communist groups at the time of the Spanish Civil War, was, in its author's words, 'Aristotelian, empathy-drama', a deliberate exception among his work. Piscator's *War and Peace* project, though destined for the St James's Theatre, never got off the ground. Reinhardt staged *A Midsummer Night's Dream* with Oxford students in Worcester College garden, then moved on to America – though his designer Ernst Stern stayed behind (incidentally doing the Christmas decorations for Selfridge's store, one of the great London sights). This left Kurt Jooss's ballet company from Essen as the one truly exciting survival of the 1920s theatre to come our way. This group, with its excellent designer, Hein Heckroth, emigrated *en bloc* and established itself at Dartington Hall in Devonshire, one of England's most progressive schools. Its performances of *The Big City* to jazzy music by Alexander Tansman, and above all of Jooss's League of Nations satire *The Green Table* came nearer than anything else to the spirit of the Expressionist theatre and the stage works of Kurt Weill. Alas, Weill's own contribution to our theatre was a rather flabby musical to a text by Robert Vambéry called *A Kingdom for a Cow* – a short-lived prelude to the successful stage works which he was to write in the United States.

What proved more acceptable to the London theatre of that time was the handful of leading émigré actors who managed to learn the language adequately enough to get established on the English stage. This was not universally easy: Fritz Kortner, for instance, who spent his first years in London as a film actor, found the English tradition of elegant underplaying difficult to reconcile with his own powerfully expressive style, and had little success. But Oskar Homolka found parts there – and became indeed better known in London than later in Hollywood – while Friedrich Valk and Adolf Wohlbrück, or Anton Walbrook as he became, were accepted members of the London theatre world (Walbrook being now buried in Hampstead's cemetery alongside Kay Kendall's grave and Hugh Gaitskell's urn, with John Constable over the way). Above all, the English public took to its heart the waif-like Elisabeth Bergner, whom the leading impresario of the day, C.B. Cochrane, immediately treated as a star. Basil Dean having been impressed with her success in the German dramatisation of Margaret Kennedy's immensely popular novel *The Constant Nymph*, Cochrane accordingly decided to produce her in a play by the same

author. This was *Escape Me Never*, which instantly put her at the top of
the West End social-theatrical tree. Queen Mary told her she made her
cry; Noel Coward wrote 'You are fantastic!'; Lady Astor gave her a
copy of Mary Baker Eddy's *Science and Health*; the Redgraves made
her godmother to their son Corin; Bernard Shaw received her with a
cry of 'Heil Hitler!' and a private performance of 'Deutschland,
Deutschland über Alles' to his own accompaniment. It was a multiple
accolade from the high British Establishment, and to cap it all James
M. Barrie, the elderly author of *Peter Pan*, fell in love at first sight,
wished to make her his joint heiress (so her memoirs recall) and
decided to write her a play. Cochrane was delighted, and backed the
plan to the hilt, ultimately engaging Fyodor Komisarjevsky as director
and William Walton as composer, and commissioning Augustus John
and Ernst Stern respectively for the sets and costumes. The result was
*The Boy David*, with Bergner as the 13-year-old giant-killer, a work
which fell heavily and expensively flat. King George VI asked for a
special performance to be put on as part of his coronation celebrations,
but by that time Bergner was out of the country; the play was not
performed again; and early in the Second World War the actress and
her film producer husband Paul Czinner left for the United States. By
the time she came back her popularity had passed into history.

# IV

Finally there was the most universal of all arts – music. Not
only can this theoretically break all national barriers, particularly since
the development of radio and the gramophone, but great musicians
traditionally live on a semi-Olympian – or anyway wholly Ritzy –
international plane, travelling from one great musical centre to another
across continents and oceans, if not the world. This high-level traffic
however applies almost entirely to executants – soloists, singers and
conductors – rather than to the creative musician, the composer. Thus
it is only when the former are particularly committed to specific
composers or schools that such exchanges help to introduce audiences
to unfamiliar new foreign music. Worse still, the prejudices against
twentieth-century German music in pre-war England were at least as
strong as those against the corresponding visual arts. 'All those
dreadful composers ending in –*er*', Professor Edward Dent is
supposed to have said, 'Reger, Mahler, Bruckner, Pfitzner'; while

Hindemith's music was dismissed by Constant Lambert as 'sewing-machine counterpoint' and Ernest Newman – king of the newspaper critics at that time – found Weill's *Dreigroschenoper* songs to have 'the worst faults of more than one bad style and the qualities of not a single good one, even at secondhand'. Such composers were simply not accepted in the English repertoire, whose conception of the modern symphony, for instance, was determined not by Mahler but by Elgar and Sibelius. The one recognised German figure in those days was Richard Strauss, as heard primarily in *Don Juan, Till Eulenspiegel* and *Der Rosenkavalier*.

The most eminent of the musical émigrés to settle here therefore did more to raise our standards than to change our ideas. So Fritz Busch as conductor and Carl Ebert as director turned John Christie's private enterprise at Glyndebourne into one of the world's finest small opera houses with Peter Gellhorn as its *répétiteur*, while Max Rostal gave the violin teaching at the Guildhall School of Music international status. Among the singers were Ilse Wolf and Richard Tauber; among the pianists, Edith Vogel, Franz Osborn, Franz Reizenstein, Paul Hamburger and the Hungarians Ilona Kabos and Louis Kentner; the violinists Ida Haendel and Henry Datyner arrived from Poland and the young Norbert Brainin joined with three fellow-students to form the Amadeus Quartet. There was however no refugee composer of the first rank: thus our chief link with Schönberg and his school was Egon Wellesz at Lincoln College, Oxford, whose main interests lay in the rather recondite field of Byzantine music, though the Spaniard Roberto Gerhard and the Hungarian Matyas Seiber (at Morley College) became active exponents of the serialist approach. Hanns Eisler too was here several times between 1934 and 1937; he wrote music for one or two indifferent films and the Manchester production of Toller's play *Draw the Fires*; thanks largely to Alan Bush a number of political works were performed by the Workers' Music Association and other left-wing groups. At this stage, however, Eisler was remote from his teacher Schönberg, whose music was more persuasively advocated by the pianist Peter Stadlen. There were also two conductors, pupils of Schönberg who were particularly associated with this German-Austrian avant-garde and its more socially-conscious wing: Karl Rankl and Walter Goehr. Unlike such other émigré conductors as Walter Süsskind, Leo Wormser or even Karl Haas, however, they do not seem at any time to have been in a position to shape the repertoire, and their special experience of modern works was seldom used.

The most successful pre-Hitler composer of light music to settle here was Mischa Spoliansky, who provided the score for a number of films; he and Berthold Goldschmidt still remain. But there is also the very remarkable case of Wilhelm Grosz, who after a few first performances at modern music festivals in the 1920s had followed Křenek and Kurt Weill into the area of highbrow jazz, writing a *Jazzband* for violin and piano, a jazz age ballet called *Baby in der Bar* and various other original and entertaining works published (like so much else of interest) by Universal-Edition. In 1933 he left Berlin, where he was an employee of the Ultraphon record company, and came to London as a refugee. Here he set out to interest the local music publishers in his serious music, but found that he was much more welcome in Tin Pan Alley, where he was signed up by Peter Maurice Ltd (now a part of EMI) and put to work in collaboration with the song-and lyric-writer Jimmy Kennedy. The immediate result of this partnership was *The Isle of Capri*, which is said to have derived from twelve bars in his Second Piano Suite and became one of the most successful of British song hits up to that date (it is still earning sizeable royalties today). Others followed: *Red Sails in the Sunset*, *Poor Little Angeline*, *Midnight in May* (to a tune taken from Johann Strauss, with words by H. Graham) and at least two dozen more, constituting the first body of popular songs from this country to catch on in the United States. There were also some slightly more up-market songs for children written with the poet Rose Fyleman, but scarcely anything in his serious (or serious-jazz) vein, partly perhaps because he was cut off from his previous publisher by the *Anschluss* of 1938. That year he too moved on to America, dying early in the war at the age of forty-five. His work has been undeservedly neglected ever since.

In music, once again, it seems likely that what really changed our attitude to the mid-European avant-garde was neither the performers nor the composers who came to this country, but the more gradual influence of publishers, scholars and middlemen. At the heart of this process were two arrivals from Universal-Edition in Vienna (the firm which, Hindemith apart, had published the great bulk of the new mid-European music of the 1920s): Alfred Kalmus, who in due course carried on that firm's work via his own business in Soho, and Erwin Stein, Schönberg's pupil and editor, who worked for Boosey and Hawkes, the publishing house (and lessees of Covent Garden Opera House) and whose pianist daughter eventually married the Earl of Harewood, a leading figure in the post-war operatic revival. Besides these, and later to become influential in the music policies of the BBC

Third Programme under the aegis of Edward Clark (yet another pupil of Schönberg), was Hans Keller, a violinist-cum-critic of wide knowledge and passionate enthusiasm whose artist wife Milein Cosman turned many of the leading émigré musicians into familiar faces via the pages of the *Radio Times* and elsewhere. At the same time we acquired new standards of musical scholarship through such figures as Wellesz at Oxford, Hans Redlich at Cambridge and Otto Erich Deutsch, the documentary biographer of Schubert. Like the book publishers, the dealers and the art historians, these vital communicators were to become truly effective after the end of the Second World War.

## V

This question of the longer-term impact of the emigration in Britain is not a simple one, but for anyone interested in the continued vitality of our own culture it is enormously important. Even from a cursory and incomplete survey like mine – and it should be emphasised that the selection has been very subjective, resting largely on my own memories of works, events, personalities and names – it will have appeared that the immediate effects were in most cases nothing like as significant as the gradual penetration of the actual cultural apparatus: that the real change in attitude, in other words, came with the emergence in the 1950s of a new wave of publishers, art dealers, musicologists and dramaturgs who had been formed either directly or indirectly in the central European tradition. It was not that these people were (or still are) necessarily concerned to promote the literature, art and so forth of their countries of origin; the novelty, in our insular society, is that they were no longer unaware of such foreign matters, or positively prejudiced against them. Besides the art-book publishers already mentioned, who so changed our whole notion of what art books could (and should) be like, there were the younger, more general publishers who burst on our scene after 1945; men such as Ernest Hecht of Souvenir Press, Peter Owen, Max Reinhardt and George Weidenfeld, whose firms proved to be of considerable literary and scholarly significance and who now seem almost indistinguishably absorbed into the British publishing world. They are special in that they cannot help seeing England as a part of Europe, and it is largely due to their active participation that British publishers now support such international events as the annual Frankfurt Book Fair.

If you look back at the history of the reception of the continental avant-garde in England you will see that there was a wave of interest in Expressionism during the early 1920s which then petered out, with the effect that the few people actually familiar with the ideas introduced by the emigration were too often able to call them 'old hat'. Roughly speaking, it could be said that both the Bloomsbury group of the interwar years and the influential magazine *Horizon* which Cyril Connolly founded at the beginning of the 1939–45 War, were angled on Paris as the fount of all worthwhile influences, as of course were the British surrealist group. Where anything further east was concerned there was a crucial gap in understanding between the decline of A.R. Orage's magazine *The New Age* at the start of the 1920s and the rise of John Lehmann's *New Writing* in the late 1930s. And even the latter, though it certainly spread knowledge of the writing of the anti-fascist Left (including Kisch, Brecht, Kantorowicz, Regler and the young Austrian Yura Soyfer), was too much confined within the limits of a like-minded political club: you would not, for instance, find Franz Kafka there (though his main English disciple, Rex Warner, was a *New Writing* author).

Still less would you have found any such writers within the curriculum, or even on the shelves, of the average university German department. Shameful as it may now seem, the orientation of British *Germanistik* in those days was towards the eighteenth century and the middle ages; modern literature was largely ignored, and insofar as the academics themselves took an interest in it their judgements coincided far too often with those prevalent inside the Third Reich. A work such as Samuel and Hinton Thomas's still very useful *Expressionism in German Life, Literature and the Theatre* (1939) was a complete exception, and the modern reader can hardly be surprised that we lost Professor Richard Samuel to Australia soon after. Much more typically, alas, W.H. Bruford in his charmingly written *Some German Memories 1911–1961* even now looks back sympathetically at E.G. Kolbenheyer, H.F. Blunck (who had 'a difficult run as President of the *Reichsschrifttumskammer* under the Nazis for a few years'), Rudolf Binding ('completely the cavalry officer and gentleman') and Hans Grimm of *Volk ohne Raum* fame whom Bruford visited in 1936 ('an excellent opportunity of getting to know a few of the leading writers left in Germany after the coming in to power of the National Socialists and the flight of Jewish authors and/or irreconcilable opponents of the Government'), actually inviting him back to lecture in Edinburgh the next year. Admittedly Bruford also knew and liked Toller but, generally speaking, the émigrés in those days were treated as cut off from the German tradition and the periodicals in which their new work appeared were not bought for our libraries. Writers like Hans Carossa, Rudolf Alexander Schröder and Stefan George were seen as more central, borne by what Leonard Forster has called 'the sustaining power of a true tradition'. Brecht by these standards was not yet worth academic consideration, and although he has since been taken inside the portals one wonders if it is not in part because he provides such endless opportunities for research. Other fine writers have been shunted off into a critical compound called *Exilliteratur* (as distinct, presumably, from *Literatur* proper; cf. *Trivialliteratur*).

The classic portrait of an émigré artist – based in this case on the film and theatre director and occasional poet Berthold Viertel, who was here through much of the 1930s – is Christopher Isherwood's 'Bergmann' in *Prater Violet*, a novel from the *New Writing* stable. Isherwood of course was one of the small minority who knew at first hand why and how the emigration had come about. 'I knew that face', he says of the narrator's first meeting with this unknown refugee, 'it was the face of a political situation, an epoch. The face of Central Europe.' Thereafter he sees London through Bergmann's eyes, eyes formed by 'Dickens, the old German silent movies, Wedekind and Brecht':

> At the Zoo, he identified a baboon, a giraffe, and a dromedary with three of our leading politicians, and reproached them publicly with their crimes. In the National Gallery he explained, with reference to the Rembrandt portraits, his theory of camera-angles and the lighting of close-ups, so loudly and convincingly that he drew a crowd away from one of the official lecturers, who was naturally rather annoyed.

For me this conjures up not merely the memory of Hans Hess, who was in effect my own Bergmann, introducing me to countless ideas and insights about Weimar civilisation and the people who had destroyed it, but also a wider, cloudier image of young people all over England coming into contact with much the same hazardous background and stimulating cast of mind through the émigrés whom they had the luck to get to know as teachers or as older colleagues. Frank Warschauer taught, for instance, as did Lutz Weltmann, Hugh Rank from the Reinhardt-Seminar, Hugo Garten (senior German master at Westminster), Frederick Samson at the Royal College of Art, George

Brandt at Bristol, George Mayer-Marton at Liverpool ... across the whole country the effect must have been immeasurable.

Equally important – though technically outside the period of the present book – was and is the second generation of emigrants: the children of the original émigrés, who were brought up in English schools, colleges and universities and in many cases had English relatives or an adoptive family. Once again it is not perhaps their actual creative work that is so influential, though such well-known names come to mind as Frank Auerbach, Alexander Goehr, Frank Marcus, Robert Müller, Caspar Wrede and (in his capacity as an original poet) Michael Hamburger. For their special contribution has been to get inside an English skin, as it were, without disowning the particular heritage and cultural make-up of their fathers; they are thus quite exceptionally valuable as mediators in both directions. The reader should think then of Hamburger's poetry translations, of Goehr's music criticism, of Martin Esslin's initiatives as head of radio drama at the BBC, of Hannah Horowitz and her Visiting Arts Unit, of Erich Fried as a translator of Shakespeare, of Fritz Spiegl the Liverpool flautist and of the younger men like Dieter Pevsner, Thomas Neurath, Paul Hamlyn, Frank Herrmann, Tom Maschler and Tom Rosenthal who have gone to reinforce the already strong émigré influence in British book publishing; an influence typified at its best perhaps in the *Pelican History of Art*, with its debt to the broad scholarship of Nikolaus Pevsner and the designing skills of Hans Schmoller and the Swiss-based Jan Tschichold. At the same time one should remember those who have gone back to their grandparents' countries, like Georg Eisler (who with Hilde Spiel re-founded *Ver Sacrum* and stimulated the Vienna Sezession into a new lease of life) taking with them a shrewd and intimate knowledge of ourselves, sometimes in our less orthodox aspects. Both ways a lot of intangibles have altered, with the result that the kind of easy exchanges which prevail in the area of pop music are today also found on traditionally more awkward and rarefied planes.

Perhaps it is just the difficulty of penetrating the stout English hide that makes such a process, when it actually takes place, so much more profound and lasting than it would be in a more loosely integrated country. We are still a relatively homogeneous society; hence whatever we can assimilate seems likely to form part of our character rather than be a more or less interesting enclave. This has certainly been so over the centuries: the English have absorbed the Norman-French influence, the seventeenth-century Dutch, the Hanoverians and more recently the victims of the Russian pogroms, all to their lasting benefit and without feeling challenged to put up any great fight for the purity of the race or, for that matter, of the language. In other words, we have long been mongrels, and it is arguable that history's periodical efforts to see that we remain such have the effect of keeping us intellectually and culturally refreshed. Even in the Victorian age, for instance – that popular symbol of solid stability – we absorbed much that was stimulating and/or instructive from an immigrant business man called Friedrich Engels, an émigré called Dr Marx and such a mixed bag of foreign artists as (for instance) the Dutchman Tadema, the German Herkomer, the Danes Clausen and Sickert, the Frenchman Legros and the Americans Sargent and Whistler. Perhaps we need to do this kind of thing again.

I have of course been talking only of the arts. But add such other areas as the sciences, scholarship, economics and medicine, and it should be hard for even the most short-sighted nationalist – or blind antisemite – to overlook the benefits which we obtained from the emigration of the 1930s at Germany's expense. Nevertheless we are not always consciously aware of where we are going and it might be a good thing if today we could take stock and acknowledge what these people brought us. Not out of gratitude to those who were once our frequently misunderstood and sometimes neglected guests, still less out of satisfaction at our present situation (since quite enough is left us to be dissatisfied about). But once again we are now in a position of having to absorb a large-scale immigration without being mentally or culturally prepared for it; so might it not help us if more of today's Englishmen understood how rejuvenating for a rather elderly society such a development can be? This is perhaps the most important of all the issues confronting us. It would be poetic justice if one of the effects of Hitler's race policy could be to help us deal with it in a civilised and, in the long run, civilising way.

*Herbert Loebl*

# Refugee Industries in the Special Areas of Britain

## I

Throughout the nineteenth century, Britain attracted a considerable number of entrepreneurs from Germany and from central European countries, particularly during the second half of the century. Some of these made a major and permanent mark on the industrial scene. For example, the largest electrical and chemical manufacturers in Britain today developed from firms established by German emigrants. There are many examples to be found from this period, even if most of the enterprises no longer exist or cannot be recognised as separate businesses.

The reasons for the arrival of German and other continental entrepreneurs in Britain were many: Britain was the centre of industrial development in Europe at a time when Germany and other European countries had not yet changed from mainly agrarian to mainly industrial economies; it provided ample opportunities for enterprise and its doors were wide open to all without restrictions; the political climate in Germany – particularly after 1848 – was less than comfortable for Liberals and, indeed, for Jewish Germans of any political persuasion, so that it was not surprising that many of the immigrant entrepreneurs were Jewish.

It is to be noted, however, that these immigrants arrived as individuals. They were not part of a wave of refugees from political or religious persecution like the Jews from Russia, who arrived in Britain in relatively large numbers from 1880 onwards. They, too, produced an impressively large number of outstanding industrialists and other entrepreneurs. While the wave of refugees resulting from the First World War largely by-passed Britain, that created by the Nazi persecution of their political opponents and of Germans (and later of Austrians, Czechs and Poles) of the Jewish faith created a new and potentially serious political problem for Britain, which had introduced highly restrictive immigration policies in 1920.

The attitudes and policies of Britain towards refugees from Hitler's Europe have been documented in the excellent works of Sherman,[1] Wasserstein[2] and others. It is doutbful whether future research will be able to add very much of significance to the general picture, but particular aspects remain which have not been specially covered by these works. Policy towards refugee industrialists is one example.

The picture which emerges from the works cited above is a sombre one. For domestic and external reasons, British policy towards refugees was narrowly circumscribed at least until November 1938. Influential opinion in Parliament, in the press and among the public did not favour an open door, however desperate the need, and the Government did not wish to take any action which might have appeared to increase unemployment in a climate in which, despite the efforts of some economists, historians and others, it was widely believed that a causal relationship existed between immigration and unemployment. 'The theory that for every thousand aliens admitted a thousand Britons are thrown out of employment is denied alike by economic science and the plainest experience' wrote Dorothy F. Buxton and Sir Norman Angell in 1939,[3] but it was widely believed nonetheless.

This left one area in which the Government could act relatively freely: the admission of refugee manufacturers and export traders. Such action was not only in line with the principles laid down by the British Cabinet in the early days of Nazi rule – that Britain should obtain the maximum benefit from the admission of refugees[4] – it also had a number of political and practical advantages: the Government would be seen to act positively at least in this area of the refugee problem; the numbers of refugee entrepreneurs would be relatively small; some capital would be brought into the country, if not by refugees themselves then by their friends or relations abroad; exports would be increased and unemployment reduced. This would enable the Government to open the doors a little more widely to other refugees, since some sort of equation could be made between the numbers admitted and the amount of new employment created. This would satisfy all but the most diehard anti-alien and antisemitic opinion in the country.

This kind of arithmetic was indeed used when the government came under great pressure to admit more refugees, particularly following the events in the Reich on and after 9 November 1938 (*Reichskristallnacht*). From 1933 up until then no more than 11,000 refugees had been admitted.[5] The number of ventures established by refugee manufacturers was about 250 and they were clearly in an early stage of development. Yet the Home Secretary, Sir Samuel Hoare, was able to announce in the House of Commons on 1 December 1938 that 15,000 jobs had been created by these refugees.[6] A few weeks earlier Sir John Hope Simpson, the foremost expert on refugee matters of his day, had put the number at 25,000.[7] The discrepancy between the two figures may well have been due to the fact that the official employment statistics ignored factories employing less than 25 people and this was to make all early information on refugee industries somewhat unreliable. But whichever was the more accurate, both figures supported those working for a more generous refugee policy.

The Government had already indicated at an early stage in the development of the refugee problem that the doors would be open to anyone wishing to set up a factory in Britain, particularly in an area of high unemployment. In a debate in the House of Lords on 31 July 1935 the Marquis of Londonderry, for the Government, said: 'I have no reason to believe that any obstacle will be placed in the way of any individual, if he is likely to be of credit and assistance to this country, who may wish to introduce an industry into this country and give employment to men who are now unemployed'.[8]

From the beginning of Nazi rule industries were established by refugees, particularly in the London area. The numbers were small in the early years, but the tempo increased sharply after 1937. In a memorandum to the Foreign Office, intended for transmission to the Inter-Governmental Committee on Refugees, the Home Office reported on 9 September 1938 that '185 factories had been established by aliens – mainly refugees – between April 1935 and July 1938'.[9]

By February 1939 the Home Secretary was able to quote a figure of 300 factories.[10] We have been unable to find any later official figures for the period up to the outbreak of the War, when all immigration ceased except for a few special cases. We believe, however, that the number of factories started by refugees increased sharply during that time, if only because the majority of refugees from the Reich entered Britain in the seven or eight months before the War.

At this point, we must turn away briefly from the refugees and consider the economic and social situation in parts of Britain which were severely depressed. One of the ingredients of the witches' brew which led to the rise of Hitler in Germany was the business recession of 1929 and the industrial and social problems which resulted from it. While in Britain as a whole the average unemployment did not reach Germany's worst levels, there were parts of Britain where it was even higher. These were the older industrial areas, particularly the north-east coast of England, Cumberland, South Wales and the Clyde valley in Scotland, that is, the industrial areas which depended largely on coal, steel, shipbuilding and heavy engineering. What was worse, unemployment in these parts remained at a high level after a strong recovery from the business recession began in the rest of the country and showed no signs of improvement until the start of re-armament in 1936. Some profound structural changes had evidently taken place during the recession, although signs of these had already been apparent since the end of the First World War. The problem of the so-called 'depressed areas' attracted much attention, but its uniqueness in British industrial history, both in complexity and in scale, made it impossible to propose solutions based on past experience.

By 1934 Ramsay MacDonald's second National Government concluded that some special action was required, if human misery in the depressed areas was to be alleviated and the economic waste represented by heavy and chronic unemployment was to be reduced. Following a detailed investigation of these areas in the spring and summer of 1934, the first Special Areas Act was passed in December 1934. The House of Lords had changed the term 'depressed areas' to 'special areas' during the passage of the Bill. The Act provided for the appointment of Commissioners – one for England and Wales and one for Scotland – who were to co-ordinate all activities undertaken in pursuit of solutions for the problem of these areas.

One of the most fruitful results of the Special Areas Act of 1934 was the construction of factories on industrial estates and on smaller sites which were available for rent. Government-financed companies were set up in the areas concerned to undertake the construction and the administration of these factory estates. By 1937, large estates were well advanced at Team Valley, Gateshead, on the north-east coast, at Treforest near Cardiff, in South Wales and at Hillington near Glasgow, in Scotland. Smaller estates and small groups of factories were built in west Cumberland and also in the smaller places in the north-east. Not only did these factories provide a certain amount of employment relatively quickly, but it was in industries new to the areas and of a kind very different from those on which they had depended hitherto. The new light industries were to make a major contribution to the restructuring of the depressed areas and refugees were to play a significant role in this, as we shall see.

The success of the Government-owned factories was by no means a foregone conclusion at the time they were built. By definition, the depressed areas had little or no tradition of manufacturing enterprise in light industries. Neither was it certain that the available labour could adapt to the new skills, nor that women would be willing to come into the new industries, given that there was almost no previous employment for them in the traditional industries.

The Commissioners realised, therefore, that firms would have to be attracted from outside the depressed areas. As far as Britain was concerned, this line of approach proved almost totally unsuccessful: in the summer of 1935, the Commissioner for England and Wales wrote to some 5,000 firms suggesting that they might move to, or open branch factories in, one of the Special Areas. Over 4,000 firms did not reply at all and of the rest only 12 showed any interest.[11] The Commissioner concluded reluctantly that 'it had to be assumed that there was little prospect of the Special Areas being assisted by the spontaneous action of industrialists outside the Areas'.[12]

It must be remembered that British companies – unlike individual refugees – could build their factories where they chose. Although the Government took every opportunity to state that it would *like* firms to set up factories in the Special Areas, it did not have a policy of locating industry on the basis of regional need, nor of preventing a too rapid expansion in the more prosperous parts of the country, for example in the London area. Such policies, involving both 'sticks', that is a refusal to allow factory building above a certain size in some parts of the country, and 'carrots' in the form of loans, grants and preferential taxation, were not implemented until after the Second World War, although some financial inducements became available as a result of the second Special Areas Act of 1937 and through some private finance.

The Special Areas were unattractive to British industrialists for a variety of reasons, which included their distance from London, their high local taxes (a feature of all the poorer parts of the country) and the supposed militancy of their workers. The lack of response to the Commissioner's initiative was not, therefore, very surprising. In the event, most of the new factories in the Special Areas were let to local entrepreneurs on the one hand, and to refugees on the other. The need of the depressed areas of Britain to find new employment and the need of refugees to find shelter coincided. This happy conjunction was to be of benefit to both. But how did refugees actually find their way to these Areas? What were the means by which they became acquainted with the facilities offered and did they wish to go there in the first place? The answers to these questions are somewhat complex and we can do no more than sketch them in briefly.

In his second report of February 1936 the Commissioner for the Special Areas of England and Wales referred to the fact that he had been in contact with people in Germany who would have to leave the country.[13] Given the poor response of British industry, as discussed above, he was willing to obtain tenants for the new factories from anywhere. In early March 1936 the Ministry of Labour wrote a letter to the Aliens Branch of the Home Office, in which it referred to the report by the Commissioner. The letter suggested – more or less – that it should become a *condition* of admission to Britain for any alien (for 'alien' read 'refugee') who wished to set up a factory that he should do so in one of the Special Areas.[14] This letter was undoubtedly prompted by a debate in the House of Commons a few days earlier, in the course of which the problems of the Special Areas were discussed once again.

While the reply by the Home Office was cautious, it also took note of the debate in the House and concluded that 'further steps should be taken to persuade foreign manufacturers who wish to establish themselves in this country to place their works in those parts of the country where there is considerable unemployment'.

The Home Office also suggested that pressure might be brought to bear upon foreign applicants 'in some cases' by warning them that 'having regard to the present policy of HM Government, it might not be possible to agree to establishing their businesses in London or other areas proposed by them'.[15] The Home Office had no powers under any of the Aliens Regulations to make the location of a business a condition of entry. This was soon pointed out by a letter from yet another Government Department, the Board of Trade, which drew attention to the fact that 'the Government had stated categorically that it would not take powers to prohibit an individual from starting a factory where he wishes in order to compel him to go to some place where he does not wish to go'.[16]

The Board of Trade also referred to the fact that the majority of refugee manufacturers up to that time had expressed a preference for the London area, for reasons which it considered 'not unreasonable on the whole'. The reasons for this were simple and clear: more than half of the Jewish population of Britain lived in London and many refugees had friends or relations among them, as well as business contacts. They had, in any case, probably never heard of Gateshead, Cardiff, Hillington or Workington before. When starting up in a foreign country – with an absolute minimum of resources – it is natural that one does so where one has friends and contacts. Apart from this, London was the centre of the British market and those who wanted to export would find buyers from almost all important countries, and particularly from the British Empire and Commonwealth, represented there. A location other than London would merely add to the difficulties and costs of establishing themselves. Yet this was precisely what the Ministry of Labour and the Home Office wanted to achieve! The result of these discussions among Government Departments was a compromise: the letter sent out by the Home Office in response to enquiries by prospective refugees *did* mention the matter of location as *one* of the questions which would have to be agreed, but it did not make it a condition of admission.

How did prospective refugees react to this policy and why were those whom we have been able to interview under the impression that a location of their factories was, in fact, a *condition* of their admission?

The refugees who arrived before 1937 had a number of advantages. The situation in Germany was not yet as desperate as it was to become later. They were still able to travel abroad before their emigration and some of them paid one or more visits to Britain to prepare their move. Most important of all, they were still able to transfer at least a part of their assets and this gave them a certain position of strength from which to negotiate with the authorities when discussing location, particularly as no factories were yet available for rent on the trading estates being built in the Special Areas. This no doubt explains why we have not found any evidence of refugee firms in the north before 1937.

By the time the majority of refugee manufacturers were seeking admission, the situation had changed dramatically. Many of them belonged to prominent German-Jewish families who felt relatively secure – however illusory such feelings turned out to be – and who had therefore left the decision to get out of Germany until it was almost too late. When they did decide to leave, they knew that they were fleeing for their lives. This applied to Austrians and Czechs from the moment the Germans marched in. For those who had delayed applying for permission to come to Britain until the spring of 1938 or even later, all that mattered was to get out. Their willingness to go to one of the Special Areas must be seen in this context. It was, no doubt, explained to them that permission to settle in one of these Areas would be granted very much more quickly than for any other parts of Britain, including London.

If the Home Office largely achieved its objectives regarding the location of refugee industries, it was due to the speed with which permits for the Special Areas were obtained. It was not surprising, therefore, that the refugees believed that their admission was conditional on their willingness to settle in one of the Areas, and the letter of permission helped to strengthen this impression: this letter always specified where any factory was to be set up and in the cases we have studied – where the letter of admission still existed – it always referred to a location in a Special Area. For refugees the advantages of the Special Areas were real enough; few of them had more capital than they had been able to bring out of Germany discreetly in the course of a few export trips in the past, or borrow from friends or relations abroad. The availability of factories *for rent* would have been, for most, a deciding factor even if the Home Office had not pressed for a particular location. On the other hand, the markets for the goods they intended to make were generally remote from the Areas; still, refugees are not in a good position to select ideal locations for their factories.

While the Home Office applied pressure, there were a number of organisations which sought to attract refugee manufacturers to particular Special Areas. The Industrial Estate Companies set up by the Government sent representatives to Europe in order to contact potential refugees. Similarly, the local Development Organisations, which were a feature of all the Special Areas, sent their representatives on the same errands. The British Consular Offices cooperated closely, particularly in speeding up the enquiries which had to be made before anyone obtained a visa.

Any arrangements had to be confidential. The Nazi authorities were doing all they could to stop the removal of businesses abroad, particularly those with export connections. Any prospective emigrant had to give an indication of the kind of job he was likely to do in the country of immigration before he received permission to leave. The Nazi authorities knew very well that anyone coming to Britain would be permitted to accept a job only in exceptional circumstances, yet they seem to have acquiesced in the proceedings. Nevertheless, contacts with British Consular Officials and visitors from the Special Areas had to be circumspect. Application papers and mail containing any references to the intention of setting up a factory in Britain were usually transmitted by consular officials in the diplomatic bag.

The availability of capital raised a particularly delicate question.

Intending refugee manufacturers had to show that they had the minimum means available in Britain to set up factories. Official transfer of funds after 1937 was practically impossible and the penalties for illegal transfer were draconian, so that few people dared to risk it. Some devised elaborate schemes to transfer funds through export transactions, but this was possible only in the smallest firms where the owner himself handled all the books and correspondence and where there was no danger of being given away by employees. Others were able to show that funds were coming from friends or relations abroad. The problem seems to have been handled with flexibility and good sense by the Consulates abroad and by the Home Office in London. From the end of 1937 onwards, all Departments of State and the Special Areas organisations worked closely together to assist the transfer of refugee manufacturers to the Special Areas. By the spring of 1939, two out of three refugee factories in Great Britain were established in these areas.[17]

## II

Since we constantly refer to them, we must define what we mean by refugees and refugee industries – or more correctly, refugee industrial firms. 'A refugee', wrote Sir John Hope Simpson in 1938 – with reference to German and Austrian refugees and at a time when the extermination camps were not yet in operation –

> might be described as an *involuntary* migrant. He would rather remain where he is, but conditions religious, economic, political or social have rendered his life there so uncomfortable or, indeed, so unbearable, that he is forced to migrate from his home in search for more tolerable conditions of life elsewhere. His alternatives to escape may frequently be the concentration camp or suicide. His search is often rendered more difficult in that the ordinary rights of a national are withdrawn from him, he is denationalised, unprovided with the normal travel documents and left to fend for himself by any services of the State to which he belonged. He is an unwanted inhabitant of the world, unwanted in the country of his origin, unwanted by any other country.[18]

In the study we undertook between 1975 and 1978 on Refugee Industries in the Special Areas of the North,[19] we did not distinguish between those established before and after the War. Our criteria required only that the founders were admitted as refugees or, in the course of events, became refugees in the sense that they could not return to, or live in their countries of origin, that their enterprises were founded been 1937 and 1961 and that they were still in existence in the north of England on 1 November 1974.

We accepted as refugees not only those who were directly and immediately threatened by the Nazi regime in Germany and in those countries invaded by the Nazis before the Second World War but also people, mainly of Jewish origin, whose life was made difficult by the semi-fascist regimes in eastern Europe, particularly Poland and Hungary, and who were, in any case, afraid of an early German invasion. This was not long delayed in the case of Poland, and in the case of Hungary political events led to the same results as far as Jewish people were concerned. We have also included people – again mainly Jewish – who escaped from Europe after the defeat of France and few who survived the war in Europe.

Within these criteria we can now give the categories we have been able to discern from our study:

1. Firms which were set up by refugees on arrival from Europe before or during the first months of the War, who were admitted on the understanding that they would set up factories in a Special Area. Such firms may have been started by refugees entirely on their own or in partnership with British interests.

2. Firms which resulted from 1. For example, two partners may have separated, causing an additional firm to be set up. Again, sons of refugee manufacturers – in every case we have studied they were themselves refugees – may have set up firms of their own.

3. Firms which were set up in the north by refugees long after their arrival and whose presence there was unconnected with the conditions of their admission into Britain.

4. Firms which were started by refugees together with British (or foreign) working or financial partners. We included such firms only after we were satisfied that they would not have been started without the initiative of the refugee partner.

5. Firms which were started by refugees in other parts of Britain but were moved to the north under general location of industries policies after the war, or which were set up under such policies. In both cases, the existence of such enterprises in the north was due to the original admission of their founders as refugees.

6. A few cases which fit into none of the above categories, but which satisfied us that they came within our general theme.

## III

The first refugees intending to set up factories whom we were able to locate in the north arrived in 1937. They were atypical and came to – then – atypical places. The founders of a specialist firm in the steel industry, originally from the Saar, settled on Teesside even before it was included in a Special Area. Towards the end of 1937, the founder of a leather tanning company, from Hungary, decided to settle at Millom in West Cumberland, although no factory was yet available for him. The first arrivals on Tyneside – in February 1938 – were the founders of a knitwear firm, for which a factory was being built at North Shields on what was to become a small industrial estate in an area very badly hit by the closure of shipbuilding yards in the early 1930s. Their arrival was reported in the North Shields *Evening News* of February 1938 under the headline 'German family arrives to start new Tyneside industry'. This was quite common, particularly in the smaller places, where the arrival of refugee manufacturers was news on two counts: firstly, because there was the prospect of work – a most important topic for many families – and secondly, because the founders were foreigners. We have found several examples of such local reporting. To give another one, the *West Cumberland News* of 18 March 1939 reported a speech by the President of the Cumberland Development Council:

> Major Hibberd . . . welcomes the refugees who are coming here with their brains, capital and machinery. We benefit as we did when the Huguenots were forced out of France. It is significant that when unemployment is increasing, there should be this wave of refugees, victims of persecution, ready to repay in kind the shelter offered to them.

The next arrivals were two firms whose founders also came from Germany. They settled in St Helen's Auckland in south-west Durham, where a small industrial estate was being constructed. This area had suffered great deprivation even before the business recession, since coal mining, the main local industry, had ceased in the late 1920s. The majority of refugee firms, however, were established only in 1939;

this applied both to the north-east and to Cumberland. With one or two exceptions they started in Government-owned factories.

Almost none of the intending manufacturers had much money at their disposal. Most of what they had – and even then it was usually not enough – was needed for plant and machinery and for working capital. Quite a few had less than £2,000 in capital. This left very little to live on. They depended on getting their businesses off the ground as quickly as possible. Most of them bought second-hand machinery and improvised as best they could. Some firms found financial backing from local people or firms, to whom they were introduced by the authorities. The financiers were looking for new ideas and the refugees provided them. The fact that they came from countries whose inhabitants were generally considered very capable and efficient certainly helped.

Most of the refugees who came before the War were able to bring at least some of their household effects with them. The Nazis imposed penal charges for this privilege. Some refugees had difficulty in accommodating all their belongings in the small semi-detached or terraced houses they were able to rent. Quite a few of the refugees had owned substantial businesses at home. H. C. Whitehouse, the former Sales Manager of North Eastern Trading Estates, recalled that when he had visited a prospective refugee tenant of the Team Valley estate at his home in Berlin in 1937, the door was opened to him by a liveried servant! The adjustment to the new situation cannot have been easy for the people concerned. All of them had to get used to a new language and a different way of life. The proportion of those who had never before been to Britain was surprisingly high and many lacked knowledge of the markets for their products. There were all the signs that they had left in a hurry and without proper preparation – which, under the circumstances, was hardly surprising.

Some made false starts by producing goods they could not subsequently sell. Others counted on a continuation of the markets they had supplied from their original works. They could not have been considering the possibility of war, or that these markets might be closed, because in some cases this would have removed the basis of their business from the start. They quickly learned and adapted, however, and almost all of the firms they started survived and grew, in spite of many handicaps, the most serious of which was internment in 1940. The earlier arrivals helped later ones in both personal and business matters. For example, a manufacturer of cardboard boxes recalled that his first substantial order came from a refugee firm which had settled only a few months before he arrived.

Many refugees had elderly relatives with them or worried how they could get them out of Germany, Austria or Czechoslovakia. Although many made English friends fairly quickly, much of their social life was spent with fellow refugees. They were at that time still happier to converse in their native tongue, and their common fate and problems formed a natural bond.

The setting up of so many new firms by foreigners did not go unnoticed either locally or nationally. At a time when business was still slack, particularly in some trades, the anxiety of some British manufacturers was aroused. Questions were asked in Parliament, some of them couched in unpleasant language. For example, on 28 March 1939 the North Shields *Evening News* reported that a Scottish Member of Parliament, Mr D. Kirkwood, had tabled a question in the House concerning the knitwear firm to which we have already referred as the first arrival on Tyneside. The question described the promoters as a 'German-Jewish firm' and noted that a permit had been issued for an Austrian expert to come to Britain in order to train local workers. It pointed out that the Scottish hosiery industry had difficulty in keeping its factories working full-time and asked why, under these circumstances, had the foreign firm been given facilities under the Special Areas Act? In a leader of the same day, the *Evening News* wrote:

> The obvious answer is that there is a crying need for new trade and if no English firm comes forward with an offer to supply it and a foreign firm does, it is only common sense to welcome the offer. . . . While little is publicly known of the details of the new factory, we accept the statement . . . that the goods manufactured will be a different line from those produced by the Scottish companies.
>
> That the latter may not be injured by the competition, if any, will be the hope of everyone. But there would be little hope of new industries being established anywhere if the existence of similar industries in one part of the country or another were to be a barrier against new enterprise.
>
> The promotion of the knitwear undertaking promises to create employment in a district where it is badly needed.

This was almost certainly not the only occasion when the establishment of a refugee firm had to be defended in this way.

The trade unions had similar problems. They were quite unused to dealing with light industries and to the girls and women employed in them. Furthermore, they looked askance at small firms, which were unusual in the Special Areas of the north with their heavy industries, because they were notoriously difficult to organise. It was not surprising that trade union secretaries allowed themselves some wild language and made quite baseless accusations. But these jarring notes did not ring out for long. Within a few months, the whole country would have quite different – and much more serious – preoccupations: the outbreak of war.

# IV

Few refugees appear to have considered that the War might present them with further problems. In a sense, the failure of the policy of appeasement meant that the world at last understood the menace posed by the Nazis and was now rallying to the side of Hitler's opponents and victims.

In contrast to 1914, when every German living in Britain was suspected of being a spy, an entirely different situation prevailed in 1939. Public sympathy was on the side of the refugees and even the Government realised that it was confronted with quite a new problem. It desired to give the refugees the maximum amount of liberty; at the same time, in the interests of national security, it had to sift out any spies and Nazi agents who might use the guise of refugee as a cover for their subversive activities.[20] To deal with the problem, the Government set up special Tribunals. One hundred and twenty of these were appointed and it was their task to classify aliens of an enemy nationality into three categories: those in category A were deemed to be suspect and interned; those in category B remained at liberty subject to certain restrictions, particularly on travelling, while those in category C were given considerable freedom and their Aliens Registration Certificates were stamped 'Refugee from Nazi Oppression'. While some tribunals were over-cautious and thereby caused refugee industrialists a great deal of extra worry and trouble, because they had been put into category B, those in the Special Areas of the north appear to have had no such difficulties. They were all classified under category C.

Their problems lay in a different direction. At the onset of the War, most raw materials coming in from abroad were rationed on the basis of use in the year before the War. Since few refugee manufacturers in the north had been operating for a whole year, they found themselves without the necessary raw materials. A small number went out of business, once all substitute materials had been exhausted. The majority of firms changed over to the production of goods which were either needed directly for the war effort or were considered essential for the civilian population. This reduced, even if it did not entirely remove, the difficulties of materials allocation. The changeover in production was not easy, but most firms seem to have managed reasonably well, being helped by the fact that it was gradual rather than sudden. By the early summer of 1940, most of the firms concerned were on a war footing.

At that time the War was going badly for Britain. Perhaps because of this, the government policy towards the refugees underwent a dramatic revision, a subject dealt with at greater length elsewhere in this volume. Here it is sufficient to note that, within a week of the capitulation of Holland on 10 May 1940, all male German and Austrian refugees were arrested throughout Britain, regardless of their classification. In the north, nearly all the refugees, as industrialists, were in category C. The shock of finding themselves once more in prison, guarded by soldiers carrying rifles with mounted bayonets, was heightened by the irony of their situation: having escaped with their lives from the Nazi Reich, they were now suspected of being the agents of their tormentors, in spite of having been fully screened before being admitted to Britain.

It is beyond the scope of this essay to discuss the details of the internment period, which, for some, lasted as long as two years. What concerns us here is how the young firms survived while their founders and managers were away in internment camps. At first, the wives of some of the interned manufacturers tried to carry on, until they too were forced to leave within the month. One or two firms moved temporarily out of the area and the women carried on the business. In other cases, friends, foremen or newly-trained local managers tried to do the same. Several of the businesses, however, had to close down. The financial position of most of the firms, particularly those of the later arrivals – and of the families concerned – rapidly became disastrous. Since they had arrived with barely enough to start their business, the interruption caused by internment and the uprooting of their families strained the finances of some beyond breaking point. Some of the women and children who went to London had to be supported by charities for the first time in their lives.

Within a few weeks, both the internment order and the conditions under which refugees were being held sparked off a number of heated questions and debates in both Houses of Parliament, in spite of all the desperate preoccupations of the Government and the country. The Government was forced to give way and the internment order was gradually put into reverse gear. The whole affair appears to have been a gross blunder, although perhaps an excusable one under all the circumstances.

Release from internment began in September 1940, but it was a slow and erratic process. Some refugee manufacturers from the north were among the first to be released. Others – often partners or close relatives of those released – were detained for a year or more, for no discoverable reason. Most of the refugees returning from internment had to rebuild their firms almost from the beginning. Those whose firms were not engaged on work of national importance found that their factories had been requisitioned during their absence and their plant and machinery stored. Gradually, refugee firms were drawn into war production. So that they and their firms could undertake such work, they were required to obtain Auxiliary War Services permits which were entered onto their Aliens Registration Certificates. Refugee manufacturers – like other refugees – were also recruited for Civil Defence activities. Slowly, the sense of alienation created by internment disappeared as they were gradually accepted into the community.

# V

Even a brief essay on refugee industries in Britain in the period from 1937 onwards would be incomplete without some reference to the Refugee Industries Committee. Established a few months before the War by a number of prominent public figures, mainly Members of Parliament, this remarkable organisation was originally intended to assist refugee manufacturers from Czecho-slovakia. Its first name was the Committee for Development of Refugee Industries. By 1941 its name had been changed to the Refugee Industries Committee and, by the end of 1947, to the Committee for Development from Overseas.

The Committee quickly became recognised as the national organisation for refugee industries, who found in it a powerful advocate with ready access to both ministers and government departments. Its membership was wholly British and this proved to be of great value, particularly under the circumstances arising out of the war: it saw to it that the new firms received reasonable allocations of scarce materials; it helped to procure labour permits and export licences; it was active during the internment period and it arranged for questions to be asked in Parliament in particular cases. Later, it succeeded in obtaining an easing of the many restrictions imposed on all aliens of enemy nationality, particularly those affecting movement, which were especially irksome to industrialists. Some police authorities kept refugees waiting up to ten days for permission to travel a distance of forty miles!

From 1942 onwards the Committee arranged annual conferences in London, at which representatives from the local Refugee Industries Associations – it is believed that there were eight of these during the War – could meet each other and members of the central committee and its executives. On these occasions they were also able to meet representatives of government and to discuss their problems with them. On the whole, these problems seem to have received sympathetic consideration. Speeches made by highly-placed well-wishers helped to boost the morale of those present. The Committee also effectively combated the xenophobia which persisted during the War and increased towards its end. There was a fairly strong lobby pressing for the return of all refugees to their countries of origin after the end of the War and it required much skill and determination on the part of the Committee to neutralise this lobby. With shortages of labour after the War rather than the expected unemployment, the need for defending refugee industries became less important and the Committee began to draw attention to their achievements, both on the radio and in the press. At the same time, the Committee started to assist the 'second wave' of refugees who wanted to set up factories, including those who had served in the armed forces, those who had no opportunity to start before the War and those few who came after the War.

The most important part of the Committee's work during the last year of the War and after it ended was concerned with the naturalisation issue, a matter on which all Government replies up to then had been vague. Refugee industrialists became increasingly concerned about their position when the War ended. We have already referred to the lobby calling for a general repatriation. But quite apart from this, it was feared that a blanket naturalisation of all those who wanted to stay in Britain – and this certainly included almost all industrialists – was unlikely even if the principle had been accepted, because the machinery of the Home Office was not geared to deal with the relatively large numbers involved. Naturalisation had been suspended during the War, resulting in a large backlog of applications.

In the event, naturalisation was granted with a speed which surprised most of the people involved. Industrialists (and other categories of refugees, for example ex-servicemen) were able to make priority applications, so that they could travel abroad in search of export orders. Within three years of the end of the War, naturalisation was almost completed. The period of total absorption of refugees was beginning and, as far as refugee industrialists were concerned, the Refugee Industries Committee played an important part in achieving this satisfactory outcome.

# VI

In the following pages we will attempt a qualitative and, as far as possible, a quantitative evaluation of the contribution made by refugee industries in the north of Britain,[21] large parts of which remain 'Special Areas' today, although the designation has now changed. Firstly, however, let us look for a moment beyond the statistics and turn the spotlight briefly onto the men who created the enterprises. It has been observed that the case histories of these men have almost the quality of an epic. The Oxford Dictionary defines an epic as a poem 'narrating continuously the achievements of one or more heroes'. The implication is that the achievements referred to were obtained after great struggles. This definition is not inappropriate to the picture revealed by the case histories.

The mere fact of their safe arrival in Britain was already an achievement for some. Once here, they had to feed and clothe their families in the knowledge that they had nothing and nobody to fall back on if things went wrong. They struggled with a new language, with strange customs and with markets they did not know well, if at all. The different origins, backgrounds and experiences of the founders formed a microcosm of European light industry. At one end of the scale, there were entrepreneurs who tried to continue skills developed by their families over several generations; at the other, there were professional men with no previous business experience who tried to earn a living by making relatively simple products. There were false starts which would have discouraged men of lesser courage. For many, internment destroyed the tender plant they had nursed to modest health and yet another start had to be made! A few created important new markets but lacked the financial resources to carry on, only to see others reap the benefit. There were firms which could not support two founders and their families, so that one of them had to leave! In one such case, the departing partner established a new business which today counts its sales in millions and which has branches and factories in several countries overseas. One could go on picking out such fascinating details. Altogether, the case histories present a record of courage, imagination and hard work.

## Number of firms involved

Our study shows that the number of refugee manufacturing concerns established between 1937 and 1961 in the northern region (north-east and Cumberland) was seventy-six. Of these, twenty-two firms were no longer in existence in the region on our reference date (1 November 1974). It is noteworthy that only three of these twenty-two firms failed in the ordinary course of business. The rest ceased to exist for a variety of reasons, which included war-time conditions (lack of material or the transportation of the founder overseas during the internment period), retirement of founders and acquisition by other firms and subsequent transfer to other parts of the country.

## Number of founders and employment generated

Fifty-four of the firms established by refugees in the north-east of England before the end of 1961 were still in existence on 1 November 1974. Some 100 founders, many of whom were no longer alive at this time, were involved. The total number employed in the region by these firms was 16,932. We have been able to cross-check the employment figure with the Department of Industry and, after making some necessary statistical adjustments, we found that the official figure coincided with ours to within 4.2 per cent.

We took no account of the indirect employment generated by these firms through the purchase of goods and services in the region. In fact, because of the influx of many new industries into the region since the War, it became possible to obtain an increasing range of goods and services throughout the region. It follows that the indirect employment created by refugee firms in the north has increased over the years. While we cannot quantify it, it may well amount to 15–30 per cent of the direct employment.

We have also omitted any employment created elsewhere in Britain as a result of the establishment of these refugee industries in the north, as well as employment resulting from the setting up of new production lines within existing British firms by refugees who did not start their own factories; there were certainly several such examples in the area.

When we consider the relatively small number of founders and take into account their minute resources, we must come to the conclusion that the amount of employment created represents a considerable achievement. Numbers apart, refugee industries had a qualitatively beneficial effect on the labour market; many new skills were introduced and training problems were solved. In the course of this, the adaptability of the work-force was demonstrated, particularly that of men who had grown up in entirely different industries and trades. Furthermore, the kind of industries established by refugees needed girls and women, for whom there had been practically no job opportunities in the region before 1937. The successful integration of female labour into the productive economy was to have important implications for the postwar development of the region. The original fears that female employment was irrelevant in the Special Areas with their high male unemployment proved to be largely unfounded. Indeed we were able to establish, with the help of the Department of Industry, that the fifty-four surviving refugee firms employed rather more male than female labour: the exact ratio was 1.2:1.

Many managerial employment opportunities were created of a kind which had been difficult to obtain in the pre-1937 economy of the north, so that this was a desirable development. Furthermore, it seems that a fairly large proportion of refugee firms engaged in activities usually described as R and D (research and development). Unlike branch factories – which form the major part of the new postwar industry in the north – refugee firms carried on most of these activities 'in house' and so created professional and technical positions.

## Size of firms, by numbers of employees

The Report of the Committee of Enquiry on Small Firms (Bolton Report)[22] defined small manufacturing firms as those employing 200 people or less. Our analysis shows that by this definition thirty-four firms (63 per cent of refugee manufacturing firms in the north in existence on 1 November 1974) could be classified as small. The Bolton Committee found, however, that the average employment in such firms in Britain was only twenty-five. By contrast the average employment of the thirty-four refugee firms was 109. It is beyond the scope of this article to investigate this discrepancy, or to try to explain the apparently better performance of refugee concerns in the small manufacturing field compared to the same category of British industry as a whole.

The following Table shows the relative employment figures for the fifty-four firms still in existence on 1 November 1974:

| No. of firms | (%) | No. of employees | |
|---|---|---|---|
| 1 | 1.85 | 5 — | 10 |
| 4 | 7.41 | 11 | 50 |
| 13 | 24.10 | 51 | 100 |
| 16 | 29.64 | 101 | 200 |
| 34 | 63.00 | | |
| 11 | 20.35 | 201 | 500 |
| 6 | 11.12 | 500 | 1,000 |
| 3 | 5.53 | Over | 1,000 |
| 54 | 100.00 | | |

## Types of industries established by refugees

Our study shows that, except for the chemical industry in West Cumberland, refugee firms established in the north were in the light industry sector. Those set up before the War began with very small resources; so small, indeed, that it is difficult to understand how they survived and prospered. They clearly depended on skills, on the knowledge of a specialised market or product (often acquired only after the start of a venture) and on the ability and the will to sell. All these attributes, however, would have been of no avail had it not been for the tenacity and the ability to improvise displayed by the founders and their staffs.

With one or two exceptions, the industries set up before the War were not in advanced technologies but in relatively ordinary products which had either not been manufactured, or were not readily available, in Britain. The War itself determined the kind of products which were needed, or were permitted to be made. When we consider the postwar enterprises a somewhat different picture emerges; while clothing and hosiery manufacture, for example, still represented a high proportion of new ventures, some new firms now appeared to be both more capital-intensive and in more advanced technologies like electro-chemical engineering, chemicals and plastics. In the case of some new enterprises, new markets were discovered for the products of more traditional industries, such as, for example, paper-converting.

When the pre-1939 industrial estates had been established, it was expected that many, if not most, of the new factories would produce goods for local consumption, i.e. goods which up to that time had been imported into the region. This was seen as an essential part of the strategy for strengthening the economies of the Special Areas.[23] In the event, this was found to apply to only one refugee firm. Their products were specialised and therefore found a national rather than a local market; most firms developed export markets. Goods made for national retailers did find their way back to the region but in only a single case studied, a firm of cardboard box makers, did we note the intention on the part of the refugee firm to serve mainly a local market.

*Types of industries established by refugees in the*
*Special Areas of the north, 1937–61 (surviving firms only)*

| | |
|---|---|
| Adhesives | Knitwear |
| Boilers and radiators | Leather goods |
| Brushes, including artists' brushes | Leather, tanning |
| Building materials | Mechanical handling |
| Buttons and dress ornaments | Millinery |
| Car accessories | Packing materials |
| Chemicals, fine | Paper converters |
| Chemicals, industrial | Plastics, converters |
| Clothing | Plastics, foam |
| Curled hair | Plastics, manufacturers |
| Electrical accessories | Pumps |
| Electro-chemical engineering | Safety belts and helmets |
| Electronic controls | Scientific instruments |
| Fabric and cloth | Slag and scrap recovery |
| Foodstuffs | Small metal ware |
| Footwear | Spectacle frames |
| Furniture | Sports goods |
| Gifts and novelties | Sports wear |
| Gloves, hosiery | Toys and fancy goods |

As already stated, most firms appear to have had at least some export business, some selling a large proportion of their output abroad. A few firms produced goods which had been at one time almost exclusively imported into Britain; artists' brushes, for example. The export performance of some of the firms was recognised both by Queen's Awards to Industry, five of which were earned by refugee firms between 1966 (when the award was instituted) and 1974, and by appearances in the Honours Lists. Six founders or members of their families appeared in these Lists up to the end of 1974; four of these were named for export achievements.

## Choice of location

As we have seen, the choice of location for refugee manufacturing ventures founded after 1937 was, in practice, restricted to one of the Special Areas. Not only was it much easier to obtain permission to settle in Britain after agreeing to set up an industry in one of the Special Areas, but by the autumn of 1937 the first factories *available for rent* on trading estates and elsewhere were ready for occupation. Furthermore, a range of sources of financial and other assistance were available, in principle at least. In the event, only ten of the forty-two refugee firms established before 1939 in the north received any direct financial assistance.

What we will examine here is why the firms we have studied chose the Special Areas of northern England rather than those of Wales or Scotland. Objective factors appear to have played a small part: in the north-east, the availability of a suitable raw material (for example, sand), the nearness of the Scandinavian markets and financial backing from local interests were reasons given for the choice. Other factors, however, seem to have played a much bigger role: the prior settlement in the area of friends or relations; the presence of a sizeable Jewish community and of religious institutions, particularly the existence of an Institute of Jewish Studies (Yeshiva) at Gateshead; the personalities and the salesmanship of the secretary of the Tyneside Industrial Development Board and of the Sales Manager and other officers of North Eastern Trading Estates Ltd.; or simply chance.

In west Cumberland, we know of only one case among the early arrivals where an objective factor operated: the suitability of local water persuaded the founders of a leather tannery to set up at Millom, a remote place in a remote area! Again, the personalities of the officers of the development organisations seem to have played a major role in the choice of location.

In the period January to September 1939, the remoteness from London and the absence of any large towns which might become targets for enemy aircraft became factors in the choice of west Cumberland, and the prior settlement of friends or relatives again played a part, both before and after the War. Given, in addition, that communications were not good in parts of the north-east, for example in south-west Durham where the earliest arrivals settled, and even less adequate in west Cumberland, we must conclude that objective factors played little part in the choice of a Special Area in the north.

The choice of location of some of the postwar refugee firms was based on considerations and requirements which applied to all industry and which therefore require no examination within our context.

## Suitability of location

It is tempting to speculate as to the suitability of the location of refugee firms which were established before the War and which were induced by the Home Office and other Departments of State to establish themselves in the north.

We know that before the policy of exerting pressure on refugees was adopted in the summer of 1936, most of them expressed a preference for the Greater London area for reasons which, as we have seen, the Board of Trade considered perfectly reasonable.[24] Certainly very few refugee firms established before 1937 were located in the Special Areas and we have not come across a single firm on the east coast of England (or west Cumberland).

For the majority of firms the choice was between four locations of almost equal unsuitability (South Wales, the south-west of Scotland, west Cumberland and the north-east coast of England). There were, of course, some advantages; these included lower wage rates, a generally lower cost of living and the availability of factories for rent. Refugee industries might well have grown faster and to greater importance in the London area and in some other places. Nevertheless, they prospered – reasonably in most cases and outstandingly in a few – *in spite of their locations*, to which they adapted from the beginning.

From the standpoint of the national economy it might well be that reasonably successful and stable firms in those parts of the country where they are badly needed, are of greater importance than outstandingly successful firms in London and in a few other places where prosperity is accepted; we must conclude that Government policies were more far-sighted than appeared at the time they were formulated. The War itself made a location in the north – particularly in west Cumberland – more desirable, because the danger, disruption and stress caused by the bombing of London and other large centres was thereby, in the main, avoided. Location became less important as firms became established and as communications improved after the War, although by this time the founders who had borne the early inconveniences of a location which was less than ideal, had either died or retired.

## Importance of refugee industries in the Special Areas of the north

The relative importance of refugee industries on the north-east coast and in west Cumberland can best be illustrated by reference to the unemployment figures for the two parts of the region at the end of 1934, i.e. at a time when the business recession was almost over and when the north found itself left with a huge structural unemployment problem.

|  | *Unemployment*[25] *in 1934* (A) | *Employment by refugee firms in 1974* (B) | $\frac{B}{A} \times 100\%$ |
|---|---|---|---|
| Durham & Tyneside | 176,862 | 10,552 | 5.96% |
| West Cumberland | 13,530 | 6,380 | 47.15% |
|  | 190,392 | 16,932 | 8.89% |

We see, therefore, that refugee industries were relatively much more important in west Cumberland than on the north-east coast as a whole, although their importance in some districts in the north-east, for example in south-west Durham, was much greater than the overall figure for the north-east would suggest.

We did not consider it necessary to investigate the total sales of the firms studied and accepted the approximate figures we were given. Some firms were unwilling to release their sales figures. Our estimate for the total sales of refugee manufacturing firms in the north in 1974 is £140–150 million. Similarly, we estimate their exports to have been about £40 million in that year, £20 million of which was accounted for by a single firm.

## 'Spin-Off'

In an important work on industry in depressed areas published just before the Second World War, Dennison pointed out that where the industrial structure of an area was one of a limited number of industries, interconnected with each other – and this was certainly true for all the depressed areas of Britain – there is only a small probability of diversification and development of new industries from old. He showed that in the newer industrial areas in the south-east of England, by contrast, there was a 'continuous process of the emergence of new forms of economic activity'.[26]

We asked about half the firms in our study about any known 'spin-offs', that is, about employees or partners in the firm who were known to have set up new manufacturing firms of their own. We were told of a fairly large number of cases, although we made no attempt to make an exhaustive investigation. The examples seemed strongly to support Dennison's theory. It is, of course, a fairly general experience that small and medium-sized firms generate relatively more spin-off than large ones. This may be because the leadership displayed by the founders, where they are still in control, is 'catching' or, at least, is seen as being capable of emulation. The sparsity of means available to most refugee manufacturers and the high degree of improvisation required in order to survive in the early stages may have played a particularly instructive role.

## Status of surviving firms

Since the end of the War, many of the larger British firms have grown by acquiring smaller firms. While the same trend remains discernible in other industrial countries, the taxation system in Britain, which made it difficult for family concerns to be passed on to the next generation, frequently resulted in the necessity of disposing of a business before retirement or on the death of the founders.

Refugee firms were subject to the same pattern of development, and the more significant ones were therefore of interest to larger industrial interests in Britain. It is not surprising, therefore, that thirty-three of the fifty-four surviving refugee-founded firms had been acquired by 1 November 1974. In one sense, this may certainly be considered a success, because the buyers must have believed that they were obtaining a business, valuable in its own right, not dependent on the personality of its founder, as is so often the case with small firms.

## Outlook

The importance of refugee industries in the Special Areas of England, Wales and Scotland is now much less in relation to such industries in Britain as a whole than was the case in 1939. In spite of the 'stick' and 'carrot' policies of successive postwar Governments, a large majority of refugee-founded manufacturing firms in Britain are now located outside the Special Areas. It is doubtful whether more than 15 per cent of the employment created by refugees in the manufacturing sector is now located in the Special Areas and the share of those in the north is unlikely to be more than 5 to 7 per cent of the national total.

As far as stability is concerned, we have already noted that in the north only one or two of the firms concerned depended on a local market. The number of firms which have the kind of plant which might be considered immovable are few. From the point of view of the Special Areas, the risk remains that refugee-founded firms might be moved away from them after acquisition, particularly since almost all of the new owners are based outside the Special Areas.

The favourable grant, loan and tax policies in the Special Areas – now called Development Areas – have so far prevented a widespread removal of the acquired firms by their new owners. In some cases, the special skills gained by the work force over many years have proved to be a stabilising factor, but the possibility of removal is always there, particularly in times of economic difficulty. A number of firms have been moved already in the cause of rationalisation of production and overheads, and the process seems to be accelerating.

On the other hand, we know of cases where the new owners have made very substantial new investments in the acquired firms. Nevertheless, it is probable that the factors making for removal are more important than the new investments, at least at the moment of writing (late 1980).

Those refugees who arrived in Great Britain as children before the War are now reaching an age where new starts are increasingly less likely and, with the opportunities now available of starting relatively small factories anywhere in the country, we can say that the peak in the number of refugee-founded firms in the Special Areas of the north – and the situation is unlikely to have been different in the other Special Areas of Britain – was probably in the middle of the 1960s, and that the number of firms founded by refugees in Special Areas will inevitably decline.

In the short term, given a return to economic expansion, continuing growth in the employment provided by the remaining firms may compensate for such a decline. In the longer term, however, the contribution made by refugee-founded industries to the solution of the structural problems of the Special Areas of Britain – problems which remain acute – will decline.

## VII

The contribution made by refugees to the British industrial scene *as a whole* has not, to our knowledge, been studied so far. It would, in any event, be a formidable undertaking.

Up to the War, at least, this contribution was made largely in the Special Areas, i.e. those parts of Britain which were in the most urgent need of new employment. We have fairly accurate and comprehensive information on this contribution in the Special Areas of the northern region, including case histories of all the firms involved. In principle, such information should also still be obtainable from the Special Areas of Wales, Scotland and in Northern Ireland. But even before 1939 there were important refugee industries outside the Special Areas. Specialist firms in the chemical, rubber, leather tanning and machine-tool industries, to mention but a few, were established in London, Birmingham, Leicester, Manchester and other places.

Since the end of the War, and especially since the naturalisation of former refugees was completed in the late 1940s, the industrial activities of former refugees have become so intimately fused with those of British industry as a whole that studies attempting to isolate their contribution would now be very difficult indeed. We *do* know that by 1947 there were at least 1,000 refugee manufacturing firms. They are believed to have employed about 250,000 people.[27] This indicates a threefold increase since previous official figures were quoted in February 1939.[28] But we would merely be guessing if we attempted to estimate the number of manufacturing firms established by refugees since then.

One *particular* reason why refugees in Britain showed such a marked tendency towards industrial activity is revealed when we consider the composition of the refugee population in Britain at the outbreak of War in 1939; *one-third* of all adult male refugees from Germany and Austria had been manufacturers in their own countries.[29] This means that there must have been between 4,000–6,000 former manufacturers among the refugees – a heavy loss to German and Austrian light industry. Of these, no less than 1,040 had been in the textile industry, 836 in the manufacture of clothing, 225 in industrial chemicals and 502 in the manufacture of leather goods. We shall leave aside the question of why British admission procedures favoured former manufacturers.

When we look for *general* explanations for the achievements of refugees in the industrial field we touch upon more fundamental questions. It may be possible to generalise from a wide range of examples about the enterprise shown by minorities and immigrants, particularly involuntary immigrants who, by definition, were members of minority groups in their countries of origin. The evidence on which such a generalisation might be based can be seen with particular clarity in the development stage of industrial countries and, more recently, in under-developed countries.

Elkan, in his *Introduction to Development Economics*, notes the entrepreneurial role played by minorities, often of immigrant origin, in such countries and points out that the degree of enterprise shown by them is higher than that shown by the population among which they live:

> Development depends on people who are enterprising. Frequently – but not invariably – an initial upsurge of development is attributable to the enterprise exhibited by some minority group of the population – Chinese in South East Asia, 'Levantine' in West Africa, Asians in East Africa, Parsees in India, Samurai in 19th-century Japan, or Non-Conformists in 17th-century England, What they share is neither a common race nor a particular set of beliefs that might predispose them to entrepereneurial aptitudes. They do, however, have in common minority status of 'deviance' and perhaps the resulting feelings of insecurity propel them forward towards economic success in a way that distinguishes them from the rest.[30]

Ninety per cent of the refugees who came to Britain were Jewish or of Jewish origin, as defined by the Nazis. These refugees were, in a sense, *deviants* twice over: they belonged to a minority in the countries from which they came and where, in accordance with Elkan's account, they had already displayed strong entrepreneurial aptitudes. Their status as insecure strangers in a foreign land was superimposed on the attitudes with which they arrived.

This double *deviance* may well be part of the explanation for their remarkable enterprise.

# Notes

1. A.J. Sherman, *Island Refuge: Britain and Refugees from the Third Reich*, London, 1973.

2. B. Wasserstein, *Britain and the Jews of Europe, 1939–45*, London, 1979.

3. N. Angell and D.F. Buxton, *You and the Refugee: The Morals and Economics of the Problem*, Harmondsworth, 1939, p.141.

4. Cabinet Papers 27, Conclusion 8, 12 April 1933.

5. Hansard, Parliamentary Debates, 342, 2172.

6. *Ibid.*

7. 'Can Refugees be an Asset?' *Planning*, 216, Political and Economic Planning, 14 January 1944, p. 4.

8. 1st Report of the Commissioner for the Special Areas of England and Wales, House of Lords Debates, 98, 999.

9. Cooper to Under Secretary, PRO FO 371/22534, W 12173/104/98, 9 September 1938.

10. Sir Samuel Hoare to the Society for the Protection of Science and Learning, 'Refugees: Their Contribution to English National Life', 6 February 1939 at University College, London.

11. Commissioner for the Special Areas of England and Wales, 2nd Report, Cmd. 5090, HMSO, London, 1936, p. 5, § 13 and 15.

12. *Ibid.*, p. 6, § 17.

13. *Ibid.*, p. 17, § 59.

14. Besso to Sir Ernest Holderness, Ministry of Labour, ET, 1315/1936, 11 March 1936, Home Office Aliens Records.

15. Internal Memorandum, Home Office, 30/6/41, 13 March 1936, Home Office Aliens Records.

16. Hansard, Parliamentary Debates, 309, 2201.

17. See n.10.

18. J. Hope Simpson, *The Refugee Question*, Oxford Pamphlets on World Affairs, No. 13, Oxford, 1939, p. 3.

19. H. Loebl, 'Government-financed Factories and the Establishment of Industries by Refugees in the Special Areas of the North of England 1937–1961', M.Phil thesis, University of Durham, 1978.

20. 'Judex', *Anderson's Prisoners*, London, 1940, p.19.

21. The following is based on the results of a study of all the refugee industries in this area, undertaken between 1975 and 1978 (see n.19). Our material was very comprehensive, but we cannot give details of individual firms here.

22. Report of the Committee on Small Firms, Cmd. 4811, HMSO, London, 1971, p. 3.

23. Commissioner for the Special Areas of England and Wales, 1st Report, Cmd. 4957, HMSO, London 1935, p. 80, § 203.

24. Fennelly to Cooper, Board of Trade, IM 995/36, 15 April 1936, Home Office Aliens Records.

25. Source: Commissioner for the Special Areas of England and Wales, 1st Report, Cmd. 4957, HMSO, London 1935, p. 94, App.1. The figures refer to 26 November 1934.

26. S.R. Dennison, *The Location of Industry and the Depressed Areas*, London, 1939, p. 95.

27. 'What has the Refugee Industrialist done?', *Director*, November 1947, p. 42.

28. See n.10.

29. A. Stevens, *The Dispossessed: German Refugees in Britain*, London, 1975, p. 293.

30. W. Elkan, *Introduction to Development Economics*, Harmondsworth, 1976, p. 33.

# Rainer Kölmel

# Problems of Settlement

*German-Jewish Refugees in Scotland*

While tens of thousands of refugees from National Socialism settled in London after 1933, some thousands found refuge in Scotland. Although their experience was in many respects comparable to that of their fellow-sufferers who were dispersed throughout the world, it was also related to specific conditions in the society which received them and was therefore in some ways unique.

This essay[1] examines one particular aspect of the history of German-Jewish refugees in Scotland: the extensive activities of various relief organisations, particularly Jewish ones, and the refugees' own initiatives in the creation of an institutional framework on the fringes of a society which, during the war, remained largely foreign to them.

## I

Geographically, Scotland was further removed from the fateful developments taking place on the Continent than was London. Nevertheless, the tradition of making the best of every situation, and refusing to believe the worst, was common throughout the British Isles.[2] Contemporary press reports give the impression that the population was, at best, very inadequately informed concerning the developments in Germany. This applies particularly to the first half of the period during which the National Socialists were in power. Local newspapers in Scotland spoke of antisemitism as a feature of the

German character with which the Jews in Germany would have to come to terms.[3] As late as 1939, plans for the annihilation of the Jews were being described as mere propaganda.[4] Naturally the Scottish public had access to more information than appeared in the local press, but national press reports generally followed a similar line. Thus press reports alone were unlikely to stimulate either protest movements or even a willingness to undertake relief action.

The Scottish Jews played a prominent part in enlightening the Scottish population about the way the situation was developing in Germany. They were the first to appeal to the public on this issue directly, and not only via the media. It was discussed for the first time in the Jewish Representative Council (JRC) in Glasgow on 16 March 1933, and on 27 March the calling of a protest meeting was suggested.[5] From this time onwards, the Jewish community bore the main, if not the entire, burden of refugee work.

The Scottish churches held their first combined protest meeting on 6 December 1938 in the Assembly Rooms on the Mound in Edinburgh;[6] almost simultaneously (on 9 December) the Glasgow Chamber of Commerce held a meeting which led to the Lord Mayor of Glasgow's Relief Fund being established on 15 December.[7]

The remarkable relief work undertaken by Glasgow Jews in particular is related to the nature of their community. This had grown enormously following a large influx of immigrants from Eastern Europe at the turn of the century. At the end of the nineteenth century, there were approximately 1,000 Jews in Glasgow;[8] by 1921 there were 14,000, making Glasgow the fourth largest Jewish community in Great Britain.[9] The experience of antisemitic persecution in Eastern Europe shared by the Glasgow Jews represented an enduring link between them. They also gathered valuable experience at the time of their own immigration, experience which was to benefit later German-Jewish refugees.[10]

It was some time before the Jewish community in Glasgow became fully aware of the dangerous position of the Jews in Germany and of the consequences for the whole of the Jewish community.[11] This is not surprising, for the German Jews themselves only gradually became aware of the implications of National Socialist racial policies. In addition, the Glasgow Jews were predominantly Eastern European in origin and did not feel particularly close to the German Jews. Some prominent members of the Glasgow Jewish community had had previous experience of the relations existing within the German Jewish communities: '. . . because there (in Leipzig in 1924) I found there was a certain – how could I put it – I don't want to say hostility – a certain resentment among the Jewish community there between the "Ostjuden", the Polish Jews who came, and the natural German-born Jew with a long tradition'.[12] But these prominent members of the Glasgow Jewish community maintained contact with Germany through their international connections, and therefore had a direct interest in what was taking place in National Socialist Germany. It was these people who were later to lead the protest movement and who initiated the relief measures which followed.[13]

Opposition to Nazi Germany was initially limited to verbal protests and a boycott of German goods. This was probably because, in the first years after Hitler's seizure of power, the wave of immigrants was not expected to reach Glasgow. However, as early as 27 March 1933 the Glasgow Jews were discussing the establishment of a fund to assist the settlement of German Jews in Palestine.[14] During 1933 Glasgow and Edinburgh themselves were facing problems which had arisen as the result of the National Socialists' racial policies. Several professional people who had come to Scotland to take the university examinations necessary for them to work in Great Britain required financial assistance. One month after the Academic Assistance Council was established in London, a similar initiative took place independently in Glasgow.[15]

The first sums of money collected in Glasgow were transferred to the Central British Fund in London; for the time being, no separate Glasgow fund was set up. However, separate application was made to London for a part of the money to be returned to be used for the support of German-Jewish academics in Scotland. This request for funds for a particular purpose points to a dilemma which existed until 1939 – that the people who collected money in Glasgow and other parts of Scotland could not determine the purpose to which it was to be put. Aid for refugees was organised centrally from London for the whole of Great Britain. This led to conflicts when, for example, the Scottish Jews were expected to carry on their work without financial support from the central fund.[16]

In fact, every financial demand made on the Jews in Glasgow was a greater burden than similar demands made on Jews in London. The economic differences generally apparent between the north and the south of Great Britain were even more accentuated in the case of the Jewish communities of Glasgow and London.[17] This is not the place to discuss regional differences; suffice it to say that in 1936, more than 50 per cent of the Jews in Glasgow lived in the Gorbals (a slum area)[18] and that many of them were unemployed and themselves dependent on assistance from the welfare organisations of the secular and religious communities.

A wave of antisemitism[19] in a number of British cities, including Glasgow, also contributed significantly to the general uncertainty. There were no clashes with Mosleyite fascists such as were common in the south, particularly in London, but anti-Jewish placards appeared in public places, and the Jews in Scotland felt that they had sufficient reason to mount a 'defensive action'. It was, however, only undertaken with the greatest of caution.[20]

The relatively low degree of integration of the immigrants from Eastern Europe, the economic depression with its far-reaching consequences, particularly for the population of Scotland, and the existence of antisemitism all understandably reduced the Scottish Jews' readiness to support refugees from National Socialism. Against this background, the meaning of the statement made to Parliament on 21 February 1933 by the Home Secretary, Sir John Gilmour, becomes clear. He emphasised that immigrants could only be admitted if their settlement in Britain was consonant with the interests of the country, and that these interests must predominate over all other considerations.[21]

The factors which contributed to the British government's restrictive immigration policy applied to an even greater extent in Scotland. Predominantly, there was a conflict between two concerns of seemingly equal importance – on the one hand, the desire to help the refugees, and on the other, to preserve the jobs of British citizens.[22] Some suggestions for the resolution of this conflict were manifestly absurd. The idea of settling refugees in the sparsely-populated areas of the Scottish Highlands appeared in several Scottish newspapers, and not only in the letter columns.[23]

One solution which was often discussed, especially in Scotland's Jewish circles, was to settle the German-Jewish refugees in Palestine. These deliberations were not made with the aim of shirking responsibility. The Jews were attracted by this solution primarily because they themselves considered that real freedom from persecution was possible only in the Jewish homeland, Palestine.

The Jewish community in Glasgow was a Zionist stronghold. Accustomed to the status of a persecuted minority, the Glasgow Jews had, after their experiences in Eastern Europe, become realists: 'They were realists of the sort who dreamed of the re-birth of Zion'.[24] Thus plans for the settlement of German Jews in Palestine, and all the deliberations about making emigration possible, can be explained initially in terms of their own hopes for the future. On the occasion of an appeal by the Central British Fund, the *Jewish Echo* wrote:

> The Jewish tragedy in Germany has proved definitely that there is no hope for the Jewish people but the establishment of their national home, Palestine.
>
> On this aim all our activities must be centred and particularly our work for the rehabilitation of the stranded German refugees. Jews must persistently demand their right for national survival. The earmarking of our refugee fund subscriptions for Palestine is an excellent means of demonstrating this legitimate demand.[25]

In January 1939, when this appeal appeared in the press, there were already hundreds of refugees in Scotland and the Jewish community's assistance already went far beyond the raising of funds and the spontaneous protests of the time after the seizure of power. However, the first relief measures undertaken between 1933 and 1938 were not organised on a formal basis. Individuals set up informal committees which assumed responsibility for certain tasks. There were many such committees in the Jewish community, taking on a variety of tasks. Thus the exact date of the foundation of the Glasgow German Jewish Aid Committee, for example, can no longer be established. One of its founding members described its work as follows:

> When it came to the refugees, we appointed a sub-committee, who were responsible for refugees. Then we extended it – then you don't look for democracy for representing – you get different people who have different influences and who can help you. So we made the nucleus of a committee and say – I'll mention a name – Heilbronn, Heilbronn was a man who was here for the best part of eighty years. But he came from Germany, some of them came from Holland so they had connections, and they were influential people, so we brought them into the committee.[26]

Finding support for this work was necessarily a slow process. It was supported by institutions in London, by prominent representatives of British Jewry,[27] and – tragically – by National Socialist policies. As persecution intensified, the interest of the mass media also increased.

Between 1933 and 1936 there was little evidence of the Committee's work. This was primarily because the majority of the emigrants to leave Germany in the first wave did not need assistance, being sufficiently provided for through their own contacts and private means. The restrictive immigration policy of the British government proved successful, as the first German-Jewish immigrants were not a burden on the British or Scottish population. This situation could not continue, however, when persecution was renewed after the *Anschluss* (annexation) of Austria in March 1938 and especially after the pogroms in November of that year.

The most important decisions continued to be made in London. The government responded to the new influx of immigrants by re-introducing the visa system for aliens holding German or Austrian passports, which made flight practically impossible for many Jews.[28] The relief organisations began cooperating more closely with each other and with the government.[29] With this change in the situation, however, the significance of the regional committees increased. For many Jews from Germany and Austria, particularly for those who had no contacts other than those provided by the voluntary relief organisations, the success of their flight from Germany or Austria depended on the efforts of these organisations to find people prepared to adopt child refugees, to offer apprenticeships in agriculture or industry for young refugees, and to find jobs for domestic servants. Apart from this, British citizens prepared to give a formal guarantee of maintenance had to be found for cases which the Committee itself could not sponsor.[30] The Glasgow committees and other relief organisations in Scotland worked with some success in this field.

The Glasgow Jews worked particularly actively for child refugees, the work of their specialist committee[31] being by no means limited to fund-raising. As early as 1934, efforts had been made to find foster-parents for Jewish children from Germany from within their own ranks, or in the rest of the Jewish community. The British government facilitated the immigration of child refugees after the November pogroms and a mass immigration of children began, organised by the Movement for the Care of Children from Germany.[32] It seemed that the number of potential foster parents in Glasgow could not meet the demand and that new ways of dealing with the provisional reception of the children would have to be found. Towards the end of 1938 a decision was made to establish a home for child refugees in Glasgow to accommodate the children until foster parents could be found. This home was opened on 9 March 1939.[33]

The largest project undertaken within the framework of child refugee aid in Scotland was the creation in Whittingeham of a training centre to prepare children for further emigration overseas, particularly to Palestine. Viscount Traprain, the nephew of Lord Balfour, the Foreign Minister who had become famous for his statement on Palestine in 1917, had put the Balfour estate at the disposal of this project. The Whittingeham Farm School, as it was officially called, was opened on 9 June 1939, with a total of 160 children in its care. This project too was largely financed by the Jews of Scotland.[34]

The Glasgow Jewish Refugee Children's Aid Committee was responsible for the welfare of a total of more than 300 children. Some of them were reunited with their parents or relatives, others went to Israel. Many moved to England and only a few remained in Glasgow, probably because, as in Dr Johnson's times, their best prospect in Scotland was the road which led to England.[35]

The activities of the relief organisations did not come to an end with the outbreak of war. The committees in Glasgow, in particular, continued to be burdened with large amounts of work. The refugees who had come to Glasgow before the war needed to be looked after, as did those who were now forced to move to Glasgow from the 'protected areas', for example, Edinburgh. In this way, more than one hundred domestic servants came to Glasgow, where they had to be found new positions. The children from the Whittingeham Farm School also had to move in order to avoid being interned.[36]

The mass internment of male refugees meant that large numbers of their dependants were suddenly left without a breadwinner. The committees were able to help out here and their representatives also played an important role as witnesses before the tribunals set up to determine who was to be interned.[37] They were the true advocates of the emigrants before the tribunals, fulfilling this function with great devotion. Many of the emigrants, having arrived in Scotland through private initiatives, had not required the assistance of the committees and only now became aware that there were people prepared to assist them and who even, surprisingly, had exact records about them.[38] In many other cases, of course, the relief organisation had followed the refugees from their starting-point in Germany to their arrival in Scotland, helping them to procure residence permits, to find jobs or opportunities to train or continue their education and providing some with finance to continue their journeys (£100 for adults, £50 for children).

The committees possessed a great deal of information about individual refugees, but this did not automatically lead to a close relationship between the refugees and their protectors. Although the committees could still be called upon to act as intermediaries, the refugees were now largely left to their own devices and were, to a certain extent, isolated. This may be illustrated by the experiences of some of those who found work as domestic servants.

## II

As has already been mentioned, the job situation in Scotland remained very depressed during the 1930s. There was, however, one area in which the number of jobs available far exceeded the number of people looking for work: domestic service in private households. Domestic servants were hard to find even in the 1930s in Scotland; in July 1939 there were 580 vacancies registered with the Domestic Bureau.[39] The Home Office issued only ten work permits per week, and this was far too few to fill all the vacancies.[40]

Before the arrival of the refugees, many German girls had taken advantage of the opportunity to learn English while working as 'mothers' helps' (a system similar to the postwar *au pair* scheme). Unlike the refugees, however, they had come to Scotland voluntarily. In many cases this difference was not taken into account, and the refugees were regarded, as were the mothers' helps, simply as cheap labour.

Very few of the women refugees who became domestic servants in Scottish households did this voluntarily. Some, however, were willing and able to adapt themselves to whatever work was offered. Difficulties often began on their arrival in Scotland, but were not necessarily caused by their inexperience of the kind of work which was offered to them. Problems were caused more by the customs of this strange country, with which the refugees had not yet become familiar, even if it was only a strict observance of the Sabbath:

> And I went to those people – there – as a maid. There was nobody to meet me at the Central Station. What was I to do? I couldn't even speak the language? . . . It was a Saturday. They were orthodox Jews, she says, 'I wrote to tell them', she says, 'not to come on a Saturday'. You know? So I arrive, right in the middle of a Saturday, and she was so rude to me! So what could I do – you can't say anything. She was so crazy, my God! What I went through.[41]

Conditions which had been arranged in advance had to be adhered to. Thus, for example, one of the women interviewed had succeeded in getting her son into Britain without a visa, but was not permitted to keep him with her in a household in Edinburgh. He had to be put into a home.[42] Communication between the refugees and their employers was often made difficult because most of the refugees did not speak adequate English:

> I was treated very decently. I was there for six months, I couldn't speak very much. I had a dictionary and with – oh, that was a dreadful time! . . . and I was very depressed too. Then I thought to myself, there's no point in crying, I have to learn English.
> *Question:* And where did you learn English?
> I read the newspapers which my employers took, the headlines. If you really have to, you learn anything. And the cooking and everything. I mean, I couldn't even cook what they wanted.[43]

The refugees did not know the language, were unfamiliar with the customs, their cooking did not please the British palate and the work was hard:

> It was an enormous farmhouse, I think it had twelve rooms and a huge garden. . . . And that was before Hoovers, so she would say to me, for instance, today we'll beat the carpets, shall we? Then the carpets, the heavy carpets, would be carried outside into the garden – the yard, we would call it – and beaten with a beater, with a carpet beater, something you don't even know of. Things like that, and huge amounts of washing, and everything, no machines, nothing.[44]

All this, however, was not as bad as the degrading situations in which some individuals found themselves.

The subjective feeling of degradation was not restricted to those refugees who could remember the times in Germany when they themselves had had domestic servants.

> And I really must say, they wanted to exploit us all! At home, we'd all had maids of our own. And it wasn't so easy, suddenly to become maids ourselves. But they made no allowance for this, I must say.[45]

The refugees initially found themselves at the bottom of the social structure, and in some cases, the employers let the new arrivals feel this without any consideration for their background.

> I don't know any names. It was an isolated spot in the Highlands.

And there was only one bus, I think, which went twice a week. So that I could leave to go to Edinburgh to work as a servant, if necessary. Wednesday was always the day off for servants, and Sunday too, I think. Then a general's wife wrote to me, saying that she would employ me. Work began at 7 am. I would have to make seven open fires and then clean the silver, the house-chambermaid's work. In the afternoons, I could do some sewing as well, because she had heard that I was skilled at sewing, and at 11 pm she mostly goes to bed and then she likes to have a massage.[46]

Although unpleasant memories of the time refugees spent as servants predominate, there were some who adjusted well:

I mean, I come from a household where I didn't clean my own shoes. And if you suddenly have to do it, then you do it, don't you? No, I didn't have any difficulties with these people. In any respect. They had two small children, who were quite nice. I mean, I ate in the kitchen, but, to be honest, nothing mattered much to me.[47]

But there were also cases in which there could be no question of humiliation or exploitation:

Very rich people. Both sons were in the army, and I had a wonderful position there. I didn't have to do any heavy work, the gardener did that. The master of the house did the fires, I even had my own sitting-room.[48]

The situation was particularly difficult for those refugees in service who had to live in remote areas of Scotland. Those who lived near the centres, Edinburgh and Glasgow, at least had the opportunity to meet other refugees on Wednesday and Sunday afternoons and talk about their worries and needs. A residential home in Colinton Road served as a meeting-place in Edinburgh, while in Glasgow refugees would meet on Tuesday evenings at the Zionist Centre,[49] before the rooms of the Society of Jewish Refugees and the Refugee Centre were made available for such gatherings.

In a number of instances the refugees had already attempted, before the outbreak of war, to get other employment. This reflected the dissatisfaction which obviously existed among them. Such social tension resulted firstly, from the persecution experienced by the refugees in National Socialist Germany and secondly, from the inability of some of their 'hosts' to recognise and allow for the loss of status suffered by their German-Jewish domestic servants. Naturally, such discrimination was not limited to those in domestic service.

This unfortunate situation was aggravated by a widespread failure to recognise that it was German Jews and not National Socialist Germans who were seeking refuge in Scotland. Many people misunderstood the special position of the refugees and were therefore unable to differentiate between Germans:

> I shall never forget, Gerald, my son. I was in the Botanical Gardens with the pram, and I always spoke German to him, and a lady in the Botanical Gardens heard this. She said in quite good German: 'Oh, you speak German?' and was surprised that she had never seen me at the German Consulate. She asked if I went to the German Consulate when evenings for German-speakers were held there. I had to explain why I didn't go to the German Consulate, and she couldn't understand the distinction. The Scots are so kind-hearted, they just cannot understand it.[50]

With the outbreak of war, in the storm of indignation directed against German aggression, these misunderstandings intensified into an undifferentiated hostility to all things German. Several of the people interviewed suffered as a consequence:

> I will tell you something else, when I came here in the year 1939 – '39 I came here – I was telling people that the Germans were so well armed – they have got thousands of this and thousands of that and you know what people used to say to me – I'm a fifth columnist – I'm a spy. That's what they said to me.[51]

It was refugees who were in close contact with the population, especially those employed in private houses, who were most exposed to public anger:

> . . . they had four sons in the British army and one of them was shot down by the Germans and I got the blame for that. I find the Scottish people very nice people and I wouldn't change my life but at the time of the war they hated us, they could not understand the difference between a Jew and a German.[52]

Several domestic servants even lost their jobs because of the Scottish population's lack of understanding:

. . . and when the war broke out, this couple was not too keen to have
– although they were Jewish – they were not too keen to have
German people on their premises and they lost their job.[53]

Some of the refugees attempted to avoid discrimination by denying
their national identity:

> When the war broke out, I was still working in Edinburgh. Then
> this lady came and said, 'You are Hitler!' At first, I didn't know
> what she wanted. I didn't know that war had been declared. Then
> she said: 'war'. I had to look up the dictionary to find out what 'war'
> is. Then, for example, my son, who was at school, came home with a
> torn overcoat. I asked him: 'What happened to you?' 'Well, I got a
> big hitting. The boy thought, I am German, but I told him I'm
> Polish.' I said: 'You're not Polish'. But what could I do. He said, 'I
> think it is better, I tell them I am Polish'.[54]

Another interviewee behaved in a similar way in an air-raid shelter
during a German air-raid:

> Then I thought, it would be really stupid if I had to go to prison
> again – I'll just say I come from Holland and leave it at that. And
> that is what I did. And naturally I was then accepted as part of the
> group.[55]

The inability of large sections of the Scottish public to recognise the
special situation of the Jewish refugees from Germany was also revealed
in the general view that the government's internment policy was
harmless. In the first months of the war, those in government circles
did not appear to be quite certain why and against whom they were
really fighting. They acted, therefore, in accordance with the tradition
established in past wars, which had been fought essentially for national
and imperial power. An individual's legal position was therefore
regarded as being determined by his or her formal nationality.[56] As a
result, all the emigrants were suddenly declared 'enemy aliens', the
majority of them having barely had time to get used to being refugees
in a foreign country. The provisions made for internment and the
internees' experiences in the camps need not be discussed here, but the
experience of internment had a strong impact on many refugees. In the
camps, some of them were exposed to considerable political
influences,[57] and many had their educational horizons broadened.
Some, too, made contacts which they maintained after internment.

For the majority, however, this was a period of considerable psychological strain. The shock of the outbreak of war meant that relatives and friends who had remained behind in Germany were exposed to the terrible certainty of persecution without the option of flight. Anxiety about their own future was an equally heavy burden.

When the policy of internment was reversed by the British government,[58] the refugees made the pleasant discovery that they were needed after all. They were able to join the military forces[59] or do other forms of war service. For many, this was the first opportunity to get any kind of work, while many women were now able to give up their positions as domestic servants and take up other work, for example, in the armaments industry. Such jobs could not be chosen freely but this disadvantage was accepted, especially as the British population was similarly affected by the war. The majority of the refugees were no longer condemned to be idle. Even though they had not achieved employment commensurate with their social and educational backgrounds they were, at least provisionally, integrated into the working community and therefore no longer so isolated from their British neighbours.

## III

In practice, however, conditions in industry and in society as a whole were not yet conducive to social integration. The refugees still felt most comfortable, and closest to their lost homelands, in their own homes. Curt Rosenberg described his wife's first contacts with working life in Scotland:

. . . and found a similar position in Glasgow. It was a large tailor's workshop producing women's uniforms. Her job was at the sewing-machine. There were large rooms with a lot of people and a lot of noise, dust and dirt. She really got to know proletarian working conditions there. She accepted this with her usual courage, but it wasn't nice, she was always looking out for something else . . . It was especially difficult because her new job was considered 'essential work', and could not be left without special permission from the Labour Office, which was difficult to get. So she stayed where she was for quite some time. I often used to pick her up from work and would wait for her in front of the house in the city centre, in a narrow and rather unpleasant-looking street near the Clyde. After work, the female workers would pour out. They were mostly very young girls who looked pretty dirty and unkempt. As a class they were below the shop employees, but gradually she even got used to these surroundings and found that in general, these workers had better characters than the shop girls with whom she used to work. But our beautiful home where we could spend our evenings comfortably, and our Sunday walks, compensated us.[60]

The author of these lines then noted, with astonishment, that they met only very few people on their walks, 'because the Glaswegians are not as fond of walks in the open as are the Germans'.[61] He thought that the external appearance of the Scots was not very different from that of the Germans,[62] but that the environment was strange, as the people interviewed generally agreed: 'It was terribly strange. Yes, it was very strange. Life here was very strange'.[63]

It is quite understandable that in this situation most of the refugees initially stayed within their own social community.[64] A representative of the Jewish community in Glasgow who has already been quoted, described the situation as follows:

The refugees came, you see, to talk over old times, and the *Gemütlichkeit*. And you must remember as follows – no one is that perfect – each one lives in the past, looks in the mirror of time and he sees himself. Each man might say to himself, or each woman for that matter, I've just come from Düsseldorf, I've just come from Mannheim, the war will finish, and I'll go back, because I'm a stranger here – I am truly a refugee. So it's better to keep together, and to retain each one's own culture, one's own interests, one's own language, one's own behaviour and so on because I don't know, tomorrow I might be able to go back. So you keep yourself to yourself.[65]

Communication between the emigrants and the society which received them was naturally difficult because the emigrants did not yet have an adequate command of the English language. In fact, many of the refugees regarded their stay in Scotland during the war as temporary. Some of them intended returning to Germany, while many were on the waiting list for an entry visa to the USA and, in any case, immigration into Great Britain was often conditional upon the refugees' moving on.

In many cases, the social circles in Scotland to which the refugees had access through their employment were not the same as those to which they had belonged in Germany. One of those who was involved expressed this succinctly: 'During the whole war – well, really, we stayed amongst ourselves'.[66]

Initially, the refugees met in private homes. Two sisters by the name of Türk, who had come from Frankfurt and settled in Edinburgh made their own rooms available for gatherings: 'In Edinburgh there was a – there were not so very many refugees, and there was a family called Türk, two sisters, and they held open house. And every Friday evening about forty people would go there'.[67] There were similar private meeting places in Glasgow:

> Our home became more or less a meeting place. Everybody tried to hear the same language, they were not versatile with the language yet and whatever worries they had they talked over the evening so they very often came up to us, you know, just leisurely without invitation, you know, we tried to make them at home.[68]

These private meetings continued throughout the whole war. At the same time, more formally organised associations came into being. Their origins and the functions they fulfilled will be reconstructed briefly here.

The first public meeting place was the Student International Centre in University Avenue, Glasgow, where a very mixed group gathered. In this 'international' context they could meet without renouncing their national identities and without fear of discrimination. These meetings resulted in the formation of four organisations, each different in character. Many refugees became a member of more than one of the groups.

On 4 August 1939 the *Jewish Echo* reported the foundation of an Austrian Jewish Club in the University Union. This was the first association organised by German-Jewish refugees. Six months later (at the beginning of 1940) the Society of Jewish Refugees (SOJR) was formed. During the first few months of its existence, this society also met at the University. Founded by the pharmacist E.I. Levy, the dentist Dr. H. Hirsekorn, and the medical practitioner A.J. Ehrlich (all three Berliners) the society soon became extremely active and obviously met an urgent need of the Jewish refugees in Glasgow. By the beginning of 1941, a year after its establishment, the society had 200 members.[69] When it moved later into its own premises it ran a restaurant there, serving 'continental' food.

In 1940 other refugees had come together, independently of the

Society of Refugees, to organise a welfare fund. The appeal made on the occasion of its foundation read:

> The undersigned refugees, people who already in Germany endeavoured to help their co-religionists when in need, have come together to address the following appeal to all refugees living in the Glasgow area. The war and all it has unavoidably brought with it have increased the Glasgow aid committee's tasks at a time when its income is decreasing. We refugees want to show our co-religionists living in this country that we are determined not only to accept help, but also to make our contribution towards relieving need within our group. Fortunately many of us have found not only political protection here, but also employment, and it is to these that we primarily address our appeal.[70]

The fund was originally called Glasgow Refugee Voluntary Help. Lend a Hand. It later changed its name to Refugee Mutual Aid Society (RMAS).

The relationship between these German-Jewish organisations and Glasgow's Jewish community is interesting. On the occasion of the RMAS's annual meeting in May 1943, it was felt necessary to point out that the fund was intended only as additional aid and that it did not want to compete in any way with the Glasgow Refugee Committee's activities.[71] This remark can be traced back to an argument which had taken place between the representatives of the refugee community and the Glasgow Jewish community in the autumn of 1941, when the SOJR had made a collection for members in need.[72] Joseph Sachs, a member of the Glasgow Jewish Aid committee, and Dr A.I. Ehrlich felt it necessary to clarify their different points of view, Sachs asking why such an additional fund was necessary.[73] On receiving Ehrlich's explanation that the fund aimed to help refugees independently of the aid committee,[74] Sachs replied that the existing committee provided adequate aid;[75] the Jewish community in Glasgow objected above all to the expression 'refugees in need'.[76] In his reply , Ehrlich pointed out that there were refugees who, in personal matters, would prefer to turn for help to other refugees who had experienced the same plight. He explained further that 'our aim in Glasgow is to take our own modest share in the responsibility for refugees which, so far, the Glasgow Jewish Refugee Committee, . . . has borne alone so willingly'.[77]

Although in the long term the Jewish refugees and the resident Jewish community developed a reasonable understanding, there were for several years acrimonious arguments between the two groups. The

*Jewish Echo* served as a platform for these arguments. The foundation of the Austrian Jewish Club was enough to provoke criticism. A leader-writer in the *Jewish Echo* commented that, in view of what German and Austrian Jews had suffered, it was reluctant to criticise but the unfortunate victims of Nazi brutality had apparently not yet learned their lesson from the tragic events in their fatherland. The writer was of the opinion that it would be to their own benefit if these victims of persecution were to unite with their co-religionists, lay aside their aloofness and assimilate with the eastern Jews who were settled in Glasgow. The idea of an Austrian club in Glasgow was foolish and the leader listed the numerous Jewish organisations which already existed in Glasgow and which the Austrian Jews could join. As far as language was concerned, the majority of the refugees already spoke quite good English, many also spoke Yiddish. The leader finished on a rhetorical note: if a refugee club was necessary at all, why should it be a German or an Austrian one? Such an undertaking would always be a reminder of the Austrian and German Jews' failure to realise the ideal of assimilation.[78] The leader expressed disappointment at the refugees' clearly demonstrated lack of interest in the Glasgow Jews' organisations. Eventually, many Glasgow Jews assumed that the refugees did not want to be friendly with them. But according to Curt Rosenberg, it was not their German aloofness which prevented the refugees from making use of the facilities offered by the Jewish community in Glasgow.

> The Glasgow Jews took just as little interest in us. On the contrary, they to a certain extent resented the German-Jewish refugees. Most of the Glasgow Jews had come from Russia or Poland; their families had emigrated in the 1880s and 1890s, at the time of the pogroms there. Earlier, German Jews had looked down on them; now they avenged themselves by being very reserved towards us.[79]

In any case, the Glasgow Jews made no secret of their resentment. A leader by Dr Aaron Rosmarin, Editor of the *Jewish Spectator*, entitled 'What every Jew should know' expressed clearly why they despised their co-religionists. During the Russian Diaspora, in spite of repeated pogroms, intellectual and spiritual life had not only survived but also increased in strength, providing the Russian Jews with a strength and a refuge. The German Jews, meanwhile, had increasingly given up their Jewish culture and identified themselves with the Germans. At the same time they had begun, like the Germans, to despise their fellow

Jews. Eventually it reached the stage when German Jews regarded it as a tragedy if their daughter were to marry an *Ostjude*; they even preferred a match with a Christian family. In this process the values of Jewish culture had been forgotten and the German Jews had claimed Goethe and Kant as their own in place of them. When they lost all this under National Socialism, they had had nothing left to cling to: 'He suddenly realised that he was a man without a culture for his soul and without a land for his body'. German Jews' misfortune lay less in the physical strength of the enemy than in their own spiritual weakness. 'The German Jew's tragedy is not so much the result of Nazi brutality, as of his lack of a spiritual fortress such as Russian Jewry had.' Rosmarin saw the Jewish way of life, its culture and customs, as the Jews' strongest weapon against persecution and oppression. He did not see assimilation as a solution to the Jewish problem.[80]

This article provoked a reaction from Karl W. Aron, who wrote a letter to Rosmarin saying that it was unfair to attack a person who was already down. Many refugees, including Aron himself, were being told constantly by British Jews that they deserved their fate because they had forgotten they were Jews. Even if it were true that the German Jews had despised the Eastern Jews, it did not help matters for the Eastern Jews now to behave in the same way. Aron pointed out that the impact of the persecution they had suffered in Germany was worse than anything which had happened in Russia, where Jews were accustomed to persecution, while in Germany it had occurred suddenly and unexpectedly. Added to this, flight had been easier for the Russian Jews, as there had been no restrictions on immigration to the USA or to Great Britain. Aron firmly rejected the accusation that the German Jews had no real culture of their own. He called the German Jews the best organised Jewish community in the world. It was true that the German Jews were proud of German culture, but this was not to be identified with German culture under Hitler. He asked why German Jews should not take pride in German culture; after all, he had never met a British Jew who was not proud to be a British citizen. He agreed that assimilation would never solve the Jewish problem, but everything depended on what was understood by assimilation. The Eastern Jews too had discarded their eastern robes and had stopped speaking Yiddish when they settled in the West. Aron deplored the fact that at a time when so many forces were being mobilised against the Jews, one section of Jewry felt itself to be superior to another. He suggested, finally, that both groups, residents and refugees, should lay aside their mutual contempt.[81]

Less than two months later, the discussion was renewed. On 1 March 1940 an article with the title 'Are the Jewish Refugees Doing Their Duty?' was printed in the *Jewish Echo*, their duty being seen as cooperation with those Jews who 'had held out a helping hand'. The author established that a large number of German and Austrian Jews were keeping aloof from the Jewish community of Glasgow, claiming as their reason that they had not yet received an invitation into the community. An invitation was regarded as absolutely necessary and should be forthcoming immediately. Nevertheless, the question of why the German-Jewish refugees were still proud of German culture remained. Had not this culture produced millions of egotistical, cunning and aggressive *Übermenschen* (supermen) who had readily made themselves available as the tools of a rapacious and criminal regime? In conclusion, he pointed out that there was a club for Austrian refugees in Glasgow, the membership of which was largely Jewish. Why was there no purely Jewish refugee club? The writer of the article was obviously unaware of the existence of the Jewish refugee club, the Society of Jewish Refugees, which took this opportunity to introduce itself to the Glasgow Jewish community, and to reject some of the accusations which had been made.

Both Dr Hirsekorn and Dr Ehrlich replied to the article summarised above in a letter to the editor which appeared in the *Jewish Echo* on 16 March 1940, under the heading ' "Society of Jewish Refugees" (Glasgow)'. The authors acknowledged that the refugees had received a great deal of help from the Jewish circles in Glasgow, but maintained that this help could not 'encompass the entire personal life of the refugees'. Experience had shown that many problems could only be solved by a group of people with a common experience of suffering. Most of the young refugees, and many of the adults, had not yet adapted sufficiently to their new environment to face an uncertain future without personal help. An organised association of refugees was necessary to facilitate their participation in the rich life of their new home. This required a full knowledge of the country, its customs and habits, and its language. Only a collective effort could enable them to achieve this successfully. Some of the functions and aims of the society were therefore to improve its members' knowledge of English, to introduce refugees to their new environment, to play sports, to give financial support in special cases and to promote Jewish cultural and social life in general. The authors of the letter emphasised that they themselves had come to this country as Jews and that the Society's aim was not to further German culture, but culture in general and Jewish culture in particular. The name which the Society had chosen, long before the article had appeared in the *Jewish Echo*, was proof enough of this. In other respects, they agreed generally with the conciliatory tone of the article. However, the Jewish community had been misinformed: there was in fact no 'German organisation' in Glasgow. How, therefore, was it possible to draw conclusions about the attitudes of the German refugees?

The authors then pointed out that the small numbers of refugees who had come to Glasgow at the beginning of the emigration had been successfully absorbed into Scottish society. But now larger numbers were involved, and the problems of so many individuals could only be solved by an organisation. The Society aimed to promote cooperation between Jewish refugees, wherever they came from, and the Jewish community in Glasgow. As far as assimilation was concerned, the authors took no responsibility for the history of the Jews in Germany.

We experienced our fate as Jews, came to this country as Jews and felt responsible for the Jewish refugees who were living in Glasgow. We are determined to prevent the gradual mental and physical decay which is inevitable if there is a lack of personal support in a country which is still strange to them.

The Society saw itself as a self-help organisation. In spite of this and further attempts at clarification, on 22 March the *Jewish Echo* repeated its accusation that the majority of refugees were keeping aloof from the Glasgow community. They did not go to the synagogues and, what is more, the names of those refugees who had become rich in Glasgow were missing from the community's balance sheets. In principle, however, the foundation of the Society of Jewish Refugees was welcomed because it was based on Jewish principles.

# IV

The Society of Jewish Refugees had set out its aims clearly, but another organisation for German-Jewish refugees in Glasgow had a less clearly defined function. The Glasgow Refugee Centre was established in 1941 and later changed its name to the Scottish Refugee Centre.[82] The core of this particular organisation was formed by the Austrian Centre, modelled on similar centres which existed in

London.[83] A youth club for Czechoslovakian, German and Austrian refugees also moved into the Centre's premises in Pitt Street, later at 358 Sauchiehall Street. This youth club was particularly active and attracted a large number of young people who had found neither the Society of Jewish Refugees nor the Austrian Centre a suitable meeting place.[84]

The first reports about the Centre did not mention political objectives. Before its opening, the *Jewish Echo* discussed the position of the many intellectuals among the Jewish refugees. Some of them had adapted to local conditions and their cultural needs were met by Zionist organisations, the local youth movement and the Jewish clubs. The Centre, however, was intended to cater for the many who remained culturally isolated.[85]

Unlike the Society of Jewish Refugees, the groups which were affiliated to the Centre often addressed themselves to the Scottish public. An event entitled 'Onward Culture' took place on 31 December 1941. The programme emphasised the fact that many of the refugees had remained outsiders in Glasgow, even though they had Scottish friends in whom they took great pride, and that while the refugees felt the need to maintain social links with the people with whom they shared a common past, the Centre was to be a place where they could also meet their Scottish friends. The programme did not point out the importance of Jewishness to those refugees who gathered at the Centre.[86]

Another event, this time with the motto 'Festival of Nations', was held on 23 August 1941, under the patronage of the wife of the Lord Mayor of Glasgow, Lady Dollan. The following appeared on the invitations:

> The refugees from Nazi oppression are working side by side with their Scottish colleagues to produce the weapons to liberate Europe from Hitler's tyranny, they fight together against the common enemy. Let this festival be a demonstration of international comradeship! Let this festival be a demonstration of faith in victory![87]

A group of young people from the Centre performed on various occasions, at events in Glasgow as well as in other Scottish cities.[88] This group of refugees did not split up into different national organisations until late in 1942, when political and ideological commitments began to appear.

By the beginning of 1943 there was a regional branch of the *Freie Deutsche Jugend* (*FDJ*–Free German Youth)[89] in Glasgow, while a local branch of the *Freier Deutscher Kulturbund* (Free German Cultural Union) had been established at the end of 1942. Curt Rosenberg describes why it was set up:

A special organisation, a local branch of the Free German Cultural Union, was to be established for those German Refugees who were not satisfied by the activities of the Society of Jewish Refugees. This was all the more necessary because, apart from the Jewish refugees, quite a few non-Jewish political refugees from Germany had gathered. They included workers but also a former editor, a writer and a former Communist member of the Reichstag. The SOJR did not provide a suitable forum for them. Thus the German Cultural Union fulfilled a real need.[90]

On 12 December 1943 a local branch of the *Freie Deutsche Bewegung* (Free Germany Movement) was also established.[91] In London, attempts to unite had not led far, but in Glasgow there was successful cooperation as late as August 1943, when the SOJR, the Free German Youth, the Free German Cultural Union and the Free Austria Movement all worked together to organise a mass 'Unity Concert'.[92]

What happened in Glasgow and the Scottish provinces has very little relevance for the history of the German Socialist movement in exile. It therefore seems a more fruitful line of enquiry to examine the relationship between the refugees and their organisations, than to investigate their theoretical objectives which were, in any case, obscured by the war.

The Refugee Centre was primarily a place where social gatherings took place. The presence of political refugees suggests a certain political orientation, but politics were not the main attraction. People went to the Centre because it had a restaurant which served cheap and, most importantly, 'continental' food. People went there:

because there was a restaurant, so in that sense people met and I mean during the war, any restaurant where you got food and especially food to your liking, that was a great attraction and I would say most people were attracted by that sort of thing, the dancing and the social events.[93]

The restaurant, dominated by the Austrians, was the focal point of the Centre. Politics was seldom the topic of conversation:

The majority were refugees who were at a loose end with language
difficulties here anyway and that was the only way they could spend
a Sunday afternoon or a Saturday afternoon to get some strudel and
a bit of music but it was as innocent as that.[94]

Thus the Centre was a 'nice little place, where everybody met' (I45)
and although most people knew that political activities took place
there, they were not predominant. It was a place where refugees could
spend their time instead of sitting in their bed-sitters alone (I50), a
place where familiar smells assailed them (I42) and a place to meet
friends. Many friendships, and even marriages, were made there.

The young refugees especially shared a need for orientation, and a
strong desire for education.[95] Curt Rosenberg directed the cultural
activities of the Refugee Centre:

> I also frequently advised the FDJ when they held functions,
> especially an evening devoted to Heine, which I subsequently
> attended. . . . Among the refugees [in Glasgow], there were not
> many who had a thorough knowledge of German literature,
> philosophy and history, but there were many who had a very strong
> desire to find out something about them. I must say that in this
> respect the 'Aryan Germans', who mostly belonged to the working
> class and had come here as political refugees, were better than the
> average refugees. Jewish young people, however, were an exception
> and were at least equally enthusiastic. There were many likeable
> people among them: young married couples, young men and young
> women. They mostly came from good middle-class families, were
> well-educated, had good manners, and adapted well to their new
> lives. They had particularly decent attitudes and many of the young
> girls and women were very pretty.[96]

With few exceptions, the political refugees had firm ties with the
German Communist Party (KPD) in exile. Although they did not
advertise this, it could not be concealed for long in the intimate
atmosphere of the emigrant society of Glasgow.[97] The statements of
several of the people who were interviewed, who went to the Refugee
Centre only rarely, if at all, can be understood in this context: 'It was
because of politics, Communism. There were some people here, they
were Germans too, they had left Germany only because they were
Communists, not because they were Jews'.[98] If the political trend was
obvious to outsiders, it did not deter those who frequented the Centre:
'Yes, unfortunately. Its political function was – There were mostly

Communists there. But, it didn't seem so "off". I was never a Communist, and was never really aware of it'.[99]

The accuracy of Rosenberg's description of the youth group is confirmed by the interviewees. The group comprised members of a generation which had not completed a proper education in Germany. In most cases, Jewish organisations were the first to offer alternative educational courses, directed largely at preparing young people for emigration to Palestine. Judaism and Palestine were the solutions which could be offered to young people in search of a future: Scotland did not feature in their expectations or as the target of their flight. They were there simply by chance. These young people could not be expected to accept this fate. Recollections of persecution were still fresh although the younger refugees knew very little about its causes. Answers to questions about fascism and the ultimate liberation of the Jews were certainly not to be found by remaining in Scotland. The Scottish Jews shared the young refugees' lively interest in everything concerning Zionism, although the origins of their common interest were quite different, while the Glasgow Jews were not familiar with the emotional world of the German youth movement. Neither could the young expect much from the older Jewish refugees, to whom Zionism seemed to be a form of protest, and who were so attached to their German homeland that in spite of the persecution they had suffered they had left it only with heavy hearts.

It is therefore not surprising that, at least during the early years of the war, the atmosphere in the clubrooms of the Society of Jewish Refugees seemed somewhat stifling to the younger generation. The clubrooms were seen as a place of nostalgia as well as a social meeting place for their parents' generation.

The Refugee Centre was livelier, with singing and music and heated discussions about the future:

> . . . but I wasn't really terribly happy until I made contact with the Refugee Centre first in Pitt Street, and then in Sauchiehall Street, where I met youngsters like myself who were uprooted, who were searching, who were looking for something, you know.[100]

Young people went there in spite of their parents' advice to the contrary:

> I know my parents used to say, you know that's quite a left-wing club you go to and I said nonsense, nonsense because I was not a

bit interested and I didn't want to know, all I was interested was that I could meet some young people of my age and I was quite happy with that, I didn't want to get involved.[101]

However, most of the young people organised in the youth group did not resist political involvement. After all, one of the reasons they went to the Centre was to seek answers to a whole range of questions:

Questions such as what had all this been about, you know, Hitler coming to power and the war breaking and where was all this leading and what was going to happen and in those days socialism certainly seemed a way out of all these difficulties and so our activities at the centre and the cultural activities were geared towards widening our knowledge about what that really meant and we had some marvellous programmes. We participated in a young group of actors and we participated in a choir and when the War broke out we went right up to the north of Scotland where we took songs from Czechoslovakia, songs from the Spanish War, from Germany and then we had 'Sprechchöre' but we didn't only do that, we wanted to let the Scots know how much we appreciated living here. We recited Burns at them with rather strange accents and they bore with us with a great deal of pleasure and even more tolerance.[102]

Political activity also included writing pamphlets and discussions, which 'were on socialist principles, dialectics, and definitely, you could feel it'.[103] The aim of keeping the young refugees together and preparing them for a return to Germany was also political

because those people at that time felt that fascism was a plague and that that plague would one day die and once that had died they would go back and I remember the feeling which I didn't altogether share but which I think I understood, the feeling which we had when we sang a song like 'Moorsoldaten'.[104]

The political refugees assumed that they would eventually return to Germany, indeed many of the young Jewish refugees regarded it as their duty to return. 'Actually we thought it was our duty to go back and build up Germany, you know, in the right way.'[105]

## V

The relationship of most of the Jews to the Centre was based, inevitably, upon a contradiction. If they discerned the ideology of the people who backed the Centre, they were tacitly supporting an institution for which Judaism as a philosophy had no relevance. Consciously or unconsciously, they were contributing to the sprritual destruction of Judaism. Refugees in the Centre supported Marxism and German culture rather than Judaism; there could be no question of piety in the Centre. 'None of us went to the synagogue. It stands to reason, if one was in the Communist Party – a Communist, anyway, then one was an atheist. Probably that was the easiest thing for the Party to accustom us to'.[106] In any case, few of the refugees were deeply religious and the reproaches made by the *Jewish Echo* certainly contained an element of truth. But a commitment to Judaism did not reveal itself only in attendance at the synagogue. Membership of the Society of Jewish Refugees, for example, which emphasised its Jewishness, offered an opportunity to demonstrate publicly a commitment to Judaism. Another possibility was to join the special Jewish units of the British armed forces, and thus combine a demonstration of commitment with an active fight against German fascism.

During the war, most of the people interviewed had turned away from the Centre and the hopes for the future propagated there. Their relationship with the Jewish community in Glasgow became closer and the bitter arguments between the refugees and the Glasgow Jewish public were a thing of the past.

Reconciliation between the refugees and the Glasgow Jewish community received a clear impetus when, in late 1942, the 'final solution' of the Jewish question became public knowledge and the full extent of the brutality of the National Socialist system was recognised. The refugees' anxieties, and especially their deep concern for relatives who had remained in Germany, were understood much more clearly. The Glasgow Jews could understand that a communal feeling had developed on the basis of common suffering in the past; it had developed among the Glasgow Jews themselves. It was no longer possible for the refugees to contemplate returning to Germany. It therefore seemed even more necessary to develop closer relationships with the Jewish community in Glasgow.

This did not eliminate all the differences between the new arrivals and those Jews who were already settled in Scotland, however much they would have liked to ignore them. A speech made by Rabbi Rosen to the Society of Jewish Refugees suggests this:

> Perhaps there was a time when German, Polish, Russian, and British Jews each possessed something unique, and this no longer exists. Today there are no longer German Jews, Polish Jews, Russian Jews or British Jews, today there are simply Jews.[107]

Naturally, after having lived in Scotland for several years, most of the refugees had learnt English, which facilitated communication with the society which had originally seemed so foreign to them. They had moved closer to the Jewish community in Glasgow, or had established contact with it via Zionist organisations. At the same time, the Society of Jewish Refugees continued to exist, probably even expanding after the Refugee Centre closed. Nevertheless, many of the former German-Jewish refugees now began to cultivate a private circle of friends, because they had more comfortable living conditions and were therefore less dependent on community organisations.

> We then began to meet in our own homes because you know once we were married, of course, we had our own homes and the centre was still used but I think less than it had been and it was no longer so important to meet there because people were beginning to integrate and to settle down.[108]

To sum up: participation in war service, whether by joining the Pioneer Corps, the armed forces or the Jewish Brigade, or by doing other essential work; reconciliation with the indigenous Jewish community via Zionist organisations; acquisition of the English language; familiarisation with Scottish customs and, often, the decision to make Scotland a new home; a general improvement in living conditions and a reduction in the level of economic dependence on the relief organisations – all these were factors contributing to the high level of integration into Scottish society achieved by refugees from National Socialist Germany by the end of the war.[109]

## Notes

1. This essay is based largely on the results of a research project undertaken between 1976 and 1979. The paucity of written sources, and a desire to include in the investigation the personal experiences of those concerned, suggested the use of oral history methods. For the methodology, see R. Kölmel, 'Die Geschichte deutsch-jüdischer *Refugees* in Schottland' (Ph.D. dissertation, Heidelberg, 1980), particularly pp. 5–31. Quotations are taken from the transcripts of the interviews.

2. A. Sharf, *The British Press and the Jews under Nazi Rule*, London, 1964, Foreword.

3. *The Scotsman*, Edinburgh, 10 April 1934, cited in Sharf, p. 34.

4. *Evening News*, Edinburgh, 7 March 1939, cited in Sharf, p. 90.

5. Minutes, Jewish Representative Council, Glasgow, JRC Archive, 16 March and 27 March 1933.

6. Gl/3/41, Strathclyde Regional Archives, Glasgow.

7. *Glasgow Herald*, 16 December 1938.

8. D. Daiches, *Glasgow*, London, 1977, p. 139.

9. M. Freedman, *A Minority in Britain*, London, 1955, p. 77.

10. There were relief organisations, initiatives for the protection of 'enemy aliens' during the First World War, and help in settlement. See C. Bermant, 'Anatomy of Glasgow', in M. Mindlin and C. Bermant (eds.), *Explorations: An Annual of Jewish Themes*, London, 1967, pp. 99–106.

11. The *Jewish Echo* (a Glasgow weekly) had shown concern about the threat of National Socialism as early as 1930. Cf. an article with the title 'Who is Adolf Hitler?', *Jewish Echo*, 17 October 1930.

12. Interview with M.G., JP, 8 February 1978, p. 3.

13. Minutes 16 and 17 March 1933; thereafter, meeting of Jewish businessmen on 29 March 1933 to organise the boycott, JRC Archive. A boycott of German goods was still considered the best form of protest in 1935, see Minutes, 12 September and 13 October 1935, JRC Archive. The second generation of immigrants was particularly active in the organisation of this boycott; Jewish Representative Council, *50 Years*, Glasgow, 1964, p. 11. See also 'Buy British–Boycott German', *Glasgow Herald*, 29 May 1933.

14. Minutes, 11 May 1933, JRC Archive. By 8 June 1933 £1,800 had been collected; in 1936 the sum had grown to £27,000. Minutes, 2 April 1936, JRC Archive.

15. On 11 May 1933 the JRC discussed the proposal made by Professor Carewe (University of Glasgow) to raise funds for scholarships for German-Jewish scientists. Minutes, 11 May 1933, JRC Archive.

16. In August 1934 the Gertrude Jacobson Orphanage was approached by a relief organisation in London to take in and possibly arrange adoption for eleven German-Jewish children. The authorities responsible were prepared to accept the children, but wanted a guarantee from the relief organisation in London that they would undertake responsibility for the children after the age of fourteen. The authorities in Glasgow went so far as to express their opinion that the children would be better looked after in London than in Glasgow.

This illustrates the tension which existed between the regional authorities and the central authorities in London, who accepted funds collected in Glasgow into the central fund, and then called upon the Glasgow Jews to support the children without any contribution from the central fund. This double burden was felt to be intolerable. JRC, *50 Years*, p. 10, and Minutes, 27 August 1934, JRC Archive.

17. M. Flinn (ed.), *Scottish Population History*, Cambridge, 1977, p. 458; R. M. Titmuss, *Birth, Poverty and Wealth*, p. 90, cited in R. Mitchison, *A History of Scotland*, 2nd ed., London, 1977, p. 402; I.H. Adams, *The Making of Urban Scotland*, London, 1978, p.175.

18. Minutes, 8 October 1933, JRC Archive.

19. Reference to the spread of Nazi propaganda by Reinhold Hoops, lecturer at Glasgow University, JRC, 21 April 1934; insurance companies refused to insure Jews, JRC, Minutes, 7 October 1934; letter to the editor, *Glasgow Evening Citizen*, 27 January 1935.

20. At a meeting of the JRC, Dr. Salis Daiches suggested the formation of a Defence Council. Minutes, 8 June 1933, JRC Archive.

21. A.J. Sherman, *Island Refuge: Britain and the Refugees from the Third Reich 1933-1939*, London, 1973, pp. 27–8.

22. *The Scotsman*, 11 January 1936.

23. Sharf, p. 197.

24. JRC, *50 Years*, p. 7.

25. *Jewish Echo*, 20 January 1939.

26. Interview M.G., JP, p. 11.

27. Several prominent public figures came to Scotland to emphasise the importance of the appeal for funds. The Marchioness of Reading and Viscount Bearsted, for example, came to Glasgow in April 1936 for this purpose; *Jewish Echo*, 24 April 1936.

28. Sherman, pp. 86–93.

29. German Jewish Aid Committee, Annual Report, 1939, p. 16; see also J. Lettner, 'Aspekte der österreich-jüdischen Emigration in England, 1936-1945' (Ph.D. dissertation, Salzburg, 1972), typescript, pp. 21–2.

30. Sherman, p. 125.

31. As a result of the friendship between the Heilbronn family and Rebecca Sieff, several Jewish women met at the Heilbronns' house in Glasgow in 1934. They formed a women's committee along the lines of the Women's Appeal Committee in London, which had the objective of fund-raising and preparing girls and boys from Germany for settlement in Palestine. This was in tune with the general aims of the Glasgow Jewish community outlined above. N. Bentwich, *They Found Refuge: An Account of British Jewry's Work for the Victims of Nazi Oppression*, London, 1956, p. 24; interview M.G., JP, p. 11; *Jewish Echo*, 24 January 1936, 3 March 1936.

32. Sherman, pp. 183–4.

33. *Jewish Echo*, 30 December 1938, 6 January 1939, 17 March 1939.

34. Mrs M.T. Mann and Mr A.M. Levenson at a meeting of the German Jewish Aid Committee about the financing of projects, *Jewish Echo*, 30 December 1938, 14 July 1939.

35. Bermant, p. 100.

36. *Jewish Echo*, 13 September 1940.

37. Of the 112 tribunals set up in the whole of Great Britain, six were in Scotland.

| Tribunal | Men | Women | Total |
|---|---|---|---|
| Edinburgh | 201 | 329 | 530 |
| St Andrews | 15 | 34 | 49 |
| Glasgow | 350 | 483 | 833 |
| Aberdeen | 35 | 53 | 88 |
| Dundee | 11 | 27 | 38 |
| Elgin | 35 | 41 | 76 |
| | 647 | 967 | 1614 |

*Source:* General Purpose Committee, Gl/3/41, Strathclyde Regional Archives.

These figures show that the refugees were concentrated in the large cities. This was even clearer after the internments and after the exclusion of the refugees from the 'protected areas', which included Edinburgh, Dundee and Aberdeen. The majority of the refugees who remained in Scotland settled in Glasgow. This explains my concentration in this article on developments in Glasgow. As Liaison Officers before the tribunals, the Glasgow Jews could build on their experience of internment policies during the First World War, when they had given guarantees for the unassimilated members of their community (*Jewish Echo*, 6 October 1939). They were thus in a position to discharge their duties both conscientiously and confidently. After more than 1,200 cases had been processed, an interim report of 24 November 1939 stated that more than 99 percent had been recognised as 'refugees from Nazi oppression'. Minutes, 16 December 1939, Gl/3/41, Strathclyde Regional Archives.

38. 'Refugee Joint Consultative Committee', Circular No. 14, 27 September 1939, Wiener Library. The police too had access to information about every refugee. 'There are very few British citizens about whom so much is known', F. Lafitte, *The Internment of Aliens*, Harmondsworth, 1940, p. 41.

39. The Domestic Bureau had been established on the initiative of the Quakers and was responsible for the placement of women and married couples as domestic servants in Scotland. It opened under the management of the wife of Professor Max Born in December 1938 at premises in Stafford Street, Edinburgh. Initially the work of the Bureau was limited to coordinating the work of the various committees which placed domestic servants (Edinburgh Jewish Refugee Aid Committee and Christian Council for Refugees). From 20 June 1939 on, all cases were processed independently by the Bureau. Its welfare activities included the opening of the Scottish Domestic Hostel for Refugees at 77 Colinton Road, Edinburgh, on 2 August 1939. Domestic servants were introduced to their work in this hostel, which also provided a social centre where they could meet on their free days. After Edinburgh was declared a 'protected area', the Domestic Bureau moved to Glasgow, where it found accommodation in the premises of the Jewish relief committee in Queen Square. A total of more than 1,200 cases were processed by the Domestic Bureau. Work permits were received for more than half of them, but only about 300 eventually reached Scotland. Minutes, 27 November 1939, Gl/3/41, Strathclyde Regional Archives, *Jewish Echo*, 9 May 1941; interview,

Margarete Gal, transcript, pp. 4–6, 19–21.
40. Bulletin of the Scottish Christian Council for Refugees, No. 1, July 1939, p. 8.
41. I(nterview) 16, G(erman), pp. 15–16. Transcript in the possession of the author.
42. I51, G, p. 3.
43. I51, G, p. 4.
44. I9, G, p. 8.
45. I9, G. p. 6.
46. I19, G, p. 4.
47. I22, G. p. 6.
48. I37, G, p. 8.
49. 39 Queens Square, Glasgow, see *Jewish Echo*, 4 March 1939.
50. I31, G, p. 20.
51. I52, E(nglish), p. 6.
52. I45, E, p. 3.
53. I49, E, p. 4.
54. I51, G, pp. 11–12.
55. I37, G, p. 10.
56. G. Leibholz, 'Die völkerrechtliche Stellung der "Refugees" im Kriege. Eine Betrachtung der britischen Internierungpolitik während des letzten Krieges', *Archiv des Völkerrechts*, Vol. 2, No. 2, Tübingen, 1949, pp. 129–59, esp. p. 135.
57. '. . . in a sense what was much more important and much *tiefgreifender* was in fact meeting the Germans who were not Jews, that is the political refugees who had a tremendous sense of organisation who ran, I would almost say, an entire school system on Onchan, stretching from arithmetic, geography, philosophy, Marxism, Leninism, the bleeding lot and these people had a profound and lasting and perhaps now when I look back partly, only partly, I would underline this, partly tragic influence on me.' I41, E, p. 26.
58. Cmd. 6217; new editions in August 1940, Cmd. 6223, and October 1940, Cmd. 6233. The refugees had to complete a form after their release from internment. 'I had to fill in my prison record and it said have you ever been in prison, before, if so, give details and it said time and I said November 1938–December 1938, Buchenwald concentration camp on charge of being a Jew, then I said June 1940 to present day, such and such internment camp, charge of being a German.' I41, E, p. 25.
59. Interned refugees were released on joining the Auxiliary Military Pioneer Corps. Cf. N. Bentwich, *I understand the Risk*, London, 1950. For the internment, see also P. and I. Gillman, *'Collar the Lot!' How Britain interned and expelled its wartime refugees*, London, 1980, and R. Stent, *A Bespattered Page*, London, 1980.
60. C. Rosenberg, 'Aus der Emigration', eye-witness report, typescript, Glasgow, 1956, Wiener Library, PIIIi (England), No. 226 (No. 3010), p. 52.
61. *Ibid.*, p. 48.
62. *Ibid.*, p. 10.
63. I32, G, p. 19.
64. Of course, there were exceptions here too, as the following example illustrates: '. . . but my father who was kind of a religious man and so was my

mother, they immediately made contact with the synagogue and it really wasn't all that long before my father had a kind of position of authority, he became one of the synagogue elders so to speak.' I42, E, p. 4 (The father of this interviewee was born in Poland.)

65. Interview M.G., JP, p. 22.

66. I22, G, p. 23.

67. I7, G, p. 8; W. Waldstein and H. Gal, *Österreichische Komponisten des 20. Jahrhunderts*, Vol. 5, Vienna, 1965, p. 28.

68. I27/28, E, p. 4.

69. *Jewish Echo*, 3 January 1941, 28 February 1941.

70. This appeal is in the possession of Mrs Elli Gruber, one of the signatories. The author has a copy.

71. *Jewish Echo*, 28 May 1943.

72. *Ibid.*, 18 October 1941.

73. *Ibid.*, 31 October 1941.

74. *Ibid.*, 7 November 1941.

75. *Ibid.*, 21 November 1941.

76. *Ibid.*, 5 December 1941.

77. *Ibid.*, 19 December 1941.

78. *Ibid.*, 11 August 1939.

79. Rosenberg, pp. 50–1.

80. *Jewish Echo*, 5 January 1940.

81. *Ibid.*, 19 January 1940.

82. The Glasgow Refugee Centre was opened on 24 January 1941 under the patronage of several Scottish public figures including Sir Daniel Stevenson, Dr M. Anderson and W. Anderson. The Centre had many facilities: a library, meeting rooms, a canteen and a café, as well as two rooms for the temporary accommodation of refugees in difficulty. *Jewish Echo*, 11 June 1941.

83. E. Kolmer, *Das Austrian Centre, 7 Jahre österreichische Gemeinschafts-arbeit*, London 1945, pp. 2–3. The author points out, however, that there were small differences: 'Although Glasgow is a city with a population of millions, only a small, if very active colony of daring Austrians settled here, so far north. Not only do you know everybody by name, you also know their shoe size, date of birth, etc.' See also G. Knepler, *Five Years of the Austrian Centre*, London, 1944, p. 2.

84. Kölmel, pp. 216–18.

85. *Jewish Echo*, 6 December 1940.

86. A copy of the programme is in the possession of the author.

87. *Ibid.*

88. Edinburgh, 25 November 1941; Aberdeen, 10 December 1941.

89. *Freie Tribüne*, Vol. V, No. 9, 28 April 1943.

90. Rosenberg, pp. 55–6.

91. *Freie Tribüne*, Vol. VI, No. 1, January 1944; Rosenberg, p. 63.

92. *Freie Tribüne*, Vol. V, No. 8, August 1943.

93. I14, E, p. 10.

94. *Ibid.* p. 12.

95. The declared aim was to fill the gaps in the refugees' general education. Regional conference of the FDJ, Glasgow; *Freie Tribüne*, Vol. VI, No. 3.

96. Rosenberg, p. 63.

97. See n. 82.
98. I31, G, p. 17.
99. I19, G, p. 9.
100. I42, E, p. 7.
101. I50, E, p. 5.
102. I42, E, p. 6.
103. I49, E, p. 12.
104. I42, E, p. 8.
105. I15, E, p. 12.
106. I22, G, p. 19.
107. *Jewish Echo*, 16 June 1944.
108. I42, E, p. 11.
109. For the problems of integration, acculturation and assimilation, see Kölmel, pp. 285–309, and the essay by M. Berghahn in this volume.

# Marion Berghahn

# German Jews in England*

*Aspects of the Assimilation and Integration Process*

## I

'Assimilation' has become well-established as a key concept in German-Jewish history. The Jews of Germany have always been regarded as particularly well-assimilated, and as possessing a high potential for assimilation, in contrast, for example, to the Jews of eastern Europe. Particularly amongst Jews themselves it is quite usual to classify not only whole groups of people, but also certain persons within the group or the family, according to the extent to which they are assimilated. As a rule, type and intensity of religious observance provide the yardsticks by which assimilation is measured. It is generally assumed that the greater a person's indifference towards the Jewish religion, the more assimilated he or she is. From this it follows that the more 'unreligious' a person is, the more 'un-Jewish' and

*This essay is based on a social-anthropological study, conducted over several years, of German-Jewish emigrants in London. The following analysis draws on approximately 180 interviews, each of several hours duration, with representatives of three generations, other biographical material, and historical studies of the German Jews in general and the emigration in particular. Numerous private and official functions, which the author was able to attend as a 'participant observer', also proved to be very useful.

This study was financed by a grant from the Social Science Research Council, and its publication by Macmillan in London as a book, with the title *German-Jewish Refugees in England – The Ambiguities of Assimilation* took place in 1984. The author would like to take this opportunity to express her gratitude to all the emigrants and representatives of the German-Jewish organisations, without whose kind hospitality, patiently given information and advice this study would not have been possible.

'German' he or she is; and the more 'Orthodox', the more 'Jewish'. However, after only a few interviews it was obvious that the process of assimilation is not so simple. 'Deutschtum' (German-ness) and 'Judentum' (Jewishness), to use Herman Cohen's terminology,[1] in no way formed an opposition, and the attachment to both was mostly independent of religious observance. Academics as a group provide a good illustration of this. They often display an indifference towards religious customs and Jewish community life, but it would be wrong to draw general conclusions from this about a lack of identification with Judaism as a whole.

Belief in the German Jews' high potential for assimilation also presented a problem in another respect. The conviction that the Jews were different from other Germans in nothing but their religion was based on this belief. Applied to the situation in England, it led to the expectation – held by many German Jews of the older generation – that the process of assimilation is completed by the third generation at the latest, turning Jews of German descent into English people of the Jewish faith.

The interviews soon showed that this assumption also is too simplistic and does not deal adequately with the real situation. It became apparent that their Jewishness meant a great deal to many of the emigrants, but not in the sense of a religious confession. Further, the assimilation process did not take the expected direction. A surprisingly large number of third generation, that is, of those who were born in England after the war, felt a need to distinguish themselves from their English environment, culturally and psychologically.

These observations suggest that it is necessary to re-examine the concept 'assimilation' and its application to social and cultural developments within the German-Jewish community. This concept has been used as though its meaning is self-evident, although it has hardly ever been defined exactly in the context of German-Jewish history. It therefore seems appropriate to investigate the concept 'assimilation' in the light of modern sociological research.

In a sociological sense, assimilation signifies a cultural rapprochement among ethnic groups. Often the concept is extended to include the socio-economic sphere;[2] but as these two processes are not necessarily connected, it seems more useful to differentiate them conceptually. In this essay, therefore, 'integration' will be used to refer to social and economic integration into the wider society.

Traditionally, assimilation is regarded as inevitable when ethnic groups live in close proximity to each other, as, for example, when a minority is surrounded by a culturally different majority. Until recently, it was considered equally inevitable that it was only a matter of time before the minority would be culturally absorbed by the majority.[3] This is based on the 'simplistic view . . . that geographical and social isolation have been the critical factors in sustaining cultural diversity.'[4] Usually this led to the conclusion that cultures cannot survive if geographical and social divisions disappear and minority cultures merge into the culture of the majority – a process which in the past was regarded as desirable anyway.

This view can be partly explained by the fact that 'culture' has been generally defined in terms of institutions, customs and traditions, particularly religious ones; that is, in terms of clearly identifiable elements.[5] In addition, there was the conviction mentioned above that geographical isolation was a precondition of the survival of cultures and that cultures disintegrated when the boundaries disappeared. Consequently, this concept of culture could not deal adequately with the situation in the USA, for example. Here a 'multi-ethnic' society has developed in which there are no geographical divisions between ethnic groups and, in addition, members of individual groups have abandoned many traditional customs. This applies particularly to religious customs which, as in the case of Judaism, were mostly regarded as being identical with culture. As the minorities continue to exist as identifiable groups, however, the generally accepted concept of culture is obviously inadequate. Therefore, an attempt was made to identify factors which were more appropriate for dealing with the phenomenon of ethnicity. The anthropologist A.L. Epstein sees the basis of culture as a strong 'emotional attachment to the ethnic group' and this affective tie 'is all the more powerful because it is rooted in the unconscious'. He introduces the terms 'intimate culture' for this personal relationship, and 'public culture' for the more concrete elements of culture.[6] Another anthropologist, Frederick Barth, makes a similar division, but gives 'private' culture precedence over 'public' culture. According to Barth, the most important function of public culture is to différentiate between different groups. He points out that the public culture can change, just as the composition of groups themselves can change, and sees ethnic identity as more important for the continued existence of the group. On the one hand, ethnic identity is based on external symbols such as 'dress, language, houseform, or general lifestyle' and on the other, on 'basic value orientations: the standards of morality and excellence by which performance is judged'.[7]

In attempting to define culture, then, it is not enough to look for concrete customs and institutions. According to this view, patterns of behaviour, attitudes and value systems are more important. That is: the decisive factor in cultural behaviour is the way in which events in the outside world are perceived, events which then influence the type of response. As standards of value and behaviour are formed virtually from birth by the child's upbringing and education, they form so integral a part of a person's nature that most people never become consciously aware of them, and they therefore remain largely beyond their control. It is certainly possible to become aware of the culturally determined roots of one's world view, but it is very much more difficult to influence or change them.

This 'world view' expresses itself on three levels: on the first, it creates order in a universe whose nature is chaotic; on the second level it functions as a link connecting people of similar perceptions, creating in this way social or ethnic groups or categories within the larger society; on the third level it shapes the relationships between the individual and the institutions of the wider society.

To paraphrase Kant: there are no 'objective' situations; individuals always judge situations on the basis of previous experience and knowledge, and react accordingly. This applies both to the sphere of immediate personal relationships, and to the area in which cultural contacts between ethnic groups take place. In the context of our topic, this means that we should not expect to find members of a minority integrating elements of the majority culture unchanged into their own culture. Instead, they interpret them in the light of their own cultural background, and then assimilate them to their existing cultural heritage.

In this way, the original ethnicity is also altered. Because we are dealing with the process of a re-interpretation here, the term 'assimilation' takes on a different meaning. Normally assimilation is understood to be the adaptation of a minority culture to the culture of the majority, that is, as a process which goes only in *one* direction. Assimilation in the sense of a re-interpretation, however, means the opposite: the adaptation of the new to the old. As the 'old' culture is also subject to changes, this process does not proceed only in one direction. According to this view, traditional ethnicity develops into a new form which combines within itself elements of its original form, and elements of the culture of the wider society, but is identical with *neither*.

How do these rather general considerations relate to the specific case of the German Jews? It should be clear by now that the assimilation process is more complicated than is generally assumed. This applies to the assimilation of Jews in Germany as well as in England or in other countries of refuge.

The Jews of Germany did not simply become Germans encumbered with a few reminders of their Jewishness.[8] It is equally unjustified to see them as members of a Jewish nation who simply adapted to their non-Jewish environment in various areas.[9] In both cases, assimilation becomes nothing more than an addition of Jewish and German, even if the two elements are given different weight in the two interpretations. The important point is that – since the emancipation – an ethnicity has developed which combines Jewish and German elements in a very specific way: it is identical with neither one nor the other, but represents something completely original, a unique identity.

A similar development can be observed among Jews in other countries.[10] It explains the tensions, or at least the feelings of strangeness which exist between Jews of different ethnic origin. The estrangement between German Jews and the Eastern Jews which can still be felt today, as we shall see, is a particularly well-known case. The Jews of Germany, however, were among the first to undertake the transformation from members of the Jewish nation to an ethnic minority within a wider society. The main feature of this process was secularisation, which enabled social, economic and cultural adaptation to the wider society.[11] Secularisation did not originate in an arbitrary striving for conformity in a non-Jewish environment, but was set in motion by economic, political and social factors which were the result of historical developments in the seventeenth and eighteenth centuries. Reference is frequently made to an affinity between many elements of German and Jewish culture. This affinity is in fact striking, and perhaps explains the particular intensity with which this process of transformation was undertaken on the part of the Jews. On the part of the non-Jews, antisemites frequently denied the existence of any affinity, and they even regarded the Jews in Germany as 'artfremd' ('of alien blood'), but this does not change the historical reality of the process. Although the movements hostile to the Jews eventually prevailed, this does not legitimate them. After all, at different times in the history of Germany, Social Democrats, Communists, Catholics, even modern artists have also been regarded as 'vaterlandslose Gesellen' ('un-German fellows') or as 'undeutsch' (un-German). The German-Jewish ethnic minority was as much a part of German society as were these groups.

## II

Only when the situation of the Jews in Germany in 1933 has been grasped in its full complexity, can one appreciate what their expulsion from Germany during the National Socialist regime meant to them. They were not only robbed of their social and economic existence, but at the same time, lost a large part of their cultural basis. These two aspects must be seen in conjunction for a correct understanding of the assimilation process in the countries of refuge. We will first turn to the external circumstances of the Jews' flight from Germany and to the problems which accompanied the establishment of a new existence in a foreign country.

There has been much speculation about the motives behind the choice of particular countries of refuge. There is no doubt that the USA was by far the most popular choice, and many emigrants who are British citizens today would have liked to become Americans, had the War not prevented them from continuing their journey to the USA. According to personal communications received from refugees, many made their decision on the basis of business relationships and friendships, or connections with relief organisations such as the Society for the Protection of Science and Learning or the Society of Friends.[12] A surprisingly large proportion had English relatives; that is, members of their family who themselves or whose ancestors had migrated from Germany to Great Britain in the nineteenth century or at the beginning of the twentieth century. Connections with these family members were now re-activated. Help, perhaps in the form of guarantees, was often given only after many urgent letters of request, and even then, sometimes not more than was absolutely necessary was offered. In other cases, help was given generously and family contacts were renewed. One of the most important motives in the choice of Great Britain as a country of refuge was the transport of children organised by British private citizens: an unparalleled achievement which probably saved the lives of no less than 10,000 emigrants.[13]

The early emigrants were mainly political refugees and academics. Some were government employees who lost their positions as early as 1933, and this in many cases had made the decision to emigrate easier. Businessmen were relatively untouched during the first years of the National Socialist regime, and many migrated to Britain quite late. Of course, there were some far-sighted businessmen who began methodically to develop their connections with Great Britain soon after 1933, and who were therefore able to emigrate with their families under much more favourable conditions than would have been possible later. Not only was it easier to get permission from the British end to migrate, but at that time it was still possible to take large sums of money out of Germany.

The situation was incomparably more difficult for emigrants in 1938/9. Many arrived with huge trunks full of clothes – to the great surprise of their English hosts. The German refugees did not match up to English conceptions of what refugees were like, but trunks of clothes, not to mention the legendary 10 *Reichsmark* allowed for the journey and permitted to be taken out of the country, could not cover the costs of daily living.

The biggest problem was caused by the fact that, due to the worsening economic situation, the British government granted only a very limited number of work permits during the thirties. Permits were granted only for domestic service, for specific educational courses and training programmes, for example, in agriculture, and for occupations which promised to be useful for British industry, such as the establishing of factories. As a result of this restrictive policy, the majority of the emigrants saw themselves condemned to be idle and abandoned to a life of frustration and poverty, which forced many to accept 'charity' from relatives or relief organisations. During my conversations with emigrants, it became obvious how difficult this was for them, as most came from well-to-do, or at least financially secure backgrounds. The aim of freeing themselves from a situation which was felt to be humiliating and regaining their independence spurred on many of the refugees. The older ones searched tirelessly for work, and the younger ones worked hard and achieved highly at school and university. Many of the younger refugees, however, had to forego a university education with heavy hearts, for financial reasons, and often also because of a certain desire for independence. Some still regret the lack of a university education today.

The significant and active role played by women in the process of adapting to English life is remarkable. In many cases they were the family's major support – financially and emotionally. It was the women who, under the difficult conditions caused by lack of money and extremely cramped and insecure living conditions, repeatedly overcame the problems of daily life without complaining. Beyond this, they developed considerable efficiency and skill at improvising when it came to finding opportunities for working and earning money, whether legal or illegal, in order to feed their families or boost the meagre family budgets. As a rule they were more successful at this than many men, whose occupational skills were, in general, much too specialised.[14]

On the whole, it seems that women coped better, psychologically and practically, with the trauma of flight. It was frequently women who had urged flight from Germany and who had undertaken the complicated business of giving up houses and winding up their affairs. But it was not only in times of crisis that German-Jewish women proved to be admirably equal to the occasion. After the war, as life gradually returned to normal, they played an equally important role, working with their husbands to build up businesses or helping them in other ways to find a niche in the economic life of the country. To the present day, the successful work of countless societies and charitable organisations owes much to the active support of German-Jewish women.

While in many cases, traditions well established in Germany were carried on here, the achievements of German-Jewish women refugees during the prewar and war years are particularly noteworthy because they were often forced into a lifestyle for which, it would seem, they were totally unprepared. Most of them had come from well-to-do backgrounds and only rarely had they been without sufficient household help, so that many had first to acquire basic housework skills such as cooking. For women, then, emigration involved a particularly radical re-adjustment.

The situation in the academic world, which can only be mentioned briefly here, was comparatively favourable in the thirties. While in non-academic circles a considerable loss of status had to be accepted, as, for example, when established businessmen were forced to go into service as butlers, or when – as was almost invariably the case – women from middle-class backgrounds worked as domestic servants, the lot of university teachers was often better. The Society for the Protection of Science and Learning (SPSL), which had been founded in 1933, helped many scholars to find employment in British universities and other research institutions. British academics even donated part of their salaries to give scholars from the Continent the chance to work in English universities. The assistance available, especially for the elderly and the sick was, however, limited. The number of British universities, and consequently the number of positions vacant, was relatively small in the thirties. Apart from this, the SPSL deliberately pursued a restrictive admissions policy in order to counteract anti-German resentment among British academics. Many refugees therefore received only temporary appointments if they found employment at all, and the majority of them had to go to the USA to find a permanent appointment. The Society again assisted them in this. Not all but many of those who remained behind soon felt at home in British academic life, and within a short time quite a few achieved great standing as scholars.[15]

This is not to suggest that individuals did not experience difficulties in adjusting.[16] But the liberal atmosphere of the universities, especially when compared with that of German universities at the time, offered some compensation for these difficulties. Undoubtedly the international character of academic pursuits, particularly in the natural sciences, played an important part in this. In many cases, contacts had already existed between researchers in Germany and abroad before 1933, and this naturally facilitated integration.

Doctors and lawyers, on the other hand, had to face almost insuperable difficulties for a long time. The professional bodies feared competition and therefore displayed great hostility towards the registration of immigrants. As a result, only a few immigrants were permitted to practise in Britain until after the end of the war. Lawyers faced additional difficulties because the training they had received and the procedures to which they were accustomed were different from those in Britain. Those who could not work in the field of international law or in reparations were often forced to change to other academic areas, or to work as accountants, writers or journalists. As an occupational group, lawyers were probably the hardest hit by expulsion from Germany. It is not surprising, therefore, that a high percentage of lawyers returned to Germany after the war.

In trade and industry, German and Austrian Jews again demonstrated their remarkable adaptability and energy. Many took up the British government's offer of support for the establishment of business enterprises in the designated Special Areas, in certain western and northern parts of Great Britain. This is discussed in greater detail in another essay in this volume.[17] Indeed, the emigrants' willingness to settle in these areas was often made a condition for the granting of residence permits. Thus many refugees were in a position to support themselves soon after their arrival in Great Britain. In addition thousands of new jobs were created at a time of economic recession, in areas where they were badly needed. Several hundred firms were established, mainly producing textiles, chemical and pharmaceutical products, and toys. Jews from the Continent soon played such a large part in the diamond and fur markets that during the thirties London developed into the international centre of these trades. In other areas too, there was a noticeable upturn in British industry, due largely to the introduction of new methods of production and to the opening up of new markets. In England, many emigrants continued to use business connections with foreign customers which they had already established in Germany before they left, thus benefiting British industry.

In spite of considerable obstacles which initially had to be overcome by almost all emigrants, they achieved much in many fields which cannot be discussed in detail here. Among the most striking achievements were those made in the field of classical music, as every regular listener to Radio 3 can confirm. If the quality of the contributions made by Jewish immigrants from Germany and Austria to the economic, intellectual and cultural life of Great Britain were to be assessed, the result would undoubtedly show that the immigrants made a much larger contribution than one would expect from a group forming such a small proportion of the total population. But do statistics reveal the whole truth? Was the process of adaptation really as smooth and painless as it seemed from the outside and when viewed retrospectively, in terms of its results? This brings us to some socio-psychological aspects of the assimilation and integration processes.

Firstly, mention should be made of the frequently recurring outbreaks of antisemitism which hampered the migrants from fitting into the new society socially, economically and emotionally. Although the achievements and merits of the immigrants were often acknowledged, this attitude was by no means common to the entire British population. The antisemitism which appeared openly here and elsewhere originated in professional jealousy and xenophobia, and, in places, it took on alarming forms, continuing long after the Second World War. The Jews of England were repeatedly forced to take defensive measures, such as the publication of pamphlets like *Are Refugees an Asset?*[18] It is easy to imagine what a devastating effect it must have had on the immigrants to discover xenophobia and antisemitism in Britain, after they assumed that they had finally escaped from them.

Numerous interviews with Jewish emigrants living in Great Britain showed that they were aware of widespread antisemitism in their private lives in Britain, although direct attacks on Jews were reported relatively rarely. Mostly, antisemitism manifested itself in 'stupid remarks', such as the dubious compliment that one was not 'typically Jewish', etc. – remarks which, although they were irritating, were felt to be innocuous. Several people interviewed expressed awareness of the fact that the coloured population, the primary target of racist hostility, had so far cushioned them. In general, though, they were convinced of the fundamental decency of the English people, and were confident that the liberal traditions of England would retain the upper hand – although some expressed doubt, because 'after all, we believed that in Germany too'.[19] It is interesting that very similar observations were made in interviews about experiences of antisemitism in Germany before 1933. There too, it mostly manifested itself in individual cases, and antisemitic remarks made by a teacher, or bullying of Jewish children were mentioned frequently.

The majority of the emigrants had not been discouraged by the various forms of antisemitism they encountered in England; after all, in principle, antisemitism was nothing new, and they had learned to live with it. But it was not easy to forget their flight from their traditional homelands, and the marks left by the experience were still discernible in the new lives they established outside Germany. On the one hand, this experience was regarded as positive: through it, one had been torn out of the complacent satisfactions of a bourgeois existence and forced to prove oneself anew, even if the lost prosperity and the comfortable life of the 'German' times were occasionally remembered nostalgically. Apart from this, conversations with the refugees often showed that the knowledge that they had passed this test so successfully gave them a certain amount of satisfaction and helped to restore their self-respect, sorely wounded by the continual insults of antisemitic propaganda.

On the other hand, there can scarcely be a single German Jew who survived without psychological damage the traumatic experiences first of Nazi rule and then of the flight, with all its fears and anxieties; not to mention those who went through the hell of the concentration camps, whether for some weeks or for several years. Added to this were the problems, frustrations and uncertainties with which they had to struggle in the process of building up a new existence. Perhaps fear for relatives and friends, and often parents, who were left behind in Germany, was an even greater burden. It was hard to bear the disappointment of not being able to arrange their departure from Germany, and later the despair and pain when, in the mid-forties, the dreadful end became more and more apparent – pain which could be eased only a little by the passage of time. Persecution mania, depressions, insecurity and feelings of inferiority were further results of the traumatic events of the past, results which are often still apparent today.[20]

The numerous suicides during the first years of the emigration should not be forgotten either; nor should the many older people who could not get over the loss of their homes and their way of life, and who died of a broken heart.[21] For many of the older people today, the loneliness of old age is increased by the feeling of being a stranger in a society in which culturally, and in terms of attitudes they do not feel at home, despite their gratitude for the sanctuary received.

While many of the German Jews' traumatic experiences described so far were shared by other persecuted minorities in this or in similar form, the German Jews also faced another very specific conflict: did not these emigrants have 'two souls within one breast' – a German one and a Jewish one? This meant that after the German Jews' expulsion from Germany, they found united within themselves, as it were, both the persecutor and the victim. It was inevitable that this situation should lead to conflicts with the world around, and within the individuals concerned. It meant that the German Jews encountered not only anti-*Jewish*, but also anti-*German* sentiment in their everyday lives. It was a sadly ironic situation: they had to leave Germany because they were Jews, but in the countries of refuge they experienced suspicion and hostility because they were seen primarily as Germans. This attitude led, logically, to their internment by the British government; it was also expressed in the classification of Jews from the Continent as 'enemy aliens'.[22] All this took place in spite of their energetic but largely fruitless attempts to combat the general ignorance about the seriousness of the situation on the Continent. Apart from this, they anxiously attempted, by good conduct, to avoid drawing attention to themselves, and many tried to play down their German origins as much as possible; by, for example, avoiding the use of the German language.[23]

Given that anything German was suspect in the new environment, how did the Jews deal with the German element in themselves and their ties with the country and the people who had caused their misfortune? Here again we must distinguish between Germany as a centre or point of reference in social or political terms on one hand, and in intellectual and cultural terms on the other.

The Jewish emigrants were so much a part of Germany that it is easy to imagine how painful it must have been for them to become at all aware of the 'German-ness' in themselves as something separate. In many interviews with older emigrants, their bewilderment and indignation at the National Socialists' action of branding them as strangers in their own homeland is still expressed today. It is well known that awareness of the National Socialists' seriousness about their antisemitic goals spread only very slowly, although this is not true for all German Jews. Among some groups and individuals and most radically among the Zionists, the process of loosening ties with Germany, at least as a national homeland, had begun earlier, in reaction to growing antisemitism before and after the turn of the century. For the majority, however, the process of separation, and thus virtually the state of homelessness, began with forced segregation after 1933. A strong feeling for Germany as a home could scarcely develop among young people who experienced only Hitler's Germany, and whose childhood was spent under the shadow of the events that followed 1933. For many of them, therefore, emigration was nothing less than a liberation.

For most of the Jews who left Germany, at least for most of those living in England, the break with Germany has remained final; the majority seem hardly ever to have seriously considered returning. For most of them, the Federal Republic has no particular significance; at best, they display a reserved interest in it. Because most of them no longer have relatives there, close personal ties are also lacking. In addition, Germany has changed so much since the war that it is not easily identifiable with the country which the emigrants remember: 'Berlin is no longer Berlin' was a common remark. Feelings of national loyalty are restricted to England – if nationalism of any sort is not rejected totally because of its destructive potential. The emigrants go to Germany on business trips, for personal reasons, to visit friends from old times, in some cases to visit relatives or family graves, or they search for traces of their childhood and youth. Some of the people interviewed 'confessed' that they feel very comfortable in Germany again now, but have a guilty conscience about this and do not dare to admit their changed feelings openly. On the other hand, many swore to themselves never to set foot on German soil again and have kept their oath to this day.

There is a similar range of feelings towards the Germans themselves: the emigrants are predominantly reserved towards the Germans, their distance deriving from a very deep distrust of every member of the older generation. In addition, the older emigrants are often still bitter; today, however, downright hatred is less frequent. As one member of this generation explained: 'How can I hate the

Germans; my worst enemies, but also my best friends were Germans'. The attitude of the older generation is predominantly ambivalent. In spite of the bitterness, some still have close and cordial relationships with individual Germans, old and new friends.

Among the second generation, ambivalence also predominates: here too, distrust determines their attitude towards the Germans, without excluding friendly relationships with individual people. Some members of the second generation, however, feel an implacable, almost uncontrollable hatred, which is found in this intensity neither in the first, nor in the third generation.

This attitude is only too understandable if one remembers that the members of this generation were, in many ways, hit hardest by National Socialist persecution. As children, in the years which are of such importance for intellectual and emotional development, they were torn away from their parents' homes and their homelands, and subjected to experiences which overtaxed them emotionally. Many of them had lost their parents and other relatives in the cruellest way. In several cases, the circumstances of war had caused personal separations and estrangements. Often, the children were burdened by watching their parents suffer under difficult living conditions. In addition, they had to grapple with their own problems of adapting to a foreign environment at a stage in their development generally characterised by insecurity and feelings of inferiority. Their experiences meant that they grew up and became independent early, but often the price they paid was a 'normal' childhood and youth. Many of them lamented this loss with great bitterness. For most, time has softened feelings of revenge and hatred; others have deliberately attempted to overcome these feelings because, as several expressed it, they realised that they would damage their own souls, but have no effect on those at whom their hatred was directed.

For the third generation, that is, those who were born after the war, the situation is less problematical. They are more distanced from the events of the thirties, and therefore their feelings towards Germany are more neutral. They often find it difficult to identify their parents and grandparents with the victims of a persecution which has become a part of history. When confronted directly with the atrocities, in a film, for instance, they often feel personally involved. In general, however, they tend to see the persecutions less as a specifically German matter than as the product of particular historical and social conditions which would also have led to similar atrocities elsewhere, as was the case during the Inquisition, for example. Germany holds a certain attraction for them as a country in which to travel and study, but it is revealing that Israel is even more popular.

Generally speaking, then, it was relatively easy to loosen bonds with Germany as a homeland in a geographical and national sense, or rather, it was made easy by the events of the time between 1933 and 1945. But what about the 'other' Germany, whose cultural and intellectual traditions meant so much to the Jews in Germany; traditions which had become such an integral part of their way of life and which could not easily be uprooted?

This is not to say that it has not been attempted. On the contrary: to judge from my conversations with emigrants, the majority initially attempted to sever every tie with Germany and to assimilate completely into English life. Many of the older emigrants, however, soon realised (and the internment frequently led to a certain disillusionment) that all the good will in the world did not help: their obvious accent and their way of life could not simply be shed. In the eyes of the natives, they were clearly marked as foreigners. As their English neighbours were generally friendly and treated them with respect, however, it was comparatively easy to accept their status as 'Continentals'. Mostly surrounded by friends from German days, 'the crowd', they lived essentially the same life as before their emigration. Often enough, they still possess furniture and crockery from Germany, which give their homes an unmistakably Continental atmosphere. Eating habits too have hardly changed.

A highly developed sense for 'culture' and refinement must also be regarded as characteristic of German Jews: a passion for collecting objects of art and a lively interest in literature. While Goethe, Lessing, Heine and Thomas Mann are still the most popular authors, some of the emigrants also read German post-war literature in the original and follow with interest the course it has taken. In recent years, the desire to read and speak German has been re-kindled among many emigrants. This phenomenon is not only a symptom of old age, as might be expected, as with increasing age ability in a foreign language decreases; younger people too have a similar interest. Love of music and the theatre continues unabated, and when an ensemble or orchestra from Germany or Austria performs in London, the audience acquires an unequivocally Continental air, recognisable in the correctness of dress, which continues to be a strongly-held value. Many reveal an equally strong interest in Jewish history and, in particular, in accounts of the lives and achievements of German Jews who suffered a similar fate.

The numerous religious, social and cultural institutions which were founded during the period of emigration, and which continue to flourish, played a significant role in maintaining the continuity of the German-Jewish way of life. The most important of these are the Leo Baeck Lodge, the (Liberal) Belsize Congreation, the (strictly Orthodox) Munks' Congreation in Golders Green and, not least, the Association of Jewish Refugees from Germany and Austria. In this context, it is interesting that the German-Jewish institutions originally attempted to amalgamate with Anglo-Jewish institutions. But cooperation was not very successful because conceptions of the purpose and functions of these institutions were too diverse for the Jewish community. The 'Continentals' thereupon founded their own institutions which have preserved their German character for successive generations, up to the present day.[24]

While it is not surprising to find cultural continuity in the first generation, in spite of ambivalent feelings towards their traditional homeland, it is all the more remarkable in the second generation, because this generation tried like no other, sometimes desperately, to become English, not only because of the hostility to all things German mentioned above, but primarily because of the reluctance of most children and young people to be different from those around them. In regard to language, they were successful. In many other areas of daily life, the obliteration of the traces of their German origins – where it was attempted – did not, in general, succeed.

Apart from a few exceptions, members of this generation declared that they by no means felt themselves to be English and that they were aware of being strongly marked by their German-Jewish background. Frequently this realisation came as the result of a trip to Germany, where attitudes and behaviour which seemed familiar made them aware of their own cultural roots. German influence reveals itself not only in an emotional life which is more expressive than the English one; the members of this generation perceive the sense of order, efficiency and punctuality, their work ethos and the seriousness which they see as typifying themselves, as specifically 'Teutonic' and as the thing which most clearly distinguishes them from the British people. They are perfectly well aware that the astonishing socio-economic success of their generation in particular is in large measure due to this 'German efficiency'. The achievements of their group fill them with satisfaction, but not necessarily with pride. They prefer simply to register the heritage of their backgrounds as a fact. Their feelings towards their country of origin are much too ambivalent for them to perceive these 'German virtues' as an unmixed blessing.

This generation's relationship to the German language is equally ambivalent. In most cases they have a good command of German, although English is undoubtedly their first language, without being their mother tongue. They do not necessarily keep up German out of love for it as a language, or because of its familiarity, as is generally the case with the older generation, but rather because it is useful to have another modern language; quite a few earn their living as German teachers. In those cases in which an aversion to Germany has developed, it creates a peculiarly schizophrenic relationship to the German language.

On a more concrete level, English cultural influences can barely be discerned. The majority of the emigrants' friends, particularly their closest ones, come from the same milieu. Eating habits clearly reveal German customs as, for example, in individual dishes or in the retention of the cold evening meal, at least at week-ends. Very few have introduced English 'tea'. Occasionally, English dishes have been adapted, but the international cuisine generally found in middle-class households today clearly predominates. It is significant that English eating habits, including mealtimes, have so to speak, been left out.

These brief remarks might produce the misleading impression that this generation lives in an ethnic ghetto. In spite of their emotional distance from the English lifestyle and mentality, members of this generation often emphasised that they felt completely at home in English society; they have many good acquaintances, and often true friends among the English, and their common school, university and work experiences have made them familiar with English society. Certain characteristics of the English lifestyle are highly valued – as they are also by the older generation – and the relative lack of them in German society is criticised. The main one is 'decency', as mentioned above, but they also include fairness and the inclination to moderation. The precision and clarity of the English language is especially valued in contrast to German, which so easily inclines towards obscurantism.

If they do not feel English, most do at least feel British, even if it is a particular brand of Britishness. Some Jewish emigrants are unhappy about this 'particular brand' and still hate the German part of their make-up. Most of those interviewed, however, did not experience this duality of ethnicity and nationality as a conflict, but as something enriching. In many cases, this attitude is the result of a learning process. As mentioned above, the desire for assimilation at any price was particularly strong in the first, but was also present in the second generation: quite obviously a result of the 'enemy alien' syndrome. A reversal began to appear as early as the fifties, when several members of this generation established a group which, significantly, they named *Hyphen*: they refused to deny their cultural origins, but at the same time aspired to a synthesis with English society. Hyphen aimed to create opportunities for people with similar ideas to establish contact and to meet socially, and to reduce feelings of isolation.[25] It seems that this process of turning away from assimilation as an ideal is still continuing. Repeatedly, interviewees who had almost completely distanced themselves from the German-Jewish community, either because of intermarriage, or from other motives, mentioned that awareness of their origins had become much stronger in the past few years. They expressed a growing need to take more intensive interest in this subject, and to acknowledge it openly. One argument is that they are so certain of their assimilation that they can now afford to recognise the 'unassimilated' elements in their make-up.

How does German-Jewish ethnicity develop in the third generation? Statements about this generation must be made with caution, because it was not possible to interview more than thirty-two members of this group and no supplementary material, such as biographies or general works, was available, as was the case for the preceding generation. Only a separate study could provide more concrete results. But the prevalence of certain attitudes among the young people interviewed was so striking that they seemed to be more than merely coincidental.

One example is the remarkable fact that thirty-one of the thirty-two interviewees stated that they did not feel English, or not in the first instance English; they did not feel German either, which agrees with the observation made above that this generation has a neutral attitude towards Germany. Its members have no particular affinity, either for the bad or for the good. But an astonishingly high number chose German as a subject at school and quite a few chose to study German history in order to find out more about the origin and fate of their forebears. Others have a special interest in the history of their own family, but not in the history of Germany as a whole.

When asked what they feel themselves to be, the majority of those interviewed replied that in the first instance they are Jews. Closer questioning revealed, however, that in most cases their Jewish consciousness has its roots in a lifestyle which clearly displays Continental elements: not only eating habits taken over from their parents and a predilection for certain German dishes, which are enough to make them seem 'different' to their English friends, but also a similarly developed interest for cultural things. Further, the observer finds similar attitudes to work and to achievement and the trend, almost typical of German Jews, towards a university education. Added to this is the awareness of their non-English extraction and thus of the fact that their parents are different from those of their English friends. For this reason, marriage partners and close friends are often chosen from young people with a similar background. The reason frequently given is that 'then one does not have to explain so much'.[26]

On the one hand, this Continental Jewish identity has its roots in their origins; on the other hand, it is strengthened from outside by the antisemitism found in the wider society. Every one of the younger people interviewed is aware of its existence, and many of them have experienced it personally.

They also set themselves apart from English Jews. It must be emphasised, however, that for a large number of those who were interviewed, these distinctions have become blurred, so that often they did not know the origins of their Jewish friends. It is remarkable, however, how often the interviewees expressed a strong feeling of 'ethnic alienation', something already familiar from Germany. They mostly traced this back to different cultural interests and religious behaviour.

As far as the latter is concerned, the feeling of strangeness is expressed primarily in what could be called a methodical or philosophical attitude towards religious traditions and customs. Orthodox and non-Orthodox German Jews often hold the opinion, as did their parents and grand-parents, that Eastern European Jews adhered too mechanically to Orthodox customs and did not think enough about their meaning and significance. This could lead either to an obsession with *Kaschruth* on the one hand, or to a greater laxity on the other. Jews of German descent, by contrast, either deliberately rejected certain customs such as *Kaschruth* because they regarded them as meaningless, or kept them very strictly, 'because we know exactly what we are doing, and why' – this is the explanation given by a member of a 'German' community in which the heritage of German Orthodoxy has been retained in almost pure form. Interestingly enough, there is a great interest in this community among younger Jews, many of whom are applying for admission.[27]

Whether or not the views on Judaism expressed by the German Jews and their descendants are both correct and justified is not at issue here. In this context, the important thing is the fact that traditions have been continued and that, together with other attitudes, they constitute a unity which we have called 'German-Jewish ethnicity'. As for the chances of the future survival of this type of ethnicity, the possibility cannot be excluded that as the German component becomes more diluted, the remaining Jewish element will ultimately combine with the Anglo-Jewish element, in spite of all the differences which continue to exist. On the other hand, it was emphasised at the beginning of this article that although particular movements within German culture provided a driving force for German-Jewish culture, it was never identical with German culture as a whole, but always retained its own individuality. This is confirmed by the results of recent research into the continuity of ethnicity and ethnic identity. If one further takes into account the pressures to which the Jews in Germany were subjected (and which they withstood) to give up their ethnicity, then there is some reason to believe that these traditions will survive. After all, in England the Jews are permitted to be what, in the final analysis, they could not be in Germany: German Jews.

## Notes

1. H. Cohen, *Deutschtum und Judentum*, 40th ed., Giessen, 1923.

2. See, for example, M.M. Gordon, *Assimilation in American Life*, New York, 1964.

3. See, for example, 'Assimilation', *International Encyclopedia of the Social Sciences* I, 1968.

4. F. Barth (ed.), *Ethnic Groups and Boundaries. The Social Organization of Culture Difference*, Bergen, 1970, pp. 9–11.

5. A.L. Epstein, *Ethos and Identity*, London, 1978, p. 92.

6. *Ibid.*, p. 111.

7. Barth, p. 14.

8. See, for example, G. Mosse, *Germans and Jews*, New York, 1970, p. 113; P. Gay, *Freud, Jews and other Germans. Masters and Victims in Modernist Culture*, New York, 1978, pp. 93, 95.

9. See, for example, H.S. Levine, 'Als amerikanischer Jude in Deutschland', H.M. Broder and M.R. Lang (eds.), *Fremd im eigenen Land. Juden in der Bundesrepublik*, Frankfurt, 1979.

10. J. Katz, *Out of the Ghetto. The Social Background of Jewish Emancipation, 1770–1870*, Cambridge/Mass., 1973, pp. 1–3.

12. See esp. *Ibid.*; Katz, *Tradition and Crisis. Jewish Society the End of the*

*Middle Ages*, New York, 1961; R. Rürup, 'Emanzipation und Krise', in W. Mosse and A. Paucker (eds.), *Juden im Wilhelminischen Deutschland, 1890-1914*, Tübingen, 1976, p. 37.

12. N. Bentwich, *The Refugees from Germany, April 1933 to December 1935*, London, 1936; *Rescue and Achievement of Refugee Scholars*, The Hague, 1953; *They found Refuge*, London, 1956.

13. See K. Gershon, *We came as Children. A Collective Autobiography*, London, 1966.

14. G. Tergit, 'How they Resettled', in Association of Jewish Refugees (ed.), *Britain's New Citizens. The Story of the Refugees from Germany and Austria*, London, 1951, p. 62.

15. Verbal communication from Miss Esther Simpson, for many years the secretary of the Society for the Protection of Science and Learning.

16. Information received from emigrants. To date, there are no studies of the integration and impact of academics from the Continent in Great Britain. There are only studies from the United States: for example, D. Kent, *The Refugee Intellectual*, New York, 1953; H. Pross, *Die deutsche akademische Emigration nach den Vereinigten Staaten, 1933-1941*, Berlin, 1955, D. Fleming and B. Bailyn, *The Intellectual Migration. Europe and America, 1930-1960*, Cambridge/Mass., 1969; H.S. Hughes, *The Sea Change. The Migration of Social Thought, 1930-1965*, New York, 1975. For the situation of lawyers, see Z.M. Reid, 'Contributions to Science and Art', in Association of Jewish Refugees (ed.), *Britain's New Citizens*; see also N. Bentwich, see n. 12.

17. See the essay by H. Loebl in this volume.

18. 'Are Refugees an Asset?', PEP Pamphlets, London, 1944. See also D. Buxton, *The Economics of the Refugee Problem*, London, 1933; the volumes of *AJR Information* from that time and the Annual Reports of the *Trades Advisory Council*, London, 1943-9, give a good idea of the antisemitic movements of the time.

19. See also C. Holmes, *Anti-Semitism in British Society, 1876-1939*, London, 1979; K. Lunn (ed.), *Hosts, Immigrants and Minorities. Historical Responses to Newcomers in British Society 1870-1914*, London, 1980; G. Lebzelter, *Political Anti-Semitism in England 1918-1939*, London, 1979.

20. H.B.M. Murphy, 'Practical Measures for Refugee Mental Health in Britain', in *The Bulletin of the World Federation for Mental Health*, 4/4, 1952; Klaus P. Fink, 'Victims of Political Racial Persecution', in *Nursing Times*, 22 March 1979, pp. 496-9.

21. Verbal communications from emigrants.

22. For the internment, see the essay by M. Seyfert in this volume.

23. German-Jewish Aid Committee (ed.) 'While you are in England. Helpful Information and Guidance for Every Refugee' - a pamphlet issued in two languages in 1939 - is instructive.

24. See, for example, C.C. Aronsfeld, *Leo Baeck (London) Lodge 1953. The First Thirty Years*, London, 1975; Walter Schwab, *B'nai B'rith. 50 Years of Achievement, 1926-1976*, London, 1976; New Liberal Jewish Congregation Belsize Square, 'Our Congregation - The Twenty-Fifth Anniversary, June 1964'.

25. I would like to take this opportunity to thank Peter Johnson, who generously gave me material and information about *Hyphen*. See also the

article by another founding member of *Hyphen*, E. Sheldon, 'The Younger Generation', in Association of Jewish Refugees (ed.), *Britain's New Citizens*.

26. This is not to suggest that Jews of German descent only marry within their own community. Any discussion of marriage among German Jews in Great Britain can only be based on speculation, because there are no data. The information given by emigrants themselves, purely subjective impressions, suggests that the rate of intermarriage in the third generation is as high as 50 per cent. This estimate, however, seems very high and probably reflects anxieties about the continued existence of the group. In the USA, where the marriages of minorities are studied more systematically, the Jews, for example, have the lowest rate of intermarriage. See, for example, R.J. Reeves Kennedy, 'What has Social Science to say about Intermarriage?', in W.J. Cahnmann (ed.), *Intermarriage and Jewish Life. A Symposium*, New York, 1963.

27. A well-known Rabbi described the differences in a similar way: I. Maybaum, 'German Jews and Anglo-Jewry', in Association of Jewish Refugees (ed.), *Britain's New Citizens*.

# Notes on the Contributors

**Marion Berghahn,** D.Phil., Ph.D. Her publications include *The Image of Africa in Afro-American Literature*, London, 1977; *German-Jewish Refugees in England. The Ambiguities of Assimilation*, London, 1984; now an academic publisher; lives in Leamington Spa, England.

**Francis L. Carsten,** D.Phil., D.Litt. Oxon., FBA 1971. Masaryk Professor of Central European History at the University of London 1961–78; among his many publications are: *The Origins of Prussia*, London, 1982; *Fascist Movements in Austria. From Schönerer to Hitler*, London, 1977; *War against War. British and German Radical Movements in the First World War*, London, 1982.

**John Fox,** Ph.D. He is an editor of *Documents on German Foreign Policy 1918–1945*, London, and has published *Germany and the Far Eastern Crisis 1931–1938*, as well as several articles on Nazi policies towards the Jews.

**Anthony Glees,** Ph.D. Lecturer at Brunel University; his publications include *Exile Politics during the Second World War. The German Social Democrats in Britain*, Oxford, 1982.

**Gerhard Hirschfeld,** D.Phil.; Fellow of the German Historical Institute, London. His publications include: (ed.) *The 'Führer-State': Myth and Reality, Studies on the Structure and Politics of the Third Reich*, Stuttgart, 1981; (ed.) *Social Protest, Violence and Terror in Nineteenth- and Twentieth-Century Europe*, London, 1982;

*Fremdherrschaft und Kollaboration. Die Niederlande unter deutscher Besatzung*, Stuttgart, 1984; a study on the emigration of German academics from the Third Reich is in preparation.

**Lothar Kettenacker**, D.Phil.; Fellow and Deputy Director of the German Historical Institute, London. He has published, i.a., *Nationalsozialistische Volkstumspolitik im Elsass*, Stuttgart, 1973, and edited *Das 'andere Deutschland' im Zweiten Weltkrieg. Emigration und Widerstand in internationaler Perspektive*, Stuttgart, 1977; a study on British planning for postwar Germany (1939–45) will appear shortly.

**Rainer Kölmel**, D.Phil. Lecturer at Edinburgh University; he is the author of a history of the German-Jewish refugees in Scotland during the Nazi era.

**Herbert Loebl**, OBE, MA. Engineer, founder of enterprises in the areas of precision engineering and electronics; he is the author of a study of refugee industries in the Special Areas in England, 1937–1961; he currently works as an industrial consultant.

**Conrad Pütter**, MA. He has published numerous articles on radio and exile; a reference work on broadcasting by the German-speaking emigrants, 1933–1945, is in preparation.

**Michael Seyfert**, D.Phil. He works as a freelance journalist for various German radio and television stations; he is the author of a study of the literature of German-speaking refugees in British internment during the Second World War (to be published soon).

**Bernard Wasserstein**, Ph.D. Professor of History at Brandeis University; his publications include: *The British in Palestine*, London, 1978; *Britain and the Jews of Europe 1939–1945*, London, 1979.

**John W.M. Willett**. Writer, co-editor of the English edition of Brecht's works; his publications include: *The New Sobriety 1917–1933. Arts and Politics in the Weimar Period*, London, 1978; *The Weimar Years*, London, 1983; *Brecht in Context*, London, 1984.

# Index

# Index